THE NAZI PERPETRATOR

THE NAZI PERPETRATOR

POSTWAR GERMAN ART AND THE POLITICS OF THE RIGHT

PAUL B. JASKOT

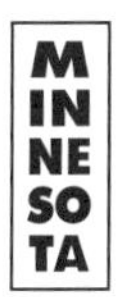

University of Minnesota Press
Minneapolis
London

Publication of this book has been aided by a grant from the Millard Meiss Publication Fund of the College Art Association.

MM

The University of Minnesota Press gratefully acknowledges financial assistance provided for the publication of this book from the University Research Council at DePaul University.

Portions of chapter 2 were published in "Gerhard Richter and Adolf Eichmann," *Oxford Art Journal* 28, no. 3 (2005): 457–78. Portions of chapter 4 were published in "Daniel Libeskind's Jewish Museum in Berlin as a Cold War Project," in *Berlin: Divided City, 1945–1989*, ed. Philip Broadbent and Sabine Hake, 145–55 (New York: Berghahn Books, 2010). Portions of chapter 5 were published in "The Reich Party Rally Grounds Revisited: The Political Resonance of the Nazi Past in Postwar Nuremberg," in *Beyond Berlin: Twelve German Cities Confront the Nazi Past*, ed. Gavriel D. Rosenfeld and Paul B. Jaskot, 143–62 (Ann Arbor: University of Michigan Press, 2008).

The views or opinions expressed in this book and the content in which the images are used do not necessarily reflect the views or policy of, nor imply approval or endorsement by, the United States Holocaust Memorial Museum.

Published by the University of Minnesota Press
111 Third Avenue South, Suite 290
Minneapolis, MN 55401-2520
http://www.upress.umn.edu

Library of Congress Cataloging-in-Publication Data
Jaskot, Paul B., 1963–
    The Nazi perpetrator : postwar German art and the politics of the right / Paul B. Jaskot.
    Includes bibliographical references and index.
    ISBN 978-0-8166-7824-2 (hardback)
    ISBN 978-0-8166-7825-9 (pb)
1. Art and society—Germany—History—20th century. 2. Art and society—Germany—History—21st century. 3. Architecture and society—Germany—History—20th century. 4. Architecture and society—Germany—History—21st century. 5. War criminals—Germany. 6. History—Psychological aspects. I. Title.
    N72.S6J35 2012
    701´.0309430904—dc23
                                                                2012031601

Printed in the United States of America on acid-free paper

The University of Minnesota is an equal-opportunity educator and employer.

20 19 18 17 16 15 14 13 12   10 9 8 7 6 5 4 3 2 1

For Rob

CONTENTS

ABBREVIATIONS

CDU	Christian Democratic Union
CSU	Christian Social Union of Bavaria
DVU	Deutsche Volksunion, German People's Union
ECA	Economic Cooperation Administration
FDP	Freie Demokratische Partei, Free Democratic Party
FRG	Federal Republic of Germany, West Germany
GDR	German Democratic Republic, East Germany
IAC	International Auschwitz Committee
IBA	Internationale Bauausstellung, International Building Exhibition
IMT	International Military Tribunal
KfdK	Kampfbund für deutsche Kultur, Fighting League for German Culture
LA Berlin	Landesarchiv Berlin
NPD	Nationaldemokratische Partei Deutschlands, German National Democratic Party
NSDAP	Nationalsozialistische Deutsche Arbeiterpartei, National Socialist German Workers' Party, or the Nazi Party
SDS	Sozialistischer Deutscher Studentenbund, Socialist German Students' League
SED	Sozialistische Einheitspartei Deutschland, Socialist Unity Party
SenKult	Senatsverwaltung für Wissenschaft, Forschung und Kultur
SPD	Sozialdemokratische Partei Deutschlands, Social Democratic Party
VB	*Völkischer Beobachter* (People's observer)
WBG	Wohnungsbaugesellschaft, Residential Building Society

POLITICAL HISTORY AND POSTWAR GERMAN ART

Franz Schönhuber, like many twentieth-century Germans, had a complicated and variable relationship to the Nazi past.[1] Born on January 10, 1923, in Trostberg an der Alz in Oberbayern, Schönhuber worked his way through the Nazi youth organizations, became a party member in 1941 and willingly enlisted in the Waffen-SS. During the war he helped train French Waffen-SS volunteers for a division called "Charlemagne." At his denazification trial after the war, he was labeled a "fellow traveler" (*Mitläufer*) and released; he settled into a life as a journalist. Schönhuber, like most postwar Germans, deemphasized his Nazi past. His image as a successful postwar journalist stood in opposition to the silence over his role as a former member of the Waffen-SS, a criminal organization according to Allied justice and most of the world's opinion. By 1975, he was the head of the Bavarian Information division of the prestigious Bayerische Rundfunk, served as a TV moderator, and achieved a degree of popularity. In the meantime, his politics tacked to the right. He joined the Christian Social Union (CSU), the Bavarian equivalent of the Christian Democratic Union (CDU), West Germany's dominant conservative political party. The powerful Bavarian minister, Franz Josef Strauss, took Schönhuber in as a member of his trusted circle of advisers ("Franzensclub"). All seemed to be going well.

But his Nazi past eventually complicated his relationship with his employer and the CSU. As rumors circulated about his former position within the Hitler state, Schönhuber decided to address any questions head-on with an autobiographical account, *Ich war dabei* (I was there), published in 1981. His book excused aspects of the past and the National Socialist leadership. By mid-1982, the Bavarian Journalists Association dismissed him from its board, and he lost his Bavarian broadcasting job. He turned further right, helping to found the new party of the Republikaner (Republicans), which officially came into being in November 1983. The Republikaner achieved surprising success as a right-wing party in the 1989 vote for the parliament of the European Union. He and five other party members went to Brussels, where they forged links with, among others, the French right-wing ideologue Jean-Marie le Pen.[2] This success in a national election was not to be repeated. Schönhuber changed course in 1994 and secretly crafted on his own an agreement with Gerhard Frey, the head of the extremist German People's Union (DVU), a party with open Nazi sympathies. Such a strategic alignment came as a shock to the Republikaner Party faithful, and after much pressure Schönhuber resigned in December 1994. Given this uneven history, Schönhuber's relation to the Nazi past can be characterized in different ways and within specific temporal contexts: his role as a functionary for the Waffen–SS, his postwar ideological pronouncements on the past, and his strategic alignment with more overt neo-Nazi voices played out at particular moments of public debate. These positions stood in stark contrast to his initial identity after 1945 as a journalist supporting a West German democracy opposed to National Socialist principles.

Schönhuber's biography obviously has a place within the political history of twentieth-century Germany. He is, however, completely absent from the art historical literature. After all, why should he be included? Art historians have found right-wing movements and politicians in the postwar era uninteresting and not much help in interpreting their chosen subjects. They have instead focused, as just one example, on mining ever more closely the interlocking philosophical claims of Joseph Beuys and his inner circle.[3] Yet consider another German artist working at the same time as Beuys and ignored by art historians: Paul Mathias Padua was a painter famous in the Nazi period and collected by its elite leaders. Martin Bormann, for example, purchased his notorious *Leda and the Swan* (*Great German Art Exhibition,* 1939), an image that shows the swan ravishing a seemingly contemporary woman. But Padua's career did not end in 1945. He continued to work actively and even received a gallery exhibition in 1965 that fêted his career and recent work.[4] Scholars, though, have given no notice to this art historical event. As with Schönhuber, art historians have little to say about the continuity of Padua's activity as an artist during and after the Nazi period. In an era that sought so fervently to determine who was to blame for the genocidal policies of the Nazi regime, why does the public exhibition of an artist so well connected with the Nazi past go unremarked?

Naturally, it is not the case that Beuys is irrelevant to a history of post-war German art. Rather, a more comprehensive analysis of the politics of the right gives a more synthetic understanding of postwar German culture, one that also includes the likes of Padua. All artists and architects after 1945 operated within the context of evolving concepts of the Nazi past. Schönhuber's biography is only one example of how conservative and extreme right-wing politicians radically influenced this context. But artists and architects also engaged with or reacted to the maneuvers of the right. A look at the dynamic interplay between artistic communities and broader political forces can help us formulate a more complete interpretation of the functional and evolving intersection of art and German politics after World War II.

Understanding this intersection in twentieth-century Germany requires a firm grasp of the specific history of National Socialism. We have long known the effect of the Nazi Party (Nationalsozialistische Deutsche Arbeiterpartei, NSDAP) on German society, with tentacles extending back into the roots of fascism after World War I and forward into the neo-Nazi groups and antisemitic pronouncements of recent years. In the art history of postwar Germany, however, scholars have surprisingly undervalued the variety of ways this Nazi past wove in and out of the production of art and architecture. Certainly, the crimes of party members and willing accomplices help explain memorial art at the sites where victims suffered, a natural focus of the contemporary scholarship.[5] The explosion in the past few decades of Holocaust memorials as well as the concomitant depth of historiographic analysis of these spaces and places dedicated to victims is, though, only half of the art historical problem. Postwar art formed a more complicated nexus with the diverse ways in which Germans understood and used the Nazi past. Scholarship should work to avoid the isolation of art historical debates that give an often distorted or oversimplified view of what specific aspects of the Nazi past engaged artists. The particularities of Nazi biography, policy, or event have much more to say as evidence for artistic and architectural choices. This book expands scholarly categories of evidence, widens the field of interpretation, and deepens our knowledge of the profound intersection of politics and art in postwar society. It proposes a new way, an extended and integrated way of viewing the relationship of art and architecture to the Nazi past.

Such an expanded field of inquiry foregrounds a mostly unacknowledged subject in art history: the Nazi perpetrator. As Raul Hilberg explained in a now-classic definition, "The perpetrators were people who played a specific role in the formulation or implementation of anti-Jewish measures. In most cases, a participant understood his function, and he ascribed it to his position and duties."[6] More broadly, substantial numbers of Germans, men and women, implemented the National Socialist policies against European Jews and other groups, and after 1945, their agency within and relationship to these policies were variably labeled criminal. James Waller has described this problem of genocidal perpetrators in social-psychological terms related to the internal disposition and external situation of any individual. For Waller, people who become perpetrators can have three sometimes overlapping identity traits: a specific cultural belief system that helps, for example, construct an "other"; an ability morally to disengage that provides psychic distance from an action or event; or a rational self-interest in an outcome for pecuniary, professional, or other motives. In combination with situational factors such as the socialization of individuals within a specific institution or the importance of group identity, these psychological characteristics help to explain how ordinary people can do extraordinary evil.[7] This general analysis of perpetrators takes on catastrophic proportions for Waller especially "when the distinctions between war and crime fade," as was the case in Nazi Germany.[8]

In historical rather than social-psychological terms, the shifting definition of *criminal* behavior and identity markers such as those Waller describes could be highlighted at different moments in public debate. These changing categorizations came to determine who was or was not a perpetrator. Diverse postwar audiences could consider criminal agency very narrowly, as at the International Military Tribunals at Nuremberg, or broadly enough to encompass all Germans who did not actively resist. People like Schönhuber, in this regard, could fall in- or outside this ideological and judicial range depending on the temporal and political context.[9] In addition, political discussions of the continued presence of perpetrators influenced art and architecture just as efforts to memorialize victims did. My argument makes the impact of these historical players and the debates about their actions less abstract in the analysis of postwar German art. How postwar audiences interpreted the dispositional character of particular Nazi era subjects played an especially important role in these debates.

Such an agenda means insisting on knowledge not only of the multifaceted and nefarious details of Nazi policy and the variety of its perpetrators but also of right-wing politics both before and after the war. Right-wing politics—from moderately conservative to extremist—often led to public debates about individuals and groups from the past who could be called perpetrators in the present. After all, those who espoused a liberal or left-wing position claimed rationally that their politics rejected the fascist debacle of the past. Germans who maintained right-wing beliefs, however, had a more difficult position to hold, as evidenced by Schönhuber's biography. On the one hand, many (although not all) disavowed the conflation of conservative positions with fascist ones; on the other, they sometimes shared biographical connections to or maintained some ideological convictions with that very Nazi past that they wished to promote in the postwar present. Distancing themselves from some elements of the Nazi past while embracing other points of continuity became a balancing act for many conservative voices and a target, real or perceived, of their liberal critics. Artists, architects, and other cultural actors lived with these frequent debates, and not surprisingly, they too sometimes engaged in or were influenced by the question of who could be called a perpetrator in the past or the present. An expanded analysis of the politics of the right gives a more nuanced understanding of the experiences of German artists and architects who participated in cultural dialogues that involved the changing status of the Nazi perpetrator.

One result of this triad between perpetrators, artists, and conservatives is that the following book is, at least before reunification, very much a West German story, with few notable exceptions. East Germany after all lacked a publicly acknowledged conservative politics. Further, the founding myth of the Communist leadership of the German Democratic Republic (GDR) had always been that fascism was an extension of capitalism and, hence, only a problem for the Federal Republic in the west. As Jeffrey Herf has put it:

> The meaning of coming to terms with the Nazi past [in the GDR] was simple and straightforward: smash capitalism. The Communists had always claimed that capitalism contained the roots of Nazism. Because these roots had been ripped up in the Soviet zone of occupation but were being replanted in the Western zones, the possibility of a renewed fascism now lay outside, and only outside, East German borders in Western Germany. Antifascism was now directed against the West German present. It no longer referred exclusively or even primarily to the Nazi past.[10]

Given this context, GDR citizens did not engage in debates about who was or was not a perpetrator in the past or the present. Those criminals in the past could easily be defined as all who had willingly helped the Nazi state, while the present remnant of this group existed only in the west. This attitude ignored the fact that both moderate and extreme supporters of even the genocidal policies of the Nazi regime found a place within the GDR. Certainly, this official position could not stamp out all reflection on these historical subjects, and especially in some films and literature, there were occasional attempts to culturally engage the highly sensitive issue of how the GDR present connected with the Nazi past. Such was not the case, however, with architecture and painting on the whole. So, for example, in 1953 the state-run Bauakademie's journal featured a translated article on the U.S. art scene by Soviet sculptor Vera Mukhina with the German headline of "Entartete amerikanische Kunst" (Degenerate American art).[11] Seemingly unaware of the parallel with the 1937 *Degenerate Art* show, the art establishment displayed an extraordinary tone deafness as to why such words like "degenerate" conjured up the worst of the Nazi art project. As a rule, few historical debates about criminal agency occurred in the Cold War east. In this political geography, GDR artists and architects had no definition of the perpetrator to address.

The Nazi perpetrator figured in West German conservative debates in very particular ways, and we can lay out several of these that overlap in this book up front. For example, by the late 1950s, important discussions about the Nazi past occurred in conservative circles regarding what perpetration meant. Who did what, who was a perpetrator, and how should legislation or judicial measures deal (if at all) with them? As with many aspects of that history, these definitions were not fixed but were rather fluid. All manner of conservative and right-wing politicians manipulated the concept to project a strong distinction (real or imagined) between their contemporary activities or biographies and those of individuals in the National Socialist state. Such an approach tended to dovetail with and legitimate international Cold War policies as implemented in the Federal Republic.

For much of the postwar period, the CDU exemplified this position. The party's dominance in office as well as the fact that some of its members were former Nazi officials gave it an ambiguous and difficult relationship to the past. Bringing the CDU into art history reveals how cultural production and the party's policies can be mutually illuminating, an assertion of particular importance in the governments of the two major CDU postwar chancellors, Konrad Adenauer and Helmut Kohl. Further to the right, the rise particularly since the 1980s of neo-Nazi activity, of hooligans and new parties that called on aspects of their predecessors' ideology for legitimacy, posed a threatening set of problems for Kohl and the Federal Republic. Such challenges garnered major attention from the state during and after the end of the Cold War. Integrating these conservative and political debates into art history complements the important burgeoning literature on the memorialization and memory of victims. We gain a more comprehensive sense of the subtle inflections of postwar cultural production through analyzing the complex resonance of debates about the perpetrator.

The central function of political and social struggle within these debates is fundamental to the analysis of culture during this period. To take but one example, we have long known of the importance of the confrontation of the younger generation with the older, which converged in particular in the battles of 1968. In that confrontation, scholars have noted the role of Joseph Beuys, the interest of Anselm Kiefer, and the participation of innumerable other artist activists. But what do we know about their fathers and mothers? Should art history address the development of a postwar conservative consensus that activists targeted for their generational conflict? What did these artists mean when they called their professors fascists? Taking these questions seriously, as seriously as the activists at the time did, foregrounds the real substance of the political debates and the complexities of the struggle over describing who was or was not criminally connected to the past. This book attempts to avoid projecting the paper tiger of the "right" onto a self-satisfied narrative of artistic resistance. Political struggles constitute important elements of any society; it is high time we integrated this truism as a central pillar in the structure of any art historical analysis. Many important areas of art history have already done this.[12] My project does the same here in new investigations of postwar art of the Federal Republic.

Historiographically, scholars working on cultural themes have addressed the Nazi past and postwar society predominantly in three distinct ways. First, they have focused on the question of institutional and biographical continuity between the National Socialist era and West Germany after 1945. German scholars have taken the lead on this work, and they have foregrounded the central question inevitably of moral responsibility and the issue of culpability.[13] Second, writers have also produced particular case studies of artworks and architecture that take up the Nazi past. Many German and non-German scholars have focused on the analysis of key sites and projects that thematize social memory and memorialization of the victims. The literature on this subject is vast and particularly interdisciplinary, especially deriving from historical and literary scholarship.[14] I also bring this well-known work into my study to see what it can tell us about art and architecture. In turn, though, a focus on different kinds of cultural questions brings a new emphasis to our understanding of established postwar historical narratives and nuances our analysis of the perpetrator as a social and political category. Finally, art historians have produced many important monographs on artists that examine how the conception of their work relates particularly to the philosophical implications after 1945 of Auschwitz as the irrational endgame of modernity.[15]

Yet art historians still tend to isolate individual artists or architectural geographies (particularly claiming Berlin as the part that stands for the German whole). Further, they rarely address the relevant political history of the right that could help to explain the import of a specific work at a specific time for a localized audience. Instead, philosophical themes take center stage as do, more recently, crucial issues surrounding how German art relates to an increasingly globalized market.[16] For interested readers, I respond to this literature most directly within the endnotes to avoid frequent interruptions of the historical analysis. But complementary to this editorial strategy, the book as a whole argues for a more precise political and institutional history to get at the centrality of the Nazi perpetrator to cultural interpretation. This argument gives the development of state policy, the institutional context for art and architecture, and ideological debates about the perpetrator within the structure of postwar society their due as art historically important themes.

More broadly, my analysis resituates art in the Federal Republic with regard to the profound and particular social crisis posed by the history of the Nazi state and the atrocities of the Holocaust. Postwar artists did not isolate themselves from this crisis or treat it as an abstraction around which they could build artistic and architectural cultures of innovation. By ignoring the often tedious and careful work required to research the specific institutional conditions and terms of debate in full, we have, at best, a partial history of modern art. Artists and architects engaged the experience of victims as an intricate conceptual problem, but they also addressed the political implications of the changing status of perpetrators. The political dynamics of the former Nazi state had obvious and crucial ramifications for subsequent artistic culture. In this regard, my main question rests not on the value or complexity of art but rather its interrelationship with a nexus of structural, governmental, and ideological interests related to the variable reception of the Nazi perpetrator.

Taking key examples from West Germany and, after 1989, reunified Germany, this project questions the relationship between artistic culture and state policies as well as conservative party politics, past and present. In so doing, I reevaluate high-profile moments in postwar German art and architecture. Three factors established conditions that would form a set of possibilities, which in turn influenced political and artistic work after 1945: the agency of individuals within Hitler's party, the policies they implemented, and the extremes of oppression pursued. I have organized the book to address multiple aspects of the resulting nexus of art and politics by looking chronologically at art historical figures and specific public debates. However, rather than following a standard art historical trajectory, I have instead chosen to emphasize important postwar political conflicts about the Nazi perpetrator that have determined my particular artistic case studies.

The first chapter introduces a political history that focuses on the characteristics of the Nazi perpetrators themselves. What range of actions did postwar audiences label as criminal in order to define the category of the perpetrator? I begin with an analysis of the Nazi Party to ground our study in the particularities and complexities of that political institution. Focusing on culture not as an ideological cipher but rather as intellectual work of strategic use, I argue that the NSDAP developed a series of different relationships to art that after 1945 helped constitute a typology of the perpetrator. So, for example, Nazi leaders found the work of Heinrich Wölfflin, perhaps the most well-known art historian ever, useful in surprising ways. Through an analysis of Wölfflin's appropriation as, simultaneously, the party rose to power, I explore how the strategic use of cultural policy for racist ends came to define one aspect of criminal behavior recognized by postwar audiences. From the perspective of political history, what becomes interesting is how specific party officials bridged the gap between culture and politics at particular times and in particular ways. Only by seeing the variety of approaches to culture can we begin to understand how the perpetrator could become itself a varied and fluid category after 1945.

Having established the foundational intersection of National Socialist political history and art history, the subsequent chapters of the book move to the analysis of postwar artists and architects and their relationships to the criminal Nazi past. Chapter 2 foregrounds an expanded definition of the perpetrator in the late 1950s and early 1960s, and how it came to dominate political reactions to the Nazi period in the immediate postwar society. The question of the perpetrator as an ordinary functionary rose with real clarity in this moment, the period of immigration for Gerhard Richter from East to West Germany. His move also marked a radical change in his artistic production. Richter took up the complex social response to bureaucratic and everyday perpetrators in his new focus on large black-and-white paintings, many of which grapple with the ambiguous status of these specific individuals in postwar society.

Chapter 3 takes on the postwar generation's conflict with its fathers and mothers up through the late 1970s. At that time, the confrontational approach to the past by students in the streets became increasingly entangled with its opposite, the very different use of that past by conservative politicians. Anselm Kiefer's work addresses the changing terms of debate, and understanding the shifts in his painting helps us to clarify widely held ideological positions that regarded the Nazi perpetrator in a very different light. Chancellor Kohl, among others, took up a variation on these new positions, which he made clear in his rise to power in the early 1980s and in his Cold War policies. For Kohl, as for Kiefer, the question of the perpetrator could be subsumed or supplanted by the mystifications of culture, which indicated a very different response to the Nazi past than that of Richter. Here the relationships of art to politics and politicians to culture are mutually clarifying.

Shifting to architecture and the high-stakes debates in Berlin, chapter 4 begins with the pre-1989 history of the Berlin Jewish Museum as it culminated in Daniel Libeskind's competition-winning design. The meaning assigned to this structure by the government, the architect, and the local community was defined predominantly in Cold War terms, terms that decidedly shifted with the fall of the Berlin Wall in November 1989. Through the process of reunification, the architecture of the Jewish Museum became subject to ideological and economic pressures that substantially changed its form and its significance. In particular, the rise in racist attacks and neo-Nazi violence influenced how politicians and the public alike discussed the building. These individuals were not so much concerned with an actual continuity with the past as they were with a real fear of a revival of fascist practices and beliefs in the present. Contemporaries' anxiety about the possibility of neo-Nazis using a strategic relationship to past perpetrators to foment new forms of violence and racism modified as well the interpretation of cultural production, including Libeskind's building.

Contrasting with this high drama in Berlin, chapter 5 concludes the book with an analysis of the regional center of Nuremberg and its architectural remnants from the Nazi period to today. Looking across time at the changing definition and use of Albert Speer's Reich Party Rally Grounds, I show the variability of political debates about the past within both conservative and liberal circles. The most recent debates have resulted in the utilization of the category of perpetrator as an agent of the past, in opposition to and no longer active within contemporary society. Here, as elsewhere, critics and artists did not consistently apply the same terms within these debates across different media or at diverse sites, and an analysis of Nuremberg highlights the distinction from Berlin. This chapter functions thus as a summation of the argument concerning the variable political receptions of the criminal past that occurred in the Federal Republic since 1945 and formed the background for the changing status of the Nazi perpetrator.

One clear message comes out of this analysis: Scholars must treat the entirety of National Socialist Germany as much more central to understanding modern German art than has previously been assumed. While this past is not always the main or only question, it is more crucial than art historians have suggested for explaining a variety of artistic strategies and the development of particular architectural projects. This is true even for works that have been at the core of many considerations of the postwar period. We need to account not only for the history of artistic resistance or conceptual ambiguity but also for a political history of the right as a part of the art historical equation. The shadow of the perpetrators of genocidal crimes looms large here. Right-wing actors and events also have an explanatory power for the functional understanding of art. We know this well when we analyze the art and architecture produced in Nazi Germany itself. However, Hitler's rise to power in the late Weimar Republic, as well as the necessity of dealing with the enduring impact of the party's policies of oppression in the Federal Republic, needs to be taken more seriously. The political debates about the Nazi perpetrator influenced the conditions of artistic production and these debates were in turn inflected by events surrounding specific works of art and architecture. Seeing this as a dynamic historical process underscores the assertion that understanding social struggle is a fundamental component of any critical history of art.

NATIONAL SOCIALISTS AND ART
BECOMING THE PERPETRATOR

IN THE POSTWAR PERIOD, THE TERM "PERPETRATOR" became relatively easy to throw around. But who were these National Socialist perpetrators? Were their actions so clear and separate from those of other Germans who helped implement policies of oppression but were perhaps less ardent, less committed, or less focused on the same ideological agenda? National Socialist leaders used alliances with a broad range of interests and social groups tactically and practically to enact their sometimes conflicting, sometimes complementary goals. In this strategic environment, specific party elites could either emphasize the uniqueness of a particular National Socialist position and action or blur the line between their interests and those of a more moderate conservative bent. Such a historical coalition between Nazi officials and nonfascist, mostly conservative voices troubled the postwar waters of those who either ignored or engaged a definition of the perpetrator as a social phenomenon. Indeed, the shifting tactics used by Nazi officials in the past made the perpetrator as a postwar term a matter of public and political debate. The constantly changing definition became of tactical importance to artists and critics as well as the politics of the right and the left, both of which contended with the Nazi past. The multiple and often simultaneous definitions of the perpetrator made for a polyvalent category connected selectively back to events and actions in Hitler's Germany.

Whether you considered your neighbor, gallery dealer, or colleague a perpetrator after 1945 was confounded in part by the many ways in which Nazis themselves used everything at their disposal—including culture— before the end of the war. Hence, we need to keep the range of Nazi-era historical actions in mind in order to understand how postwar audiences discriminated carefully between these actions to designate who in the past they thought was criminal and culpable. This chapter introduces the various historical points of engagement between National Socialism and art, from the Weimar Republic to the immediate postwar period, to identify the typological characteristics subsequent German audiences had at their disposal for the construction of the category of perpetrator.[1] As we have known for some time, Nazi officials focused to a surprising degree on the relationship between politics and art, so laying out various cultural positions makes for a good case study of the array of possible categorizations available to the post-1945 audience.[2] Tracing the spectrum of these relationships reveals the multifaceted actions and beliefs that postwar artists, architects, and critics would use to help form the social understanding of the perpetrator. These differing historical relationships crystallized into a variety of choices for postwar artists and politicians alike who evoked particular defining characteristics to describe who they considered as responsible for National Socialist policy.

Historically, we can talk about three broad (if often overlapping) categories into which the Nazi use of culture fell—strategic, ideological, and functional. The strategic use of culture encompassed the selective and instrumental involvement of art, architecture, and art history in specific Nazi policies. Concomitantly, culture's ideological role buttressed the racist and imperialist goals through various representational works intentionally or unintentionally mobilized to justify state and party interests. And finally in functional terms, vast numbers of individuals involved in Nazi institutions utilized the bureaucratic absorption of cultural production as a means to an end, as one tool of many to implement seemingly nonartistic policies. In the immediate postwar era, the German public, aided by the Nuremberg Tribunals, added a fourth categorical relationship that also subsequently became operative: journalists, politicians, and artists, among others, increasingly defined culture as oppositional to criminal policies and racist ideologies of the recent past. Laying out these four relationships of National Socialism to culture helps us understand how these positions would become useful in the postwar attempts to rationalize the new category of the perpetrator. The various constituencies defining who was or was not guilty created a messy affair, with sometimes distinct and at other times simultaneous use of these general characterizations.

Analyzing the variety of Nazi relationships to culture helps clarify how postwar categories of the perpetrator could conceptually coalesce in art, art history, and beyond. Prior to 1945, Nazi elites, slipping between conservative and fascist positions at specific moments to advance their agendas, engaged art and art history to their political advantage. Sometimes it behooved Nazi officials to link themselves to a generic conservatism or traditionalism, while at other times distinguishing themselves from more moderate positions and social groups became important. As a result of this dynamic, many artists, architects, and art historians after 1945 worked with and responded to the changing categorization of who was a supporter of National Socialism. The clarity of this categorization blurred and shifted as various historical events before, during, and after the Nazi era came into focus.

This chapter concentrates on four moments in the relationship between Nazi policy and culture in order to organize the range of choices postwar audiences selected from to develop a definition of the perpetrator. Beginning in the heated electoral battles of the late Weimar Republic, the actions of key Nazi politicians highlight the *strategic* use of culture as they engaged notable figures and institutions in their cause. Once in power after January 1933, the party elite shifted their attention from consolidation of a conservative mass base to purging the state institutions of supposedly unreliable individuals, foregrounding the *ideological* definition of who was or was not acceptable. And when the war began in 1939 and the Nazis attacked, even in this moment of war and, subsequently, genocide, they found other *functional* means of making use of art. At this extreme, even SS architects at Auschwitz, for example, engaged a clear use of culture to enact their political mission.

Throughout the Nazi era, the relationship between politics and art changed, and specific Nazi individuals made those changes possible. That few of these individuals were labeled as perpetrators in the postwar press or political debates, either in West or East Germany, is the concluding story at the end of the chapter. In spite of how Nazi leaders put art to many uses, including the most criminal, such actions remained obscure in the initial Cold War cultural politics on either side of the Iron Curtain. Culture and fascism seemed to be *oppositional* positions. This categorization would not be politically and hence artistically questioned until more than a decade after the conclusion of World War II.

Some of the examples analyzed here are well known in art history, while others are on the whole absent from the literature. The spotty coverage of topics related to Nazi Germany indicates that there is still art historical work to be done.[3] By highlighting the variety of ways the Nazi elite used culture for destructive ends and how those relationships were submerged in the immediate postwar world, I introduce us to the push and pull of National Socialist politics, a crucial component of why specific aspects variably surfaced within right-wing political debates and public culture in the Federal Republic. A supple and historically sensitive account of the shifting sands of Nazi cultural policy sets the stage for the dynamics of its postwar reception and manipulation. This focus highlights the move from an abstract to a concrete analysis of political history and what that might reveal about specific artistic debates relevant to any interpretation of postwar German art and the Nazi past, especially within the Federal Republic.[4]

Electoral Politics: The Strategic Use of Art and Art History

The long Nazi influence on twentieth-century art became most apparent initially in the give and take of electoral politics well before Hitler came to power. In the early phases of the party's development in the Weimar Republic, the NSDAP was not as yet seriously focused on elections. Instead, its followers were committed to violent overthrow of the government, such as had been attempted by Hitler on November 9, 1923, in the Beer Hall Putsch in Munich. Since the party held that the entire Weimar democracy was a sham, members had little need for elections other than as moments of increased agitation. For most of 1924, Hitler was in prison writing *Mein Kampf*, and in the December national elections the Nazi Party garnered a mere 3 percent of the vote. In the mid-1920s, there were other matters for Nazi leaders to think about than the electorate.[5]

This situation would dramatically change beginning in 1927 as Hitler pushed the party to engage more tactically in electoral politics and, following this, the party became interested in developing a cultural policy. Corresponding to this shift in party politics was a growing concern with prominent cultural figures and institutions. We can chart these shifting positions in the main voice of the Nazi Party, its official newspaper edited by Alfred Rosenberg, the *Völkischer Beobachter* (People's observer [VB]), a source that has been of surprisingly little interest to art historians. The *VB* chronicled the party and the actions, speeches, and arrests of its most prominent members. In general, articles emphasized political episodes in inflated prose, either the constant hammering on the corruption, incompetence, or betrayal of the current government or the persecution and successes of the heroic Nazi fighters. In addition to these expected stories, the writers also tried to appeal to a broader spectrum of interests by including articles on cultural events such as plays, films, and contemporary art exhibitions, as well as regular features on sports, a women's section, and a monthly horoscope. Rosenberg's editorship as well as the party affiliation guaranteed daily antisemitic vitriol as well as a constant stream of attacks on the specter of Bolshevism and developments in the Soviet Union. But it did not mean that all authors, features, or even advertisements consistently shared this same vision. You could have, for example, a scathing article about Charlie Chaplin and "Jewish Hollywood" in one issue and then an advertisement for Greta Garbo's *Anna Christie* ("Garbo spricht Deutsch!") for Metro-Goldwyn-Mayer in another.[6] Ideological inconsistencies aside, the articles on politics, culture, daily life, and other subjects became an increasingly effective weapon particularly as the electoral strategies became more crucial for party politics.[7] While exact circulation figures are not known, Detlef Mühlenberger estimates that by 1929 the paper had approximately thirty thousand subscribers, a number that jumped with the victories of the September 1930 elections and reached at least one hundred thousand by 1931.[8]

The panache of literary discussions, music reviews, and art criticism legitimated the party and balanced its more virulent racist and anti-Communist agenda. Important to emphasize here is the fact that the party did not have a coherent cultural ideology, only an agenda that addressed culture within the strategic context of electoral politics. A key example of how the *VB* and other party institutions used culture strategically to extend the mass base of the NSDAP can be seen with the appropriation and racialization of the prominent art historian Heinrich Wölfflin. Wölfflin was most well known for his influential book *Principles of Art History* (1915), in which he advocated a schematic comparative study of formal typologies to understand fundamental distinctions between European Renaissance and Baroque art. This book was groundbreaking and further cemented his career as the leader of the emerging field of art history. Ultimately, it would land him in the prestigious professorship in Munich, where he stayed until he left for Zurich in 1924.[9] Hence, he was long gone from Germany by the time the Nazi Party began to take elections seriously, and thus seemingly quite remote from any relationship to fascism.

While his early text remained influential within art history, specific Nazi intellectuals only took advantage of his methodological approach at the moment he was making his occasional references to race in *Principles* more overt in subsequent works.[10] In the *Kampfzeit* (period of struggle) up to the January 30, 1933, elevation of Hitler to the position of chancellor, party leaders built a mass base beyond their narrow band of loyal followers, with increasing electoral and public relations successes within the volatile political world of late Weimar.[11] At the same time, Wölfflin continued to develop his art historical interests as he finalized the text of his book *Italien und das deutsche Formgefühl* (*Italy and the German Feeling of Form;* 1931). The radicalization of party propaganda and electoral strategy would smelt this text and his art historical ideas into the most extreme racist cultural agendas of the party, setting the standard for the cultural policy of the subsequent Hitler state.[12]

In *Italy and the German Feeling of Form*, his analysis makes evident a much more strident *völkisch* position than in his previous work. As in his other writings, Wölfflin continued to be interested in categorizing forms into fundamental visual typologies. But in contrast to the diachronic comparisons in his earlier work, his development of synchronic and nationalist-based comparisons made his work much more accessible to more extreme analyses of art and race. How Wölfflin's ideas developed in tandem with others can be explicated by looking briefly at fundamental aspects of *Italy and the German Feeling of Form*.[13]

Although completed in Zurich and drawing on a lifetime of ideas and research, Wölfflin's text was very much a Munich book. It began with his Munich lectures before he moved in 1924 and relied on many examples of Italian and Northern Renaissance art from the Alte Pinakothek. In the book, Wölfflin described a series of formal structural differences between Italian and German art and architecture during the sixteenth century. His central argument concerned how Italian art and architecture were generated out of idealist and rationalist principles, whereas Germanic forms in the same period tended to be more dependent on the individual artist, the specific gesture of the body, and what he characterized as the inner rootedness of the soul. He attempted to show this distinction through a set of key couplings of formal differences between the social groups. For Wölfflin, the Germanic closeness to being expressed itself through the energy of form that contrasted with the formal stillness of the Italian artist. So, for example, Wölfflin analyzed Dürer's *Portrait of a Man (Hans Dürer)* (1500) from the point of view of the outline of the face (which is irregular) and the imbalance of form (see Plate 1). While each individual detail makes visual sense, the conceptual whole expresses the kind of unevenness that Wölfflin interprets as a corollary to inner energy. Conversely, when he turns to such Italian works as Titian's *Venus of Urbino* (1538) (Figure 1.1), the stability of the composition, the still and continuous contour of the figure, and the complementary control of shape give the painting a "classic" structure that points to a conceptual idealism unrelated to the reality in which the German artist struggles.[14] Why the difference?

> One will be able to find [the reason for the differences] in the natural bodily and movement-specific feeling of the race. . . . Northern movement occurs more abruptly, more spasmodically above all: it appears throughout to be dependent on a certain implementation of the will. Here finally lies for us the fruitful point of comparison. With all of its liveliness, the Italian gesture [*Gebärde*] (the word taken in its broadest sense) is something that appears light and effortless; *we* [i.e., Germans] always reckon with a resistance, which must be overcome,

and put all hope on a will, which would like to establish itself. Hence the worldview is essentially different.[15]

With the struggle of the internal will, the Swiss-born Wölfflin argues that "our" Germanic art tends to express an inherent desire for freedom. This freedom can also mean a freedom of form, such as an uncontrolled or irregular rhythm of the contour of a cloud or the flow of water. Such irregularity is the "irrational" Germanic will fighting against the confines of rational social norms.[16] Much more than in his previous works, Wölfflin asserted that the psychological premise of art remains in how an artist expresses her or his racial spirit through form. Form is thus not a mere problem of formalism. Rather form has social characteristics that must be seen in relation to their psychological basis in the artist.

Wölfflin's apparent apolitical nature did not hinder admiration of his ideas by Nazi propagandists or their use of his terminology and visual tactics, and they would successfully incorporate both his method and his analysis particularly of Renaissance art into aspects of their work. In the crucial years of the electoral struggles at the end of the Weimar Republic, such cultural propaganda became surprisingly central to important theorists in the party as well as strategies at the local and national level.[17] For a short time, the party's cultural agenda would directly tie one of the most important figures in art history to the most extreme antisemitism within the National Socialist elite.

Wölfflin's ideas and his use of comparative illustrations, for example, were positively engaged in the writings of Hans Günther and Paul Schultze-Naumburg, two prominent Nazi cultural figures and associates of Rosenberg.[18] Culture for them played more than an ancillary role in the late Weimar struggle to gain electoral success and political authority. Rather, Günther and Schultze-Naumburg would have an ability to make their ideas educational and state policy after the surprising electoral victories of the National Socialist Party in 1930, above all in the state elections for Thuringia. The NSDAP's Thuringian successes allowed Hitler to negotiate for representation in the cabinet, and he shrewdly chose the Ministry of the Interior. The Nazi appointee, Wilhelm Frick, initiated an activist Nazi cultural policy that included naming Günther to a professorship in Jena and Schultze-Naumburg to a post in the Weimar art academy. Each used these positions as effective pulpits for promoting their ideas but also for castigating the supposed degeneracy of Jewish and Bolshevik influences on culture that had led a pure Germany to the edge of wrack and ruin.[19] In this crucial moment, the party's cultural propaganda used their writings as a common means of attacking in racist terms the Sozialdemokratische Partei

Deutschlands (SPD) and centrist opposition. The new and prominent role of Günther and Schultze-Naumburg lifted their interpretations of the essentially apolitical Wölfflin's conclusions about art from the academic page into the public politics of the party. As a means of characterizing racialized art, both the citation of Wölfflin and the use of his methodological strategies of stylistic categorization formed important extensions of art historical thought into political practice.

These intellectual and political spheres came together at the nexus of cultural ideology and party propaganda, the *Völkischer Beobachter*. Cultural reporting functioned, on the one hand, as a legitimizing force to indicate the sophistication of the party and its audience and, on the other, as a political weapon, a seemingly neutral vessel into which Nazi leaders could pour ideological pronouncements and the tactical needs of propaganda. The 1928 special report and series of articles on the celebrations surrounding the four-hundredth anniversary of the death of Albrecht Dürer exemplified such strategies (Figure 1.2). Dürer's anniversary was naturally a big event in Bavaria, with an exhibition of his works in Munich's Alte Pinakothek as well as a large retrospective at the German Museum in Nuremberg.

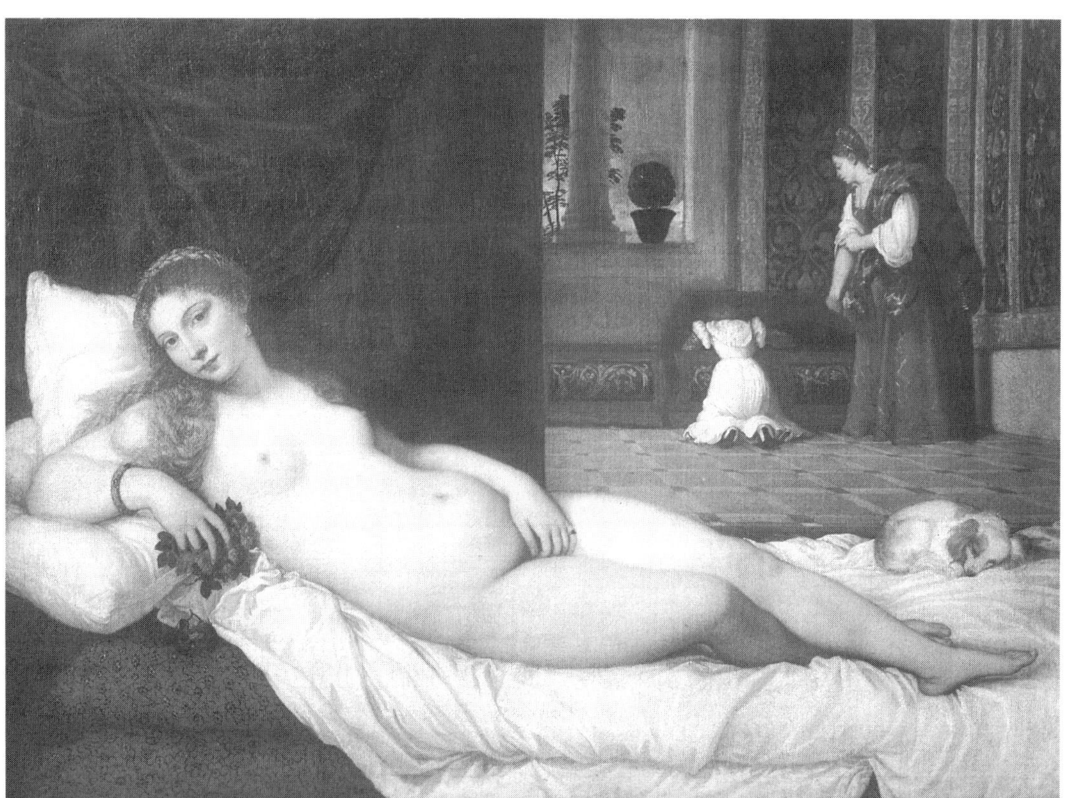

FIGURE 1.1. Titian, *Venus of Urbino*, 1538. Photograph courtesy of Zentralinstitut für Kunstgeschichte, Photothek.

Accompanying the latter, a major symposium and various other celebrations commemorated the artist, all of which were dutifully reported in the *VB*. Culminating with a full-page spread on aspects of Dürer's art and life, the cultural reporters devoted more attention to Dürer than to any other artist during the late Weimar era and used his anniversary for propagandistic ends.[20]

The seemingly neutral article on the symposium, held April 11, 1928, in the large city hall assembly room, gives some sense of the nature of the cultural reporting at this time. The report began with a list of the various honorable figures in attendance, including Wölfflin. The article briefly summarized Nuremberg mayor Hermann Luppe's remarks, who emphasized that Dürer's work reveals how the "spirit and culture from Nuremberg's Renaissance [*Blütezeit*] arise before your eyes," a phenomenon from which contemporary art can learn and gain new understanding.[21] From these remarks, the anonymous author moved to a longer summary of Wölfflin's lecture. He emphasized his assertion that art is an expression of the essential

FIGURE 1.2. Page spread for the celebration of the four-hundredth anniversary of Albrecht Dürer's death, *Völkischer Beobachter*, April 7, 1928. Photograph courtesy of United States Holocaust Memorial Museum Library.

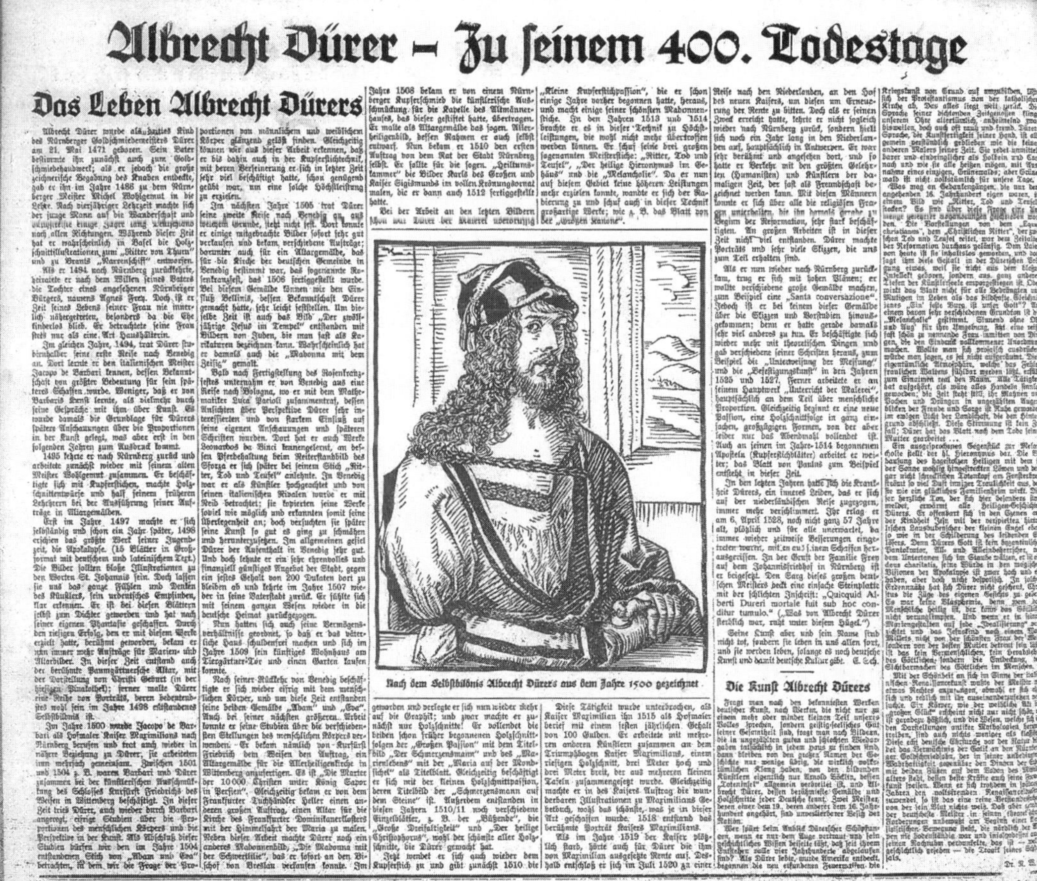

Albrecht Dürer – Zu seinem 400. Todestage

Das Leben Albrecht Dürers

Nach dem Selbstbildnis Albrecht Dürers aus dem Jahre 1500 gezeichnet

Die Kunst Albrecht Dürers

German character. While he argued that Dürer's affinities with Italy had clearly influenced the artist's drawing technique and strength of line, nevertheless "the German view [of things] could only be expressed [*aufgehen*] in pure plastic figures."[22] The "warmth and movement" of the German character distinguished itself from the still classicism of the Italian, which Dürer found "distasteful" (*unschmackhaft*).[23] Here, Wölfflin clearly outlined concepts that he finalized in his subsequent 1931 text. But as summarized and selected, the *VB* author's assessment of the mayor's and Wölfflin's commentaries *only* emphasized the essentially expressive nationalist character of German art as transparently embodied by Dürer. Any other subtlety of their ideological positions or racialized attitudes was lost.

In the grand scheme of art criticism, this is fairly innocuous conservatism even for its time and place. Within the context of the pages of the *VB*, however, such reporting had its clear legitimizing function, promoting claims of cultural knowledge for the publisher and reader alike. These positions also softened the rabid racist nationalism in articles in the same issue with a cultural chauvinism that Rosenberg and other authors of the paper easily could see as concomitant with their positions. Indeed, Rosenberg used the same tactic in his most famous work, *The Myth of the Twentieth Century: An Evaluation of the Spiritual-Intellectual Confrontations of Our Age*. The second half of this work focuses on German art, and he cites both the positive examples of Günther and Schultze-Naumburg but also Wölfflin as the only art historian used to legitimate the racist screed.[24]

As in his newspaper, Rosenberg's process of blending conservative with radical extremes extended, though, from the pages of the daily to political practice. At the 1927 Party Rally in Nuremberg, Hitler tasked Rosenberg with founding and developing what would eventually become the Kampfbund für deutsche Kultur (KfdK; Fighting League for German Culture). The KfdK dovetailed the seemingly milder *völkisch* nationalism exemplified in the Dürer art reporting with the more radical cultural propaganda of the Nazi leadership. The alliance of NSDAP positions with the coalescing German cultural order in the pages of the *VB* became a crucial weapon through the KfdK particularly leading up to the spectacular electoral successes of September 1930.

As Ernst Piper makes clear, when the NSDAP searched for electoral legitimacy it transformed itself from the revolutionary true-believer party of the 1923 Munich putsch into a carefully organized mass-based party that could appeal to a broad public.[25] While it never achieved a majority, with the September 1930 elections it became the second-largest party after the SPD, and by July 1932, it had garnered the largest bloc of voters in the election. The expansion of its base in the late Weimar Republic played an important role in its successes at the polls, as did the economic crises of the Great Depression and the internal dynamics of the state.[26] Within this political context, organizations like the KfdK focused on the main function of bringing leaders together from within and outside the party and creating a forum for cultural activism. From 1929 to 1932, the KfdK held at least twenty-one different events throughout Germany, including musical and poetry evenings and lectures on contemporary art and architecture. The KfdK's critical and condemnatory tactics ironically succeeded best in the very democratic conditions of the volatile elections of the late Weimar period, which also accounts for its more diminished importance in relation to other cultural organs once Hitler had come to power.[27]

The KfdK evidenced its attempts to bridge conservative and radically racist interests in the January 11, 1929, front-page *VB* article (unsigned but presumably by Rosenberg) that announced its formation and purposes. The author carefully linked, for example, generic conservative pro-German feelings recalling the heroic struggles of World War I with specific virulent antisemitic positions through citation of figures like Paul de Lagarde, a nineteenth-century theologian and orientalist whom Rosenberg respected.[28] The article further emphasized such linkages in its last section, a list of forty-seven prominent cultural leaders and politicians with opinions from "all directions" that had pledged to carry forward this "struggle for German spiritual freedom" ("Kampf um deutsche Geistesfreiheit"). In addition, another list included the thirteen members who made up the KfdK leadership. In the former list, expected names appear such as the racist Adolf Bartels, as well as cultural figures who supported the National Socialist cause like Winifried Wagner. The latter list registered committed Nazi followers, particularly those linked to Rosenberg, such as Schultze-Naumburg, Othmar Spann (who gave the first KfdK public lecture), and the 1905 Nobel Prize winner for physics, Philipp Lenard, an early follower of Hitler.

And yet among the supporters some surprises of more neutral cultural figures also occur. Above all, we find next to Wagner the name of Professor Heinrich Wölfflin of Zurich. It is now clear that his friend Elsa Bruckmann put his name on the list without his knowledge, so this is not about any particular attitude of Wölfflin's. Quite to the contrary, he distanced himself from this extremism.[29] Yet Bruckmann's action emphasizes an important point: the party and its members would make strategic alliances at whatever cost in the heat of this moment to cement their association with such a prestigious name and expand their cultural reach. In addition, Elsa and Hugo Bruckmann (the publishers of *Italy and the German Feeling of Form*) had not only committed themselves to the list of those willing to work on this explicitly conservative and racist agenda but also joined the leadership committee of the KfdK. It was in their house in Munich that Rosenberg held many of the initial meetings to form the group.[30] In this most important of electoral periods, party leaders could selectively tie the ideas sprinkled throughout Wölfflin's early writings and systematically in his 1931 book, as well as the status of the art historian, to their own social and intellectual network firmly aligned with Rosenberg's wing of Nazi racist ideology. Through these means, the Nazi propagandists politicized Wölfflin's work and used his essentially conservative position on a national style to legitimate the internal political goal of expanding the Nazi Party into a mass movement. This strategy also furthered the external need to present the party to a public with all the legitimacy that a group of well-heeled and nonmember supporters could provide.

Cultural politics was particularly crucial at this time in the Nazi struggle for power owing to the importance of Rosenberg and his interests as editor of the party newspaper, the ability of Frick to make room for Schultze-Naumburg and Günther in teaching positions after the 1930 Thuringian elections, and, finally, the emphasis on the KfdK as a highly touted propaganda organ of the party. Wölfflin's engagement with questions about art, nationalism, and race at exactly this time, as well as key party ideologues' citing and using parts of his work in their racist tracts, speaks to an intellectual confluence of conservative art history with reactionary positions. Further, it indicates the means by which Nazi officials politically and ideologically leveraged his specific thought and social position for the good of building a mass party. Not surprisingly, the only full review of any book by an art historian to appear in the pages of the *VB* during these years also marked this confluence: Wölfflin's *Italien und das deutsche Formgefühl*, reviewed by Franz Hofmann on October 11/12, 1931.[31] This series of appropriations of the cultivated art historian for the use of party politics illustrates how flexible and effective a strategic approach to culture could be for the party's goals of undermining democracy through any means at its disposal.

Consolidation and Radicalization: The Creation of the Ideological Enemy through Art and Propaganda

My example here of the strategic use of Wölfflin highlights how the relationship between specific cultural figures, artworks, and production could change dynamically based on political considerations that developed within the Nazi Party over time. After Hitler became chancellor, the National Socialist agenda shifted immediately from electoral politics to consolidating total power in the state. This meant a new emphasis on the exclusion of seemingly unreliable individuals from state institutions (including art schools and universities) and replacing them with solid party members and fellow travelers. Both exclusion and inclusion were based on racist and political ideological criteria, even though these criteria remained flexible enough to allow for exceptions. Such an ideological use of cultural institutions to promote particular positions and individuals became ever clearer as the party succeeded in consolidating its power. By 1936, when Hitler was confident enough in Germany's strength (and the weakness of its democratic and Communist enemies) to begin planning for war, art could be used to extend a policy of exclusion. Artists and art bureaucrats utilized art exhibitions in particular as part of a general policy to demonize key social groups, which in turn legitimized the need for an upcoming German attack on these very peoples. For the German Jews, the concrete propaganda policy of dehumanization also worked as a crucial step toward their eventual murder. The 1937 *Degenerate Art* exhibition exemplifies this agenda. Here, party cultural leaders focused on the central role of instantiating ideological criteria to identify large groups of unreliable artists who could in turn be related to the population as a whole.[32]

The overt shift from institutional exclusion of individuals to a propaganda campaign that targeted large populations was a change in degree, not kind. Nazi politics had always advocated both, but the emphasis in 1933 rested more with the question of purging state bureaucracies whereas after 1936 the ideological campaign carried more weight for cultural policy as a whole. Take the example of the Bauhaus, the fabled Weimar art school that the party targeted in virulent purple prose during its electoral struggles. At the moment in July 1933 when the school's teachers decided finally to close the institution for financial reasons, the Gestapo sent a letter. The letter, surprisingly, did not emphasize the Bauhaus's supposed Bolshevik internationalist or Jewish agenda that had been so much part of the *VB* propaganda. Instead, the Gestapo demanded the dismissal of individuals, unreliable faculty like Wassily Kandinsky and Ludwig Hilbersheimer. The school could have stayed open if Ludwig Mies van der Rohe and the other faculty had agreed to these terms and found the financial resources they needed.[33] The Bauhaus, so prominent an enemy in pre-1933 propaganda and a frequent subject in art historical discussions of Nazi Germany, almost completely disappeared from Nazi artistic debates and state policy after Hitler was named chancellor.[34]

This moment reveals how the relationship of the Nazi leadership to culture changed over time. In 1933, they focused on getting rid of the other political parties or dissident unions that had plagued them in the Weimar

Republic; but at the state institutional level of art schools like the Bauhaus, there was not a significant need to get rid of the institution itself, only to purge members based on ideological criteria. Such a move was consolidated in the April 1933 Law for the Restoration of the Professional Civil Service, which allowed state officials to remove anyone they deemed suspect, a tool the party could use to replace those people with its own members. This law proved helpful for the party to deprive Bauhaus professors of past and present key positions or commissions, irrespective of their political beliefs. Hence, Paul Klee was out as a professor at the Düsseldorf Academy while party member Franz Radziwill was in.[35] Key principles of *Gleichschaltung* (bringing into line), such as party loyalty and privileging party members in central positions of authority, worked against prominent modernist artists and architects who had achieved a certain amount of career success by the late Weimar. With few exceptions, post-1933 political attitudes toward art focused on individuals, not on artistic institutions as a whole.

Since the party had consolidated its hold on major cultural institutions in the early years of rule, it is perhaps not surprising that any references to these former enemies were few and far between in the infamous 1937 *Degenerate Art* show. Instead, the organizers of this exhibition emphasized an ideological agenda by massing seemingly problematic individuals into large groups that formed the target of hatred and fear. As Christoph Zuschlag has argued, the *Degenerate Art* show in Munich resulted from the cultural policy of specific Nazi propagandists as well as a series of smaller precursor exhibitions *(Schreckenskammern)* that began almost as soon as the Nazis came to power. The Munich exhibition, which featured more than a hundred artists and their artworks, was rapidly organized in the summer of 1937 to be a counterpoint to the first *Great German Art Exhibition* at Paul Ludwig Troost's newly opened Haus der Deutschen Kunst. Adolf Ziegler, the painter in charge of the fine arts division of Goebbels's Reich Chamber of Culture (Reichskulturkammer), led the effort assisted by leading cultural figures like the "old fighter" propagandist Hans Schweitzer (a.k.a. "Mjölnir"). As is well known, the show featured sensational wall text that not only detailed how much Weimar state officials had paid for this "unhealthy" work but also made frequent references to the Jewish and/or Bolshevist nature of the artists and their work. (Ironically, only one artist, Otto Freundlich, featured on the cover of the catalog, was actually both Jewish and a Communist.) The propagandists clearly meant to defame the Weimar democracy that had patronized such art as well as give visual evidence of the potential corruption of Jewish, Communist, and other "degenerate" types. It made a visual case for rooting them out of German society for good.[36] Naturally, removing Jews and leftist agitators from Germany also necessitated defending German borders against their encroachment, including in a preventive military strike. Not coincidentally, the exhibition came at precisely the point in which party leaders began radicalizing anti-semitic policy, expanding the categories of those deemed ideologically cor-rupt, and state officials were preparing for war.[37]

The *Degenerate Art* show was just as strategically used and timed as the tactics we have seen from the party in the late Weimar Republic. However, there were also other connections to those years of electoral com-petition that help clarify the ideological function of art for Nazi policy. Zuschlag points to three important factors that highlight the connection to Weimar: political precedents, continuity of personnel, and ideological con-sistency with other elements of Nazi propaganda. In relation to politics, Frick's early elevation in Thuringia set the stage for the pattern of cultural censorship. Already, by April 5, 1930, Frick had passed a law against the "Negro culture" of jazz, and followed this with censorship of books and films. In November 1930, he sponsored the first "cleansing" action of a museum, giving the order to remove works by Otto Dix, Lyonel Feininger, Käthe Kollwitz, Karl Schmidt-Rottluff, and other Modernists from the Weimar Landesmuseum. Frick established a line of action that Nazi leaders would make the basis of their censorship of art after coming to power, and particularly after 1937. Further, in terms of the continuity of personnel, Zuschlag asserts the important precedent of the KfdK. While the KfdK was not institutionally very central to cultural propaganda after 1933, the new government often took up personnel who had been part of the Nazi regional organizations for work in local censorship and "cleansing" actions. The KfdK provided a ready roster of trustworthy Nazi supporters for addi-tional work in cultural production.[38]

I wish to focus, though, on the ideological precedents of the show and tactics employed. The *Degenerate Art* show not only emphasized core racist concepts of the party but also used a variety of visual and textual design strategies in its catalog to highlight the totalizing connection between indi-viduals and racialized social groups. At its most basic, the construct of the exhibition came clearly from the *völkisch* cultural propaganda of Rosenberg, Günther, and Schultze-Naumburg. They had already emphasized and pop-ularized the categorization of different kinds of "pure" German art and the contrast with the "degenerate" art of Jews, the criminally insane, and others. Yet organizers not only used negative stereotypes in wall text and catalog to contrast with positive "German" art that had featured so prominently in the cultural line of the *VB*. In particular, the curatorial approach to the art (especially in the accompanying catalog authored by Fritz Kaiser, a member of the Reich Propaganda Directorate [Reichspropagandaleitung]) also borrowed specifically from Schultze-Naumburg's racist emphasis on visual categorization and comparison.[39] The visual techniques helped cement the total claims of the exhibition, as the visual and textual arguments made a seamless whole.

While Schultze-Naumburg had been publishing contrasting "good" and "bad" images of architecture since before World War I, he more overtly racialized his writing after becoming a lecture star with the KfdK. Particularly in his influential book, *Kunst und Rasse* (Art and race) (1928), he used these comparative visual techniques in the negative and antisemitic chapter, influenced partially by the popularization of Wölfflin, who also used the design of his book illustrations to lay out typologizations of form. In contrast with the connoisseurship methods he used in other chapters on positive German art, in the antisemitic sections Schultze-Naumburg draws on comparisons of "degeneracy" that are showcased in cropped photos and page layouts similar to Wölfflin's (Figures 1.3 and 1.4).[40] Here, though, Schultze-Naumburg aimed the blending of conservative art history with radical politics at the stark textual and visual creation of artistic enemies from opposite ideological perspectives, the one German and the other a threatening and unhealthy foreign presence.

FIGURE 1.3. Page spread for Wölfflin's *Italien und das deutsche Formgefühl* (1931) with Titian (left) and Burgkmeier (pages 126–27).

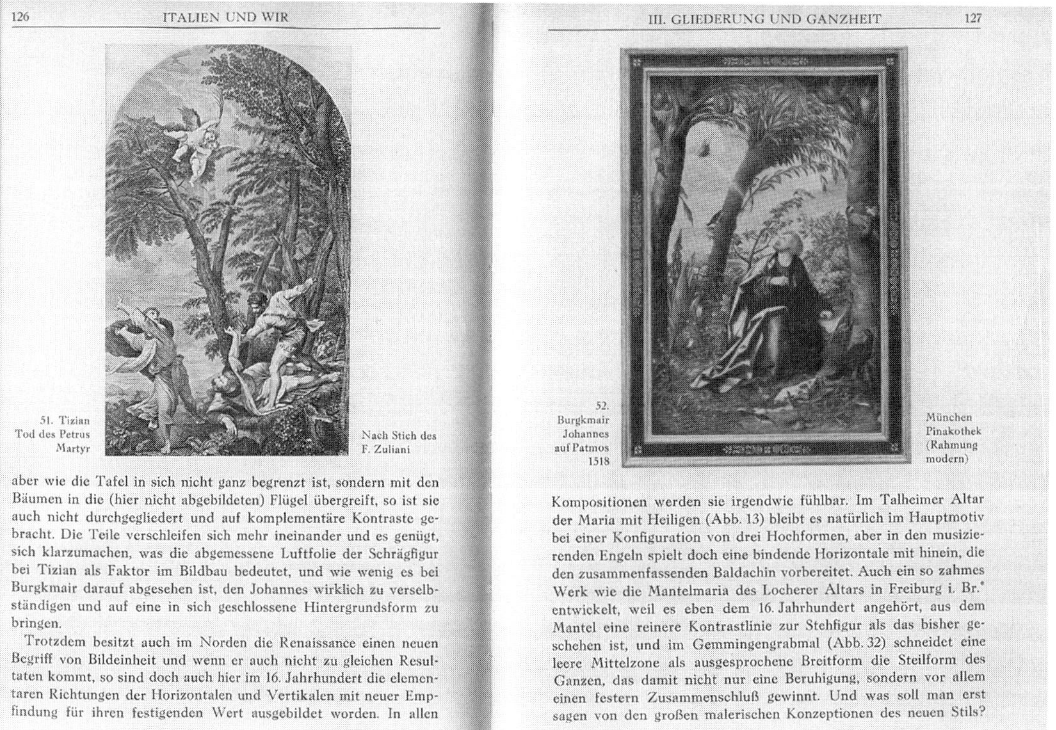

126   ITALIEN UND WIR

51. Tizian
Tod des Petrus
Martyr

Nach Stich des
F. Zuliani

aber wie die Tafel in sich nicht ganz begrenzt ist, sondern mit den Bäumen in die (hier nicht abgebildeten) Flügel übergreift, so ist sie auch nicht durchgegliedert und auf komplementäre Kontraste gebracht. Die Teile verschleifen sich mehr ineinander und es genügt, sich klarzumachen, was die abgemessene Luftfolie der Schrägfigur bei Tizian als Faktor im Bildbau bedeutet, und wie wenig es bei Burgkmair darauf abgesehen ist, den Johannes wirklich zu verselbständigen und auf eine in sich geschlossene Hintergrundsform zu bringen.

Trotzdem besitzt auch im Norden die Renaissance einen neuen Begriff von Bildeinheit und wenn er auch nicht zu gleichen Resultaten kommt, so sind doch auch hier im 16. Jahrhundert die elementaren Richtungen der Horizontalen und Vertikalen mit neuer Empfindung für ihren festigenden Wert ausgebildet worden. In allen

III. GLIEDERUNG UND GANZHEIT   127

52.
Burgkmair
Johannes
auf Patmos
1518

München
Pinakothek
(Rahmung
modern)

Kompositionen werden sie irgendwie fühlbar. Im Talheimer Altar der Maria mit Heiligen (Abb. 13) bleibt es natürlich im Hauptmotiv bei einer Konfiguration von drei Hochformen, aber in den musizierenden Engeln spielt doch eine bindende Horizontale mit hinein, die den zusammenfassenden Baldachin vorbereitet. Auch ein so zahmes Werk wie die Mantelmaria des Locherer Altars in Freiburg i. Br.* entwickelt, weil es eben dem 16. Jahrhundert angehört, aus dem Mantel eine reinere Kontrastlinie zur Stehfigur als das bisher geschehen ist, und im Gemmingengrabmal (Abb. 32) schneidet eine leere Mittelzone als ausgesprochene Breitform die Steilform des Ganzen, das damit nicht nur eine Beruhigung, sondern vor allem einen festern Zusammenschluß gewinnt. Und was soll man erst sagen von den großen malerischen Konzeptionen des neuen Stils?

Following Schultze-Naumburg, curators categorized the art of the 1937 show stylistically in terms of either shared lapses of individual artists in concept and technique or works whose ideological agenda revealed their makers' racial degradation. Group 1 in Kaiser's catalog, for example, focused on those non-Jewish artists who distorted the body through portraiture, featured in such diverse comparisons as Dix's *Portrait of Radziwill* (1928) and Schmidt-Rottluff's sculpture *Red Head* (1917).[41] In group 7, however, the African ("Neger") as a racial ideal, Kaiser fell back on a more collective stylistic classification of examples. Instead of individual artistic efforts, he focused on shared attributes as transparent visually to a degenerate concept of race. He followed this with his presentation of Jewish artists in group 8 and their equally shared preferences for distortion of the body (Figure 1.5). The booklet ends with a discussion of "art bolshevism."[42] Hence, when the catalog turned to questions of the denigration of race, Kaiser, drawing from the pattern of criticism well established by Schultze-Naumburg, used the stylistic typologization of works in order to argue for a visually coherent category of bad art. Typologizing form was well suited

FIGURE 1.4. Page spread for Schultze-Naumburg's *Kunst und Rasse* (1928), with illustrations of modernist artists compared to the physically handicapped (pages 96–97). Photograph courtesy of United States Holocaust Memorial Museum Library.

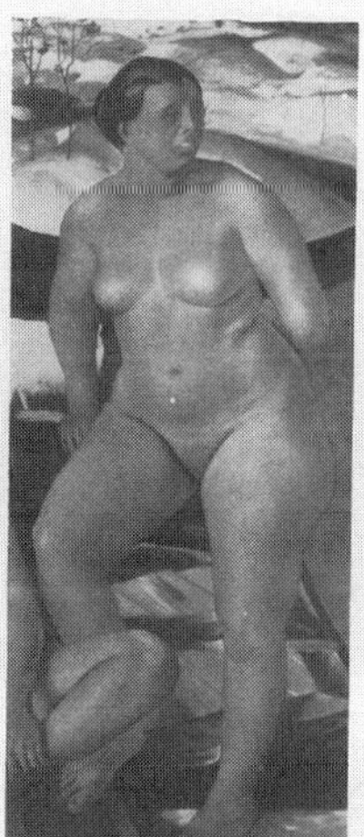
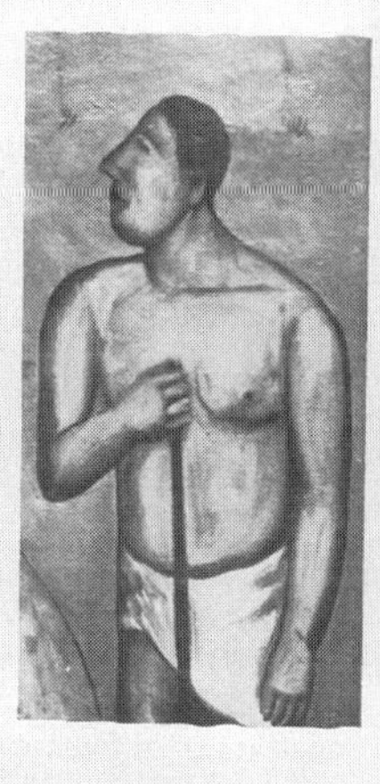

Abb. 145. u. 146. Ausschnitte aus Bildern
der „modernen" Schule

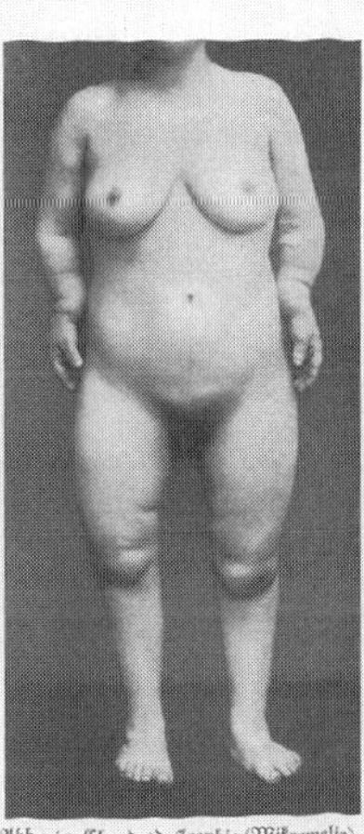

Abb. 147. Chondrodystrophie (Mikromelie),
degeneriert

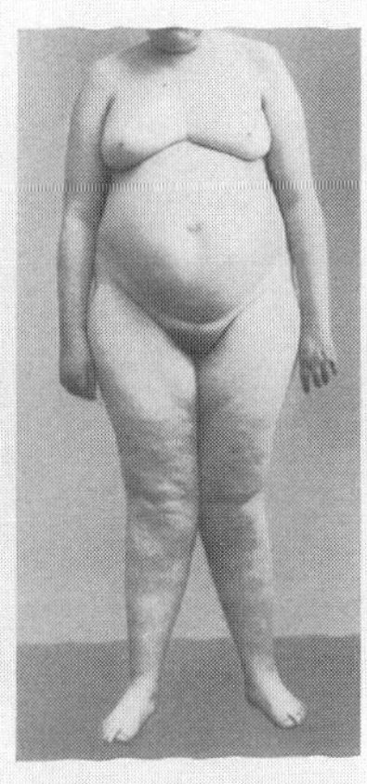

Abb. 148. Idiotie, Fettsucht

belegten, und für die Kunst im allgemeinen mehr diejenigen übrigblieben, die neben einseitigen Begabungen allerlei Züge von Entartung trügen und vielleicht durch die vermeintliche Ungebundenheit des Künstlerberufes und manches andere angezogen würden, die also eine ungünstige Auslese im Volkskörper darstellten.

Es gäbe endlich noch eine vierte Möglichkeit, doch muß diese schon nach ganz kurzer Untersuchung ausscheiden: daß nämlich die Kunst sich aus pädagogischen oder agitatorischen Gründen einseitig einstellte. Wohl gab es eine Zeit, in der die Kunst die Rolle des sozialistischen Wanderpredigers übernahm und in Schilderungen des menschlichen Elends zum

Mitleid und damit wohl auch zur Abhilfe rufen wollte. Aber um einen derartigen Mißbrauch der Kunst zu demagogischen Zwecken handelte es sich hier sicher nicht, denn Künstler und anscheinend auch die Allgemeinheit der Betrachter fühlten sich durchaus wohl in dieser Luft, in der Gleiche sich zu Gleichen fanden. Seltsam genug, daß diese Kunst auch ganz gutgläubig von den Schulen hingenommen wurde, die nun ihre Jugend sogar mit einer Kost fütterten, die man pornographisch nennen muß, wenn man diesen Begriff nicht stark beugen will. Den Versuch, ihnen den „Helden" in bildlicher Form zu zeigen, wie es bei Völkern, die noch die Ehrfurcht kannten, wohl Gebrauch war, dürfte mit diesen Bildern nicht gut möglich sein.

to the creation of the totalizing function of ideology that naturalizes and essentializes the social group associations, a crucial goal of the *Degenerate Art* show. Hence, Dix might be guilty as an individual German, but Freundlich was racially dangerous as an "other."

At the same time, the institutional critique so strategically important in late Weimar no longer made the necessary political point, given Nazi control over state and, increasingly, private spheres. For example, the Bauhaus makes no appearance in the *Degenerate Art* show catalog, a point also exemplified in the exhibition itself. Of the hundreds of works on display, Oskar Schlemmer, Klee, and Kandinsky, among other Bauhaus artists, were featured (note that the organizers did not gather works systematically throughout German collections). Nevertheless, in all the hundreds of wall texts that we know, the Bauhaus is mentioned only once, as a label for a Kandinsky work that associates him with the "Communist Bauhaus in Dessau."[43] Instead, the wall text and installation, in addition to references to Dada and Expressionism as styles, used "Communist" and "Jewish" as the most frequent sobriquets associated with all the artists. Collective identities became even more central than they were in earlier stages of party propaganda.

FIGURE 1.5. Page spread from the catalog for the *Degenerate Art* show, 1937 (pages 20–21). Photograph courtesy of Charles Deering McCormick Library of Special Collections, Northwestern University Library.

menschliche Figuren zu sehen, die wahrhaftig mit Gorillas mehr Ähnlichkeit haben als mit Menschen. Hier gibt es Porträts, gegen die die ersten geschichtlich bekannten Versuche der Menschendarstellung in steinzeitlichen Höhlen reife Meisterwerke sind. Aber auch für solche Schauerstücke wurden, wie die Ankaufspreise ausweisen, noch vor wenigen Jahren höchste Preise verlangt und bezahlt.

Gruppe 8.

In einem kleinen Raum sind hier der Abwechslung halber einmal nur Juden vertreten. Damit keine Mißverständnisse entstehen, sei bemerkt, daß es sich hier nur um eine kleine Auswahl aus den zahlreichen jüdischen Machwerken handelt, die die Ausstellung insgesamt zeigt. Die großen „Verdienste", die sich die jüdischen Wortführer, Händler und Förderer der entarteten Kunst zweifellos erworben haben, rechtfertigt zur Genüge diese „Sonderehrung". Hier findet sich u. a. auch „Der neue Mensch", wie ihn sich Jud Freundlich erträumt hat. Dort

Das Judentum verstand es, besonders unter Ausnützung seiner Stellung in der Presse, mit Hilfe der sogenannten Kunstkritik nicht nur die natürlichen Auffassungen über das Wesen und die Aufgaben der Kunst sowie deren Zweck allmählich zu verwirren, sondern überhaupt das allgemeine gesunde Empfinden auf diesem Gebiete zu zerstören.

Der Führer
bei der Eröffnung des Hauses der Deutschen Kunst.

20

Drei Kostproben von jüdischer Plastik und Malerei

Die Titel lauten:
„Selbstbildnis", „Der neue Mensch" und „Kopf".

Die Juden heißen:
Meidner, Freundlich und Haizmann.

But of course, this too corresponds to changing views of the party leadership. By 1937, state schools had been consolidated under the Nazi regime and troublesome personnel had been sent packing. Hitler had set his eyes on the East and on the racial agenda that his view embraced.[44] By then, as he managed plans for the war, the new need was to clarify the enemy for the coming fight. The *Degenerate Art* show did not need to attack the Bauhaus or its stylistic and pedagogical innovations; the exhibition instead needed to highlight those artists who the Nazis assumed in their work or in their person exemplified the sick racialized body or the threatening internationalist political agenda. Both collective enemies were central targets once the German military crossed the Polish border in September 1939. The *Degenerate Art* exhibition, as the most-visited art exhibition of all time, clearly helped support this goal.

Imperialism and Genocide: Implementation of Oppressive Policies with the Functional Use of Art

With the war, naturally, these propagandistic uses of visual culture increased as well as became more varied with the state's military strategies and successes or failures.[45] However, the war also highlights how useful art could be not only for legitimating but also for actively implementing state and party policies through the incorporation of cultural production into institutional development. This functional role of art becomes most clearly apparent in large-scale architectural planning. Such planning played a crucial role, for example, in the development of the imperialist and genocidal ambitions of the most notorious National Socialist site, the SS concentration camp at Auschwitz. Here the strategic or ideological uses of art, while still present, were secondary to the imperative of creating an efficient and stable environment that would enable German expansion in the East and its control or murder of the millions of supposedly inferior and threatening people that stood in the way of this goal. In this respect, the imperialist war drive and the racist genocidal policy were complementary and interrelated terms, and cultural decisions helped cement or support the link.[46]

While central to the historical literature on Nazi Germany, concentration camps have with few exceptions been almost entirely absent from the architectural scholarship on the period. Most likely this is a result of the relatively banal and vernacular architectural world of the camps that has been deemed visually less complex than other state building, even if its historical significance is obviously profound.[47] Little could be more architecturally obvious, for example, than the layout of all the labor and death camps (excepting the Operation Reinhard camps of Belzec, Sobibor, and

Treblinka) in a traditional plan of regularly spaced pavilions. Whatever the variations, this plan has a long history as a productive type, being associated with the military, social institutions, and industrial structures, among others. The organized plan *emphasizes* its relationship to production through its repetitive and rational spatial clarity. The link between military, productive, and punitive functions was made unintentionally clear in the first established *Konzentrationslager*, KL Dachau (Figure 1.6). The SS hierarchy intended Dachau as a model of order and stability, asserting their authority and ability to control the punishment of those deemed enemies of the National Socialist state. Such assertions were buttressed with the camp's first layout in 1933, which took over the form of the munitions factory that had previously existed on the site. The traditional plan of barracks for the prisoners to the east indicates the obvious need to regiment, observe, and control the penal population. This would be used by the SS in subsequent camps, and the organization of the environment and administration would be based on the "Dachau model."[48]

At Auschwitz, though, control of prisoners was only one goal, an intermediary function between either instrumentalizing their labor within the vast urban scale of agricultural and industrial concerns that grew up around Auschwitz or the equally vast scale of murdering the hundreds of thousands of Jewish and non-Jewish individuals deemed superfluous or "dangerous" to the state. In this context, the SS architects used building both to enable the enactment of specific policies and also to distance SS individuals from the brutal aspects of these actions. The distancing role that specific aesthetic and formal architectural and spatial decisions played in relation to the destructive capacity of the war and genocide increasingly served the larger goals of Nazi imperialism and, at Auschwitz and elsewhere, expanded on earlier functions of camp construction and planning. That is to say, architecture was political and economically productive.

The control and development of the spaces of the perpetrators are particularly revealing. In formal terms, the characteristic features of the SS-built environment were repetition of familiar cultural forms and the symbolic referencing of vernacular traditions. For example, two SS saunas built for the troops in November 1943 and early 1944 by forced labor draw on obvious central European carpentry traditions in the wood panels as well as the roofing (Figure 1.7). Such vernaculars can also be seen in relation to urban planning, as the garden city layout of the proposed SS housing estate west of the main camp and finalized in later 1942 makes clear (Figure 1.8). The gently curving streets contrast noticeably with the rigid pavilions of the inmates' spaces. In both cases, the familiarity of the architectural environment and its use create a naturalized connection to the noncamp lives

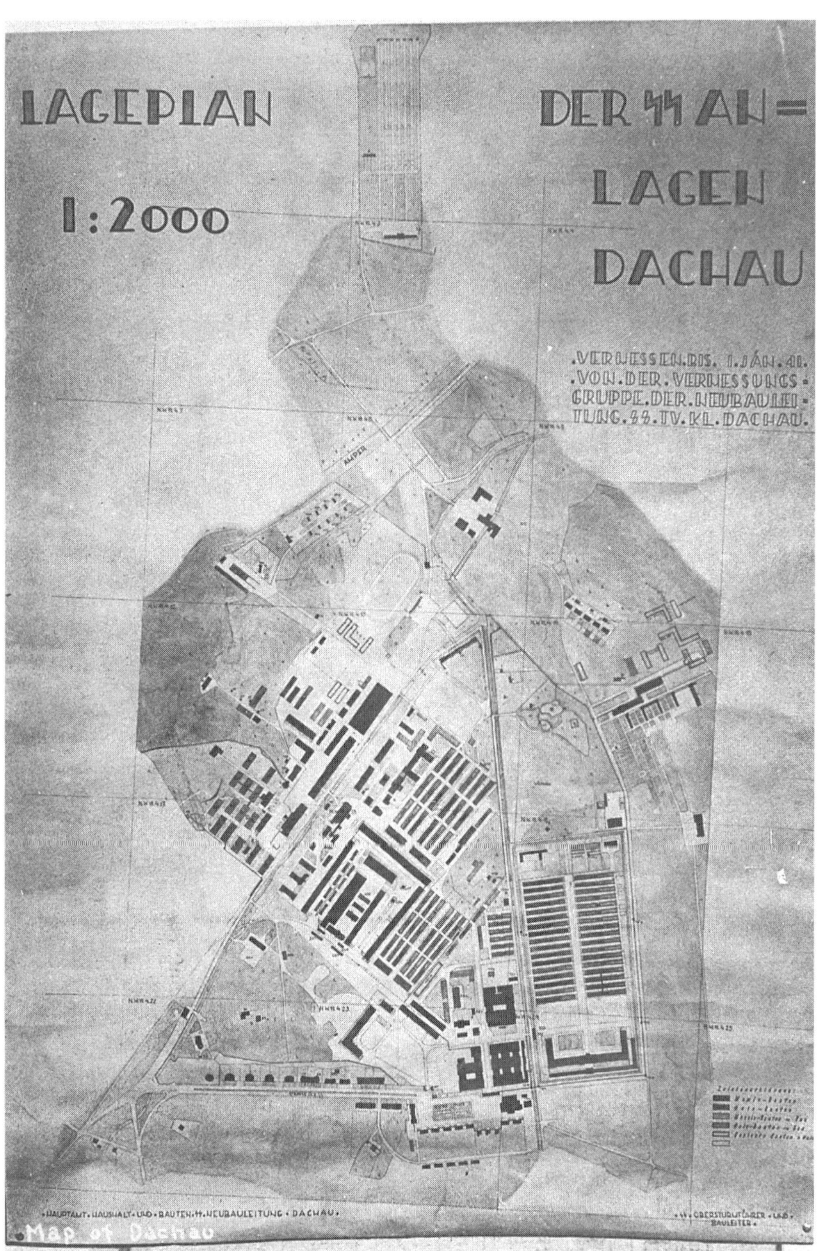

FIGURE 1.6. Plan of KL Dachau, with expanded pavilions for prisoners on the right, 1941. United States Holocaust Memorial Museum. Courtesy of Frank Manucci.

and backgrounds of SS guards and officers.[49] This architecture and planning distanced them from the productive use of thousands of prisoners in regimented forced labor at the camp as well as the implementation of the ideological agenda of genocide in the gas chambers.

Such a distancing project only works, however, if the spaces between and around the buildings are equally controlled. This was not only true for the spaces of the predominantly Jewish inmates, who existed in a world of seemingly endless organized plans. It was also true for the world of the SS. Innumerable memorandums from the increasingly centralized control of the built environment by Hans Kammler and his Amt C (Office C) in the SS headquarters in Berlin made clear that, for example, street designs in the surrounding areas of the camps should be visually unified and ordered. In addition, SS members themselves were carefully regulated in their use of specific spaces. Kommandant Rudolf Höss gave out numerous orders about where an SS member could and could not go, including, for example, strict laws about staying out of the casino in the city of Auschwitz, keeping their family members in only certain areas of the entire SS area of interest *(Interessengebiet)*, and spaces of the camp that could or could not be visited without permission. Thus, the architectural and urban environment inhabited and used by the SS outside of the spaces of their abuse of the prisoners was highly regulated, visually controlled, and tended toward buildings that emphasized familiarity and repetition of forms. These characteristics were made explicit in the orders of the Zentralbauleitung (Central Building Office) that governed the development of the space. That architects within the building administration relied on classic Modernist sources such as Ernst Neufert's *Bauentwurfslehre* (1936) for inspiration in constructing an efficient and

FIGURE 1.7. SS Zentralbauleitung, photograph of the troop sauna, Auschwitz I, circa November 1943. Courtesy of the Yad Vashem Photo Archive.

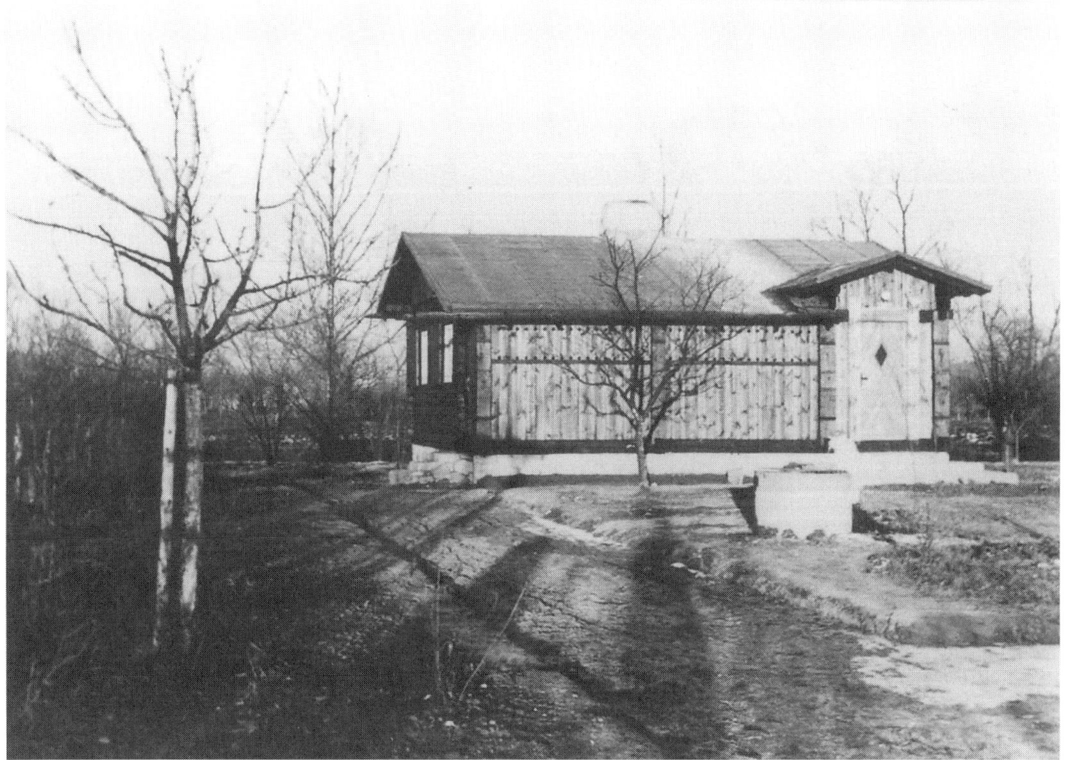

modern space proved to be no contradiction. As masters of their oppressive universe, they could separate spaces, functions, and aesthetics with impunity. They evidenced no concern for the ideological architectural debates that erupted in the late Weimar Republic that labeled such forms "degenerate."[50]

The information we gain from understanding architecture and how it enabled the SS personnel's increasing distance from production helps us clarify the essential imperialist ambitions of the Nazi war drive. These ambitions differed from the early goals of the Nazi state in consolidating its control over peoples and institutions and developing its own institutional identity and ideological positions. The principal spatial characteristics of Auschwitz not only in terms of the massive scale but also in the regulation of spaces for victim and perpetrator alike (as well as the kinds of spaces specifically for the perpetrators) indicate a different kind of function for

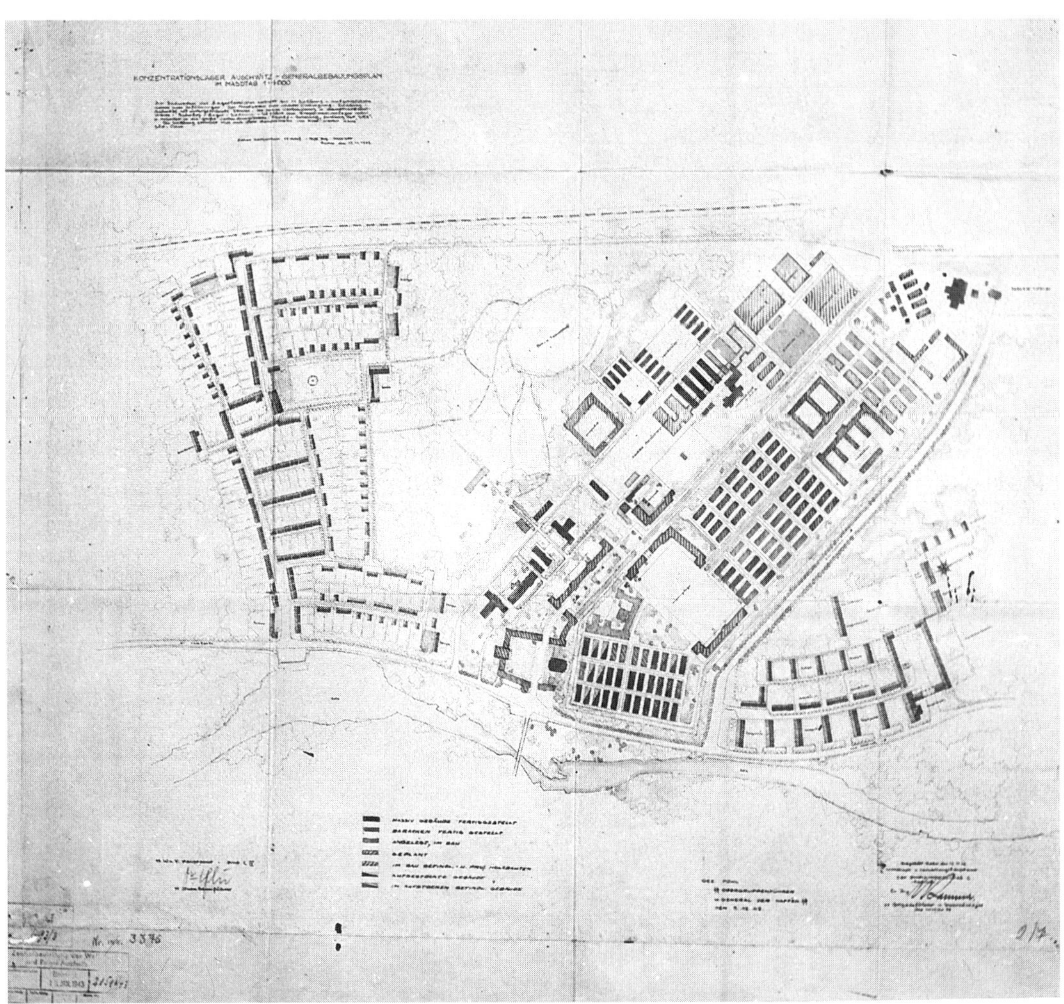

FIGURE 1.8. Lothar Hartjenstein, Final Plan of Auschwitz I, including SS housing estate to the west (left in the illustration) of the main camp, 1942. Photograph courtesy of Niels Gutschow.

the camp in relation to Nazi goals. A key function obviously was ridding the empire of racial and political undesirables through genocide and murder, both in the camps and at the fronts. But this was not merely a drive for racial purity, that is, an ideological goal. Rather, as Adam Tooze makes clear, the military campaign for control over eastern territory included the economic necessity identified early by Hitler not only to acquire agricultural estates but also to establish stable and internally controlled markets for goods and agriculture that could survive separate from the hostile world around Germany. For the Nazis, the agenda, called the Generalplan Ost, was a timetable for clearing Eastern Europe of an estimated forty-five million people to establish just such a new German political economy. Ideologically driven genocide and the war were inseparable in terms of the necessity for both to produce effectively the new political economy of Germany. Architecture at Auschwitz served each of these parallel purposes.[51]

The long-term contradictory aspects of imperialism and genocide produced unresolvable and difficult-to-maintain conditions that had to be alleviated to guarantee a productive political economy, a tactic that could be achieved with help from architecture and the cultural realm. Architecture could perform one service by functioning as a phantasmagoria for the SS personnel. The phantasmagoria is the image that allows the consumer to distance her- or himself from production, asserting an eternal and timeless essence instead of a time-bound sense of an object of labor. The illusionistic aspects of the phantasmagoria rely heavily on the repetition of the known in the guise of the new.[52] Such a logic operated for many SS spaces of Auschwitz: the SS normalized its environment through vernacular and familiar institutional spatial and architectural choices, a normalization maintained by the rigid control of interaction between the perpetrators' spaces and those assigned to the victims in the camp. Indeed and tellingly, the two aestheticized elements in the entire complex of the deadly environment of Birkenau were the vernacular decorative carpentry details on the guards' barracks at the selection ramp and also the treatment of the exterior of Crematoria II and III (Figure 1.9). Sites of power and oppression required a distancing image that drew attention away from their grotesque functions supporting the productive logic of the Nazi state. But because of this requirement, this very architectural image depended symbiotically on its relationship to that which it was meant to mask, namely, both labor and death. Distraction requires two referents, as it implies looking away from one thing to another. In the process, architecture became a functional cog in a complex and destructive political economic machine.

At Auschwitz, the architects used planning and structural decoration selectively to control the space, promote efficiency, and create points of

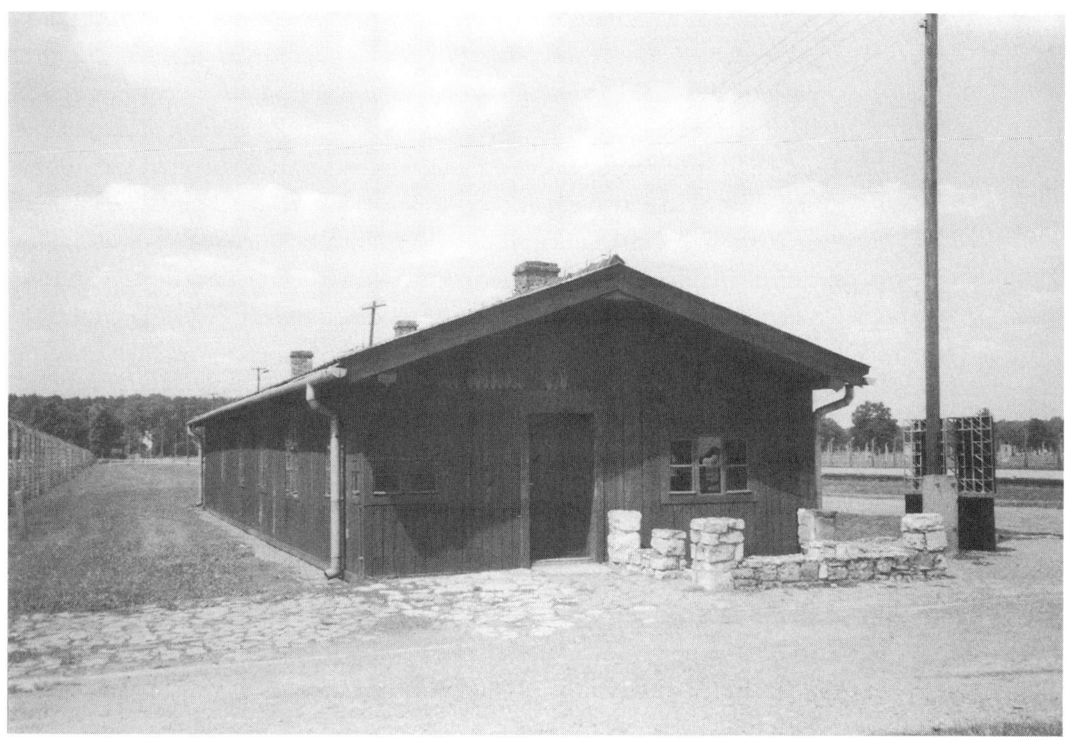

emphasis or distraction. And yet the selective use of art was always what defined the relationship between Nazis and culture. Architects at Auschwitz certainly used cultural production strategically, as in the case of Wölfflin in the Weimar period, and ideologically, such as the emphasis on art and propaganda in the late 1930s. Yet, the SS use of architecture at Auschwitz was dominated by the functional necessities of protecting personnel and advancing a Nazi imperialist agenda as well as the perceived need for the brutal murder of millions. Analyzing examples of how these three different relationships of National Socialism to culture worked helps us clarify the variety of ways in which Nazi agents could have been categorized as criminals, as active perpetrators in the postwar environment. Surprisingly, though, this interest in categorization did not arise in any significant degree until well after the war.

FIGURE 1.9. SS Zentralbauleitung, guard hut along main rail tracks within the camp, Auschwitz–Birkenau, circa 1944. Author's photograph.

Retribution: Defining the Perpetrator and the Creation of an Opposition between Art and Nazi Politics in the Immediate Postwar Period

From art history departments to the museum to the building site, the *Gleichschaltung* of cultural production in National Socialist Germany significantly legitimized and influenced the timing of radicalizing policies of oppression. As we have seen with the examples of the appropriation of Wölfflin, the propaganda of the *Degenerate Art* show and the SS architecture at Auschwitz, specific leaders and groups within the Nazi Party consciously used art and art history to promote particular agendas that increased their power and allowed them to implement their racist and nationalist goals. By the end of the war, this instrumentalization of culture included the extreme integration of architectural production with the destruction of the European Jews. Only the combined power of the Allies defeated such hubris and the wanton scale of the state's ideological and military ambitions, grinding Hitler's army to dust. The Nazi state and the vision of a cultural paradise in Germany after its potential victories had, instead, engendered the ruination of key cities through the vengeful Allied firebombings, the collapse of its political and social order, as well as the complete undermining of state-sponsored culture and cultural institutions (Figure 1.10). It seemed that nothing could be salvaged from the artists, architects, and art historians of this era as the four powers took possession of Germany and began its path toward reconstruction.

And yet, given the vast number of Germans who were party members or participated actively in some aspect of the genocide or other brutal

FIGURE 1.10. Destruction of central Nuremberg at the end of the war, c. 1945. Copyright Dokumentationszentrum Reichsparteitagsgelände.

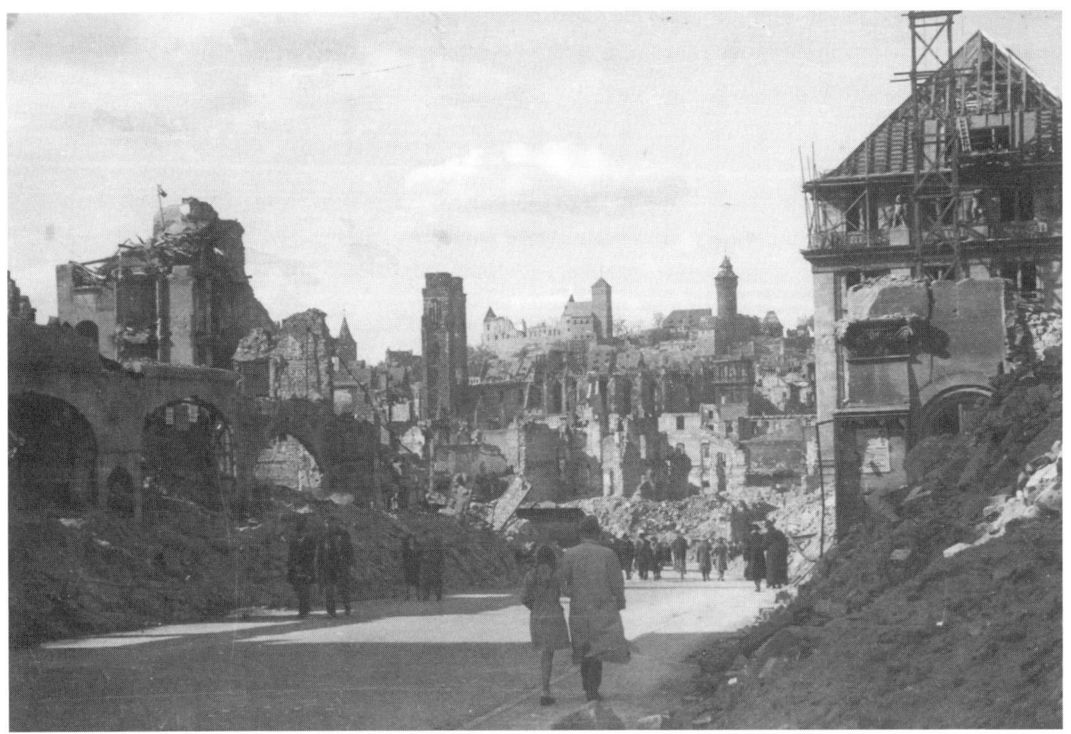

actions of the Nazi state, it is surprising to find so few of them characterized as criminally culpable or perpetrators. Internally, defeated Germany had other priorities than a subtle implementation of justice, as the Nazi drive had left a society shattered by the experience of war and radically destabilized. In Germany itself in the immediate postwar years, women dominated (seven million more women than men in the total population). The last years of the war within Germany already saw women taking on much of the burden as family heads. Millions of men faced the experience of becoming POWs with hard labor in Soviet camps, many never to return. The Soviets and their Cold War allies also expelled another approximately twelve million ethnic Germen men and women from lands settled in the east (some for generations, others as a result of Nazi efforts to move out Poles and other Slavs to make the area "Germanic" again).[53]

The forceful impact of National Socialist policies that reshaped German society did not dissipate with the collapse of the military effort after World War II. Indeed, the military campaign itself led to an immediate need to rebuild, physically and politically, the destroyed cities and institutions essential to daily life. Within this rebuilding campaign, though, occupation authorities and Germans themselves separated analysis of cultural work and criminal responsibility for the past. They were conceived of as oppositional, in spite of Hitler's clear demand that they be treated as integrated factors within his state.

In terms of the political repercussions, occupation authorities reacted to the past by condemning the policies and practices of the Nazi state and trying its leaders at the Nuremberg International Military Tribunals (1945–46). Here most clearly, the prosecution narrowed the circle of perpetrators to the few ideologically driven leaders who could be held responsible for giving orders, creating the Nazi agenda, or running the military domination of Europe. The Allies also introduced a denazification process to varying degrees as well as the establishment of bureaucratic institutions in the four zones of occupation. Those newly appointed to control the urban plans, for example, included not only architects purged from the civil service when the Nazis came to power but also leading members of Speer's architectural and wartime staff. Beyond the most elite Nazi leadership cadre who were established as criminal, the Allies often sacrificed consistency of political judgment in the face of practical need. They apparently shared the assumption that the previous regime had used cultural actors (e.g., architects) as mere tools rather than active collaborators. Hence most of these individuals were safe for postwar appointments.[54]

Yet almost immediately along with practical building measures, the impact of the Nazi past began to influence conservative political interests reconsolidating their positions in the Federal Republic. For example, in relation to party politics, the CDU—the reconfigured outgrowth of the prominent Weimar-era Catholic Center Party—discussed the recent Nazi past quite openly. Led by Konrad Adenauer, who would become the first chancellor of West Germany, CDU officials did not emphasize the singular role of Hitler and the NSDAP elite in leading Germany into the Nazi state as had been prevalent at the Nuremberg Tribunals. Identifying the perpetrator seemed of little concern. Rather, they asserted that the materialist and secular interests that had dominated Germany long before the 1930s had opened the door for the evil and irresponsible actions of the immediate past. Only the moral order represented by the Christian faiths could restore Germans to a respectable future. In this immediate postwar interpretation, the rampant materialism of capitalism was culpable for bringing the Nazis to power just as the secular worldview of the Soviet Union posed a concomitant threat in the present.[55] Such a view avoided the question of guilt, either of the leaders or camp personnel currently on trial or of the vast majority of Germans who helped create murderous policies and staff the military effort. It did mean, however, that the CDU saw an interpretation of the Nazi past as the ideological lynchpin to creating a postwar antidote and bringing the moderately conservative party to power.

While the CDU argued for a very particular interpretation of recent German history, other institutions in society, especially cultural ones, acted as though the NSDAP had had no impact on their world whatsoever. Art historians, for example, on the whole showed a profound lack of interest in questions concerning how art history had been useful for the Nazi effort. With some notable complicated exceptions, universities appointed art scholars with relatively little reflection on their relation to the party (or even their help with looting of art during the war) or little discussion of the problematic nationalism and racism in the scholarship. So, at the first German national art history conference in 1948, art historians created a sense of normality in the discipline by avoiding any mention of politics. At the second conference in 1949, scholars even organized an extended honorary session on the compromised but complicated case of Wilhelm Pinder (d. 1947) with no discussion of his nationalism or connections to the NSDAP. As with the architectural offices throughout the occupied zones, little self-reflection occurred in the public debates or writings of the immediate postwar art historians. They were busy instead reestablishing the institutional stability of their discipline, not identifying a category of art historical perpetrator.[56] The world of the criminal past and the cultural present were seen as quite unconnected.

However, in contrast to West German conservative culture that constructed itself in opposition to the Nazi past, some high-profile (if sporadic) postwar responses in the German Democratic Republic did mark a direct engagement with issues concerning the guilt of Germans and their potential role as perpetrators, as well as the suffering of the victims of the Nazi state. For example, Hubert Hoffmann reconstituted the Dessau Bauhaus in 1945 until the Socialist Unity Party (Sozialistische Einheitspartei Deutschland; SED) assumed control of this Soviet-sector city in fall 1946. At that point, Hoffmann's past as a member of the Bauhaus was overshadowed by the revelation (left off his résumé) that he had served as a city planner during the Nazi period. Eastern German officials removed him from his post. Down the road in Dresden, authorities reopened the Academy of Fine Arts in 1947 with leading antifascist artists such as Hans Grundig. His versions of *Victims of Fascism* (1946–48) explicitly figured the environment of the concentration camps with their towers and barbed wire as well as the Communist affiliation of the dead evidenced in the red triangle of the prisoner's uniform (Figure 1.11). Similarly, the first German feature film produced came from the Soviet zone, *Die Mörder sind unter uns* (The murderers are among us) (1946, dir. Wolfgang Staudte), and it thematized the criminal responsibility of the Nazi soldier.[57]

But by the 1950s, with the solidification of the Cold War, the political impact of National Socialist policies became even more concrete, while its cultural representation narrowed to a few major themes in film, none of

FIGURE 1.11. Hans Grundig, *To the Victims of Fascism,* 1946/49. Second version. Oil on fiberboard, 110 × 200 cm. Staatliche Kunstsammlungen Dresden, Galerie Neue Meister. Copyright 2012 Artists Rights Society (ARS), New York/VG Bild-Kunst, Bonn.

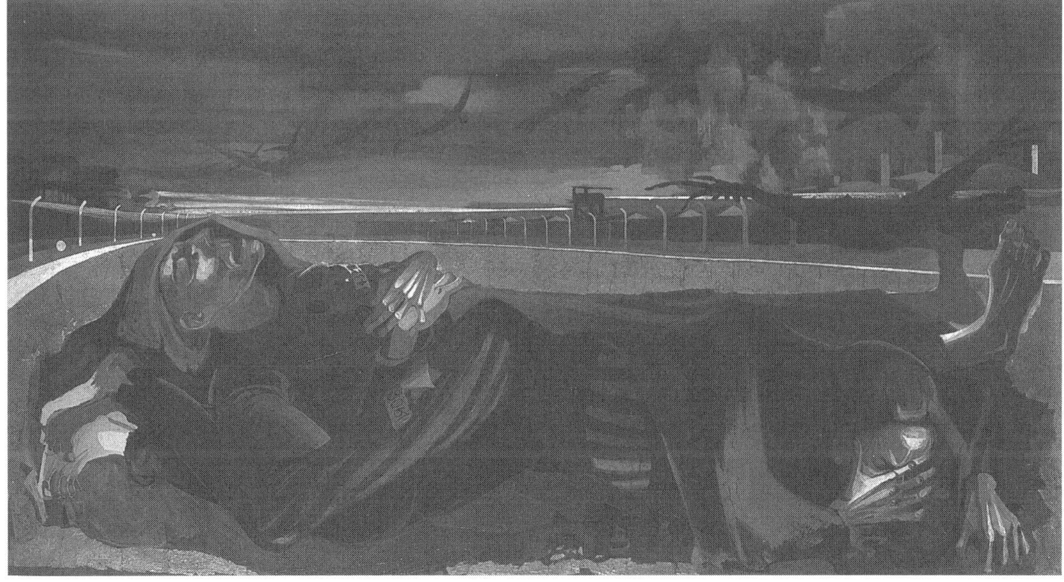

which focused on the concept of a perpetrator. (After a few initial forays like Grundig's, fine artists and architects increasingly ignored the Nazi past.) In the east, the government had already established the foundational myth of the GDR that asserted the antifascist credentials of its citizenry. From this perspective, the GDR had no perpetrators to debate. In the west, Adenauer's alignment with the United States meant bracketing further the messy continuities with the Nazi past and focusing instead on the end of the war. As Robert Moeller has convincingly argued,

> In the newly created Federal Republic, many West Germans and a large majority of the West German parliament acknowledged that the National Socialist regime had persecuted millions of innocent victims, particularly Jews. But they paid even more attention to crimes committed against Germans who were not Jews, crimes that, according to some contemporary accounts, were comparable to the crimes that some Germans had committed. The most important representatives of German victimhood were the women, men, and children who had left or been driven out of eastern Europe by the Red Army at the war's end, and those in uniform for whom captivity in the Soviet Union followed German surrender. . . . By focusing on the experiences of expellees and POWs in the Soviet Union, they could talk about the end of the Third Reich without assuming responsibility for its origins. In this abbreviated account of National Socialism, all Germans were ultimately victims of a war that Hitler had started but everyone lost.[58]

The government concentrated this debate on two groups, the ethnic German expellees and the POWs. The former proved to be an immediate presence, as upward of 16 percent of West Germany's population came from the east and settled in new housing estates in Nuremberg and elsewhere. The focus on the latter also fed the Western alliance and conservative ideology as it demonized Soviet policies and aligned the former German soldiers with their Cold War West German counterparts. Certainly, the restitution debates in parliament of the early 1950s led Adenauer and other politicians (notably, not many in his own CDU party) to discuss explicitly the suffering of the European Jews as a separate victim group and the need to help build up Israel as the new home of many displaced by the Holocaust. But, while this debate resolved itself in the reparation law of 1953, Adenauer's visit to the Soviet Union in 1955 and the conclusion of agreements with Premier Nikita Khrushchev to return all remaining German POWs proved much more significant for public discussions and the chancellor's approval ratings. In October 1955, the public greeted the last returning soldiers as both heroes and victims upon their homecoming, helping to establish the experience of Germans at the end of World War II as the primary point of political discourse concerning the Nazi past.[59] Notably, the question of perpetrators remained unasked and unanswered during this period, beyond the few identified Nazi elites who had already been tried at Nuremberg.

Filmmaking in West Germany in particular picked up on the themes of the expellees and the German soldiers in the Soviet camps in B movies and sentimental, rural-themed *Heimat* films. Art and architecture, however, went through a much clearer alignment with aesthetic and ideological debates coming from the United States and other western powers that rejected allusions to Hitler and the war and, by extension, contemporary CDU politics. In West German design, artists attempted to reestablish German products through sophisticated new aesthetics that matched the ambitions of German industry to assert itself as an international force along the models of the prewar Werkbund. In fine arts, the abstraction of Ernst Wilhelm Nay, Hann Trier, and others established itself in western academies as it did in the United States and elsewhere in the capitalist art markets (Figure 1.12). In West Germany, the rejection of naturalistic imagery in painting signaled both a distance from the works shown at the *Great German Art Shows* of the Nazi era but also from the consistent academic conventions

FIGURE 1.12. Ernst Wilhelm Nay, *Study for "Femme Rose,"* 1947. Graphite on paper, 8⁷⁄₁₆ × 11⅞ inches (21.5 × 30.2 cm). Courtesy of Harvard Art Museums: Busch-Reisinger Museum, Friends Anniversary Collection, Gift of Siegfried Gohr, 2008.214. Photograph from Imaging Department. Copyright President and Fellows of Harvard College.

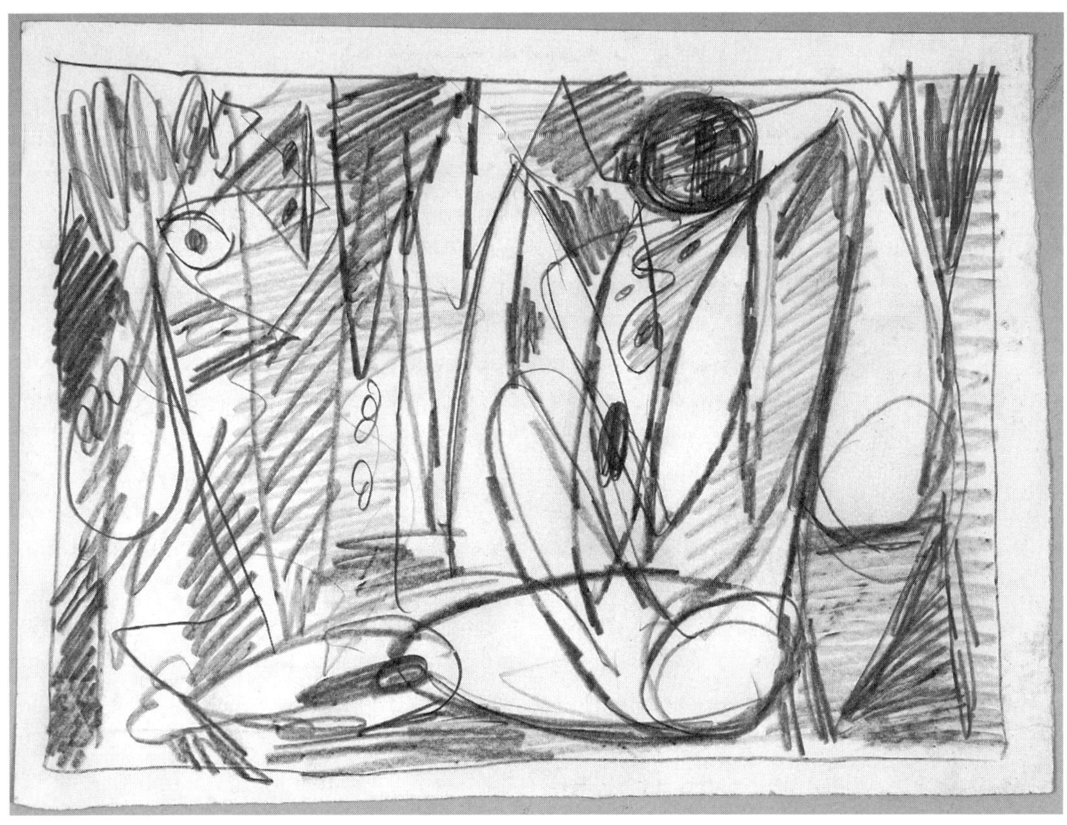

being manipulated in the Soviet east.[60] Architecturally, the steel and glass of the Weimar avant-garde became the sign for the internationalist values and antimonumental tastes of the West German state. Modernism, as a counterpart to the Socialist Realism of the east, played just as well in Bonn as it did in New York.[61] This positive assertion of German cultural values aligned with western movements complemented within the country the negative, politically critical narrative of the abuse of soldiers and citizens at the hands of the Soviets at the end of the war and into the 1950s. Art and politics could occupy different positions in relation to the past, both of which supported Adenauer's agenda. In all cases, the Nazi past was very much alive as an influence on contemporary society, but the concept of the perpetrator formed a relative silence as a real topic in culture as well as politics. Those perpetrators like Speer who did exist in name had been brought to trial and expunged from daily life in the Federal Republic. The new society supposedly represented the opposite world in all ways from that created and ruled by the fascist dictatorship.

Conclusion

Given the interest of the critics writing in the pages of the *Völkischer Beobachter*, their appropriation of Wölfflin's writing and the use of his thought in the propaganda of the party in the late twenties and early thirties exemplifies the cultural component of a broad strategy to come to power. That initial transformation of art history into electoral tactics helped establish a model of cultural policy in Thuringia and intellectual prototypes for the Nazi elites. Subsequently, these political moves conditioned the practice of the ideological demonization and degradation of specific targeted groups embodied in the example of the *Degenerate Art* show. The complicated matrix of ideas and actions, academic positions and ideologues, may have peaked with this exhibition, but it did not stop there. Rather, such a mixture of agency and ideology developed further in the instrumentalization of culture to the point of genocide in the case of SS architecture at Auschwitz. Architecture directed at the SS personnel and against the inmates and victims supported the broader and devastating goals of the state. To these three dominant relationships of art to oppressive and racist policies under the Nazi Party, I have added a fourth term of opposition, which covers the ambivalent rejection of Nazi perpetrators as an operative descriptive category for the vast majority of contemporaries in postwar German culture and society.

By foregrounding the connection or disconnect between the art world and Nazi oppressive tactics in these four cases, I have attempted to make us more aware that identifying a perpetrator and constructing a stable definition of her or his role could be a matter of choice. SED leaders in the east held to the position that dealing with perpetrators was a West German problem; categories of victims, first Communist and finally also Jewish and others, could play a role in state policy and public commemoration, at specific moments and times, but debate about the status of possible criminals from the Nazi era within the state did not occur to any significant degree.[62] In the case of the Federal Republic, however, politicians and artists alike eventually engaged a more dynamic debate about who was or was not a perpetrator, after the initial narrow category of leaders established at Nuremberg was expanded. In particular, from moderate conservative politicians to the most reactionary agitators, whether they embraced or rejected a connection to the Nazi past depended on which concept of Nazi agency they either continued to embody or appropriated as their own, or that was thrust upon them by others. The very multiplicity of identifiable positions within the party as it developed over time meant inevitably that engagements with those elements defined as criminal in a postwar world would themselves be variable. The actual and perceived relationship between National Socialists and culture, as well as the rejection of that relationship in the immediate postwar period, exemplifies this variability. When the perpetrator did become an acknowledged social and political category in the West German conservative sphere, it is perhaps not surprising that the very complexity of Nazi actions led to particular debates that left the definition especially malleable. These debates intrigued and engaged artists and architects, and their responses changed with the developing political world around them, as I detail in the chapters that follow.

The separation between the world of German art and that of politics that dominated immediate postwar history and practice in the Federal Republic would prove to be difficult to maintain. After all, even during the Nazi period, many contemporaries, including artists, found preserving a stable relationship to the party slipperier and less manageable than they would have liked. Such ambiguity and variability did not end with the demise of the Nazi state, the death of Hitler, or the trials of his leadership cadre at Nuremberg. Both the subtle and the blunt policies of the fascist state, as well as the ideological goals of key party members, continued to resonate. This constitutes the long Nazi influence on twentieth-century German art. The impact of the political strategies and tactics of National Socialist Germany reaches backward and forward from the deadly years of 1933–45. Tracing key moments in which that impact affected conservative politics also constitutes a rethinking of art in the Federal Republic. Hence, the shifting shadow of the Nazi perpetrator over politics and culture needs to be reassessed to come to a more comprehensive and critical understanding of modern German art history.

2 GERHARD RICHTER AND THE ADVENT OF THE NAZI PAST
THE PERSISTENCE OF THE PERPETRATOR

Gerhard Richter was born on February 9, 1932, at the fateful moment in which the NSDAP consolidated its electoral victories at the end of the Weimar Republic. His mother, Hildegard, enjoyed music and literature, while his father, Horst, pursued a career as a teacher. In 1936, after a period of unemployment, his father took a teaching job in the small town of Reichenau, near the Czech border, moving the family away from their home in the cultured metropolis of Dresden. With the National Socialists in power since 1933, Horst had to become a member of the party to retain his job, although it appears that he was never really a true believer. In 1942, Gerhard himself joined the Pimpfe, a branch of the Hitler Youth for boys younger than fourteen. By this time, his father had already served three years in the military, and the family rarely saw him. In 1943, Hildegard was forced to move to the even smaller town of Waltersdorf, where they sold the piano to get by and waited for the war to end. Their town became part of the Soviet Zone in May 1945 and then, subsequently, the German Democratic Republic with the division of Germany in 1949. Meanwhile, Horst came home in 1946 after the American military authorities released him from custody. Officials in the Soviet Zone did not let him return to teaching, a job forbidden to anyone who had been a member of the Nazi Party. After a period of unemployment, he found a job as an unskilled worker in a textile factory. Given these events, Richter experienced firsthand the influence of the party's disastrous politics on his life both before and after the war. Like so many of his generation, the continuity between the Nazi past and the postwar present was personal.[1]

As Susanne Küper was the first to argue, Richter deeply impressed his personal biography and that of his family on a few of his paintings that reference their actions and fate under National Socialism. Küper takes up the two key paintings *Uncle Rudi* (Figure 2.1) and *Aunt Marianne* (Figure 2.2), made in 1965 after the artist had immigrated to West Germany. For Richter, each of these works had a direct biographical connection to the Nazi past that was both revealed but also suppressed in the seemingly banal black-and-white family photos used as sources.[2] Richter painted his maternal uncle Rudi smiling and posing in his army lieutenant's uniform. He was killed in battle on the second day of the 1944 invasion of Normandy, and Hildegard Richter's family often mentioned him as a model whom the young nephew should emulate. Against this commonplace soldier's photo that belies the brutality of participation in the National Socialist military drive, the painting of his maternal aunt Marianne (with baby Gerhard) seems more private, less problematic. But Marianne also had a relation to the Nazi past: suffering from schizophrenia, she was placed in a mental institution in 1938 and died there during the war on February 16, 1945, reportedly of natural causes. It seems that the family did not ask but was aware of the many patients with mental illness whom Nazi doctors were killing in the euthanasia program, an important step toward the full-scale genocide of the European Jews. Jürgen Schreiber, working with Richter, has written an account of these biographical connections, including how his aunt was sterilized in the clinic before being murdered. However, with another turn of the screw, Schreiber discovered that Richter's first father-in-law, Heinrich Eufinger, had been a doctor active in the sterilization program. His in-laws had told the artist that Eufinger was "only" an honorary member of the SS who treated the wives of prominent officials such as Goebbels.[3] With Uncle Rudi and Aunt Marianne, willing Nazi participant and innocent victim existed in the same family, each of whom had a history exposed and yet flattened out or obscured by the seeming neutrality and banality of the family photo.

Art historians have tended to see these paintings as anomalous disruptions of Richter's broader artistic agenda to explore the status of representation. For one brief moment, the repressed Nazi past hovered just out of focus, threatening to break through the silence imposed on society by postwar Germans in the Federal Republic.[4] But looking again at the long twentieth century, I argue that the Nazi past was much more omnipresent after 1945 than art historians have supposed and that this was true of Richter's work as well. The general terms of the art historical analysis of this period emphasize psychosocial assumptions of repression and mourning.[5] Yet social historians have recognized that the immediate postwar generation of West

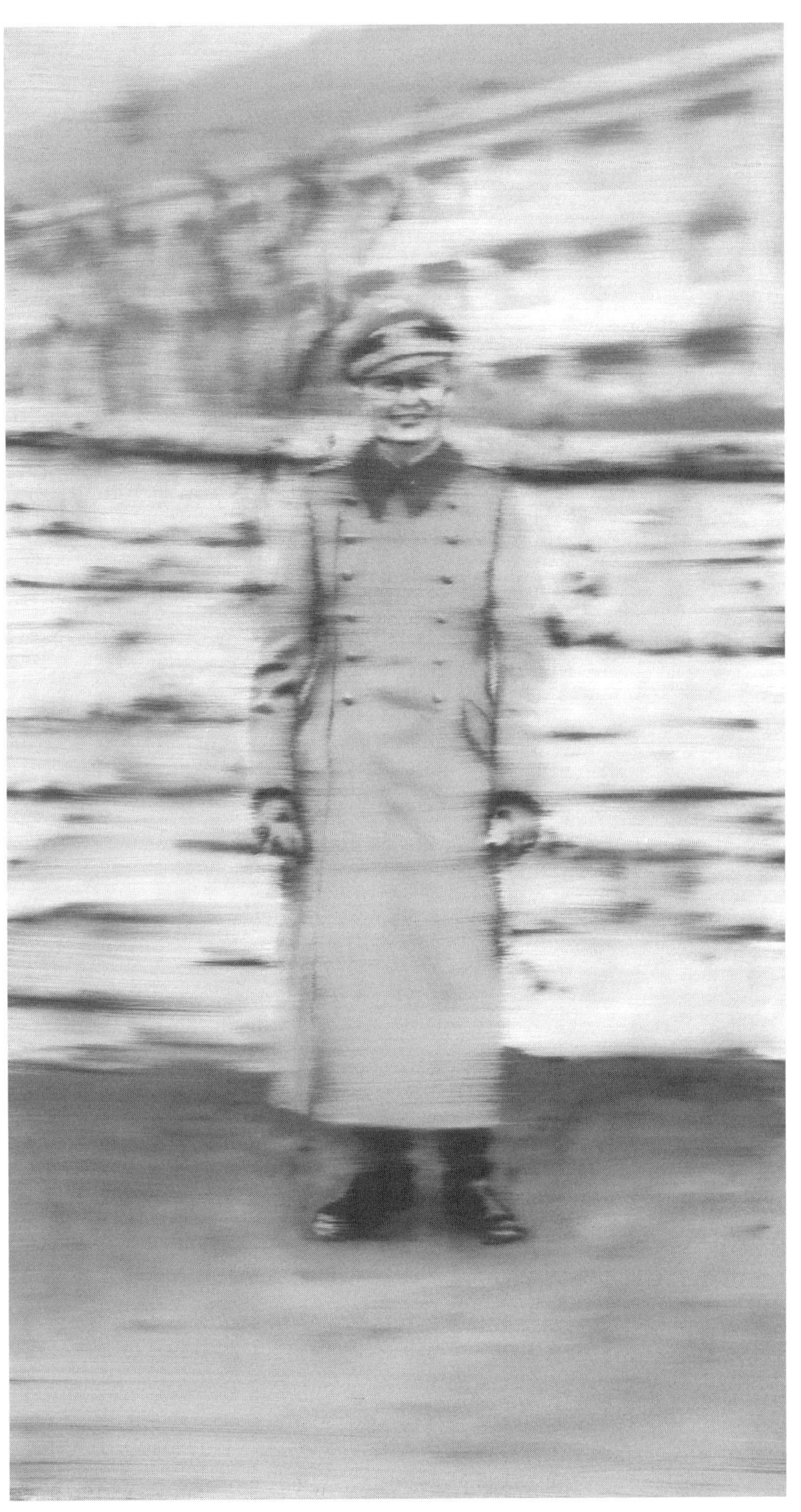

FIGURE 2.1. Gerhard Richter, *Uncle Rudi*, 1965. Oil on canvas, 34¼ × 19¹¹⁄₁₆ inches (87 × 50 cm). Czech Museum of Fine Arts, Prague, Lidice Collection. Copyright Gerhard Richter, 2011.

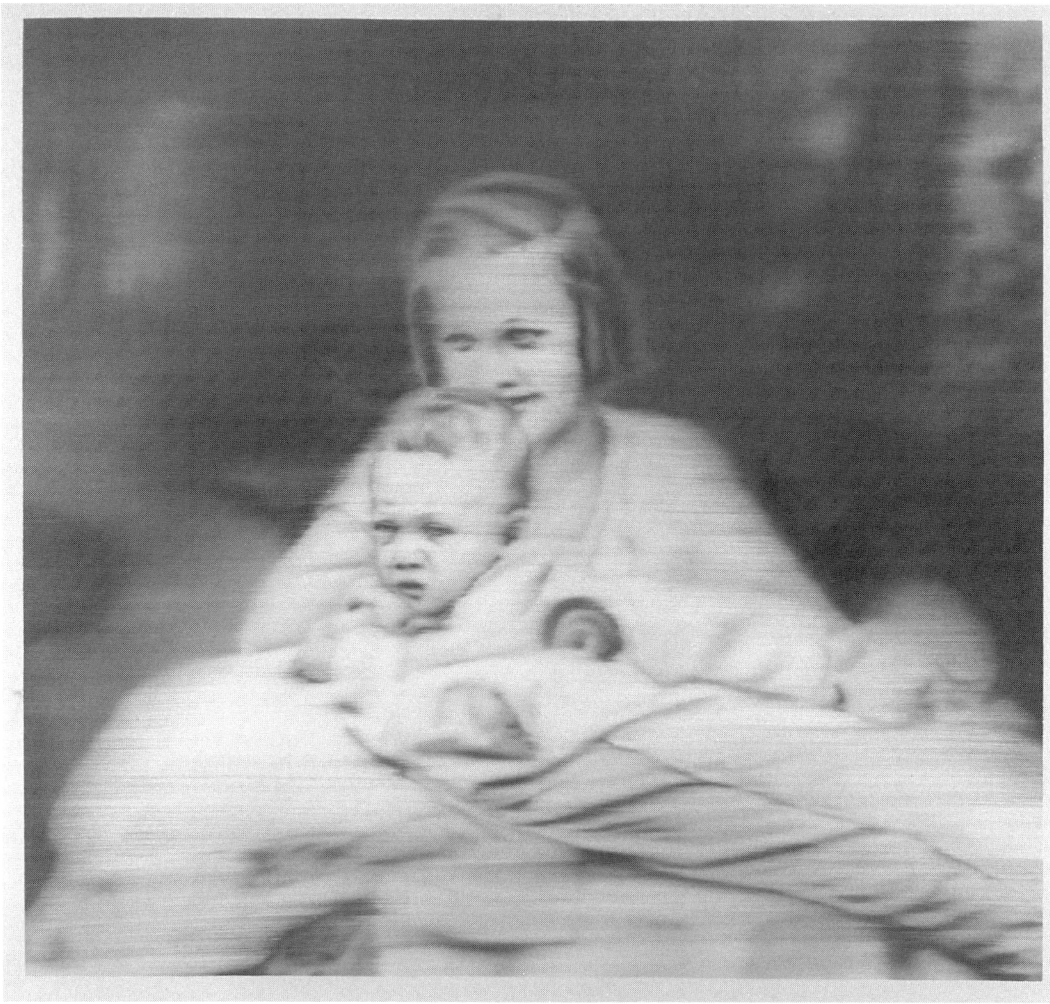

FIGURE 2.2. Gerhard Richter, *Aunt Marianne*, 1965. Oil on canvas, 120 × 130 cm. Staatliche Kunstsammlungen Dresden, Galerie Neue Meister. Copyright Gerhard Richter, 2011.

Germans actually focused on very particular aspects of the Nazi past rather than denying wholesale its impact on their current lives. As Robert Moeller has tersely stated, "Remembering selectively was not the same as forgetting."[6]

Richter was more preoccupied in his early works with the contemporary relevance of the Nazi past than scholars have previously assumed.[7] His interests resonate with particular debates about the definition of perpetrators and their status within government institutions, calling for a more precise political history of the period to help our understanding of its artistic culture. Aesthetically, scholars have long recognized his combination of both eastern bloc verist traditions of Socialist Realism as well as western market trends along with the use of the biographical sources that he collected in the panels of photos he called the *Atlas*. His interests, though, went far beyond mere artistic debates and biography. Instead, Richter's work addressed specific conceptions of agency, gender, and the family concomitant with contemporary concerns about the continuing presence of former Nazi personnel and fellow travelers in West Germany. Especially in his early black-and-white paintings such as *Christa and Wolfi* (1964), the shadow of the recent German debacle also looms large (see Plate 2).

Identifying the political terms of the debate on the significance of former Nazi personnel clarifies characteristic decisions made by Richter of both form and content. In the late 1950s into the 1960s, the West German discussion of the past shifted dramatically to encompass a more commonplace interpretation of the Nazi perpetrator and her or his continued presence in society. In particular during this initial period of Richter's work in the west, two interrelated and high-profile judicial processes significantly framed how the perpetrator was understood not merely as an ideologue but also as a regular person who fulfilled the day-to-day functional needs of the oppressive state: the Israeli trial in 1961 of former SS bureaucrat Adolf Eichmann; and the Frankfurt trial of the Auschwitz guards and officials that began in 1963 and ended in 1965.[8] These two trials were explosive events that led to a great deal of debate particularly within conservative circles about how West Germans should understand Nazi policies and former officials. While the East German party line asserted that these individuals were a problem for the FRG alone, even SED propagandists highlighted the judicial events in the west as examples of the distinctly corrupt nature of the society on the other side of the wall. The status of former Nazi personnel proved to be one of the most volatile social issues of the period, and contributed to specific scandals within the failing government of Christian Democratic chancellor Konrad Adenauer. Far from any psychosocial concept of repression, the political terms of debate concentrated on how to deal with former National Socialist perpetrators within the CDU government and society at large. Identifying these constructs and analyzing their relation to Richter's work clarifies the critical role West German culture played in expanding these political debates throughout society in the early 1960s.

By drawing on this moment of intense political and, surprisingly, art critical debate, I show that the Nazi past was anything but absent from the contemporary conditions of cultural work.[9] Hence, the interpretation of such canonical figures as Richter needs to be refocused outward toward the political history and cultural conditions of which he was a part. This move changes the assessment of central features in his early black-and-white paintings. Richter developed formal strategies and ideas about content in these paintings that engaged his West German contemporaries and their society. In addition, I briefly compare these works to one of the few examples of a well-known East German painting that also engaged the Nazi past at this moment, Werner Tübke's series *Lebenserinnerungen des Dr. jur. Schulze* (The memoirs of the Honorable Schulze, J.D.) (1965–67). Even with Tübke, though, any public discussion of this work and the debates concerning perpetrators, artistic or political, targeted the specific context of the FRG. Perpetrators, when they did (rarely) show up in East German discourse about art, were decidedly a West German problem. The west's conservative institutions, not the socialist state personnel in the east, formed the central point of reference. Hence, the interpenetration of art and the reception of National Socialist policies and perpetrators particularly deepens our understanding of West German culture and rejects the reigning philosophical concept of its collective historical repression.

THE REAPPEARANCE OF THE NAZI PAST IN ARTISTIC DEBATES IN POSTWAR WEST GERMANY

By the time Richter immigrated to Düsseldorf in 1961, some National Socialist historical events and individuals had become clear if not systematic points of reference in specific debates about West German art. These changes came along with the first significant challenges to the postwar Modernist artistic establishment, exemplified by the work of Joseph Beuys. In retrospect, one would think that Beuys, with his own experience in the Luftwaffe during the war, would choose to highlight themes that had to do with the POWs who had been so important a reference point for the Nazi past up through 1955. Yet his partially fantastic, partially accurate autobiographical account of being shot down in the Crimea, saved by Tartars, and surrounded in an environment of fat and felt (what Peter Nesbit wryly calls "the Story") only became a significant part of his self-presentation and subsequent art history after 1968.[10] Actually, Beuys's earliest engagement with the past first came with his entry for the 1957–58 international competition for a commemorative memorial at Auschwitz sponsored by the International Auschwitz Committee (IAC). Beuys's proposal centered on two gates, one placed inside the entrance to Birkenau and the other outside (Figure 2.3). Each would be an abstract shape drawn from the irregular geometric form in Dürer's famed print *Melancholia* (1514). Beuys's work, through its art historical reference, signaled the question of mourning and thus the subject position of victims as central to any appropriate German cultural response. But his conceptually abstract entry proved difficult for the international jury, chaired by the classic Modernist Henry Moore. Ultimately, they could not decide on any clear winner who could appropriately memorialize the scale of the crime. They settled on asking three finalists to work collaboratively on a project. In addition, the IAC had subsequent problems in finding enough international sponsors to pay for the eventual monument and was forced to turn the project over to a Polish government agency.[11] These tentative early steps indicate some of the difficulty in shifting the artistic interpretation of the Nazi past away from the narrative of World War II and its Cold War corollary. Beuys and a few other artists such as Wolf Vostell attempted to engage this historical moment through some initial gestures.[12] Still, the time was becoming ripe in West Germany for the "war stories" to give way to a much broader and deeply conflicted reception of the Nazi past that would also move the discussion of perpetrators into a more complex mode.

As the political context shifted, the West German art world did not silently pass over National Socialist policies and personnel, repressing them as a taboo topic. Getting some sense of how the art press most commonly referenced the past helps clarify the significance of the commonplace perpetrator as a new theme in culture and in politics after the demise of the dominant narrative concerning expellees and POWs. As I have argued elsewhere, by the late 1950s and early 1960s, artists and critics paid increasing attention to the Nazi past, albeit selectively and inconsistently. By the time Richter immigrated to West Germany, artists like Gerhard Marcks and

FIGURE 2.3. Joseph Beuys, *Design for Auschwitz Memorial*, 1957. Collage, 33.1 x 49.5 cm. Stiftung Museum Schloß Moyland, Collection van der Grinten. Copyright 2012 Artists Rights Society (ARS), New York/VG Bild-Kunst, Bonn.

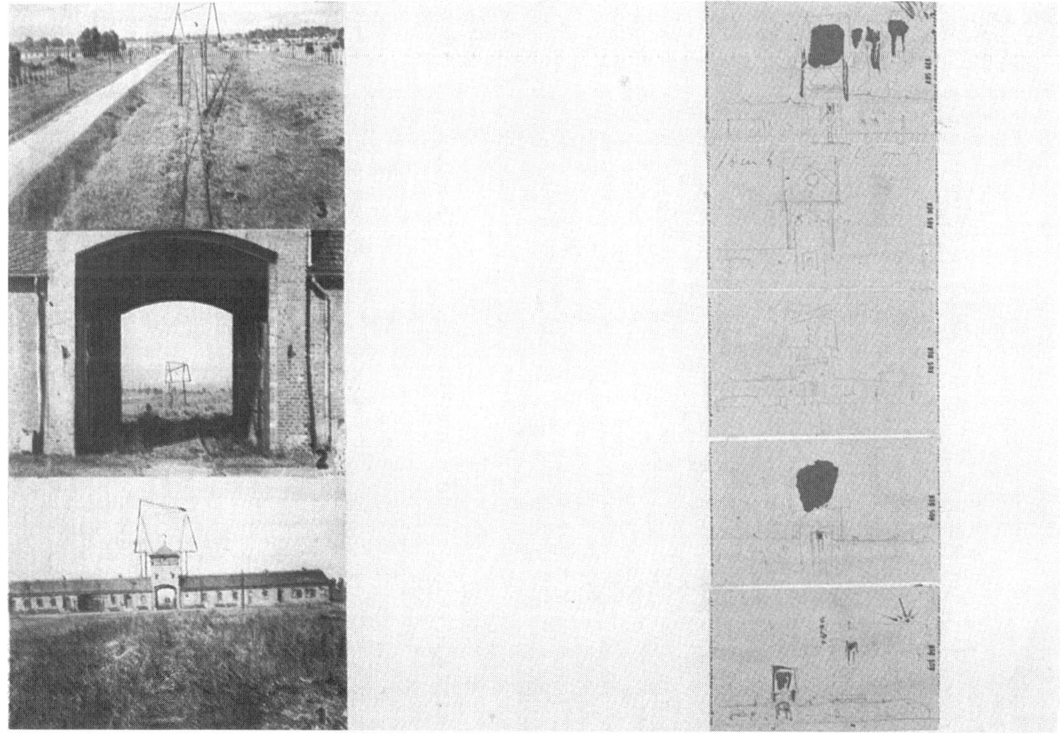

Dore Vax had already caused scandals with their explicitly critical references in their work to fascist imagery. Furthermore, journalists debated the cultural appropriateness of specific Nazi buildings, such as Paul Ludwig Troost's Haus der Kunst (1937) in Munich. And important exhibitions highlighted Jewish victims, such as the 1960 tour of *Hier fliegen keine Schmetterling* (No butterflies fly here), featuring the work of children who had been sent to the Theresienstadt concentration camp. Eighteen thousand people visited the exhibition at its first venue in Frankfurt.[13] In addition to these cultural references, Adenauer expanded his thematization of Nazi victims with a February 1960 speech of reconciliation at Bergen-Belsen, the former concentration camp. His parliamentary majority approved in May the "Law against Incitement of the People" (*Volksverhetzung*), which the CDU meant as a response to a rise in antisemitic defacement of synagogues, including one in Cologne on Christmas Eve 1959.[14] It is abundantly clear that as Richter arrived in Düsseldorf, the National Socialist past was anything but a silence in West German society or art.

The Nazi past formed a more consistent point of reference in the late 1950s into the early 1960s owing to artistic innovations that challenged the ahistorical claims of abstraction as well as the shifting public discourse on recent history such as that produced in response to Adenauer's speech. The phrases used in the art world to engage that reception varied depending on the ideological interest and historical experience of the artist, art historian, critic, or curator. Still, a shift clearly occurred as the contemporary status of past perpetrators became increasingly important in the discussion of cultural events, subjects who had been quite absent from the initial postwar responses. For Richter and other artists or critics, the presence of former Nazi Party members and supporters in families, institutions, and government offices forced the question of whether West German society had broken with or continued to sustain the criminal past.

We can gain some insight into the scope of the public awareness by looking at how art critics discussed a singularly important exhibition, using contemporary journals as primary sources. The twenty-fifth anniversary reconstruction of the *Degenerate Art* show, organized for the Haus der Kunst in Munich, became the most widely reported cultural event of the early 1960s concerning the relationship between art and National Socialist policy.[15] Running from October 25 to December 16, 1962, the exhibition—although incomplete—featured many of the artists (especially the Expressionists) shown in the original 1937 propaganda show. Most of these works had to be borrowed from foreign private and public collections. The exhibition also included a room of historical documentation that discussed the context of the earlier show.

Not surprisingly, art critics highlighted artistic quality as one consistent theme within the exhibition. They noted the generally superior worth of Expressionists and other denounced artists in comparison to those "Nazi" artists shown in the competing *Great German Art Exhibitions*. In addition to these expected aesthetic value judgments (which ignored the problem of artists like Emil Nolde who attempted to work with the Nazi Party but was still chosen for the "degenerate" exhibition), critics emphasized other points of contemporary relevance to an early 1960s audience. For example, the moderate art magazine *Das Kunstwerk* thematized the issue of generational responsibility and knowledge: "We of the older generation already know about [the multiple meanings of the term 'degenerate']. This is for us still somehow in the bones. But the youth have hardly any idea about it. So it was correctly stated in the [opening] speech that, above all, one wanted to bring young people into this exhibition, people who have neither lived this all themselves nor know anything about it from school or from their parents."[16] Notably, Otto Schrag (the author) identified the family as an important site of silence, an issue we have already seen Richter take up in his paintings of his uncle and aunt. In addition to the emphasis on generational knowledge, Schrag noted the particular strength of the work of these artists who dealt with what he described as the inner qualities of a free spirit. He contrasted this with his characterization of Nazi propaganda, which to him focused on the control of the exterior person. This distinction forced the party to expel Modernist works that did not fit the message. In relation to these postwar notions of freedom and subjectivity, Schrag explained with approval that in spite of the timing of the opening, occurring as it did at the high point of the Cuban Missile Crisis, the exhibition was well visited.

Reinhard Müller-Mehlis also discussed generational issues in the left-leaning journal *Tendenzen*, although for him (not surprisingly) a different contemporary reference point than the family or the school was of greatest concern. Müller-Mehlis described his perception of the politically motivated exclusions of certain artists from the reconstructed show, including artists represented in East German collections or still practicing in the GDR. He also noted critically the curatorial emphasis on the more moderate German Expressionists while Surrealists such as Max Ernst were underrepresented or absent. In an article in the same issue, Müller-Mehlis expanded on the generational question, although in this case it was not a matter of the responsibility of those who lived through the era to postwar youth. He emphasized rather the continuity of personnel in the Nazi state who were still active in the current Federal Republic. Müller-Mehlis named names, noting that such critics as Dr. Karl Korn, Carl Linfert, Bruno Werner, and

Dr. Karl Silex had served the propaganda purpose of the *Degenerate Art* show in Nazi Germany and now were continuing their trade in a variety of cultural and political spheres in the postwar period. For Müller-Mehlis, it was not only a question of good art and bad, censored art and supposedly Nazi art; rather he foregrounded the issue of perpetrators in our midst. Cultural figures, who had been active agents in promoting cultural policy, continued to have influence in West German artistic circles. Both biographical evidence and an analysis of continuities between the Nazi past and the current artistic culture established individual culpability or innocence.[17]

The conservative journal *Weltkunst,* like others of the art press, emphasized the quality of the artworks shown and the loss for Germany of the paintings and sculptures that Nazi officials sold off to foreign collections. But the author—Hertha Wellensiek—drew quite different lessons from the show when it came to discussing the agency of art professionals of the past and the present, in opposition to critics like Müller-Mehlis. Wellensiek argued that during the Nazi period, all "good" German artists needed to emigrate or go into inner exile, actions that had thoroughly ruined the status and quality of postwar artistic education. From her perspective, the market had yet to recover. Furthermore, and consistent with the goal of the magazine, her interest in these examples of modern art rested strongly on the provenance and original sale price of the works. But she also discussed the "good" gallery dealers and curators who had promoted this work in the face of the few "fanatics" who held power.[18] By discussing the stupidity and fanaticism of the (unnamed) cultural politicians of the Nazi administration, Wellensiek followed the line established particularly by the western powers in the Nuremberg Tribunals in which they thoroughly demonized National Socialist leaders, letting lesser but still important actors and the German population in general go without so much as a rhetorical slap on the wrist. Clearly, Wellensiek felt that clarifying the opposition between a small number of leading art world perpetrators and other Germans was part of making a satisfactory transition into the postwar era and strengthening the position of a democratic West Germany in the face of the developing Cold War.[19]

However disparate these three accounts may be in their ideological agendas, nevertheless they have several points very much in common. They all place as central to understanding the importance of the Nazi past in the West German present the question of individual agency as it relates to criminality or innocence, knowledge, and repression. In addition, they all explore whether current members of the art audience and dealers form a continuity or a rupture with the past: knowledge may or may not be passed from one generation of viewers to the next; the presence of Nazi officials in postwar cultural offices could be significant; or the contemporary art market may mark a decided break from its fascist predecessor. How do we account for the political actions of artists and art professionals in the past, and how have these individuals affected the postwar culture? Were artists and critics perpetrators, victims, or mere bystanders, and what is the role of each in contemporary culture? Whether in relation to the generational split between old and young, to an argument concerning the continuity between past and present cultural personnel, or to the cliché concerning how different contemporary West Germans were from the ideological fanatics of the past, these authors were interested in the specific relationship of the individual political actor or member of society as well as her or his relation to cultural production. The public discussion of the Nazi past and West German art returned repeatedly in those years to the emphasis on agency and the hotly debated question of continuity. Both themes hinged on authors' attitudes toward the status of the common perpetrator in contemporary society.

In his imagery that has most obviously referenced the Nazi past, Richter also dealt explicitly with issues of agency and continuity. As we have seen with *Uncle Rudi* and *Aunt Marianne*, Richter highlighted how the trace of the past figured in the painted reproduction of the family photo. He conjured up the banal presence of his uncle as a Nazi military officer and the seemingly hidden history of his aunt as victim. For him, the limits of representation marked by the smudged stroke and the ostensibly found subject matter belied issues of remembrance and personal responsibility in the face of atrocities. With these works he participated in a broad dialogue that included critics discussing the *Degenerate Art* show, politicians decrying contemporary antisemitic violence, and many others.

Yet Richter extended this theme beyond the confines of his familial biography. Within a short period after completing the two paintings of his relatives, Richter also finished his depiction of the public figure of Werner Heyde. In *Herr Heyde* (1965) we see the blurred representation of a press photo of Heyde being taken into custody by West German authorities in 1959 (see Plate 3). Heyde had been one of the doctors leading the euthanasia policies in Nazi Germany and had been living as a neurologist under an assumed name in the postwar period until authorities discovered his identity. He turned himself in, only ultimately to hang himself in his cell in February 1964 while awaiting trial. Unlike his father-in-law's activity, Richter was obviously aware of the public history of Heyde and his crimes.[20] It was quite possibly at this time that Richter began thinking about this series of three paintings. While Heyde is a social figure who publicly was viewed as a cipher for the postwar questions of guilt and the continued presence of Nazi murderers in the midst of West German society, this question of the actor within or victim of Nazi policies is also played out in the family drama of Richter's maternal uncle and aunt. But in each case, the personal and political are literally blurred, turned into popular modes of representation (family photo or journalistic image) that obfuscate a clear reading and also neutralize any specific critical line that an interpreter might take. As several art historians have noted, the blurring of Richter's paintings and their popular or familial sources clearly make the iconography ambivalent.[21] His subjects are both banal in their origin and inflated in their careful depiction as large-scale oil paintings. Richter's choices indicate simultaneously the seeming randomness of subject matter, as well as the artist's refusal to deal merely with the Modernist tropes of the formal conditions of painting itself. In spite of this ambivalence, Richter wants us to attend closely to the specific actions of these figures in order to formulate our interpretation; so, crucially, while he paints the press photo of Heyde in a blurred way, he depicts the newspaper text underneath as crystal clear, indicating both the mass media source (à la Warhol) but also the historically documented subject.

Richter used both familiar representational strategies (which incorporated the physicality of the painted surface and the illusionism of recognizable imagery) and particular kinds of sources (both personal and public). In this, he was very much of his time, engaging with contemporary practices significant in both east and west. When he arrived in Düsseldorf in March 1961, only five months before the Berlin Wall went up, he knew from his own training in Dresden the representational modes associated with east bloc Socialist Realism. Conventional Socialist Realism stressed illusionistic techniques mobilized in state-sponsored art with ideologically affirmative subject matter. His East German training provided him with the crucial skills that would become so evident in the verisimilitude he sought to bring into tension with the blur of line and surface. As Jeanne Nugent has argued, Richter had already begun to use photography in his Dresden work to structure his relationship to history. In addition, he worked in different naturalistic modes in the GDR, rather than following a strict aesthetic line, even if the range of this exploration was not the same as his later experiments in the west. Nevertheless, his aesthetic and methodological choices indicate both knowledge of and resistance to the state-sponsored Socialist Realism so important to the Dresden Academy of Fine Arts.[22]

Richter also became immersed in western avant-garde debates that at the time questioned the formal and conceptual limits of abstraction, the dominant market trend emanating out of New York.[23] These critical dialogues came to a head with the volatile discussions concerning U.S. Pop Art, provoked by several factors: a 1962 figurative painting show at the Museum of Modern Art in New York; the drop in prices for Abstract Expressionism;

Pop shows in 1963 at the Sidney Janis Gallery; and the display particularly of Robert Rauschenberg's works at the 1964 Venice Biennale. Fluxus happenings, especially in Düsseldorf, where Richter was studying and beginning to exhibit, also muddied the artistic waters.[24] Hence, in aesthetic terms, Richter's use of popular mass-market sources, the cliché of the family photo, as well as his exploration of the relationship between an indexical depiction and the formal qualities of the painted surface were in dialogue with a range of aesthetically innovative directions of the early 1960s.[25]

But internal market and institutional art world developments cannot be the singular point of reference for an analysis of Richter's work in this period. As I discussed with *Herr Heyde,* Richter interested himself in the philosophical limits of representation and the relation of painting and photography, but also distinctly West German questions of history as revealed through both formal means and choice of content. Art historians have consistently underplayed in particular his choice of specific subjects at particular times.[26] As he famously stated in a 1986 interview with Benjamin Buchloh, "The motifs [of the black-and-white paintings] were never random; I had to make much too much of an effort for that, just to be able to find photos I could use. . . . They very definitely were concerned with content. Perhaps I denied that earlier, when I maintained that it had nothing to do with content, that for me it was only a matter of painting a photo and demonstrating indifference."[27] While we cannot ignore the formal strategies, neither can we generalize or philosophize away the choice of subject as irrelevant. Indeed, we should acknowledge the prominent response in the art press to almost monthly events that reminded artists of Nazi perpetrators (such as the re-creation of the *Degenerate Art* show) coupled with Richter's own biographical connections. To do otherwise would be to underinvestigate his interest in the subject and to rip him out of precisely the debates of real relevance to an early 1960s West German public.

The Nazi Perpetrator and Political Debates about the Criminal Past

Scholars have acknowledged Richter's interest in the Nazi past, as demonstrated in the three paintings I have discussed. But these paintings are only the tip of the iceberg and merely the most obvious connection to that past. They do not indicate the full complexity of his choices related to engaging the history of National Socialist Germany. Discussions surrounding the presence of Nazi perpetrators in Adenauer's government and West German society highlighted specific political positions and associations that help us in turn to interpret other Richter paintings, which seem to have nothing to do with such a broad issue. Since the 1990s, historians have researched many aspects of this political history. Still, my contribution focuses on how the particular status of perpetrators at this moment forms a surprisingly consistent point of reference that clarifies a wide swath of Richter's work as well, especially in these early years of production after he moved to West Germany. Just as with the debates about *Degenerate Art*, central to that political history is how different groups questioned the status of the perpetrator and the issue of continuity with the West German present. The points of connection as well as distinction between the political and artistic discussions provide a range of terms that indicate the penetration of the debate on perpetrators into all areas of society.

As we have seen in the previous chapter, Adenauer's initial approach to the hot-button theme of the Nazi past was to emphasize restitution to Jewish victims, as well as to focus on the continuing question of POWs in the Soviet Union, avoiding any legislation that would require judicial action against perpetrators. Exports to Israel and financial help to the state as well as significant payments to Holocaust survivors and the families of victims formed a central component of Adenauer's policies, as did his negotiations for the return of former soldiers in Soviet captivity.[28] However, these politics had the decided effect of freeing from responsibility any individuals who participated in Nazi crimes, as no government review of their actions took place. These individuals appeared again and again in the press to embarrass Adenauer throughout his regime. Most notably, political opponents used biographical information on Hans Globke, Adenauer's chief of staff since 1949 and state secretary in the cabinet after the election in 1953, as a point of reference to shame Adenauer's administration. Globke had been in the Prussian Ministry of Interior during the Nazi era, and in 1935 he began work on legal commentaries that would become the notoriously antisemitic Nuremberg Laws. Nevertheless, after the press revealed these facts, Adenauer still held fast against removing Globke from office. Such an example makes clear that Adenauer's government was willing to pay the price of scandal by overlooking the continued presence of Nazi functionaries (above all in the judiciary and foreign service) while shoring up Cold War coalitions through restitution to individual victims and Israel. Adenauer did not so much deal with the Nazi past in any systematic way as he admitted the responsibility of its most extreme leaders through payments to its victims while he simultaneously focused increasingly on German suffering at the end of the war.[29]

But a series of occasional acts of restitution could not so easily deflect the criticism that centered on perpetrators within the Adenauer administration, and eventually the chancellor's focus on the world war and specific repayment policies gave way to new points of reference to the Nazi past.

Particularly with public and judicial events from the late 1950s and early 1960s, the discussion of former perpetrators as common citizens still living and working within West German society became heated. As Jeffrey Herf has noted, the 1958 trial in Ulm of *Einsatzgruppe* (SS mobile killing units) personnel was crucial for breaking down the postwar silence on perpetrators.[30] In this trial, it came to light that a German policeman currently serving had been involved in the murder of four thousand Jews during the war. He was sentenced to a long prison term, and journalists, lawyers, politicians, and public institutions began to debate the efficacy of Adenauer's legislation that allowed Nazi-era officials back into the bureaucracy. To combat such gross lack of oversight of former Nazi personnel, the justice ministers of the West German states set up in October 1958 the Zentrale Stelle der Landesjustizverwaltungen zur Aufklärung national-sozialistischer Gewaltverbrechen (Central Agency of the State Judiciaries for the Investigation of National Socialist Crimes). By the early 1960s, prosecutors pursued individual cases based not on the category of "war crimes" (as had predominated at the Nuremberg Tribunals) but rather "crimes against humanity." The latter focused more and more on broader categories of perpetrators and their participation in the genocide of the European Jews. The problems of expellees from the east or the difficulties faced by Germans at the end of the war and into the period of occupation no longer dominated as the sole terms in which the public discussed and remembered the past. Increasingly, the average person who had played a functional role in promoting or enacting the most criminal aspects of Nazi policy was coming into focus as the new symbol of the perpetrator.

Through the Central Agency, prosecutors began exploring various cases, including claims against the guards at the concentration camp of Auschwitz. A former inmate instigated the investigation in March 1958 by accusing a guard of murder. He filed his charge with the Stuttgart public prosecutor's office. A year later, antisemitic events also intensified the call for judicial measures. On Christmas Eve in 1959, unknown assailants defaced a synagogue in Cologne with a swastika, leading to a massive public outcry. West Germans feared that former Nazis were still active or that new extreme right-wing followers had taken up their cause in postwar society. On the heels of this event came the astounding news in May 1960 that the Israeli secret service had captured former SS member Adolf Eichmann in Argentina and had smuggled him to Israel to stand trial. These internal and external events rocked an already shaky CDU leadership and involved Adenauer in a series of national and foreign scandals that forced him to explain the continued presence of Nazi perpetrators up through his resignation from office in October 1963.[31]

Eichmann's trial in Jerusalem raised issues related to the status of individual perpetrators that were subsequently used to question the effectiveness of West Germany in breaking with pre-1945 personnel in a supposedly post-Nazi democratic society. Eichmann, as Hannah Arendt famously pointed out, proved in his trial to be the exact opposite of the caricature of the Nazi as a bloodthirsty, ideology-driven antisemite who had duped the rest of German society into submission (Figure 2.4). Rather, Eichmann's trial showcased him as a banal bureaucrat, not particularly ideologically driven nor even particularly hateful toward the Jews. He seemed recognizable

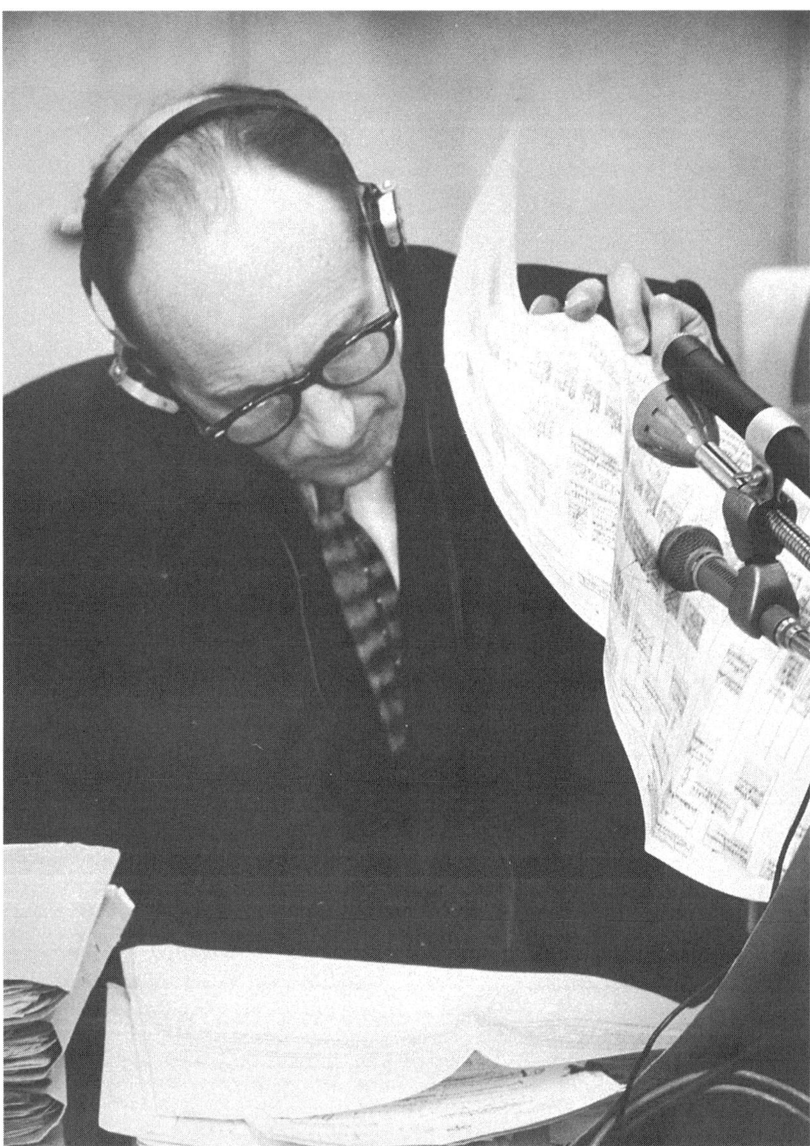

FIGURE 2.4. Adolf Eichmann at his trial in Jerusalem, 1961. United States Holocaust Memorial Museum. Courtesy of the Israel Government Press Office.

and familiar, fulfilling his functional role as part of the state apparatus. Arendt found precisely his ordinariness shocking and of most interest. For her, Eichmann could willingly participate in crimes that went seemingly beyond the ethical framework of his life because he lacked the power of self-awareness and, hence, moral judgment. She defined this ability to act, even to commit murder through pushing papers or shooting a gun, as absolute evil. But his character was simultaneously banal because it was so commonplace, not only in the world of the Nazi bureaucracy but also in the world of Israeli bureaucracy or the modern bureaucratic industrial state in general. Arendt landed in hot water particularly for this last thesis (and the implication of the guilt of the Jewish councils during the Nazi period).[32]

Tellingly for us, even while Arendt devoted most of her book to Eichmann, with the occasional dialectic asides relating to contemporary Israel and Cold War geopolitics, she also signaled some of the clear issues that would become politically relevant to Adenauer's government and the reception of the Eichmann trial in West Germany. Not only did West German newspapers discuss Nazi crimes of mass murder for the first time in detail, the testimony also greatly aided the Central Agency's work by bringing to light various Nazi and SS officials who had participated in the genocide in a variety of lower-profile, more functional roles. Eichmann's trial thus spurred on the judicial review of other perpetrators within the West German state. Prosecutors took further actions particularly against the judiciary and police institutions that held many former Nazi officials in their ranks. But while the reaction of the West German state seemed immediate, the public was nevertheless ambivalent. Arendt stated:

> The attitude of the German people toward their own past, which all experts on the German question had puzzled over for fifteen years, could hardly have been more clearly demonstrated: they themselves did not much care one way or the other, and did not particularly mind the presence of murderers at large in the country, since none of them were likely to commit murder of their own free will; however, if world opinion—or rather, what the Germans called "das Ausland," collecting all countries outside Germany into a singular noun—became obstinate and demanded that these people be punished, they were perfectly willing to oblige, at least to a point.[33]

Arendt's florid rhetoric here exaggerated the lack of public response to the past in Germany, which could be quite vocal, for example, in relation to World War II's continued impact on their lives. Her assessment nevertheless points to two crucial issues: that the public was demonstrably equivocal about perpetrators; and that the government responded to Eichmann's trial by focusing on counteracting the damaged perception of West German society in foreign states. Particularly, the CDU had to deal with the potential embarrassment of finding former Nazi criminals not in holes buried away but rather in the public sphere and at the highest levels of political power. Reducing this internal issue of perpetrators in their midst became a key motivation for Adenauer as he expanded the arrests of individual Nazi personnel and also worked to limit the systematic survey of all potential perpetrators within society. As with the critical discussion of the *Degenerate Art* show, government ambivalence nevertheless reflected new definitions of the perpetrators who could now be anywhere, a central issue in contemporary West Germany.

We subsequently know that Arendt's characterization of Eichmann as a bureaucrat without a strong ideological agenda of his own is only partially accurate. It is certain enough that Eichmann and other SS officials had limited power to set policy; but within those limitations, people like Eichmann often came up with the "innovations" that enabled and drove the radicalization of policies against the European Jews and others.[34] Nevertheless, in terms of the political reception of the trial, her emphasis on the ordinariness of the perpetrator and the crucial role of bureaucracy in implementing the genocide had clear relevance for the politics of Adenauer's West Germany. The CDU first needed to recognize guilt in order to determine who were criminals and where they were.

As the Eichmann trial was going on, the Central Agency continued to gather evidence and prepare indictments for the prosecution of the former SS guards and officials at Auschwitz. This trial opened in December 1963 in Frankfurt am Main and ran until August 1965. Journalists and lawyers also made the question and definition of the perpetrators here a central theme, but in different terms. After all, the Israeli trial had been at the intersection of international and Jewish interests, whereas the Auschwitz Trial marked the prosecution of twenty defendants by a German court using German law specific to West German political and social life. Hence, the approximately one hundred thousand people in the postwar FRG estimated to have been involved with the implementation of the Holocaust had a very practical concern with the outcome. As with the Jerusalem process, so too Attorney General Fritz Bauer attempted to make the Holocaust the central feature of the trial, and he partially did so by emphasizing the massive scale of the perpetrators' actions. After the 180 days of the trial, 254 witnesses had been heard from. Further, the trial began with a seven-hundred-page indictment as well as a supplemental three-hundred-page contextual history of the death camp, eventually published as the very influential book *The Anatomy of the SS State*. Every major German newspaper covered the proceedings, and the documentation from the trial and the press reports made for a huge and unavoidably detailed amount of information that the public could subsequently access.[35] Indeed, Richter himself closely followed the daily reports in the *Frankfurter Allgemeine Zeitung*, according to information he provided Jürgen Schreiber.[36] The CDU concept that the Nazi past should be remembered in terms of the last years of the war and the resulting victimization of Germans in the east could no longer be maintained as the focus of political debate. Particularly with the Auschwitz Trial, *Vergangenheitsbewältigung* (coming to terms with the past) took center stage as West Germans struggled with their inception of and participation in the Holocaust. They could not avoid the question of personal agency, the question at the heart of defining the functional role of the everyday perpetrator.

Still, the trial did not define the status of the perpetrator as clearly as one might expect, and a great deal of ambiguity remained about the role of these concentration camp officials and their potential relationship to other German "bystanders." Partially this resulted from the very legal limitations set on the trial itself. As Rebecca Wittmann has trenchantly argued, prosecutors needed to try the defendants under Nazi laws that stood at the time of their crimes, which meant that only the most sadistic and brutal of individual acts of violence were subject to a conviction. Ironically, guards and officials who followed the orders of their state superiors were exonerated. If you implemented the entire process of the genocide that killed millions, you were simultaneously not responsible for a crime under German law. The nature of the perpetrator was localized in his direct extralegal violence against a victim. The systemic agency, directly and indirectly, of thousands of Germans fell outside the judicial definition of criminality and thus was rendered historically neutral. As Wittmann has put it, "The German public learned to censure and denounce the sadistic excess of perpetrators of Auschwitz but to exonerate the order-followers whose crimes of complicity were never the true focus of the trial, the law, or the extensive press coverage."[37] Thus, the ideological zealot remained central as a dominant character while the functional supporter and follower was suppressed as much as possible.

We have thus two opposing understandings of the perpetrator, with the criminality of the guards on trial in Frankfurt defined quite differently from that of the bureaucratic perpetrator projected at the Eichmann Trial. Headlines and reporters for major newspapers exacerbated this situation by focusing on the most sensational aspects of the day's testimony, spending much time on the horrors of the use and abuse of human bodies in the camps while overlooking the more "mundane" day-to-day participation in genocide by camp doctors or those who were supposedly reluctant to carry out the murder of the Jews. The law complemented this view as, since the beginning of the Federal Republic, it had systematically limited the ability to try perpetrators under the terms of international human rights. Fanned by the sensationalizing press, the agency of the extreme and sadistic personnel at Auschwitz was everywhere in evidence in West Germany from 1963 to 1965 but simultaneously bracketed from the experience of "ordinary" Germans. Martin Walser, among other German intellectuals, criticized this sensationalizing tactic of the press as a distortion, and indeed other kinds of interpretations of the trial as a general lesson for Germans at all levels of perpetration appeared in letters to the editors of major newspapers. Still, the trial as a whole emphasized that the agency of the murderers concentrated specifically on individual ideologically driven acts of extraordinary violence. This was the opposite of the characterization of National Socialist officials gleaned from the Eichmann Trial.[38]

Yet, as with the diverse *Degenerate Art* show critics, a comparison of topics addressed in both the Eichmann trial and that of the Auschwitz guards and officials indicates some revealing overlaps. In the major public press reports, the Eichmann trial tended to focus more than the Auschwitz Trials on historical events such as the policies of extermination and how such themes related to the current geopolitical situation. Reporting on the Auschwitz Trials, by contrast, put more weight on issues related to the contemporary charges and indictment, that is, on judicial procedure within West Germany and whether it was fair. In terms of specific historical points, the murder of the Jews was played up much more in reports on the Eichmann trial than with the Auschwitz process. In both cases, however, 12 to 13 percent of all press accounts discussed the conduct of the German perpetrators, the most frequently mentioned theme not specifically related to the charges concerning crimes against humanity. And yet, in spite of the almost unprecedented press coverage of both trials, clear evidence exists of public ambivalence, even resistance to reading these press accounts especially in 1963–65 during the Auschwitz process. Thus, by 1965, a small part of the judiciary was almost exclusively doing the work in coming to terms with the past with a limited if important number of perpetrators dutifully reported in the West German press.[39] However, neither public forums nor CDU policies generally addressed this subject. As the CDU entered the years of the Grand Coalition with the SPD beginning in 1966, it had no particular interest in encouraging such political work at the governmental level. As in the case of art, judicial discussions of the Nazi past and resulting policies were high profile but did not result in a systematic working through of the issue. They hinged, though, on the important question concerning the status of former perpetrators haunting the West German present and their relationship to specific criminal acts.

Richter/Eichmann: The Political Terms of Debate and Artistic Work

Adenauer's regime had to face this question because of the critical responses to perpetrators continuing in their roles in the government and remaining unpunished. The seemingly banal presence of Eichmann as well as the shocking fascist brutality revealed in testimony at the Auschwitz process sharpened the public discussion on whether individual perpetrators could be the man or woman next door. Adenauer and his CDU successor, Ludwig Erhard, attempted to limit the issue to a few judicial cases, ignoring the widespread presence of criminals and former party members within society (and within the judiciary itself, for example). Further, these political events paralleled artistic discussions. Critics argued about whether the West German population and art market practices formed a democratic break with the Nazi past or a continuity with Hitler's administration (that is to say, the generational question so prominently a point of debate in the reception of the reconstructed *Degenerate Art* show). The reemergence of Eichmann and the trial of the Auschwitz guards were thus merely the most volatile tips of a much broader iceberg.

Richter began his monochromatic paintings of the early 1960s in the context of these political and artistic terms concerning the Nazi past. As we have seen with the examples of *Uncle Rudi, Aunt Marianne,* and *Herr Heyde,* Richter occasionally seemed to refer to these issues directly in his work. And yet, more broadly, these terms are much more useful than just for explaining these three paintings. In fact, our exploration of the question of the perpetrator's status helps us to clarify a wider group of visual strategies in Richter's production in the early 1960s and to interpret the social function of his work as well as the political implications of his artistic choices. In addition, the specificity of Richter's West German context for his art can also be highlighted through a comparison of his work to that of Tübke, one of the few contemporary East German artists who also responded to the scandals within Adenauer's government.

Of the sixty-five paintings listed in the catalogue raisonné for 1962– 64, at least seven have iconography explicitly related to Nazi subjects, usually military. Richter seems to have edited the catalog, for it is not complete and does not include such paintings as the one he did contrasting Communists being arrested and interrogated by Storm Troopers (SA) in 1933 with a pop image of a blond model repeated along the lower frame.[40] Also, in Richter's catalog of photographic sources—the *Atlas*—which he began keeping shortly after his arrival in West Germany, he has images scattered throughout of family members in National Socialist military uniforms as

well as scenes of military attack and aerial bombardment during the war
(Figure 2.5). Notably, images of victims do not appear until we reach the
photos he collected in 1967, which he never directly used as sources in any
of his paintings.[41] As a consistent subtheme in his early work and visual
research, Richter interested himself in both personal photos related to family members alive during the Nazi period as well as popular images of
World War II and National Socialist propaganda. In addition, he also took
an active interest in the sensational trials of Nazi personnel happening during this period. Not only did he read the press reports about the Auschwitz
Trials, he also was well aware of the brutal images from the concentration
camps, which he saw as early as his Dresden student period.[42]

The artist's interest and the volatile dialogue in the art and public
press about the relevance of personnel from the National Socialist past help
to clarify important aspects of the series of seemingly repetitive black-and-
white painted images that he completed from 1962 to 1966, the point at
which he began to experiment with a broader range of techniques and
images. I have chosen a telling example to explore, the painting *Christa and
Wolfi* (1964), one of the earliest works derived from the first four panels of

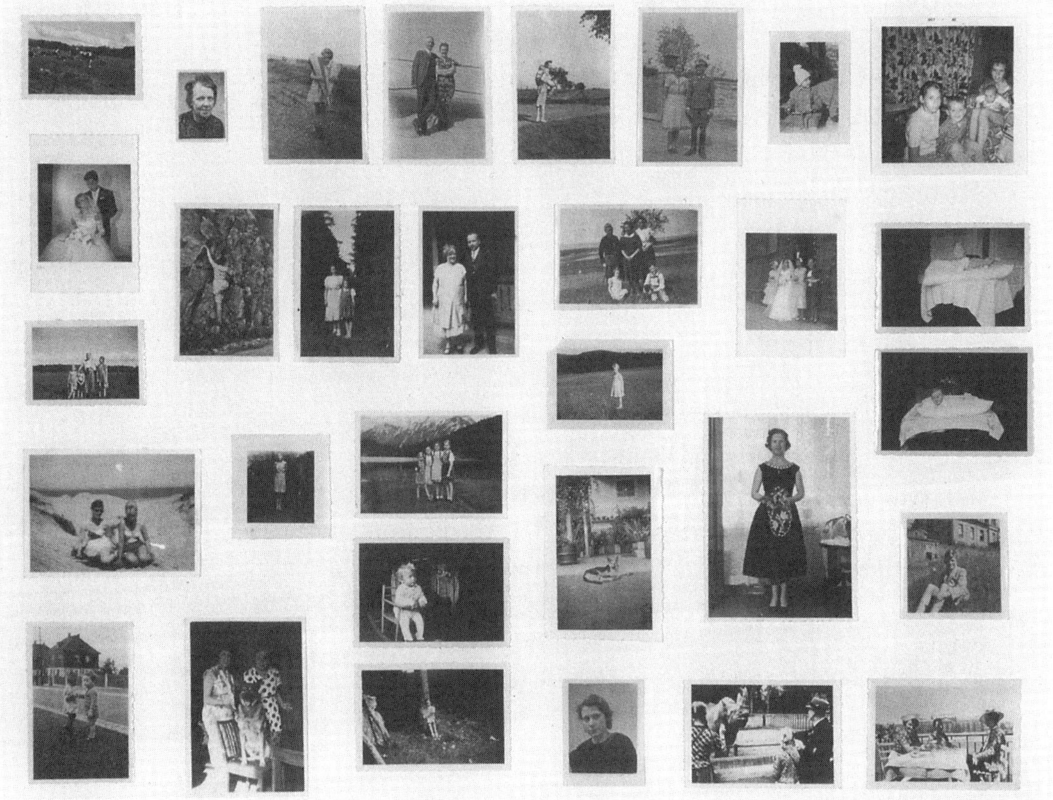

family photos from the *Atlas*.[43] *Christa and Wolfi* depicts a simple domestic scene of two women in a room with a table and a German shepherd sitting on a chair. Richter chose a photo from the third panel of the *Atlas*, which is not of his family but of his spouse at the time, Ema Richter. As with *Herr Heyde* and his other works, the painting is a version of the photo, typically blurred and cropped to emphasize certain formal issues of ambiguity and representation. But in addition, the terms established in the art and public press to debate the Nazi past clarify both the formal and iconographic strategies, which appear to have nothing to do with the world of Heyde and other perpetrators.

The subject of the painting seems appropriately commonplace. The white frame that remains on three sides of the sepia-toned image clearly evidences the origin of the imagery in a reproduction of a standard family photograph. In referencing the familiar medium of the family photo, Richter is well in line with the most contemporary artistic debates within West Germany, which, since 1962, included hefty discussions concerning the value of the challenge of U.S. Pop Art and its turn to everyday imagery. The older woman in the background is in the shadow, while the younger woman in a print dress smiles in the foreground. The family dog sits posed on the chair, staring out at the viewer. Clearly, we are meant to read this on two levels: first, on the level of a representation or rather as a painterly re-presentation of a photo; second, and simultaneously, we are meant to acknowledge its everyday imagery, its ordinariness as imagery.

Richter makes the ambivalent triangulated relationship between the everyday content of the image and the two modes of representation signified—family photograph and high-art painting—the theme of the work. The representational techniques both reveal and conceal, as does the title and even the choice of color (for color is at work here). Note that the title mentions only two subjects, Christa and the dog, Wolfi. Where is the mention of the third individual, presumably the motherly figure smoking and blurred in the background? Her mouth is little more than a slash of gray, her face wiped over paint and her features overall obscured. The artist textually and visually writes her out of the painting. She is also, of course, of the generation that would have been active during the Nazi period. Was she a perpetrator, a bystander guilty of nonaction, a possible victim who dissented? Her ambiguous presence in the image does not help us resolve this question. As a woman, she also references the important role gender played in marking the continuity between past and present. Whether as ardent Nazi mother, loyal military wife, one of the postwar women who literally rebuilt the destroyed cities, or a widow still trying to get her former party-member husband's pension, she and her generation of women were symbolic and political flashpoints around which much postwar social policy was discussed. They also mediated between the public discussion of male perpetrators (from the army to the most extreme branch of the Nazi Party) and their absence in or return to the personal world of the family. As Elizabeth Heineman has stated:

> With men at war, imprisoned, missing, or dead, women of all marital states relied on their own resources to keep their families out of danger and to make ends meet. Contemporaries marveled at this display of female competence. They also, however, feared that the war might have brought not only political and economic collapse but also the destruction of the smallest cell of social life. . . . Since they deviated so strikingly from the theoretically normative housewife, single women were considered a major social problem, and they felt marginalized by a society that promoted domesticity for women. Ironically, however, the constant problematization of their status meant that women standing alone had a relatively high profile.[44]

Richter paints her as present and fading simultaneously, just as the image seems to offer an allegory of this historical process of presence and forgetting. On the one hand, he reveals meaning in the materiality of the object (the image is decisively flat, a two-dimensional work of paint on canvas; again, note at the bottom the missing fourth photo border that breaks the illusion). On the other, the artist erases a significant singular interpretation by using the clichéd form of the fading everyday photo. The unresolved question remains: is she merely another flat area of paint in the representation of a photo, signifying nothing, or does she signal the very impossibility of reproducing the past in a moment in which the continued presence of perpetrators from her generation within the normal world of family and society is particularly loaded?

Richter exemplifies such a tension further in his depiction of Wolfi (see Plate 4). As in other paintings of the period, the artist uses a technique of selective focus, making the viewer particularly aware of the sparkle in the dog's eyes. This segment of the work has the clearest resolution. In addition, not only is Wolfi the part of the image in sharp focus but Richter further emphasizes him by painting the dog in a very cool and bright silvery-blue; for the rest of the painting, he has chosen clear sepia tones, an effect almost impossible to see in an illustration but evident in the original. Further, the dog is gendered in name and features as male, fulfilling the role of absent husband or son in the postwar domestic interior. Wolfi becomes a kind of spectral center to the composition, literally and figuratively. As such, he too seems to be nothing more than the family dog, a commonly repeated and relatively meaningless image, but simultaneously something symbolically beyond this, a resonance or trace of one of *the* brutal symbols of the SS and other Nazi perpetrators, that is, the German shepherd, or police dog (Figure 2.6).[45] I would emphasize that Richter insists on the separate formal characterization of Wolfi, signaling both his banal role as family dog, as formal representation, but also his status as a cipher (like the older woman). The ambivalence of his depiction engages both relevant themes in German art (representation vs. abstraction, popular culture vs. high art) and society (the resonance of Nazi brutality in postwar Germany). With such ambiguity, the shadow of the perpetrator hangs heavy over this interior.

But which perpetrator? The world of *Christa and Wolfi* seems not to be that of the ideological zealot but rather of the commonplace perpetrator. The absence of the anonymous male functionary, particularly those men active throughout German society, completes the world of these women and their German shepherd. The latter signals his continued male authority, but only through substitution. His social invisibility coupled with the aesthetic ambiguity signals the ambivalent response to the continued impact of his criminal past actions in the present.

FIGURE 2.6. SS Officer Karl Hoecker pets his dog Favorit in Auschwitz, 1944. United States Holocaust Memorial Museum. Courtesy of an anonymous donor.

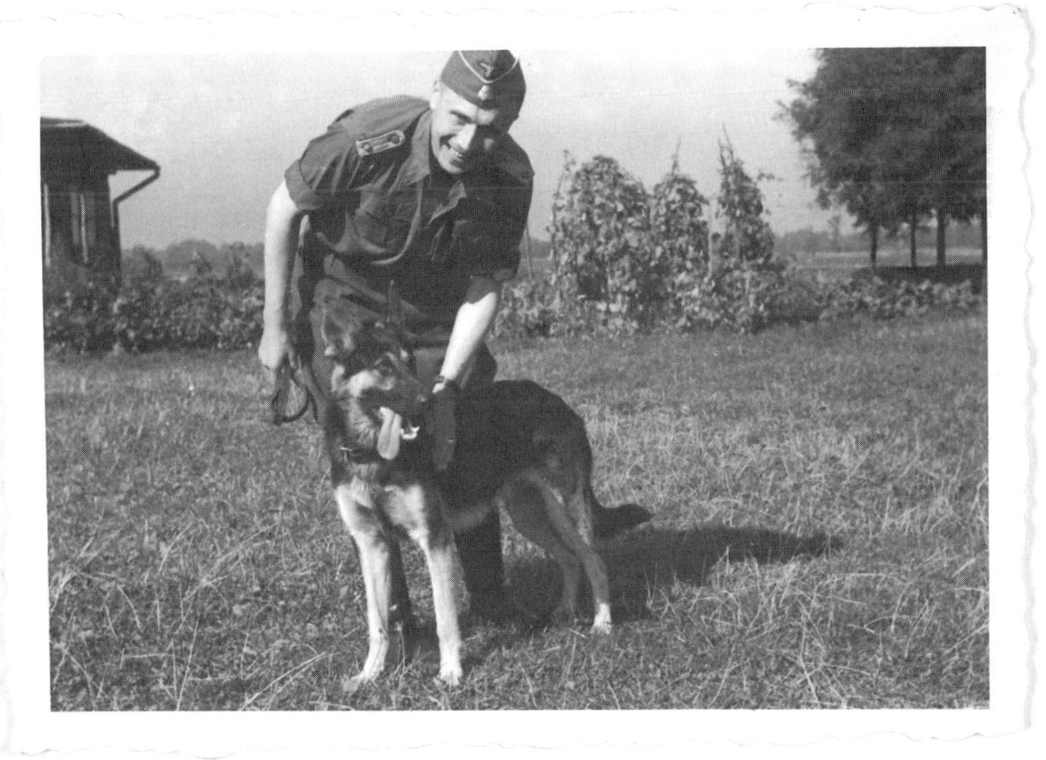

My analysis of the content and form attempts to locate Richter's choices in the historical moment of production and show how they intersect with the terms of debate used to discuss the dangerous but opaque presence of an expanded category of perpetrators in contemporary West German society. An analysis of *Christa and Wolfi* in aesthetic *and* social terms relates Richter's strategy of obscuring and revealing so prevalent in his early work to his other expressed interest in the resonance of the Nazi past. This past was simultaneously exploding in the press and the political sphere all around him, particularly as a result of the intense scrutiny of conservative personnel and their continuing institutional authority. Richter's interview with Robert Storr in the 2002 retrospective exhibition catalog helps clarify the connection. The artist denied once again any singular intent behind the choice of imagery in the black-and-white paintings. And yet, intriguingly, the artist found Arendt's phrase for describing Eichmann, "the banality of evil," a compelling choice of words for understanding the subjects in his own early work:

> In the ideal case, somebody looks at the work and asks what this is
> supposed to be and why anybody would paint such a banal object. And
> then the person comes to think that maybe there is something more to
> it, that maybe the object is not that banal after all, that maybe it is
> horrible. It stands for something . . . maybe for a terrible living room. . . .
> There was nothing but crime and misery in those living rooms. There is
> only crime and misery in general. *[Laughter]*[46]

To take Richter at his word here means to research the criminal and the banal terms of art and politics in the production and reception of his works.

We have other ways of clarifying the specificity of Richter's choices in relation to his West German context, as he was not the only artist at the time who engaged with these particular themes and politics. Surprisingly, a few notable East German painters also responded to the status and definition of the Nazi perpetrator.[47] As discussed in the preface, the official state ideology of the GDR did not acknowledge the presence of any perpetrators in the east. Still, during the early years of the GDR, some authors and directors, such as Anna Seghers and Wolfgang Staudte had broached the issue in important works, but the fine arts were relatively quiet on the subject.[48] However, at this prominent moment of Eichmann and the Auschwitz Trials, an exception to this general rule occurred. A few eastern artists broke through the SED's ideological position; significantly, though, their responses involved their take on *West* German society and its political scandals surrounding the continuity of perpetrators within CDU governmental circles. That is to say, as for Richter, western debates about what constituted past criminality still set the dominant terms of engagement even for eastern artists. Looking briefly at a prominent East German example helps clarify how these particular West German terms formed a powerful context for the artistic dialogue in which Richter engaged.

The crises within conservative FRG governmental circles, particularly the judiciary, became the focus of Werner Tübke's series, *Lebenserinnerungen des Dr. jur. Schulze* (The memoirs of the Honorable Schulze, J.D.) (1965–67). The series encompasses eleven paintings, fifteen sketches, and sixty-five drawings and studies, of which the large-scale work *The Memoirs of the Honorable Schulze, J.D., III* (1965) is the most prominent and the first work of the series shown publicly (see Plate 5). As critics recognized from the start, the images condemned the compromised West German judiciary in specific and the CDU government in general by showing a judicial everyman (evident in the generic name) who rules unthinkingly over a dualistic landscape of Nazi crimes on the left side of the painting and scenes of decadent pleasure on the right. He is a dummy, a nonthinking puppet, but also a monumental figure in his official garb with real visual and political authority. Exactly those white-collar or bureaucratic criminals (*Schreibtischtäter*) formed the heart of West German anxieties concerning Nazi perpetrators within the halls of government, either as the characterization was embraced in the Eichmann trial or obstinately rejected in the Auschwitz Trials. As Günter Meissner, a longtime supporter and interpreter of Tübke, put it in the pages of the GDR art journal *Bildende Kunst* (1966), "The work unmasks the sitting blood judges [Blutrichter] with their brown pasts who still serve today in West Germany."[49] More recently, Eduard Beaucamp, looking at the artist's sketchbooks and notes at the time, revealed that the Auschwitz Trials in particular and their revelations about West German institutions inspired the artist to begin this series.[50]

Clearly, Tübke's hyperrealistic technique put in the service of an explosive amount of iconography makes the images simultaneously both legible and obscure. We are meant to recognize many details but to find the whole a difficult if not impenetrable allegory. This push and pull of image and technique forms the foundation of Tübke's critical view of West German political institutions that claimed democratic transparency all the while hiding true criminals of the Nazi past. But this strategy, seemingly so complementary to what I have argued for Richter, also appeared to engage critically the comfortable affirmation demanded of prominent Socialist Realist artists within the GDR. On the one hand, Tübke's paintings followed East German state policy that claimed the postwar west formed a continuity with the Nazi past. On the other, their confusing profusion of imagery, as well as the combination of varied realist techniques, demonstrated a lack of clarity unacceptable to the dominant strand of art produced within East Germany. Indeed, at the time these paintings were done, the GDR Artists' Union was debating the concept and technique of realism. This debate became significant enough that Walter Ulbricht himself condemned excessively intellectualized formalism and symbolism as inconsistent with Socialist Realism at the Seventh Party Congress of the SED (April 1967). Such a critique could easily be seen as extending to the buzz around Tübke's series.[51] Like Richter, the ambivalent strategies could be critical of the specific contemporary society in which the artist worked and perhaps its own relationship to the Nazi past.

But Tübke had his defenders too, and no official policy cast him out, despite aesthetic debates at the highest level of politics. Quite the opposite. When the state found it useful, it was able to articulate through its *support* of Tübke's paintings its interest in criticizing the west and the presence of Nazi perpetrators in the Federal Republic. In Tübke's first major one-person show outside the German Democratic Republic (Milan and Munich), the catalog included an unsigned essay from the Ministry of Culture that praised the human-centered nature of his work and his optimistic representation of antifascists and others. In the one paragraph devoted to the Schulze paintings, however, the authors noted that Tübke's search for beauty often had to come about through a confrontation with the cruel and the ugly. Such a struggle was exemplified in how he took on the "reactionary powers" that still dominated in the Federal Republic through his painted "example of the Nazi judge who even today has still not lost his connection to the past."[52] Hence, for Tübke, the public reception and official political use of his work remained a matter of distancing East Germany from the corruption of West German history and contemporary politics. Whatever his critical relation to official aesthetics, his engagement with the subject of National Socialist perpetrators confirmed the position of the state. Unlike Richter's work, it was not the personal world of the family and relations between everyday (West) Germans that formed the flashpoint but rather the political competition between the states, in which the scandals within conservative FRG governmental circles were but one part. Everyday perpetrators within the family were not Tübke's subject; state institutions were.[53] In either case, though, the orientation is west. Given this focus, his use of the Nazi perpetrator as an artistic subject would remain, with few exceptions, a relatively isolated painting in the east.

In contrast to Tübke, Richter located the nexus of art and the contemporary relevance of the perpetrator within the family and common social groups. This strategy highlights the artist's specific ties to the context of

West German society and the significant debates regarding the contemporary continuity with the Nazi past. While *Christa and Wolfi* appears to be an extreme example of what Richter described as "crime and misery," other works during this period equally highlight the uneasy status of men and women in postwar West Germany, the banal and the unusual or even criminal, the private and the social. The paintings made at this time that rely on familial imagery inevitably feature male figures either as iconic and dominant central presences like Wolfi or, conversely, as small, humiliated, or grotesque creatures comparable to the older woman. Richter further populated his domestic scenes with omnipresent smiling women of multiple generations, from children to elderly widows. In all these paintings, Richter used his characteristic blur and selective focus, questioning the apparent transparency of their seemingly banal imagery.[54] Simultaneously, as he based them on snapshots, they evoked the traces of personal memory encoded in the common sign of the private photo. Richter in turn denied this personal status as a singular point of reference by his choice of a large-scale fine art format and the care he used to paint them. He employed these strategies consistently, and they engaged with an art market and West German society embroiled not only in questions of the nature of representation but also in the hotly debated social roles of women, families, and perpetrators.

Looking at other works by Richter in this period and casting a glance at the particular photos chosen in his *Atlas* makes evident his experimentation with the question of representation as it intersects with the social implications of his subjects. His work *Family* (1964) (Figure 2.7), for example, features a grouping of three women, a boy (the artist), and a girl. The boy is visually isolated to the right, while the girl and three women blend more seamlessly into each other. Furthering this compositionally gendered dynamic, the portrait *Helga Matura with Her Fiancé* (1966) shows a gigantic woman overshadowing her almost childlike husband, a relationship and characterization quite different from the photographic original. On the other hand, occasionally, Richter makes men more iconic and symbolically dominant (like *Uncle Rudi*), such as in his *Family by the Sea* (1964) (Figure 2.8), whose central figure is his father-in-law, Eufinger. While at the time the artist knew only imprecise details of Eufinger's SS past, the formality of the stock pose, as well as the undermining of the banal photographic mode through the expressive treatment of surface, still points to the kind of conceptual ambivalence Richter found compelling in *Christa and Wolfi*. These few images of clichéd male dominance, however, seem only to further point to the absence, isolation, or humiliation of men in the broader spectrum of Richter's work at the time. He often located the shifting scales, different modes of representation, constructs of female dominance and male presence or absence within the family unit, as was appropriate given many of his photographic sources.

These unresolved formal issues in the context of the social institution of the family resonate just as clearly with contemporary debates about perpetrators and the Nazi past. Perhaps his portrait of his own father, *Horst and His Dog* (1965) (Figure 2.9), is most revealing in this regard. Richter's painting shows a man of the perpetrator's generation rendered ridiculous, meaningless, and, for much of his body in this image, completely unsubstantial. The artist smeared a large proportion of the figure, now rendered as so much black and gray paint. Such an image invites the question of how this man, or any person so nonthreatening, could be criminal or live through such a criminal period seemingly without being affected. To a viewer who does not know his exact identity, he could easily have been a former Auschwitz guard, a duped bystander, or an oblivious nonparticipant. Was one of those possible pasts belied in a banal present? How can a

FIGURE 2.7. Gerhard Richter, *Family*, 1964. Oil on canvas, 150 × 180 cm. Copyright Gerhard Richter, 2011.

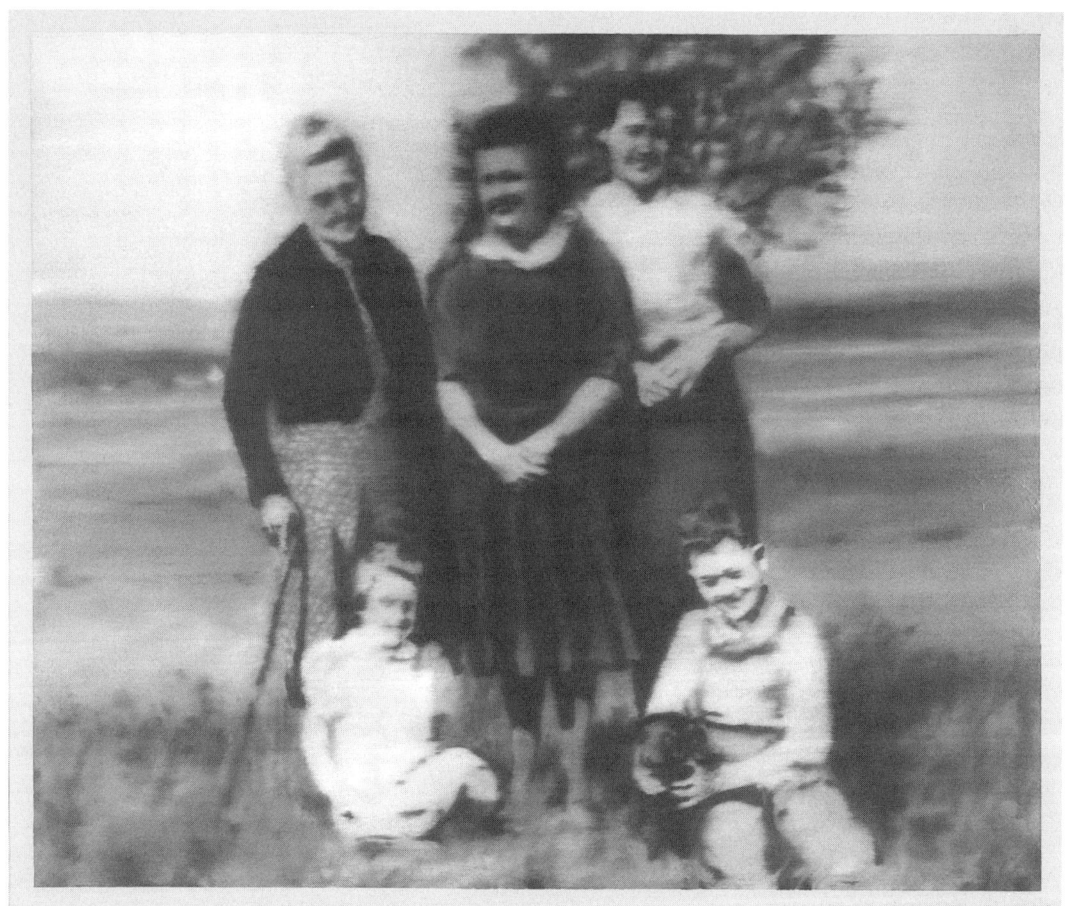

figure like this reestablish the patriarchal order in society? Richter's image could not answer such specific and definitive questions. But we can highlight the political relevance of the formal ambiguity he employs as well as his consistent interest in localizing social themes in his depictions of the family by understanding contemporary debates about the status of the perpetrator, within the CDU government and society as a whole.

When Richter turned to nonbiographical subjects, he also worked on experimenting with these formal choices and occasionally employed similar iconographic subthemes. So, for example, his portraits of *Eight Student Nurses* (1966) (Figure 2.10) show the same pattern of revealing and obscuring, repressing any significant content through the visual means of using the seemingly banal graduation photos of the students as a source. The images, though, hid the gruesome murder of the nurses by a Chicago serial killer. Like the Nazi past in his other works, the indexical form and banal subject matter signaled an ambiguous relationship to crime. But understanding the crime becomes crucial for explaining their tense intersection with contemporary society.[55]

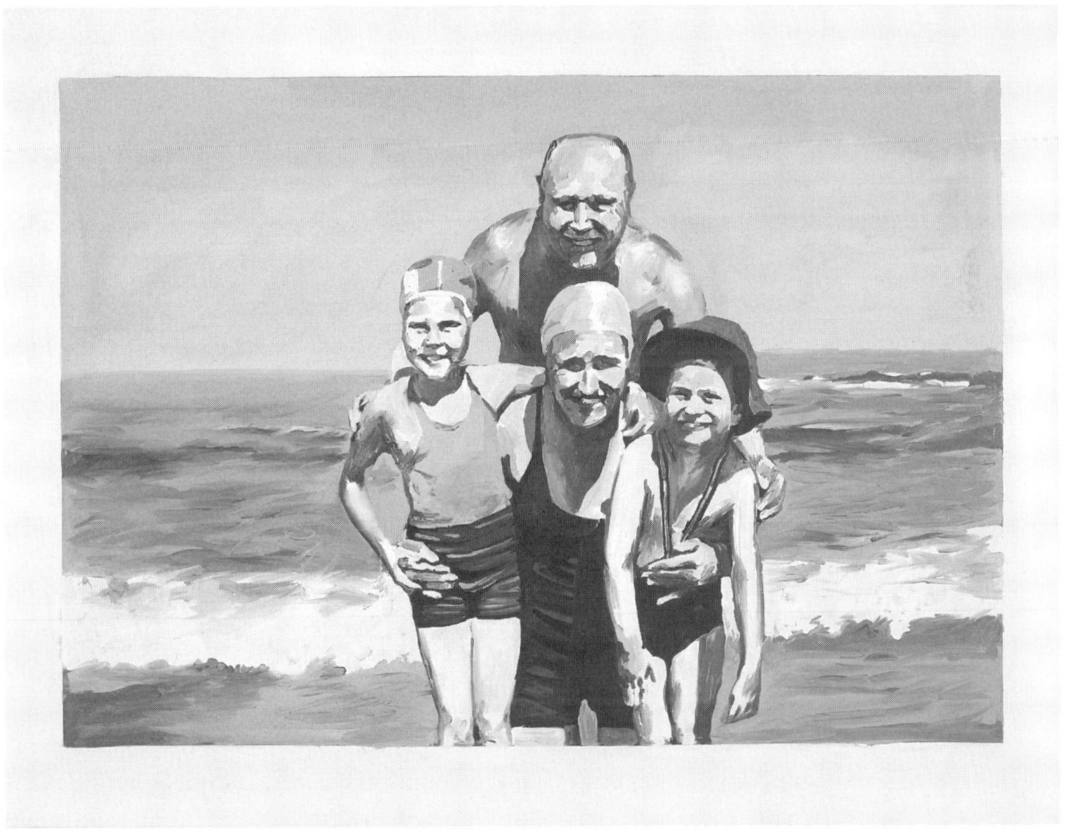

FIGURE 2.8. Gerhard Richter, *Family by the Sea*, 1964. Oil on canvas, 150 × 200 cm. Sylvia and Ulrich Ströher Collection, Museum Küppersmühle für Moderne Kunst, Duisburg, Germany. Copyright Gerhard Richter, 2011.

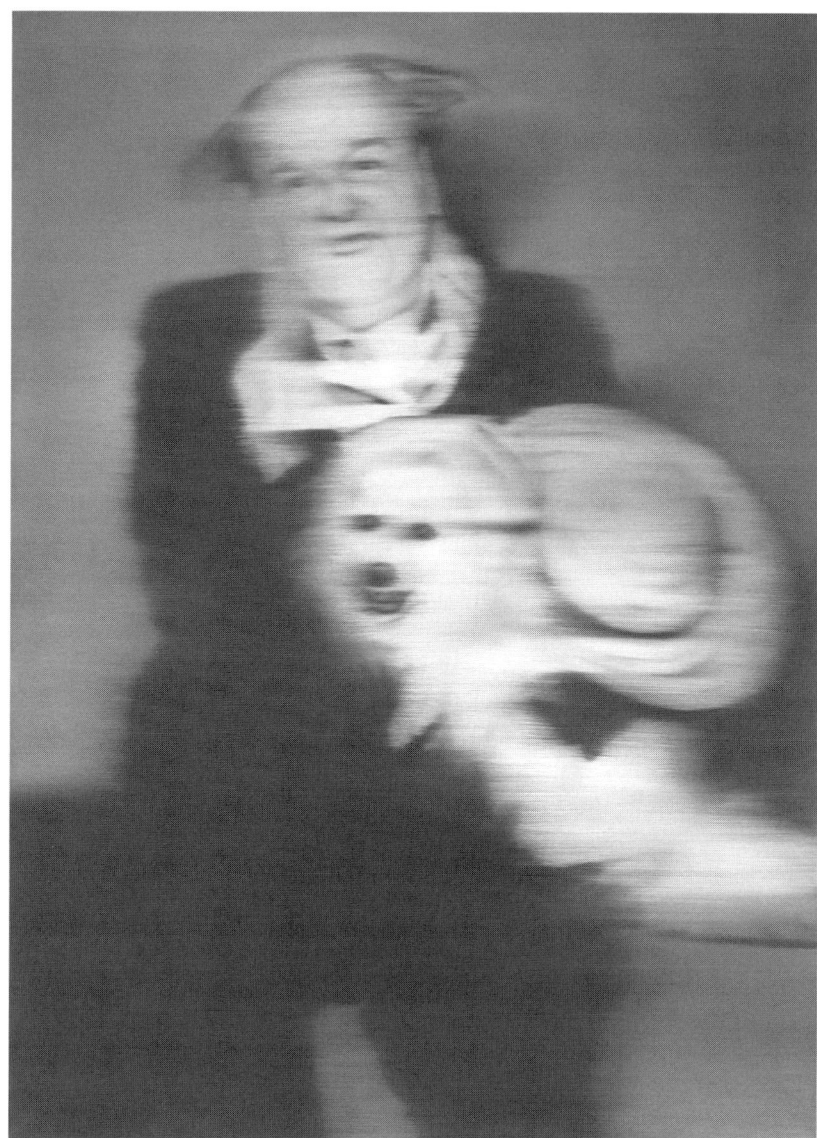

FIGURE 2.9. Gerhard Richter, *Horst and His Dog*, 1965. Oil on canvas, 31½ × 23⅝ inches (80 × 60 cm). Private collection. Copyright Gerhard Richter, 2011.

Perhaps most exemplary, *Christa and Wolfi* dynamically thematized the formal and historical contradictions that surrounded the appearance of the perpetrator amid the public trials and scandals that erupted within and around Adenauer's government. The image both reveals a common family scene and conceals that subject through Modernist facture; emphasizes and obscures generational presence; maintains itself as a personal object but also extends to a familiar social subject; and represents the reproducibility of mass media and yet signifies its unique painterly presence. Richter did not take a critical stance toward this balancing act, neither providing a dialectic resolution to this ambivalence nor signaling a valuation of the media or imagery with which he was dealing. He remained, rather, unresolved aesthetically and socially. The reference to the recent past and the use of different generations of women, as well as the specific iconography of the German shepherd, complement the broader interest Richter has shown in the Nazi period. The continued presence of Nazi personnel throughout West German society, governmental resistance in revealing these perpetrators, and the absence of public moral judgment are also useful points of reference when we bring them to bear on Richter's work in the early 1960s. Like the familial imagery upon which he drew in the popular form of the snapshot, he was both private and public, individual and social. These terms, so central to the definition of the Nazi perpetrator, help clarify not only Richter's strategies but also how political debates at the end of the Adenauer era could penetrate deeply into West German culture.

Conclusion

Richter was by no means alone in the West German art scene. In fact, members of his artistic social network, such as Sigmar Polke and the new gallery dealer René Block with whom he showed, recognized the contemporary importance of National Socialist issues as a relevant artistic subtheme.[56] Beuys and Vostell had both evidenced this well before Richter, but the loosely affiliated group also made this clear in Block's 1967 exhibition, *Homage to Lidice*. Several of the antifascist assassins of SS Security Office chief Reinhard Heydrich came from the small Czech town of Lidice. After Heydrich's death in 1942, the SS shot the men and boys of the town, and murdered the women or sent them to concentration camps; the Germans destroyed the town and erased it from all official maps and documents.[57] In Block's exhibition, artists responded to this event through a number of critical and conceptual works. Notably, Richter chose to focus on German agency by showing here his portrait of *Uncle Rudi*.

Yet by 1967, the terms of debate had changed in artistic as well as political circles. U.S. Pop Art and the challenges to conventional media were accepted strategies within the art markets of Western Europe, and artists were experimenting with ever more innovative attempts to be conceptually and aesthetically provocative. Furthermore, as is well known, artists and critics increasingly politicized such attempts through the growing crisis resulting in the global civil unrest of 1968. In West Germany, the Grand Coalition of CDU and SPD replaced the dominance of the CDU, which, in turn, was followed in 1969 by an SPD-led coalition headed by Chancellor Willy Brandt. Brandt had been a resistance fighter during the

Nazi period, and consequently the concerns of perpetrators within his government seemed less urgent than in the previous CDU administrations. In addition, as the students took to the streets, generational conflict became clear and "fascist" became a term easily used against anyone associated with official institutions. Art historians and artists would take up these new conditions in quite variable ways. In essence, the social, political, and artistic conditions were decidedly different than when Richter made his way to West Germany before the construction of the Berlin Wall in 1961.

But between 1961 and 1967, the political reception of the Nazi past clearly focused on the agency of perpetrators and how the continued presence of these individuals in West German society and conservative government circles raised a whole series of social, moral, and political problems. Such events as the Eichmann trial and the Auschwitz process concentrated these debates, as did complementary discussions in the art press, for example, the critical response to the *Degenerate Art* show. Given his own personal interests, it should not surprise us that Richter consistently used family

FIGURE 2.10. Gerhard Richter, *Eight Student Nurses*, 1966. Eight paintings, oil on canvas, each 36⅜ × 27⁹⁄₁₆ inches (95 × 70 cm). Kunstmuseum, Winterthur. Copyright Gerhard Richter, 2011.

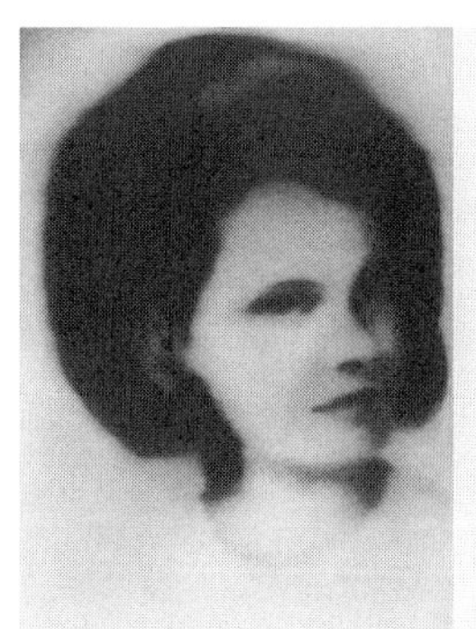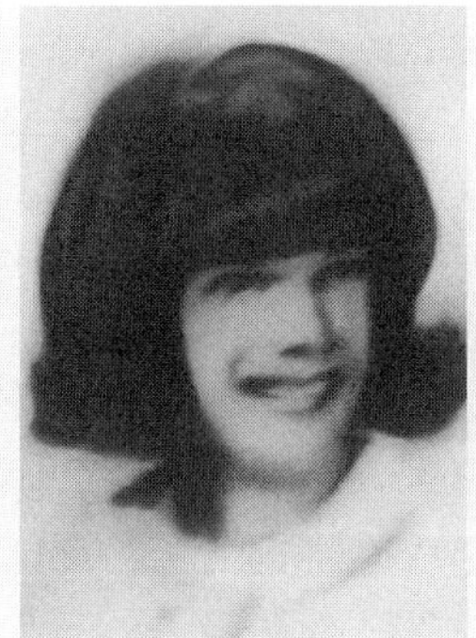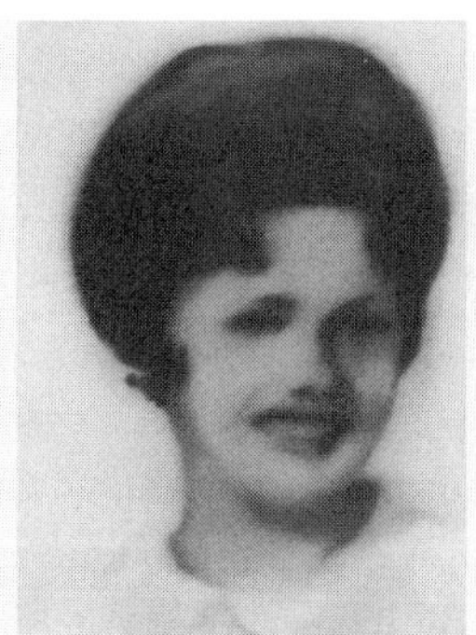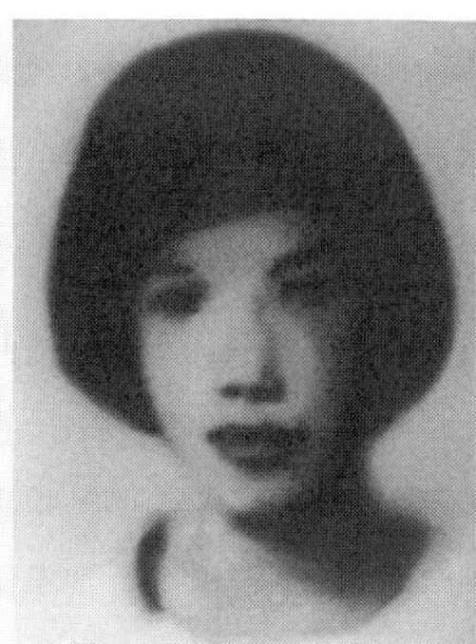

photographs and militarist Nazi imagery that engaged the recent past as a prominent subtheme in his art. These works did not reject the social or artistic terms of their society, projecting against them a radical and autonomous alternative. Rather, they engaged social and artistic debates of real consequence both aesthetically and in their indirect or direct political imagery. Richter was not alienated from the social and aesthetic world of which he was a part.[58] He exemplifies how we can use an artist developing at a crucial stage of his career to highlight the influence of conservative political debates on West German society in the early 1960s. We need to expand our field of reference to assess his contribution and that of others not so triumphantly celebrated by a market-driven art historical establishment.[59] Art historians do not necessarily need to get to know the artist better, but scholarship must attend to the broader conditions of West German artistic production, including how those conditions encompassed the changing status of the Nazi perpetrator.

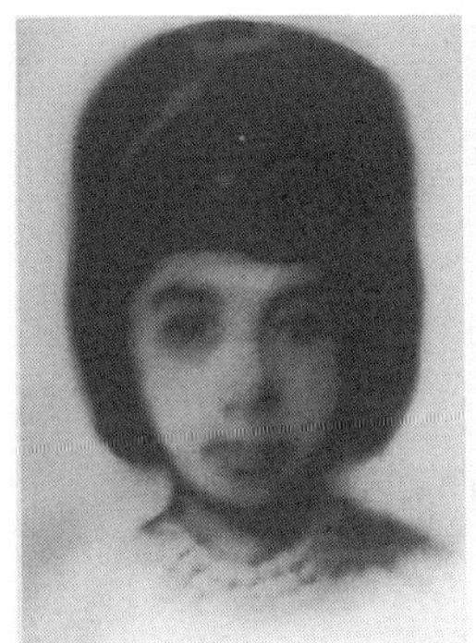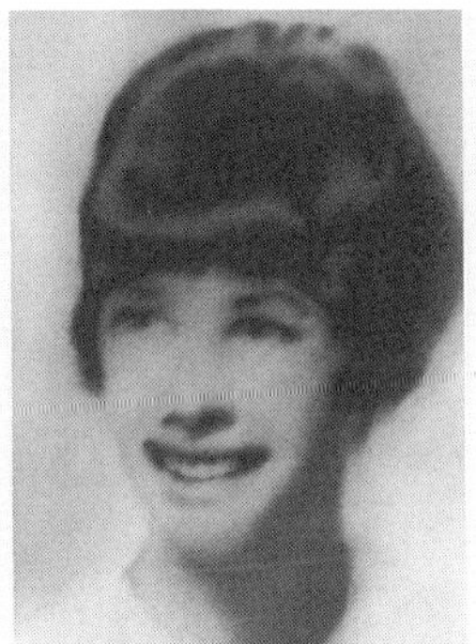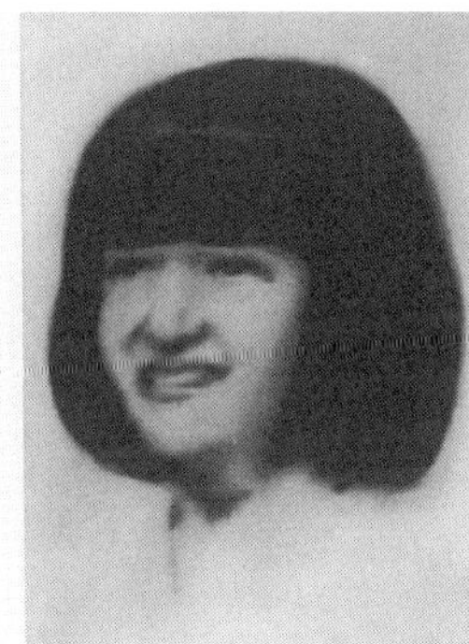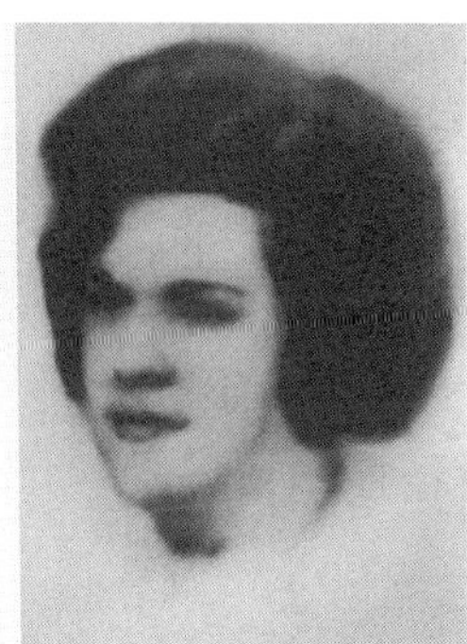

3 ANSELM KIEFER AND THE ASCENDANCE OF HELMUT KOHL
THE CHANGING PERCEPTION OF THE PERPETRATOR

> Even in right-wing circles—such as in the Hanns-Seidel Stiftung of the CSU—one begins to discover that the fine arts can also be used as a medium for transmitting the desired concept of history. Mind you, one complains that in the contemporary art of the Federal Republic there is hardly anything at hand [for such a purpose]. No wonder, given that an absence of historical awareness and "apolitical" art production were for decades guidelines for official art policy.
>
> —"Zu diesem Heft," *Tendenzen* (1984)

ALBERT KIEFER, FATHER OF ANSELM, CAME OF ARTISTIC and political age during the Nazi period. His own father had been mayor in the small town of Niederbuhl bei Rastatt before he ran afoul of the new regime in 1933 when he refused to replace the flag of Baden on the Rathaus (town hall) with the *Hakenkreuz* (swastika), an act for which he was briefly imprisoned. Buckling under this pressure, Mayor Kiefer joined the NSDAP and his son Albert joined the Hitler Youth. The latter enlisted in the Wehrmacht in November 1937 and remained active in the Thirty-Fifth Division of the army through the war. Albert Kiefer married Cilly Forster during the war, and on March 8, 1945, their son Anselm was born. Following demobilization, in December 1945 Albert was posted as an art teacher in Ottersdorf, where the family stayed for ten years. Anselm got his first art lessons from his father, who was also his first primary source for the Nazi period.[1]

Anselm Kiefer is without a doubt the most prominent postwar German artist associated with the traumatic working through of the Nazi past. Scholars have featured Kiefer in innumerable critical and historical studies as *the* artist who systematically and consistently broke any lasting taboos on the use of the world of the Nazi perpetrator as a subject in contemporary art. From his earliest artistic pieces beginning in 1969 to his triumphant and international one-person shows in the mid- to late 1980s, the steady rise of his fame also paralleled the expanding public discussion of the National Socialist past in general and Jewish victims in specific. West Germans seemed finally willing to define their country as a perpetrator society, and eventually they came to embrace Kiefer's art following his international critical successes in the first half of the 1980s.[2]

When discussing Kiefer, art historians stubbornly hold on to a relatively uninflected conception of the Nazi past that includes a generic and unexplored definition of the perpetrator.[3] Focusing on the broadly abstract terms of "repression," "melancholy," and "mourning," critics have obfuscated key dynamic conditions related to Kiefer's work, including the noticeable influence of his family's biography. In terms of my project, the particularities of the political reception of the Nazi perpetrator within conservative circles are not to be found in the literature on Anselm Kiefer any more than they were present in writings on Gerhard Richter. A precise history that includes this issue allows for a greater analytic flexibility and, as in the case of Richter, a clearer sense of the specific turns of his art.

Much of Kiefer's initial use of and success with National Socialist themes occurred in the 1970s, a period of liberal dominance in West German politics. Beginning here, we can trace how Kiefer adapted earlier concepts of the everyday functional perpetrator to his more symbolic form and content. For Kiefer, the category of the perpetrator as a historical agent begins to break down, even though personal agency still lingers as a concept in his particular visual choices. Understanding this complex relationship to the perpetrator in the 1970s helps us clarify important changes he made in his work in the early 1980s. Kiefer's project comes into sync with specific social phenomena related to conservative politics, particularly in this crucial period. In this moment as he worked on such major paintings as *Sulamith* (1983), he turned to the use of new imagery derived from National Socialist architecture (see Plate 6). This new imagery would pose a question as to whether understanding the perpetrator was an issue of articulating the agency of individuals, as in the recent past, or a matter increasingly of representation, of a turn to cultural abstraction. The tension between these two positions is palpable as he made the transition to this new phase of his career.

The early 1980s marked not only a notable artistic moment for Kiefer in West German society but also a political one when the rise of the moderate conservative right culminated in the Christian Democratic Union's leader, Helmut Kohl, becoming chancellor. For thirteen years and the whole of the 1970s, the liberal Social Democrats (SPD) led West German governments. Even extremist politics in this period was dominated by the left, including most famously the Baader–Meinhof group. However, the direction of German politics moved rightward with the rise of Kohl in the 1980s. As with Ronald Reagan in the United States and Margaret Thatcher in Britain, Kohl's election in October 1982 signaled a clear political shift in West German society, a shift that also had social and cultural implications.[4] While decidedly more liberal in his attitude toward state welfare policy than Reagan and Thatcher, Kohl nevertheless aligned Germany with the conservative Cold War politics and global financial markets, a policy consistent with that of the major Atlantic powers. Internally, as did Konrad Adenauer before him, Kohl attempted to negotiate the debate over the National Socialist past both to shore up key right-wing constituencies and to promote the first steps toward what would be called "normalization." Kohl's interest in asserting contemporary West Germany's right to be a "normal" nation again (unlike its Nazi predecessor) meant that he concerned himself with different elements of that past than had previous leaders within the CDU.

In particular, Kohl's attempt to project a new and normalized West Germany reached a fever pitch at the ceremonies in 1985 at the Bitburg cemetery commemorating the fortieth anniversary of the end of World War II. The Bitburg event was one moment in the second major postwar swell of public discussions concerning Nazi perpetrators related to specific conservative politics, culminating for scholars in the "Historians' Debate" (*Historikerstreit*) of the late 1980s.[5] At Bitburg and in other speeches in the period, Kohl used a comparative rhetorical strategy contrasting past and present in his defense of specific policies that differed substantially from earlier state positions. With this approach, Kohl significantly blurred the concept of the functional everyday perpetrator, narrowing the characterization considerably to resemble the initial postwar definition that emphasized Nazi criminal culpability only at the ideological extreme. His conception of how the contemporary West German public stood in relation to the perpetrator played a key role in his attitudes toward the past. I focus on Kohl's rise to power and his instrumentalization of history at Bitburg in order to identify how the political relationship to the Nazi perpetrator shifted in its terms and its implications, particularly with the return of the CDU to the chancellorship in the early 1980s. Kiefer's artistic strategies help highlight key tropes within these shifting terms.

Thus, in this chapter I reverse the equation used to analyze Richter: with Richter's work, tracing the political impact of a variable definition of the Nazi perpetrator was useful in clarifying his artistic strategies; with Kiefer, it is his artistic terms that clarify the instrumentalization of past criminality in Kohl's political rhetoric. While Kiefer and Kohl influenced the public sphere from two very different institutional and ideological positions, their uses of the Nazi past were grounded in parallel concerns. Identifying the artistic terms of debate helps clarify the political use of the Nazi past as power transferred from the SPD to the CDU. In this moment of political tension, the various fortieth-anniversary memorial events formed a constant backdrop and a necessary staging arena for political pronouncements on the past and contemporary Cold War interests, of which Bitburg is a prime example. Here, too, I clarify the central question of criminal agency as well as the cultural ritual of the ceremonies themselves by comparing them to the artistic debates of the day. In particular, an analysis of Kiefer can be used fruitfully to make a new interpretation of the well-known speeches of Kohl. The abstraction of the perpetrator in Kohl's conception of the past and the increasing presence of cultural representations of Nazi crimes are contiguous and mutually clarifying historical subjects, showing the breadth of debates throughout the FRG.[6] Their comparative analysis helps us understand the impact of the changing status of the perpetrator on art and in important moments of conservative resurgence in postwar West Germany.

From Fathers to Sons: The Historical Past and the Subjective Present

In the latter half of the 1960s, the Nazi perpetrator continued as a theme of the public discourse of West German society particularly within the student revolts. While dependent on a variety of different issues, from international to local, the civil unrest in this period brought to light the obvious and overt critique of the past as the new generation of sons and daughters turned against the fascist generation of fathers and mothers. In so doing, the social understanding of the perpetrator evolved as well, and artists took part as much as any other group in this dialogue. Certainly the question of the perpetrator as the functional everyman who continued her life in postwar West Germany still appeared in key public discussions up through the 1960s. But protesters and critics increasingly displaced this theme from the center of debate. Instead, they critiqued the ideologically motivated crimes associated with past Nazi personnel and fellow travelers and, in the process, painted an entire generation with these views. Ideological confrontation, not the reflection on personal or institutional connections to the past, characterized the struggles of the latter part of the decade and on into the 1970s. A brief overview of this political history provides necessary context for Kiefer's work.

In the Federal Republic, as elsewhere in the Cold War west, open generational conflict often centered on politicized groups of students. After the banning of the German Communist Party in 1956, the most prominent left-wing student group was the Sozialistischer Deutscher Studentenbund (SDS; Socialist German Students' League). The group originally sprang from the reconstituted SPD in the immediate postwar years, but by 1960 the SPD had disowned it. Increasingly, the SDS became the center of attention for public leftist critiques of West German society, and SDS leaders more and more functioned as mouthpieces for the student movement. For example, they organized an important anti–Vietnam War congress in February 1968 that was a major forum for the charismatic Rudi Dutschke and others to outline their radical agenda. The attempted assassination of Dutschke on April 11, 1968, by the right-winger Josef Bachmann precipitated the so-called Easter Trouble (*Osterunruhe*) when SDS and other leftists protested the police state. Tensions mounted and demonstrations intensified, leading parliament to pass a state of emergency decree in May 1968.[7] Such left-wing student activity was not unique to Germany, and the SDS anticapitalist and anti-imperialist agenda dovetailed with international movements of the period.[8]

Still, the specter of the recent past did inflect West German disputes differently than in Paris or elsewhere. The renewed popularity of right-wing extremist political activity seemed to confirm this German exceptionalism, specifically with the increasing electoral success of the Nationaldemokratische Partei Deutschlands (NPD, German National Democratic Party). The NPD just missed getting into parliament in the 1965 elections as it fell below the 5 percent of the vote necessary. Building off this achievement in 1966, the NPD's capture of representation in state elections in Hesse and Bavaria shocked mainstream political opinion. Ironically, in the early 1960s, the federal government had reported that right-wing coalitions were splintering and appeared to be dying out along with the final remnants of fascism. But the NPD electoral victories proved this official vision to be a fallacy. Certainly, the NPD distanced itself by necessity from direct NSDAP precedent, but still its members used specifically coded language that barely hid the connection. In its party program, for example, it committed its followers to "the natural authority of a true democracy" and also spoke critically of the lack of independence of West Germany from NATO as well as "middle Germany" from the Soviets.[9] The success of such a program at the local level and the fear that it was only a matter of time before NPD leaders entered the Bundestag gave rise to public fears of the persistence of fascism and the potential for ever more perpetrators in the halls of government.

In this context, it is no surprise that the younger generation embodied in the SDS drew overt parallels between the NPD and the former members of the NSDAP. A mainstay of the students' political program became the rubric of antifascist critiques of their parents' mainstream institutions that had allowed the extreme right once again to gain strength. The blending of the past and present became inextricable from generational shifts and anti-institutional forces. This situation foregrounded the continuing need of West Germany to deal with its perpetrators, one way or the other, to avoid a situation that many began to see as reminiscent of the breakdown in democracy at the end of the Weimar Republic.[10]

These and other political stresses on the Grand Coalition eventually led to its collapse after the September 1969 elections, in which the NPD received 4.3 percent, just short of the votes needed to gain parliamentary representation. The SPD garnered 42.7 percent of the vote and formed a coalition with the liberal Free Democratic Party (FDP); the SPD forced the CDU/CSU bloc into the opposition for the first time in the postwar period. Willy Brandt, who had been in exile during the Nazi period and had served as foreign minister in the Grand Coalition, became the first SPD chancellor. Brandt could carry forward the mantel of active opposition to the past in a way that such "inner immigration" politicians like Adenauer or his successors could not, particularly with the taint of the persistence of perpetrators within the former CDU government. In addition, Brandt's efforts led to the overt symbolic acceptance of German culpability when, in 1970, he famously dropped to his knees before the Warsaw Ghetto Memorial. Such a sign of humility and attempt at reconciliation struck a very different tone for how the state dealt with the National Socialist burden and was strengthened by foreign policies that, for example, recognized Poland's postwar borders (the Oder–Neisse Line) as inviolable. Thus, while chronologically Brandt's biography represented continuity with the 1930s as much as that of any of his contemporaries, his antinationalist policies and attempts to address collective guilt for the past drew many younger supporters—with the exception of particular segments of the left. On the whole, though, West German youth saw him as the leader of their conflicts with the older generation.[11]

These debates and conflicts were exacerbated not only within the political world of public protest but also very much so within the university world, at Freiburg, where Kiefer studied, and elsewhere in West Germany. Exemplary in this regard was the case of art history. In this discipline, fascism became a major theme for the younger generation of scholars, who used it as a weapon to distinguish themselves intellectually and politically from the perpetrators of the past. The issue burst into the open at the famed 1970

Cologne German Art Historians Congress. At this conference, a defiant group of young art historians brought together by Martin Warnke addressed openly the continuing influence of National Socialist ideology on contemporary German art history. Two crucial exhibitions in Frankfurt added fuel to this confrontational fire. The first, in 1972, centered on the reopening of the German Historical Museum's collection, which included displays of art produced under the Nazi state and wall text directly relating cultural production to class and political struggle. The second, two years later and also in Frankfurt, showed art featured in the *Great German Art Exhibitions* of the 1930s that had long been consigned to the basements. This show, coupled with the groundbreaking survey text by Berthold Hinz, as well as a small but growing literature by Barbara Miller Lane and others, established a body of research and visual materials that would form an important base for later scholars. It allowed them to assert and assess the infiltration of fascist ideology into the supposedly rarefied world of art and art history for the next decade.[12] Indeed, the very production of this work was a means of separating this generation of art historians from their conformist predecessors.

Hinz's role in the 1970 congress is worth looking at in a bit more detail, as it highlights the impact of generational conflict on the formulation of an ideologically motivated perpetrator in the world of art. His piece on the so-called Bamberg Rider (circa 1230–40; Figure 3.1) was a scathing indictment of how nationalism and racism seeped into the interpretation of this well-known statue. Based on an analysis of more than 150 texts on the sculpture, Hinz showed that it had become a famous work only relatively recently. Georg Dehio's 1890 article was primarily responsible, as he recognized the stylistic relationship between the work and that of the more prominent sculptural program at Reims. Dehio's argument prompted a series of reactionary responses from his colleagues that increasingly insisted on what was perceived as the exclusively German character of the work, a character that distinguished it sharply from French prototypes. By the Nazi period, the intellectual transformation was complete: art historians used the work to signal all that was nationalist (and anti-French) in German art as well as to embody their racial stereotypes. Most scandalously, Hinz showed through citation how such positions that reflected the art historians' enthusiasm for using their craft to promote state ideology continued unabated in the post-1945 years. Without naming names (although the written version shows that several well-known culprits included the art historians Hans Weigert and Wilhelm Pinder), Hinz nevertheless made clear that the previous generation of esteemed professors and doctoral advisers were deeply implicated in naturalizing nationalism and racism within the discipline. They had turned the science of art history into mere ideology.[13]

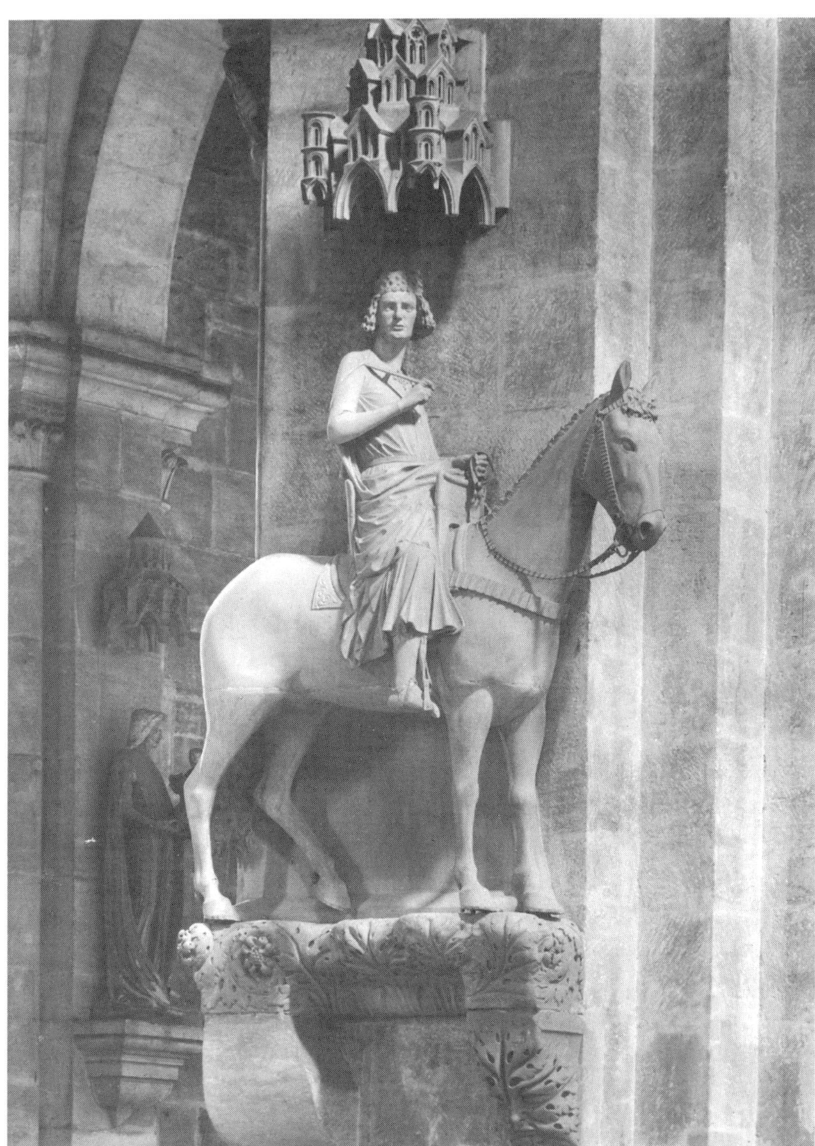

FIGURE 3.1. The
Bamburg Rider,
Bamburg Cathedral,
c. 1230–40. Courtesy
of Zentralinstitut für
Kunstgeschichte,
Photothek.

Hinz refused to name names in order to focus his argument more generally on art history as a discipline. In the record of the discussion that followed, clearly the two key factors of the debate were whether Hinz's method of reception history was even legitimate as art history, and who, exactly, he might be claiming was essentially a fascist. Professors in attendance asked "vehemently" for names and others insisted that Hinz relied only on some works of "high school teachers," not university-level scholars. Hinz defended his sources and assured his audience that they were well known. The auditorium quickly became polarized and emotions ran high.

But it is clear that the audience focused not only on the art historians who may have helped the NSDAP regime and continued in their profession after the war. In addition, outrage focused on Hinz himself, for his audacity as a young professor to use such a method to foreground his ideological critique. Those who opposed him attempted to argue that art had nothing to do with such a political criticism. The idea of generational continuity so much at the heart of debates during the Eichmann and Auschwitz trials had turned firmly to generational conflict, here and elsewhere. The previous question of what you had done in the past was secondary to whether your art historical output ideologically embodied a fascist position open to the arguments of the new generation of critical art historians.[14]

Kiefer's early artistic choices were in clear dialogue with these political and intellectual debates as well as contemporary aesthetic innovations. In his first major paintings, for example, he tended to combine various formal, iconographic, and conceptual strategies to thematize in particular the artist's relation to the recent past and its criminal policies. So, for example, in *Nero Paints* (1974), he developed his interest in the large-scale, heavily worked surfaces of Abstract Expressionism through associations with the expansive fields of the March Heath (see Figure 3.2). The fields were well-known sites of Prussian battle since the eighteenth century, and they had strong militarist and patriotic associations both in the past and the present. He related this field to the self-destructive policies of Nero; like Nero destroying his own city of Rome, here the blackened and heavily painted surface shows the burnt residue of the fields associated with Hitler's scorched-earth policy in the last months of World War II. The dripping palette in the center forms an obvious reference to the artist himself as the presenter of the scene but also as an active participant. He conflates the application of paint with applying fire to the houses at the upper right. The act of painting and the subjective gesture of the artist collapse into the historical role of the cultural producer as a participant in crimes of national self-destruction.[15] Kiefer raises moral questions: how was it possible for contemporary artists to represent previous historical atrocities, and yet how culpable were comparable artists for their actions within the recent Nazi past? In this image, the everyday role of the German and her or his continuity with past crimes seems to be emphasized.

Yet to present this message, Kiefer simultaneously used transparent imagery but also obscure form. In so doing, he brought together both the past and the present in uneasy tension; the incommensurability and yet connectedness of distinct moments of time form the heart of his artistic project. First, he dutifully records the historical crimes of the father's generation in the obvious symbolic and traditional iconography, such as the palette. But second, the son marks his own agency and inability to face up

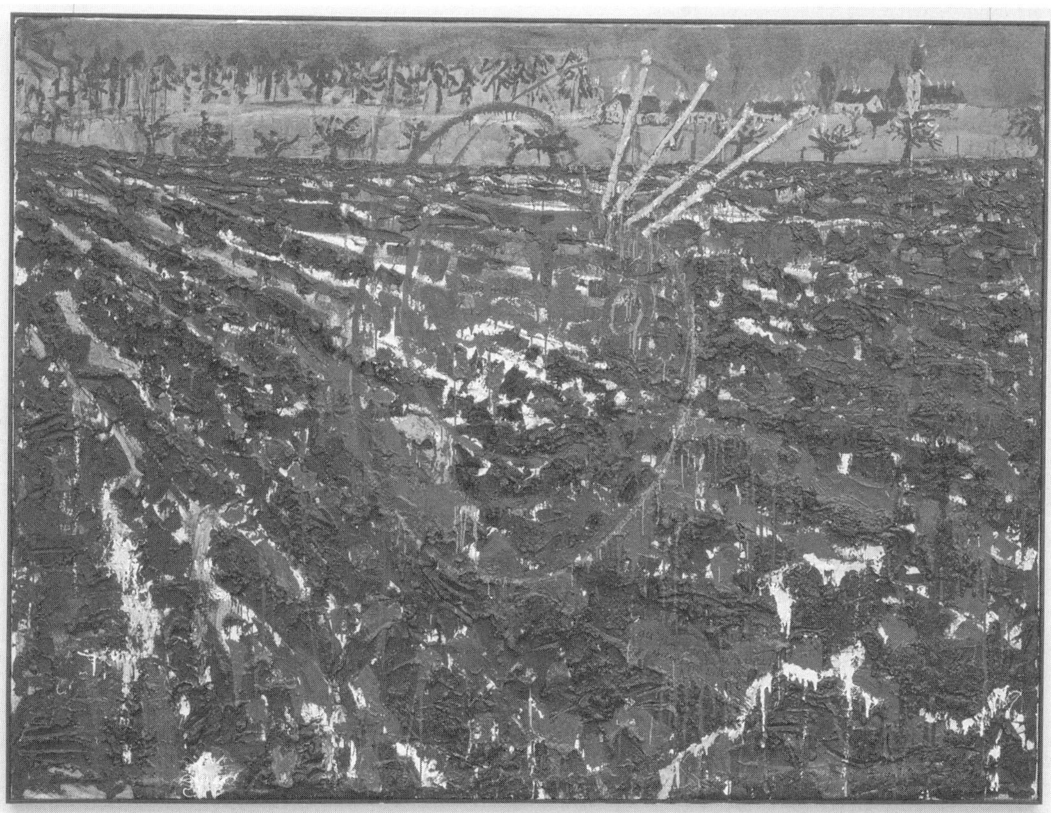

FIGURE 3.2. Anselm Kiefer, *Nero Paints*, 1974. Oil on canvas, 86⅝ × 118⅛ inches (220 × 300 cm). Photograph copyright Blauel/Gnamm—ARTOTHEK. Courtesy of Pinakothek der Moderne, Wittelsbacher Ausgleichsfonds. Copyright Anselm Kiefer.

to such a straightforward representation of the past in the personalized and obsessive facture and layering of surfaces, a clear contemporary aesthetic device that mystifies the iconographic choices. In so doing, Kiefer stages an uneasy combination of two different characterizations of the perpetrator: on the one hand, he is an ideological agent who configures the past in symbolic and allegorical terms, quite distinct from the democratic and rationalist public (especially the youth groups) that vehemently rejected the resurrection of these terms in art or in politics; on the other, he is the everyday artist who also participates in the crimes of the past, no different potentially from current citizens within West Germany.

Such a conceptual tension between form and content references as well the very real political tensions between postwar generations. To put the description of Kiefer's early project in blunt generational terms is not, however, simply to reaffirm the psychoanalytic principles of analysis that are so prominent in Lisa Saltzman's work, for example.[16] Rather, these terms also signal the relationship between Kiefer's choices and the social field of which he was a part. His take on the subject of generational tensions is quite in keeping with the range of responses of other so-called 68ers. But because of this, we need to highlight its particular historical character to avoid isolating questions of representation from the functional relations of art to institutions and audiences.

As we have seen, in the late 1960s, the big social question involving the concept of the Nazi perpetrator moved gradually from issues surrounding continuity with the past to those involving generational conflict. In this sense, not only did the parents as perpetrators surround the family life of sons and daughters, but the latter were also beginning to take things into their own hands. Still, not every confrontation was seemingly so clear-cut as Hinz's ideological critique of his art historical elders. Kiefer was not merely criticizing the criminal world of the father. Instead, his subject was the dynamic established by the son's *relationship to* the father. This includes factoring in the specific agency of each generation as it negotiated its independent relationship to the past and its criminal policies. Both the particular generational conflict *and*, by contrast, the intersection of biographical conditions of fathers and sons grounded the specific choices that Kiefer made, as well as his sarcastic handling of Nazi themes in his early work.

A surprising source, unused in art history, helps us clarify the exact nature of this response to the past and to nail down many of the confrontational interests at stake: the autobiography of Kiefer's father. Albert Kiefer tells his life story in the classic tropes of those who experienced the Nazi state firsthand. He also expands on his successful postwar artistic career, which led him into the minefield of student protest just discussed. In 1964, he was named to the Institute for Art Pedagogy (Institut für Kunstpädagogik) at the Johann Wolfgang Goethe University in Frankfurt and, in 1972, promoted to professor. Throughout his career, he maintained a commitment to naturalism and academic standards with an interest in landscape and portraiture, quite in contrast to the conceptual and painterly strategies of his son (Figure 3.3).[17]

Albert Kiefer's framing of the National Socialist past within his autobiography as well as the circumstances of his military service interest us here. His retelling of that period falls well within the exculpatory accounts that contain several common leitmotifs, including the lack of knowledge, at the time, of Jewish oppression; the fact that all military officers that he had contact with disdained and even worked against the state leadership under Hitler; and that, indeed, after all, the military served honorably.[18] Hence, soldiers and officers stood outside any definition of the perpetrator. This led him to several awkward passages, such as the sidebar that accompanies the text describing his participation as a member of the German Army's Thirty-Fifth Division in the May 10, 1940, invasion of western Europe. Kiefer notes how seemingly happy the Belgians were that the French and

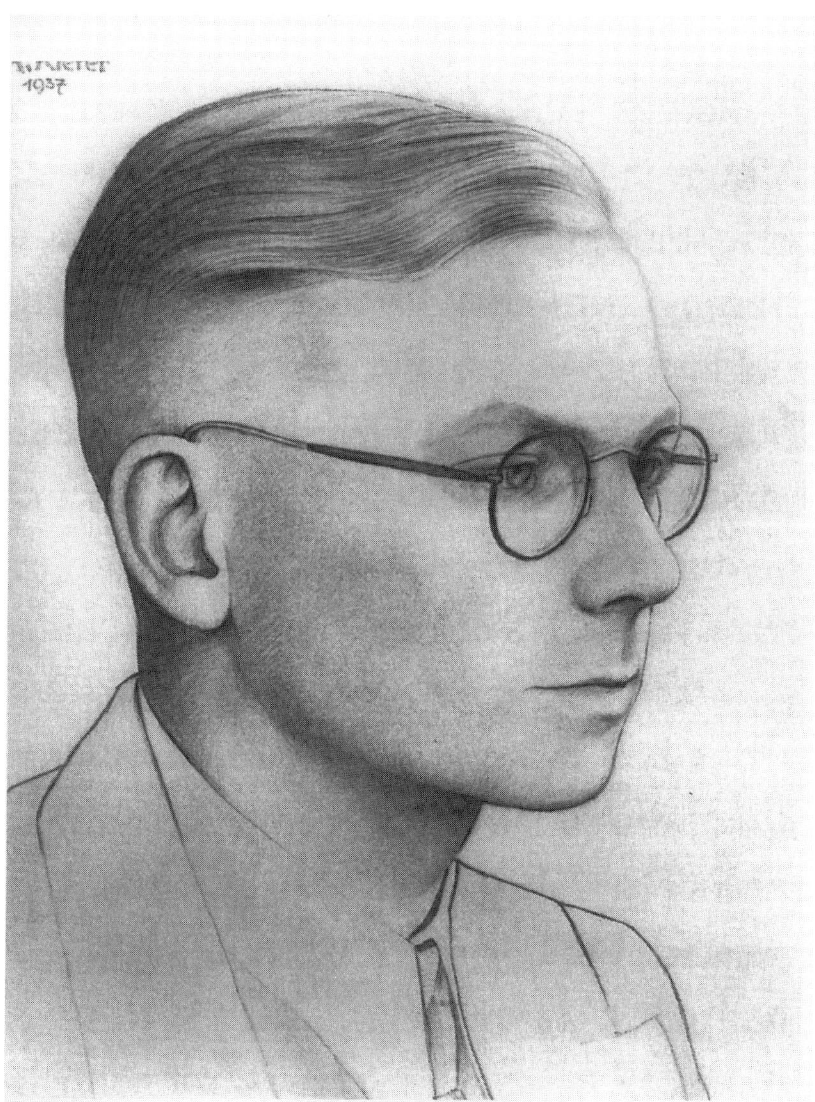

FIGURE 3.3. Albert Kiefer, *Self-Portrait*, 1937. Photograph courtesy of Professor Albert Kiefer.

British were gone and, to this day, various villagers still invited members of the Thirty-Fifth Division and their wives to festivals and special occasions.[19] While we have no reason to doubt these stories, he easily generalizes from individual selective anecdotes to characterize the actions of many of his generation as a whole. The text lacks a more nuanced understanding of the military and other German institutions under Nazi leadership. Instead, Albert Kiefer concentrates criminal agency firmly in the hands of the ideological zealots of the party elite.

Anselm Kiefer takes on precisely this unreflective subjectivity in a large number of his earliest works, and his father's biography would prove crucial in many ways for the self-fashioning of the son's artistic and ethnic identity. Although Anselm Kiefer seems to have gotten along well with his father, he nevertheless thematized the specificity of his interpretation of generational conflict through his father's autobiography.[20] When Kiefer used specific National Socialist imagery as he often did in the seventies, he referred to its ideological iconography and militarist aspirations. He produced such works simultaneously with his explorations of German myth and culture, such as his frequent reference to the Nibelungen saga. Typical of many of his generation, these works negotiated a personal critical dialogue with their fathers and mothers and, by extension, a social dialogue that characterized the broader position of the Nazi past that would make Willy Brandt's actions in Warsaw such a sensation. As a result, and in contrast to his father, Kiefer firmly linked military personnel to the most extreme policies of the Nazi state.

In particular, whether a Hitler salute at key European sites or a mocking representation of the projected invasion of England, these early works connected the political signs and myths of National Socialism to its expansionist imperialist policies. Kiefer used the iconography and fantasies of the Nazi Party true believer, linked them to the world of the soldier, and updated them for his own generation. So, the gesture of the Hitler salute (which was and remains illegal in Germany) became the shocking center of the *Occupations* series (produced 1969; published 1975; Figure 3.4). This threatening gesture was, at the same time, rendered ridiculous through the manipulation of scale, repetition of form, and setting. Here, he borrowed not only the political iconography of the Nazi salute but also the large vistas and isolated figures so celebrated in German romanticism.[21] Kiefer subverts the familiarity and nationalism of romantic painting with the insertion of the confrontational political sign. In so doing, the artist revealed how cultural traditions are also compromised through their use by political interests, and politics becomes inseparable from its cultural appropriation. In addition, through the geographical variability of the series, he linked that message firmly to the military goals of the state. The politicization of German national culture—and thus the connection between cultural work and brutal expansionist policies carried out by the military—is the particular crime of the older generation that is identified here and then mocked and ridiculed. It is not genocidal actors (the racist extremists) that Kiefer depicts but rather the seemingly more ambiguous world of the military. Whether military personnel could be described as perpetrators or whether they served and acted honorably was itself subject to debate.[22] For the younger generation, all older West Germans were tainted with fascism, as embodied by the Nazi salute, and the military as a conservative state institution was certainly no exception.

Yet such a clear distinction of one generation from the next does not completely fit with Kiefer inserting himself and his own social relations into the works. Indeed, as an added and surprising complexity, the boots, riding pants, and military coat that Anselm Kiefer wore were actually those used by his father Albert during the war (Figure 3.5). Furthermore, the *Occupations*, which form part of one of Kiefer's many book projects throughout his career, appeared as an aggressive gesture at the very moment in which the student revolts were taking this political critique of fascism into the streets,

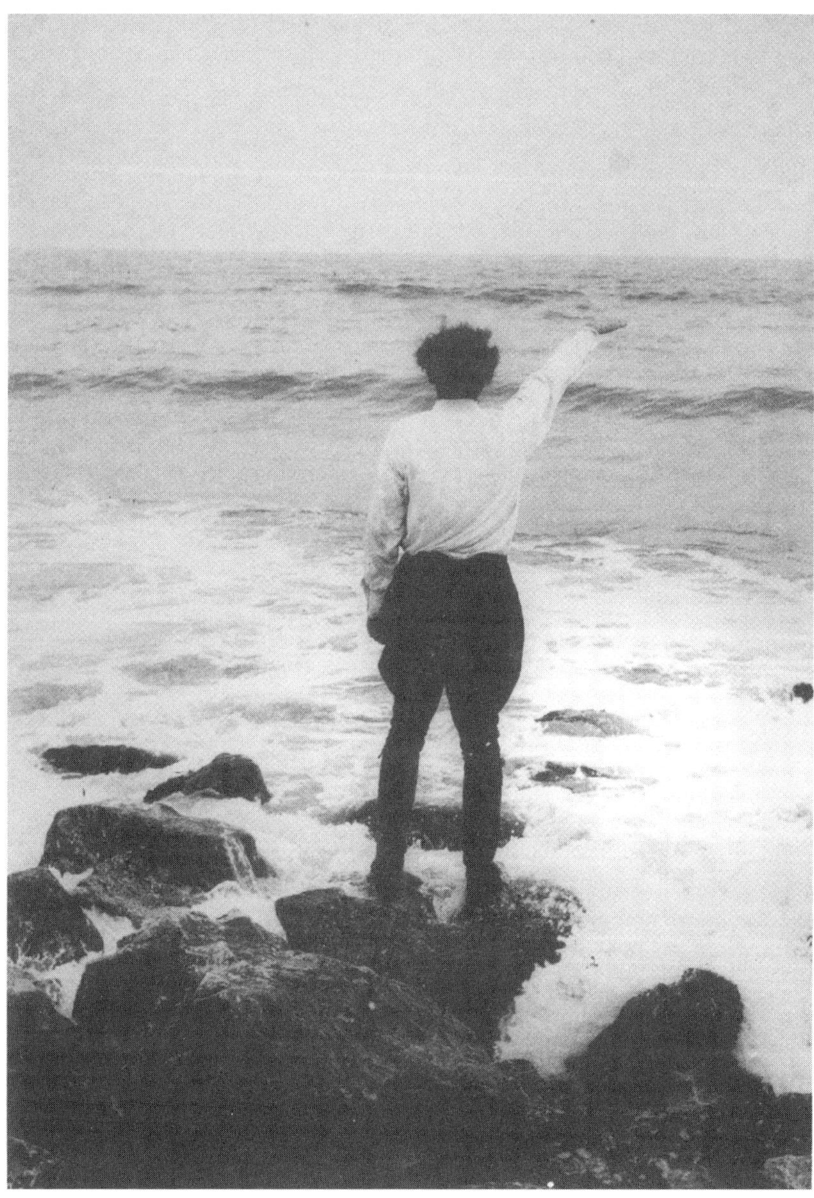

FIGURE 3.4. Anselm Kiefer, *Occupations*, 1969; published 1975. Private collection. Copyright Anselm Kiefer.

and these actions had a direct effect on his father. Albert Kiefer was deeply affected by the student revolts in Frankfurt, particularly after the radicalization of SDS activities following the 1968 attack on Dutschke. In this period, students interrupted his seminars and his anxiety increased with the success of the leftists' ever-more violent tactics. The distinction between the vast number of West Germans who had "just followed orders" and those identifiable party extremists in leadership roles became increasingly murky and meaningless to the student protesters. They thus exacerbated confrontations with the older generation who were all potentially perpetrators of the worst kind. As a consequence of the attacks on his classes, Albert Kiefer began to develop a depression that reached a crisis point in 1974.[23] His son's imagery may have been sarcastic in scale and concept, but the personal family drama also meant that Anselm Kiefer's *Occupations* directly involved the son's experience of the politics of the past through his father. They resonated with and affected the current generation of students, himself included. Members of this younger generation could neither free themselves from their own biographies nor curtail the continued presence of fascism in their institutions and daily lives.

Other aspects of Albert Kiefer's military career also marched through the early work of his son. *Operation Sea Lion* (1975; Plate 7), for example, not only involves the bathtub given to Kiefer's grandmother as part of a Nazi public hygiene campaign. It also relies on information he gleaned from his father, who served under the leadership of the Thirty-Fifth Division while its senior officers were charged with helping to prepare the invasion of England. Göring meant his "Operation Sea Lion" to begin with German domination of the air but then continue with ground invasions led by various divisions. As with his father's autobiography, Kiefer's painting thematized through its odd sources such as the bathtub the fallacy of the invasion and its bad planning. This episode thus exposed both the incompetence and the dominating imperialist dreams of the Nazi elite. Further, the three chairs in the painting relate to Kiefer's works that dealt with Christian mythology, above all the Father, Son, and Holy Ghost.[24] So, too, does the invasion of the Soviet Union ("Operation Barbarossa") figure prominently in other paintings and the autobiography. The specific biographical tensions that existed throughout West German society (here, thoroughly gendered) infiltrate any attempt by a subsequent generation to construct a subjective and autonomous artistic position. The dominant view of an ideological confrontation with the past came into conflict with a more subtle but ever-present continuity of individuals and beliefs in day-to-day society.

In these works, Kiefer marks his own status through the prominent self-representation of the artist as a member of the particular postwar

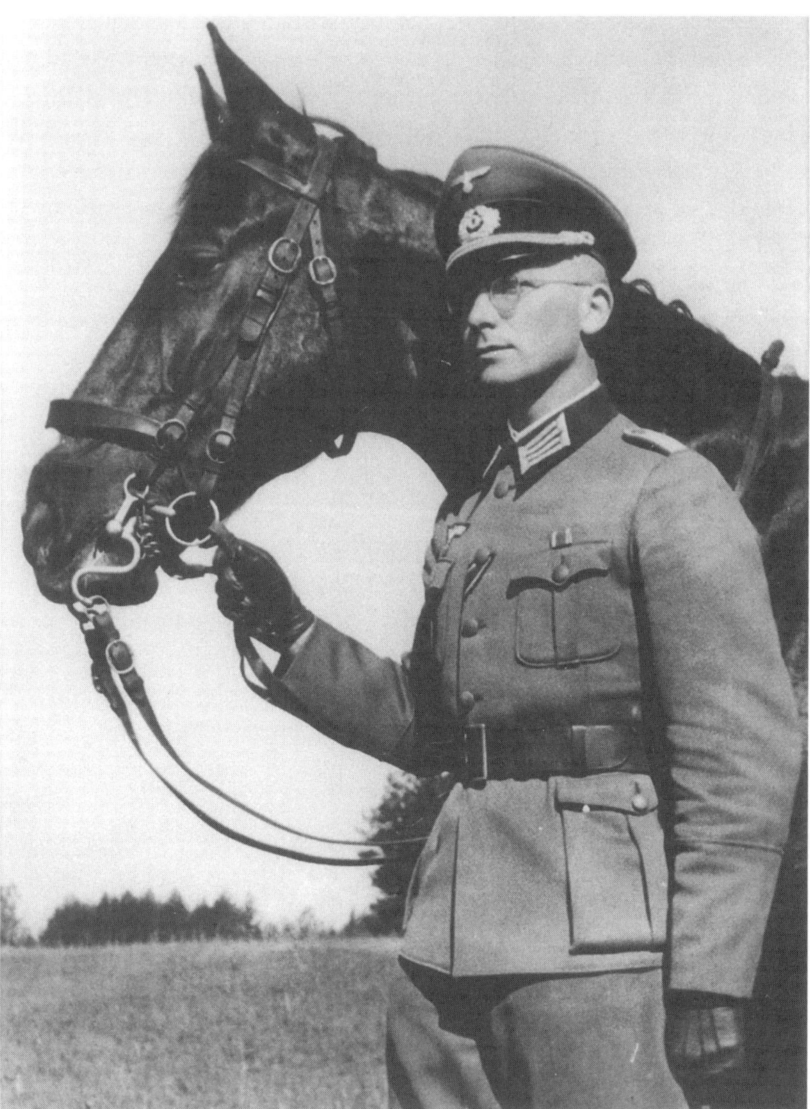

FIGURE 3.5. Albert Kiefer as a soldier, 1941. Photograph courtesy of Professor Albert Kiefer.

contemporary generation. He renders the gendered influence of fathers on their sons specifically through the nexus of culture and violence—in this regard, the almost complete absence of women in his early work is telling. In symbolic terms, he explored similar territory in his depiction of Wagnerian and other mythic themes represented in the surroundings of his own studio. For example, in *Nothung* (1973; Figure 3.6), Kiefer shows the bloodied sword in the middle of the empty studio floor, left there by the leader of the gods, Wotan, for his son Siegmund to find in time of need. With this narrative in which the absent father dooms the son to fulfill his destiny and die in the process, Kiefer asserts that the cultural actor also plays a role in the historical drama. He establishes this not only with references to Wagner but also by figuring his own artistic environment. The artist completed many works thematizing the doomed or ambivalent relationship between fathers and sons, which were shown to the public in his first major exhibition in 1973 (e.g., *Parsifal II*; Figure 3.7). Through these, Kiefer indicated the connection between clearly represented myth and obscure artistic subjectivity, historical experience and the present, the crimes of the fathers and the futile resistance of the sons. After all, Kiefer restaged the crimes of the fathers in the most inflated ideological terms in the explicitly banal environment of the son's studio. Such terms extended to the particularities of this moment in the drama within the Kiefer family as his father stood accused of being part of an entire generation of perpetrators.

Kiefer's Art in the 1980s: A Retreat into Mystification

We should not be surprised that Kiefer's historical themes and exploration of artistic subjectivity would run concomitant with political struggles in the streets that took up the reception of the Nazi perpetrator. After all, Kiefer

FIGURE 3.6. Anselm Kiefer, *Nothung*, 1973. Oil and charcoal on burlap, with oil and charcoal on cardboard, 118⅛ × 170 inches (300 × 432 cm). Museum Boymans–van Beuningen, Rotterdam. Copyright Anselm Kiefer.

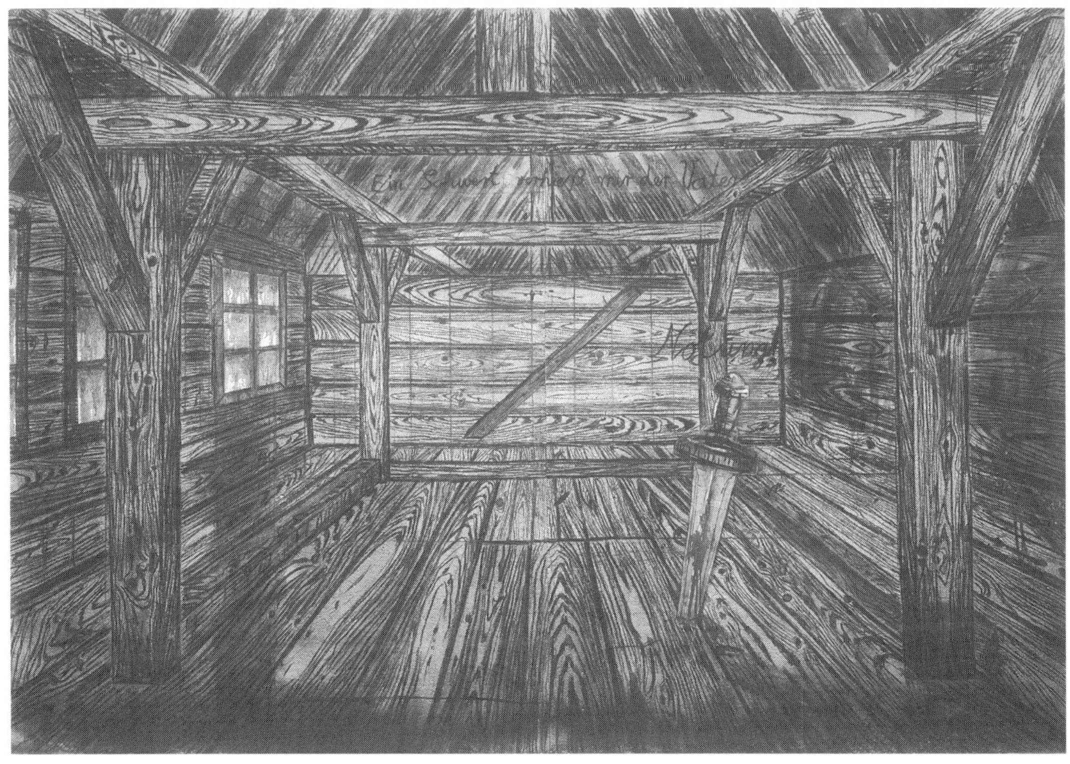

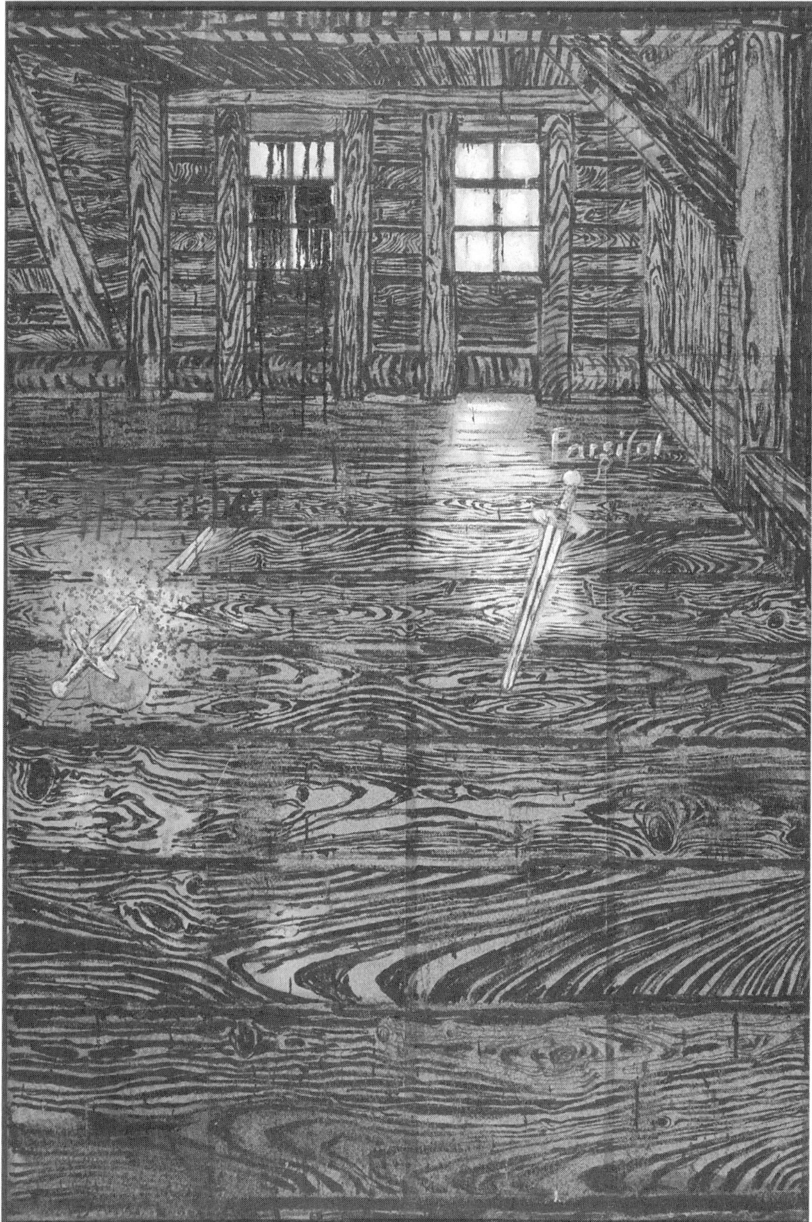

FIGURE 3.7. Anselm Kiefer, *Parsifal II*, 1973. Oil and blood on paper laid on canvas, 127 × 86 inches (324.7 × 218.8 cm). Photograph courtesy Tate Gallery, London/Art Resource, New York. Copyright Anselm Kiefer.

chose as his subject the ambiguous dynamic between contemporary cultural forces and the past criminal actions of the National Socialist state. Yet, in 1980, Kiefer began turning away from an iconography that, however ironically or subjectively, explored the political signs and militarist basis of wartime Germany grounded in the agency of his father's generation. The fascist salute, the Wehrmacht uniform, or the specific expansionist military campaign literally disappears, and as Andreas Huyssen notes, so too does the sarcasm.[25] However, eliminating these elements of his previous work from his newer paintings also removed the emphasis on generational conflict and the subject of the artist as the representative of the postwar generation imbricated in and struggling with the crimes of the parents. That is to say, the specificity of the earlier generational debates has given way to an imagery of Nazi high culture in the form of its monumental architecture and the resulting sublimation of the painter's direct connection with the past. His agency would now be marked by the expanded experimentation with surfaces as well as the symbolic presence of the palette presented here in the realm of culture, but not related to imperialist policy or familial guilt as before. Kiefer's shift in his practice would also popularize his works in the critical press.[26] It would in addition rely on a less complex conception of the perpetrator, one he increasingly shared with the critical world of which he was a part.

For our purposes, I would emphasize that the personal and social role of the perpetrator father vanishes altogether in Kiefer's work. The generational conflict had maintained a focus on the critique of the active presence of Nazi personnel and fellow travelers within West German politics and state institutions. Although different in its conceptualization of culpability, this position nevertheless paralleled and stemmed from the earlier characterization of the perpetrator we saw with Richter, namely, the potential for criminality in all levels of society, not just at the fanatical extremes. But this belief in the everyday agency of a perpetrator gave way in Kiefer's work to a more ideological and mythic understanding of how contemporary West Germans related to the Nazi past. This was the conservative turn that helps make Kiefer's work a model for explaining other areas of society in which the concept of the perpetrator was mobilized, including the rising power in these same years of Helmut Kohl and the CDU.

We can best explore this shift by analyzing perhaps the most discussed imagery in Kiefer's production, the dual female characters of Margarete and Sulamith taken from Paul Celan's poem "Death Fugue" ("Todesfuge"; 1945/ 1952). From 1981 to 1983, Kiefer produced a series of paintings that dealt with this subject by appropriating specific imagery from Celan. Celan's poem is a deeply critical and cynical view of the relationship between Jewish and Christian life that drew inspiration from his own experience with forced labor and the harsh oppression of Nazi rule. In the poem, as in Kiefer's paintings, the two women become metaphors for an exploration of the dynamic between the oppression of the Jew and the bombastic ideological claims for a doomed Christian, "Aryan" culture. While asserting this polarity, however, the majority of the poem thematizes lyrically the interaction as well of perpetrator and victim directly. These positions are crystallized, on the one hand, by the man who "whistles his hounds" and "whistles his Jews," who exemplifies the famous line "Death is a master from Germany" ("Tod ist ein Meister aus Deutschland"), and, on the other, by the Jewish "we" who must drink "black milk" and "shovel a grave in the air."[27] Perpetrator and victim participate in a surreal interaction in which the cultural tropes of dancing and singing are increasingly interlaced with the violence and power of the man over "his" Jews.

Throughout Kiefer's series, he puts at center stage the duality and interconnectedness of these twin positions in conceptual and artistic terms in the works, specifically through the figuration of the allegorical women but without any particular reference to the male "master." Kiefer's choices draw on the crucial phrase that punctuates Celan's poem: "your golden hair Margarete / your ashen hair Shulamith." In each of the images, he focuses on one of the female protagonists but always figures the other as well. So, for example, in two images titled *Margarete* from 1981 (Figure 3.8 and Plate 8), he either juxtaposes the straw signifying Margarete's hair as a vast

FIGURE 3.8. Anselm Kiefer, *Your Golden Hair, Margarete*, 1981. Oil, acrylic, emulsion, charcoal, and straw on burlap, 51³⁄₁₆ × 67 inches (130 × 170 cm). Collection Sanders, Amsterdam. Copyright Anselm Kiefer.

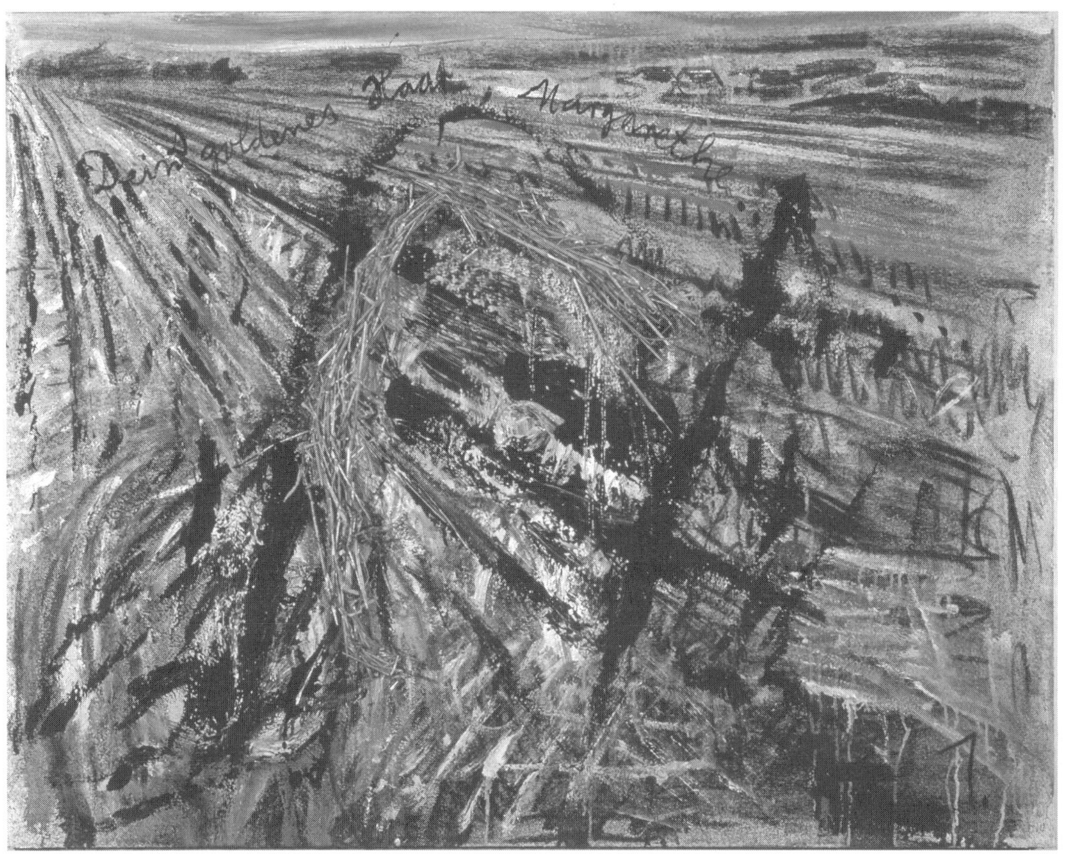

field like the earlier March Heath images (and with similar "blood and soil" overtones) or makes the "hair" plantlike as it grows from the ground. Yet in each he shadows the straw at key locations with the inky smudge of oil paint, referencing the dark hair of Margarete's alter ego Shulamith from the Song of Solomon. In addition, he complements the natural materials and organic imagery of growth with death and destruction, using somber, empty, and even burnt fields or, as in the last of the *Margarete* paintings, the flame that tops each apparent stalk. In sum, both between paintings and within paintings, there is an unrelenting presentation of oppositional symbolic forces that are nevertheless intimately codependent.[28] The destructive trajectory of German history and its opaque return in a symbolic representation form the tragic points of relation between the two.

A closer look at the most prominent painting from the series, *Sulamith* (1983), helps clarify his new emphasis on binary juxtapositions and symbolic oppositions. Kiefer's turn to Nazi architecture began in 1980 with the work *To the Unknown Painter* (Figure 3.9), and he developed that imagery here through his reference to the crypt of Wilhelm Kreis's Soldiers' Hall (1938; Figure 3.10). A monumental structure designed for Albert Speer's North–South Axis in the rebuilding of Berlin, the Soldiers' Hall was meant to celebrate the German soldier and memorialize the war dead and was the most consistently worked-on project up to the conclusion of building activities in 1943. Most likely, however, Kiefer knew very little about the building itself based on information available at the time as well as on his known lack of interest in studying the historical background of the specific works of National Socialist architecture that he appropriated.[29] More probably, his choice reflected his interest in the monument's funereal function as well as the general importance of its symbolic role to the state. Mark Rosenthal and Huyssen, among other critics, note how the darkening of the space in the painting creates a claustrophobic effect accentuated by the deep perspective. With the inclusion of the name "Sulamith" in the upper left corner and the seven-lamped altar at the far end of the hall, the memorial space functions not only as a sign of the megalomaniacal celebration of the German war dead but also as a somber reminder of the Jewish victims of National Socialist politics.[30]

In addition to the darkened setting and specific allusions, however, the artist heightened the claustrophobic effect by making significant departures from the propaganda photograph of the architectural model, which was the original source for the painting. For our purposes, I would point not only to the massive scale of the work but also to the way in which the alteration of space emphasizes the tension between the oppositional elements of the bombastic celebration of sacrifice and the mourning of victims

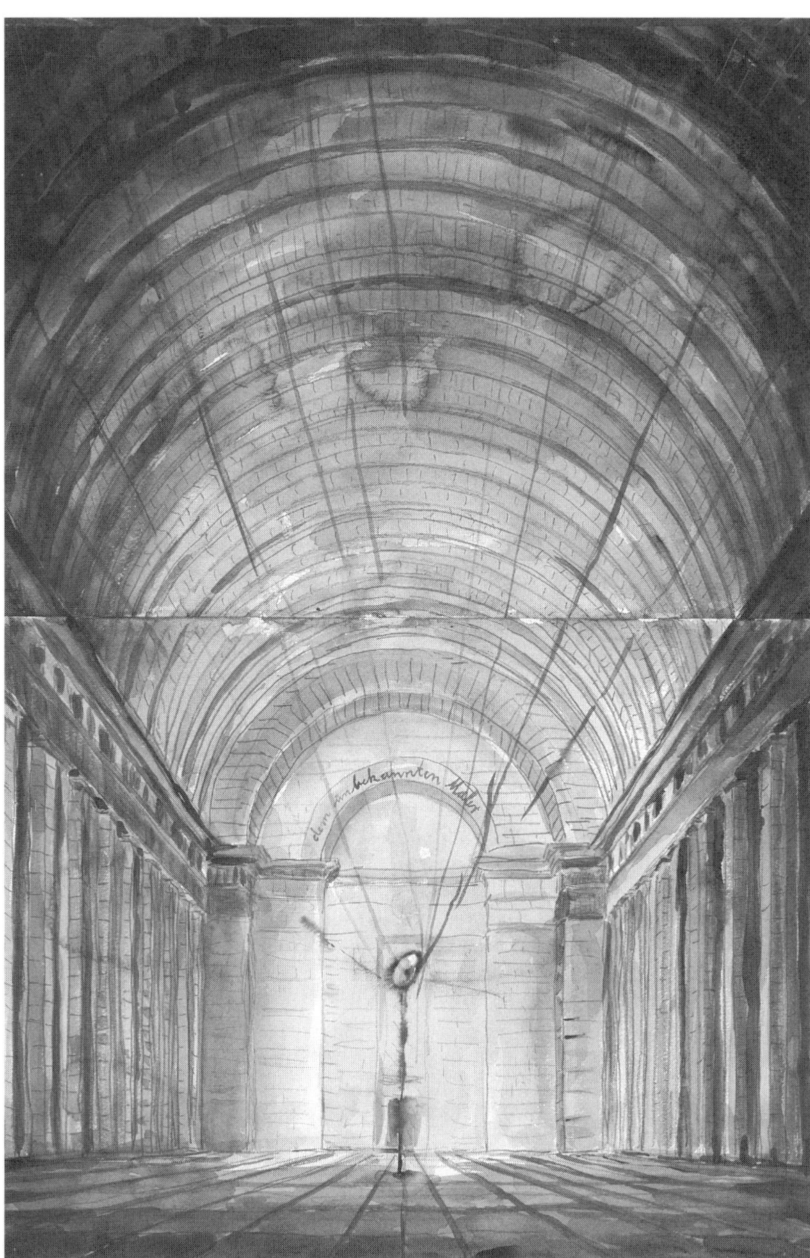

FIGURE 3.9. Anselm Kiefer, *To the Unknown Painter*, 1981. Watercolor and graphite on paper, 34⅝ × 21⅝ inches (88 × 55 cm). Private collection. Copyright Anselm Kiefer.

of racist policies. To put it directly, Kiefer makes emphatic the tense relationship between perpetrator and victim even if these positions are indicated only within the allegorical terms of the painting and through the rituals of death. Specifically, he has dramatically changed the space from the original photograph. (It should be noted that the Soldiers' Hall itself was never completed.) Kiefer added an extra bay to extend the view to the menorah-like altar and to sharpen the orthogonal lines. With this, he altered the spatial layout to be more claustrophobic and also more monumental than the original model. Kiefer emphasized with this the ideological function of the original propaganda aesthetic, its tendency to monumentalize. But as opposed to the original monolithic legitimation of German sacrifice and glory, here that ideological message of mythic dominance was intimately tied to its symbolic corollary, the ritualistic necessity of mourning the destruction of Nazi victims, the Jews. The unambiguous perspectival focus of the orthogonals on the altar makes this evident, as they both push the Jewish presence away and make it the unifying core of the composition at the same time. Perpetrator and victim are seemingly forced apart by the dramatically expanded but vertiginous space and, simultaneously, opaquely brought together in an exaggerated and loaded representation that foregrounds the cultural role of the state in memorialization.[31] Facture that has almost the character of relief sculpture and illusionistic depth, the oil paint mixed with the nonart commonplace material of straw, the juxtaposition of perpetrator and victim, death ideologically defined as sacrifice and death as racist destruction—all these oppositions make the work a profoundly disturbing whole in which Margarete and Sulamith exist in tension.

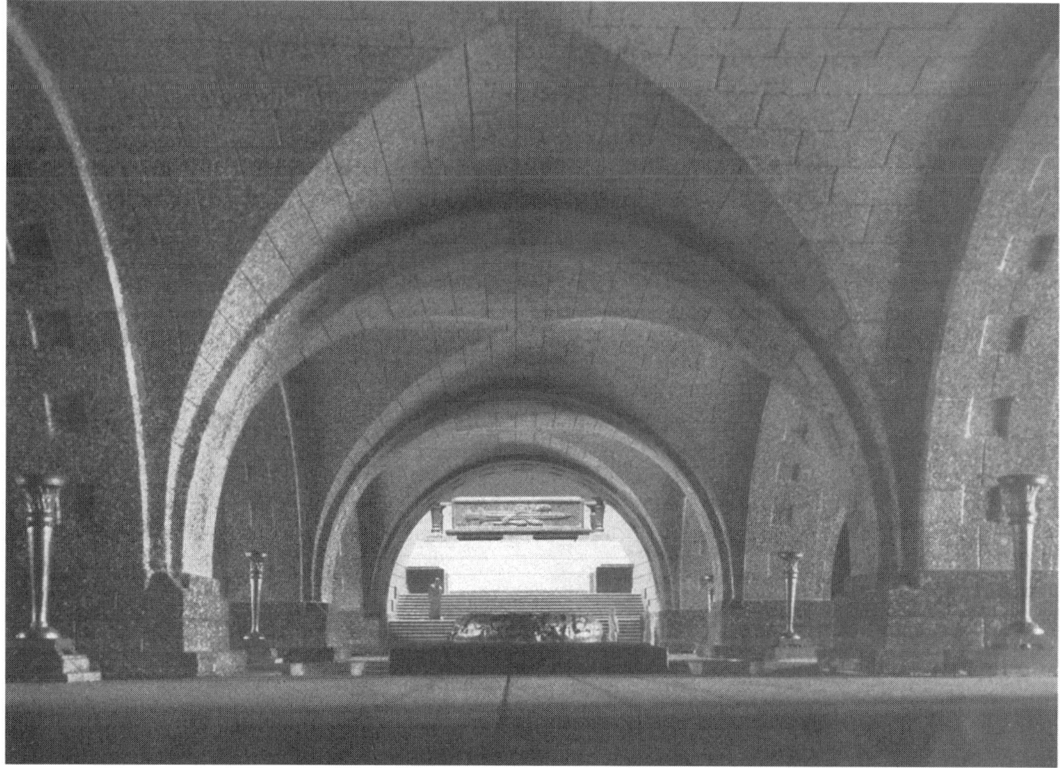

FIGURE 3.10. Wilhelm Kreis, model of Crypt of the Soldiers' Hall, Berlin, 1938. Photograph courtesy of Zentralinstitut für Kunstgeschichte, Photothek.

But I want to emphasize something more than the dualities evident in the series. For relevant here is not just the conceptual or artistic framing of the two protagonists but the nature of that framing. The binary structure also serves to emphasize the symbolic or totemic aspects of the message, with its reference points firmly grounded not in biography or politics but in culture and myth. These binaries draw our attention away from specific historical battles or policies toward their more abstract significance. Here the problem of the German past has become an epic struggle, an heir to the tragic saga of the Nibelungen. We are no longer talking about a specific self-presentation of the artist as he grapples with the conflicting feelings prompted by the criminal heritage foisted upon him by the actions of his parents' generation. Rather, Kiefer rendered the artist and German history outside a particular time or event; or perhaps more accurately, he trans-formed the historical events of the Nazi period into an expression of ritual, embodied in the form of the monumentalizing culture of the perpetrator as well as the ceremonial need to mourn the destruction of an entire people. The past still resonated and still troubled. But he no longer so emphatically blunted the dualities of the past with ironic contemporary props or settings, nor did he figure the presence of the artist (or his father) so aggressively through biographical means. Binary opposition, symbolism, cultural expres-sion, memorialization, and historical abstraction: these are the artistic terms Kiefer uses to stage his tragedy of the intertwined fate of Margarete and Sulamith. These terms avoid the more explicit political signs and the the-matization of particular militarist policies of the early works and evacuate a specific agency in favor of a cultural and allegorical turn. Kiefer developed this trend through various details in his works in the 1970s. He brought them together, though, most definitively in the architecturally inspired paintings of the early 1980s.

The West German press also marked this shift in its general reevalu-ation of Kiefer's reception. Kiefer began to show the architectural works in 1981. Just the previous year, critics had subjected him to much negative criticism for his contribution (along with Georg Baselitz) to the West Ger-man Pavilion at the 1980 Venice Biennale. Four years later, in response to a major exhibition in Düsseldorf that traveled on to Jerusalem, many of the same critics—from across the political spectrum—celebrated Kiefer's works or at least accepted them. In her study, Saltzman has analyzed this critical shift in several key texts in terms of Kiefer's career.[32] Reviewing the criticism more generally, though, critics originally labeled Kiefer in 1980 most often as "regional," "irrational," "brutal," and, pejoratively, "German." They emphasized his confrontation with accepted West German social norms by depicting the iconography of the perpetrator. In 1984, with few exceptions the critics' adjectives had changed to "expressive," "evocative," and "German," not in a negative sense but rather as a positive or at least descriptive statement about the character of his work. In other words, critics initially pilloried the artist for the active association of himself with the perpetrators in 1980; by 1984, however, they no longer perceived his project as reflecting a specific conflict or a problematic relationship to his father's generation. Rather, his paintings had become an affirmative medium for expressing a broader emotional and symbolic response to the past that embodied an acceptable national ethnic identity.[33]

A prominent example illustrates this: in the pages of the moderate-liberal *Die Zeit*, Kiefer's contribution to the Venice Biennale and his 1984 Düsseldorf show were both reviewed by Petra Kipphoff. Kipphoff's most damning paragraph in her Venice review was saved for Kiefer (although Baselitz did not fare much better): "Kiefer's subject matter as well as its applied theatricality must be simply unbearable for many whose existence the German megalomania had practically destroyed. Beyond the direct offensiveness, a play with irrationalism and brutality still remains that is covered with no form, no moral."[34] Here Kipphoff warns Kiefer of the potentially immoral base of his interest in the irrational without respect for its effects on an audience. Does his work become analogous with the perpetrators whom he thematizes? Do the paintings continue the propaganda of the past? Kipphoff highlights here the negative and dangerously confrontational Kiefer. And yet, compare this to Kipphoff four years later when discussing his Düsseldorf show:

> The high, light, empty halls under gloomy skies (a few taken directly from Albert Speer's *New German Architecture*), these oversized (but in the Third Reich real) stages for death cults and megalomania . . . are formulas of emotionalism from which, after the horror, nothing much more than the quality of a backdrop remains. . . . When one says that Anselm Kiefer has given painting back its dignity, then this phrase is only bearable because Kiefer in his best pictures describes painting anew, as a craft broken by mourning and the ambivalent presence of the already known.[35]

Although Kipphoff even repeats certain words from the first review, the second review turns many of those bad qualities of megalomania and the subject matter of Germanness into a positive artistic agenda. The artist is a neutral participant who records and externalizes the important and emotional conditions of his audience. The reviewer softened and, importantly, generalized her initial outrage over Kiefer's confrontational subjects. While critics did not discuss the specific dualism of Kiefer's works such as *Sulamith* and *Margarete*, they were nevertheless comfortable with moving their interpretation of his work away from generational conflict or shocking subject matter. Instead, they emphasized more universal interpretations that focused on the symbolic social import of his paintings. This change in the critical debate was paralleled by a remarkable growth in Kiefer's career in West Germany, leading to his triumphant one-person retrospective at the Berlin New National Gallery in 1991.

THE CULTURAL TURN IN THE PERCEPTION OF THE NAZI PERPETRATOR

The conservative direction of both Kiefer's aesthetic and conceptual interests and the terms in which his paintings were discussed belong to a broader field of artistic and political debate about the recent past and the status of the perpetrator. The conflict regarding the central question of agency shifted in the early 1980s, as did concomitantly the issues of generational continuity and responsibility for past crimes. Although Kiefer made some of the most spectacular art that recognizably engaged these issues, it was not an isolated phenomenon. Laying out Kiefer's well-known career in these new terms helps us expose trends and patterns in the cultural and ideological interpretation of the perpetrator that were contemporaneous with *Sulamith* and *Margarete*. As with Richter, we should reject the concept that we are moving from a period of repression to one of mourning and working through. Artists, politicians, and their publics debated characteristics of the National Socialist perpetrator in 1980 just as they did in the 1960s; no silence has been suddenly shattered. But attending to the particular web of terms about the past indicates the changing way artists, critics, and politicians represented those who lived it. An analysis of the shifts in Kiefer's work and its reception—with particular attention to contemporary journals as primary sources—opens up new ways to recognize similar patterns in other cultural and political responses in the period.

Silence about the Nazi past certainly did not reign over the six-year period from 1979 to 1985 that saw Kiefer's first great successes as well as the fortieth anniversary ceremonies marking each phase of World War II. The West German magazine *Art* quickly established itself in these years as a major voice within art journalism and provided a bellwether for attitudes toward the past. With its first issue in October 1979, *Art* focused on news from the museum and market world as well as longer articles on specific canonical and contemporary figures. Under the editorship of Axel Hecht, its editorial policy emphasized a well-known Modernist and avant-garde canon. The editor and authors were open to new trends, and interested in a liberal approach to free expression, but also fell back on fairly well-worn and familiar terms. In comparison to left-wing publications such as *Tendenzen*, one would expect the pages of *Art* to be more like a common survey text, full of a standard history with few references to the awkward art and years of the National Socialist regime except as they helped to highlight the Modernist masters excluded or exiled. Indeed, in the first issue, the only references to that embarrassing period were an advertisement of the Galerie Koch for the sale of Fritz Klimsch's 1937 bronze *Olympia* and the reprint of four letters from George Grosz published on the last page as interesting documents from the past (including one letter from 1941 briefly mentioning Arno Breker and Göring).

And yet, *Art* authors consistently referred to National Socialism and the Holocaust, often in articles of some depth concerning how that history affected specific contemporary artists, dealers, and audiences. In 1980, its first full year of operation with twelve issues, twenty articles and reports in whole or in part discussed the relationship between art or architecture and the criminal history of the Hitler state. These articles varied in length and depth, but displayed certain consistencies. In addition to the expected discussions of the Venice Biennale with Kiefer's and Baselitz's thematizations of German nationalism and fascist history,[36] many articles focused as well on the biographies of artists suppressed or oppressed by the regime. So, for example, in celebration of his eighty-fifth birthday readers learned of the history of Franz Radziwill's art before, during, and after the Nazi period, or of Han van Meegeren, a Dutch painter who did forgeries of Vermeer and other old masters, several of which he sold to Göring, among others.[37] Exhibitions featured the work of Peter Weiss from the 1930s, a new autobiography of Oskar Kokoschka that included his exile, as well as something of the painting career of Lothar-Günther Buchheim during the war. The latter, author of *Das Boot*, severely criticized the soon-to-be opened Neue Pinakothek in Munich, stating that he would not contribute his substantial Expressionist art collection to it or to the "monstrous" Haus der Kunst, the art museum designed by Paul Ludwig Troost for Hitler's *Great German Art Exhibitions*.[38] In general, the pages of *Art* helped define a range of artists and artistic activities victimized by the Nazi state. Although Buchheim served in the navy, he was not considered in any categorical way a perpetrator.

Into the 1980s, *Art* would continue to feature biographical articles on artists both oppressed and supported by Nazi politicians and patrons, especially those who had recently died, such as Christian Schad, Weiss, Otto Pankok, and Radziwill, as well as widows of famous exiles, among others who represented the continuity with the past. But the use of historical themes or appropriation of National Socialist imagery also played an increasing role in criticism as Kiefer and other artists became more successful in the market. Further, readers had a chance to glean a great deal of information on the general history of the Nazi period and art policy related to fascism and World War II. Frank Nicolaus, for example, in 1982 published a series of seven articles giving a substantial history of Hitler's rise to power, the suppression of Modernist artists, the *Degenerate Art* show, artists in inner exile, and those forced to leave Germany, as well as the artists who tried to accommodate and work with the regime.[39] While the series stuck to a standard focus on Modernism and summarized much information known from Hinz and others, it nevertheless represented a commitment by the journal to this period as part of the important history of modern art. (One would be hard pressed in the early 1980s to come up with its English-language equivalent in the pages of *Artforum* or elsewhere.) Other broad discussions included reviews of the London Royal Academy exhibition titled *German Art in the 20th Century: Painting and Sculpture, 1905–85*, which was complemented by an exhibition in West Berlin of forty years of art in the Federal Republic. Parallel to these more expansive historical overviews, criticism also recognized the results of National Socialist criminality through a rising number of articles on victims. These historical subjects came into focus through a plethora of new monuments and memorials constructed to commemorate the Holocaust within Germany and elsewhere. Such articles began in 1983 with reports on Ulrich Rückriem's stone monument to commemorate the destruction of the Jewish community in Hamburg and George Segal's Holocaust monument designated for Golden Gate Park.[40] In the pages of the mainstream *Art*, the biographical and occasionally overt antifascist focus on the past continued but to an ever lesser degree. Instead, authors began to favor a broader analysis of the history of art between the wars, the growing contemporary memorialization of German Jewish victims, and, most prominently, the artistic use of past events in new cultural forms. What is evident throughout the period is that readers had a wide range of exposure to the history of the Nazi past and its postwar uses that can be described as anything but "silence." Even so, the perpetrator as a category was vague in these discussions, much vaguer than in Kiefer's paintings from the 1970s.

Other art journals, however, had a slightly different emphasis than *Art*. The more conservative and auction-house-oriented *Weltkunst* focused on canonically accepted German art movements and, concomitantly, a biographical emphasis on Modernist masters who were targeted by the National Socialist cultural institutions. In this sense, it continued the kind of reporting and focus on the individual that had marked their journal throughout the postwar period, also including articles critical of anything coming out of the GDR.[41] More analogous to *Art*, the moderate mainstream publication *Kunstforum International* focused significant attention (both positive and negative) on new artists such as Jörg Immendorff, Kaspar König, and Harald Frackmann, who used motifs from German history related to the Nazi past as part of their work.[42] Relatively less space was devoted to the biographical continuities with the past or to the history of art and criminal activities during the thirties.

Not surprisingly, the most left-leaning publication, *Tendenzen*, proved to have the greatest contrast to these journals. As we saw with Richter, this publication was devoted to the critical traditions of Realism that sprang particularly from nineteenth-century French examples and Neue Sachlichkeit (New objectivity). In addition, though, many articles from the early 1980s continued the antifascist traditions of the late 1960s, highlighting artists from that generation and others who had earlier worked for the resistance (such as the printmaker Heinrich Graf) or criticizing the contemporary rise of protofascist activities. More than other journals, *Tendenzen* was inclined to publish articles that dealt with the relationship between art and specific Nazi crimes, such as describing the life of the painter Julo Levin, a Jewish artist killed in 1943 in Auschwitz. Emphasis on criminal activities and antifascist traditions kept the authors grounded in the left-wing activities of the sixties. They focused on specific examples of perpetrators, naming those artists and politicians, past and present, who had contributed to National Socialist policy. In addition, they focused many articles on antifascist artists, including East Germans such as Fritz Cremer, whom they interviewed in 1981.[43]

With increasing frequency, *Tendenzen* critics tied these discussions to the growing antimilitarization campaigns. After NATO decided in 1979 to place more nuclear-armed Pershing II and cruise missiles in West Germany, and negotiations to reduce the Soviet Bloc's arsenal failed, massive street protests broke out. They continued through the fall of Helmut Schmidt's SPD government in 1982 and the rise of Kohl and the CDU. Concern focused on this change in politics and the increasing orientation of Kohl to U.S. Cold War policies. Left-wing authors used the history of the past, marked in ceremonies for the fortieth anniversaries of events from World War II and also, beginning in 1983, the fiftieth anniversary of Hitler's coming to power, to analyze and critique the present. An editorial from March 1983 clearly laid out these potential connections. Further, the editors devoted this issue to a discussion of fascism and art, such as Ernst Antoni's "Der Faschismus will im Bild bleiben," a survey of proto-right-wing art created during and after the Nazi regime. Articles appeared in the next three numbers through 1983 highlighting Realist artists who had critically taken up specific Nazi imagery in their postwar work or the state art policies of Germany in the Nazi period. All told, this kind of more systematic attention not only coincided with the anniversaries of important events but was also prompted by the policies of Kohl's regime. In the left-wing press, the older question of political agency of the perpetrator in our midst was still firmly tied to the resonance of fascist politics in the contemporary moment.[44]

In sum, during the period in which Kiefer shifted his imagery, the critical literature in West Germany was going through its own transition. Critics were torn between leaving the question of agency and biography behind and keeping it in focus (from both conservative and leftist perspectives). Further, some celebrated the new cultural appropriation of past history while others condemned this cultural turn—particularly in large-scale painting—as an abdication of critical analysis. Finally, while conservative and moderate authors tended to separate the art market and its discussions from the political shift, more liberal and left-wing voices identified the rise of Kohl as part and parcel of how the potential for art to function in the service of fascism remained a postwar question.

In his remarkable book *Reflections of Nazism: An Essay on Kitsch and Death* (1982), the historian and survivor Saul Friedländer recognized and analyzed the ambiguity of what such a moment of conflict and transition might mean for contemporary society, as well as for the remembrance of the past.[45] We should consider Friedländer's text not as a secondary but rather as a primary source. It helps us clarify some of the main implications of the cultural turn for an understanding of National Socialist history and identify which themes a contemporary audience saw as particularly revealing and threatening in relation to changing notions of the perpetrator. His thesis addresses the increasing interest in the 1970s and into the 1980s in representing National Socialist perpetrators in film, novels, TV series, and other cultural forms. With this theme, he directly addressed the cultural discourse explicitly picked up by Kiefer and other artists and critics during a period of social and political change. Notably, while Friedländer's analysis has proved influential in historical studies, it has been surprisingly neglected in the art historical literature.[46]

Friedländer took as his evidence a small set of historical books, films, and novels that reveal "associations of imagery," which, he argued, were distinctly new and potentially troublesome. In line with Susan Sontag, he found the apparently progressive work of directors like Hans-Jürgen Syberberg or the novelist George Steiner ostensibly critical but disturbingly attractive in a way that previous discussions and representations of the Nazi past were not. In essence, he argued:

> Attention [in the new works] has gradually shifted from the revocation
> of Nazism as such, from the horror and the pain—even if muted by
> time and transformed into subdued grief and endless meditation—to
> voluptuous anguish and ravishing images, images one would like to see
> going on forever. It may result in a masterpiece, but a masterpiece that,
> one may feel, is tuned to the wrong key; in the midst of meditation rises
> a suspicion of complacency. . . . The more the worst aspects of Nazism
> are neutralized, the more the new discourse finds its way into our
> imagination.[47]

Friedländer signaled here the main terms of his subsequent critique. He
was interested in a shift in representation, from one that is less documentary and traumatic to one that is more spectacular and melodramatic. For
him, this transition moved historical analysis from objective confrontation
to emotive response. It had the additional feature of re-creating the kind of
emotional fascination in the present that was characteristic of the Nazi
past. Such a fascination hence brought us both closer to the experience of
Nazism and, potentially, further away from its historical understanding.
Friedländer leaned in this cultural analysis on the psychological effects that
have proved a consistent point of interest in his scholarship as a whole. To
him, the common cultural imagery had in it a latent logic worth unpacking.
Distinct from his other work, though, in *Reflections of Nazism,* he tried
to identify the very particular phenomenon of this historical moment in
order to send out a warning about the potential deleterious effects of this
cultural turn.

But what did Friedländer consider the distinctive features of this
moment? First and notably, the specifically psychological impact of exaggerated and dramatic representations of the Nazi past concerned him. Second, he argued that the new discourse turned away from the direct brutality
of the political violence of the genocide toward the regime's rituals, ideologies, and fascination with the cult of leadership. For him, the focus of cultural attention had altered. In this, he noted as well the inevitable loss of
the victim generation over time as a source for a continuing discussion of
the specific crimes of fascism. Such a direct avoidance of the past oppressive conditions and actions tended furthermore to "neutralize" that history,
making it consumable or seemingly distant from comparable policies or
people in the present. And, finally, the cultural turn circulated around the
dialectical relationship of kitsch and death, as the form and substance of
the new discourse:

> Kitsch emotion represents a certain kind of simplified, degraded, insipid,
> but all the more insinuating romanticism. All of us live among kitsch; we

are plunged into it up to our necks. Hence the importance and the hold this type of imagery and sentiment has on us, a hold that is formed into a frisson thanks to the counterpoint of death and destruction.[48]

Cultural producers constantly represented Nazism together with death, but not in the sense of political and active violence. Instead, the stylized and mythic death cults became most fascinating for the emotionally laden and sentimental kitsch representations, self-conscious or not. The potential revival of the emotions of fascism, if not its politics, left Friedländer to ask the important question: "Linked as it [National Socialism] is to a great extent to the rise of modernity, does this vision still run through our imagination, does it remain a temptation for today and for tomorrow?"[49] Thus the danger lies in how the cultural turn may be symptomatic of a hidden politics that could be far worse even than that of the Nazi past, if such a thing could be imagined.

As this brief excursus implies, more than a few important parallels exist between Friedländer's diagnosis and the work of Kiefer and its reception by West German art critics during the same period. They are not absolutely analogous or reducible phenomena, but homologically they respond to the same cultural symptoms.[50] In particular, they identify the central question of whether the criminal agency of the perpetrator is to be given up as an irrelevant subject in art and representation or, conversely, critically recognized. In an era of spectacular kitsch, where did the current crop of cultural production fall on this spectrum of choices? A large number of cultural actors interested in the National Socialist past addressed this question, Kiefer and Friedländer among them. The lack of attention to specific political subjects and motifs from the past is variably ignored or worried over in the different positions of artists, critics, and scholars. And finally, all these voices consistently thematized the clear sense that a new kind of representational relationship to the perpetrator, however ambiguous, was symptomatic for the culture of the day:

> And thus one perceives in the new discourse, or at least in certain of its most striking works, beneath the proposed interpretations, a kind of empty place where there is room neither for the rational interpretation of events nor for free and effective political action, nor for moral and legal responsibility in the usual meaning of the term. And if we reject, because of its simplicity, the Marxist interpretation of Nazism, and that of the revisionists because of its openly lying character, we discover, faced with Hitlerism, within the framework of a new discourse that easily encompasses positions that are apparently more classical, the failure of our ideologies and the impotence of traditional approaches.

> What remains, therefore, are those attempts at reelaboration and revocation that characterize the new discourse. Their defenders have seen in it a reestablishment of the truth, a necessary exploration, a salutary warning; their critics a nostalgia that dare not say its name.[51]

In relation to Kiefer, "salutary warning" could not be a more apt phrase to characterize his turn from generational conflict to generalized cultural memory; for Friedländer, such a psychological reinvestment in National Socialist symbols and rituals was positively chilling.

The Political Response to the Cultural Turn

Both Kiefer and Friedländer kept their focus in the early 1980s on the world of representation and cultural forms. As I have argued, for Kiefer this meant a break from the political iconography and reference to Nazi military policy that had marked his earlier work on generational conflict between the specific agency of fathers and sons. But his artistic interest in representation that highlighted a changing relationship to the Nazi past also had its corollary in politics, particularly with the ascension of Kohl and the CDU. Here, too, the terms of debate regarding the question of agency, as well as the growing importance of representational forms, took center stage. In this phase of West German history, the cultural reception of the past and the Nazi perpetrator formed a continuum with the new kinds of political instrumentalizations of that brutal period. That is to say, the context of Kiefer and the art criticism of the early 1980s cast a spotlight on specific patterns and themes related to the perpetrator that in turn may clarify particular strategies in Kohl's references to the Nazi past in the same era.

Before returning to Kohl, we can establish a control of sorts by looking at how Chancellor Schmidt addressed the issue in his term preceding the turn to the right in German politics. Schmidt's 1978 speech given at the Cologne synagogue on the anniversary of the pogrom of November 9, 1938, is exemplary in this regard. Beginning with a quotation from the prophet Isaiah concerning the transformation of a city from the rule of law to that of murder, the chancellor gave a wide-ranging speech. Notably, he included a brief but specific use of historical information about events before and during the Nazi period. He also attempted to negotiate the issues of German culpability and the potential for postwar reconciliation. In terms of the history, for example, his first short section listed the number of Jewish citizens arrested and murdered as well as the exact number of synagogues destroyed on that day forty years prior. In addition, he rhetorically ended this section with three statements beginning with "The truth is that . . ." ("Die Wahrheit ist, dass . . .") in which he described the categories of German perpetrators, bystanders, indirect witnesses, and those who were silent, including church officials.[52] His definition of those who participated was thus broad and all-encompassing, emphasizing the everyday perpetrator in our midst. He described how their crimes resulted from anti-semitism and political-economic problems long present in German society before the NSDAP came to power and of which its members took advantage. He thus emphasized the agency of party leaders and ordinary Germans alike and the continued connection and responsibility of postwar generations: "Why do we look back on all of this today? Not to distance ourselves from our own history. Not, with the finger pointing at others, to load the guilt onto someone else."[53] Conversely, Schmidt spoke of the fact that approximately two-thirds of contemporary Germans were born after the war. Contemporaries were faced with a question not of current guilt (*Schuld*) but rather of unavoidable responsibility (*Verantwortung*) as a consequence of past crimes. That responsibility extended to protecting democracy against the extremism of right and left (this is, after all, the era of the Red Army Faction). Individual citizens needed to learn, remember, and communicate that knowledge of the past. In the last paragraph, he expressed this in the metaphor of a torch (*Fackel*), a fire that must be kept lit as a symbol of the "highest worth" of the constitution: the value of the individual person and her or his freedom.[54] Certainly, such limited symbolism was commonplace in political discourse, and much of the speech was not out of the ordinary for a politician. But Schmidt made important points of reference that defined his government's approach to the past. He emphasized in particular historical facts, the need to define past and present agency in detailed terms, and the continued responsibility of citizens in the postwar Federal Republic for events of the Nazi regime.

Still, the acquiescence of the SPD and Schmidt to NATO armament policy had contributed to growing public opposition to the alliance's increasingly belligerent and militaristic stance, at the same time as the continuing unemployment crisis sapped the party's standing with its traditional supporters. These events led to significant street protest in the early 1980s.[55] Such issues allowed Kohl and the CDU to win control of the Bundestag in 1982 and to have that position affirmed by the national elections of 1983. Like Thatcher and Reagan before him, Kohl would use his office to promote both standard conservative political-economic policies and neoconservative ideological posturing in relation to foreign policy, above all the intensification of western rhetoric against the "evil empire" to the east.

As we saw with Friedländer and art criticism, Kohl's rise to the chancellorship came at a time in which the public debate concerning German

crimes of the past had begun to focus substantially on their cultural representation, rather than on the generational conflict or biography of perpetrators characteristic of previous discussions. Emblematic in this regard, for
example, was the startling success of Marvin Chomsky's *Holocaust* miniseries from 1978. In spite of its clichéd and sentimental plot and all the critical uproar it provoked, the miniseries was a gigantic success in the United
States and an even bigger success in West Germany, where one out of every
two adults watched the 1979 television broadcast.[56] The public debate on
the series, like that on Kiefer's paintings, concerned substantial discussion
of the symbiotic nature of the polarities of perpetrators and victims, and
what imagery was appropriate to represent their histories. Critics used the
discussion of the narrative to derive general principles that went well
beyond the particular generational struggles essential to the political reception of the Nazi perpetrator in the previous decade.

Similar to the art critical response to the Nazi past, the discussion
surrounding the *Holocaust* miniseries involved a broad matrix of terms
foundational to the public debate that simultaneously clarified and muddied the waters between issues of agency and the cultural reception of the
perpetrator. It was this range of positions related to the past that Kohl
tried to negotiate and exploit upon gaining power. Born in 1930, Kohl was
old enough to have experienced the National Socialist period directly, but
unlike Adenauer, Brandt, or Schmidt, he was not old enough to have played
an active role as an adult. His policies reflected a satisfaction with limiting
the culpability for the criminal past to the few main perpetrators already
known, for example, those tried at Nuremberg (i.e., the ideological zealots).
This would lead Kohl, for example, to remove the official veterans group
of former Waffen-SS members from the list of government-recognized
subversive organizations. Further, he defended public officials like Hans-
Karl Filbinger even when the press exposed his criminal past as a ruthless
naval judge.[57] We can see how he wished to distance contemporary West
Germans from culpability in an October 1985 speech he gave to an international historians' conference in Berlin: "As Chancellor of the Federal
Republic of Germany speaking at the former concentration camp at Bergen-
Belsen, I confirmed our shame, our grief, over the inhumanity of the Nazi
barbarism. But from the events of history we must also perceive that the
individual can indeed be guilty, but not the whole nation."[58] The obscuring
and abstraction of individual political responsibility, past and present,
would play a particularly central role in Kohl's public pronouncements.

Like Kiefer, Kohl established his characterization of the perpetrator over time. Still, certain patterns start to develop in his consideration
almost from the beginning. On January 30, 1983, for example, in a speech

commemorating the tragedy of the Hitler regime's coming to power fifty years earlier, Kohl laid out several key themes related to his conceptualization of the historical role of individual Germans. Speaking in the former Reichstag in Berlin in his first major speech on the Nazi past as chancellor, he named in detail certain important and heroic Germans from the past who had spoken in the building or resisted Hitler's takeover of the government, including Walter Rathenau, Friedrich Ebert, Gustav Stresemann, Julius Leber, and Eugen Bolz, among others. In addition, he listed known resistance figures like Hans and Sophie Scholl as well as Johann Georg Elser. These names were mentioned with an additional reference to Germans who did not accept the "dictatorship." Despite the inclusion of such details, it is striking that in a speech of some nine pages the Nazi Party is mentioned by name only once, followed immediately by a claim that many Germans even of this fascist period must also be seen as those who "looked to the future, who helped build our free constitutional state" in the postwar era.[59] For Kohl, while there were crimes in this former world and political authoritarianism, there were no specific perpetrators. One can see the difficult logic he faced in a key sentence on the military: "Mourning must also be claimed for the soldiers who suffered in the conflict. They suffered in order to fight for the Fatherland and to die and, simultaneously, to serve the dictatorship."[60] The slippage between mourning and serving remains only ambiguously tied to more active concepts of decision making and agency implied but not articulated in his speech.

Kohl's deletion of perpetrators from history (at best, incorporated into a few repeated references to "Hitler" or "dictatorship") would be further developed along with his emphasis on other themes and rhetorical devices such as memorialization, binary oppositions, and historical abstractions, terms that we have identified as central to Kiefer's work in the 1980s. In an important speech on April 21, 1985, marking the fortieth anniversary of the liberation of the concentration camp inmates at Bergen-Belsen, he made his more developed notion of the German relationship to the perpetrator clearer. Here, Kohl emphasized more overtly the symbolic significance of postwar acts of memory, responsibility, and reconciliation. These terms formed a repetitive leitmotiv particularly in these years marking the ritualistic memorialization of the Nazi past. Kohl had, though, made the crimes of the past more transparent than he did previously, with more direct references to "National Socialism" and Germany as a country of "murder," but notably not of murderers. In this regard, Kohl continued to void the individual role of perpetrators while acknowledging the criminal acts, all named in the nominative mode rather than in the form of verbs connected to subjects—"murder," "derision," "destruction," "horror," "crimes."[61]

Throughout, Kohl could connect this list of crimes to specific victims who had a subject position in his speech, such as Anne Frank. While Jews were the first focus of the dictatorship, other victims included Germans from all levels of society, from every arena of life. Notably, when Kohl discussed the typical bystander, he described that person as someone who did not pay attention, who looked away or who did not perceive the crimes around him or her.[62] The bystander is passive, unlike the everyday perpetrator who helped make sure the trains got to their ultimate and murderous destination. Finally, Kohl only used the pronoun "we" when it related to contemporary postwar activity in the Federal Republic, not to any activity in the past. "Us" and "them" were terms appropriate for both past and present, but also only in the most general sense for criminal and victim. From this line of argument, he could then conclude that states that participated in crimes against rights were to be condemned, a broader attack on totalitarianism that certainly also signaled his contemporaneous critique of the Soviet Bloc, which made up a significant subtheme in his analysis.

Kohl's more developed and subtle conception of the relationship of West Germans to the perpetrators of the past asserted the opposition between past and present but also used specific rhetorical strategies to abstract the perpetrator and focus instead on rituals of mourning the victim. Nowhere was Kohl's attempt to negotiate this Nazi past better exemplified than in the well-known events surrounding the ceremonies at the Bitburg cemetery, some months before his speech to the historians (Figure 3.11). In May 1985, while attending an economic summit in Bonn, and in order to shore up the NATO alliance, President Reagan (at the invitation of Kohl) honored the memory of the German war dead, including members of the SS at the burial site at Bitburg. For the chancellor, this event had significant implications, as it followed from the Allied commemoration of the landing at Normandy in 1984 (to which France pointedly did *not* invite West Germany).[63] Here as part of marking the fortieth anniversary of the end of World War II, Reagan attempted to "foster reconciliation" with the German people. In a news conference on April 18, leading up to the visit, Reagan made the following statement that sparked the international uproar about this event: "I think there is nothing wrong with visiting that cemetery where those young men are victims of Nazism also, even though they were fighting in the German uniform, drafted into service to carry out the hateful wishes of the Nazis. They were victims, just as surely as the victims in the concentration camps."[64] Reagan's attempt to blur the distinction between victim and perpetrator was part of a strategy to target the supposed real enemy of the West both in 1945 and in 1985, namely, the Soviet Union. It complemented Kohl's own position that perpetrators were to remain abstract ciphers while rituals of memorialization and the repetition of important symbolic rhetorical phrases would mark the contemporary CDU response to the past.

In terms of specific internal policies, CDU politicians used the ideological issue of mourning at the cemetery to draw, once and for all, a strong line between the Nazis and contemporary West German politics; *that* past was regrettable but over, and not to be confused with the conservative present. This strategy of "normalization" was conceived to appeal to the conservative right wing of the electorate. Kohl did all of this with the added goal of promoting a unified industrial and military policy with the increasingly multinational western bloc by sharpening the ideological confrontation with the Soviet Union. Such a government policy intersected with CDU memorializations of the victims of the past in which the distinction between oppressor and oppressed was addressed but obscured, as we have seen. In addition, these ceremonies veiled the role of state and corporate institutions in those past activities, and rendered moot the continuities

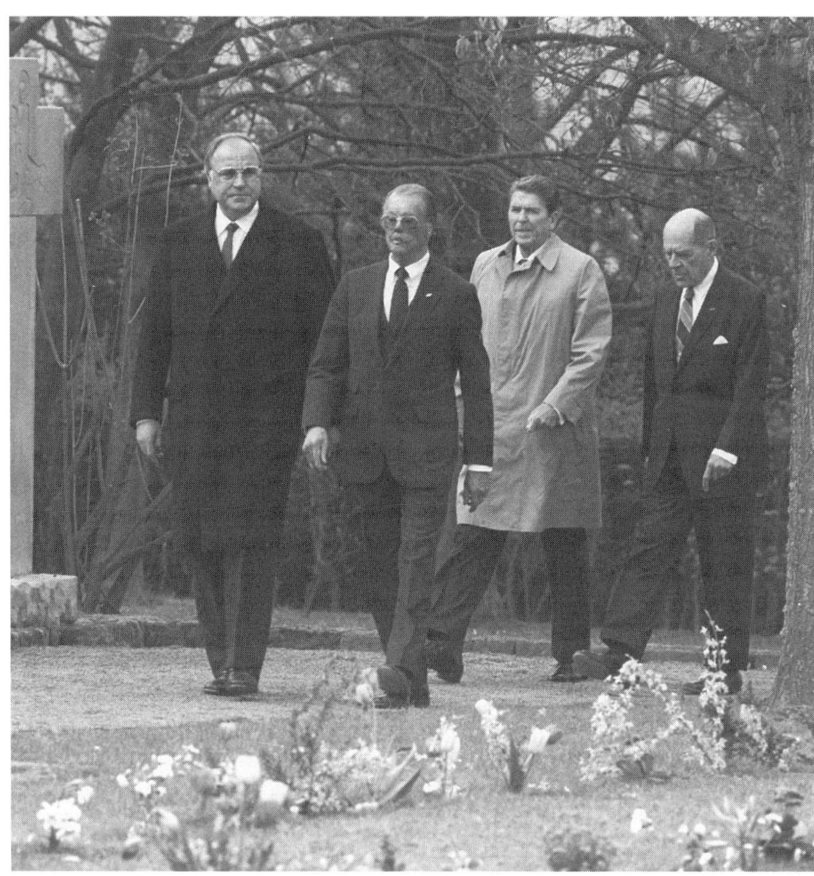

FIGURE 3.11. Chancellor Helmut Kohl, General (Ret.) Johannes Steinhoff, President Ronald Reagan, and U.S. General (Ret.) Matthew B. Ridgway visit the German military cemetery at Bitburg, 1985. Photograph by Ulrich Wienke. Courtesy of Presse- und Informationsamt der Bundesregierung.

between the Nazi era and the postwar West German order. In short, conservatives mobilized history to mourn those who had died but also ideologically construed it to distinguish between past policies and contemporary experience. Victims were real, but crimes existed separate from any concrete notion of perpetrators. For the purposes of promoting this blurred historical category, the act of official mourning in the political sphere could effectively employ the emotional spectacles that had already been formulated in the cultural realm.

Let us turn to the ceremonies and speeches of the day itself to clarify how Kohl used this instrumentalization of the past. On May 5, 1985, Reagan and Kohl began the day with a flight to Hannover from which they traveled by helicopter to visit the former concentration camp of Bergen-Belsen, a visit that was tacked on to appease severe criticism that Reagan faced. In their short speeches, each emphasized the victims of murder and genocide, the personal responsibility of Hitler as a tyrant, and the postwar reconciliation between the two countries based on democracy and military alliance. They made no mention of specific perpetrators and bystanders. From there, the two leaders flew to the small town of Bitburg in western Germany. Kohl had chosen Bitburg not only because of the Kolmeshöhe cemetery for German war dead but also because it was near a U.S. air base with approximately 10,600 U.S. soldiers and their families. An honor guard met the two leaders at the cemetery, as well as families of wartime German resistance leaders and the hastily invited World War II veterans General Matthew Ridgway, U.S. Army (Ret.), and German Lieutenant General Johannes Steinhoff (Ret.). The two veterans shook hands at the site. No speeches were given here, and as a mournful soldier's tune played during a moment of silence, the *New York Times* reporter noted that "Mr. Reagan stood a few feet from two graves with SS markings."[65] After this event, the two traveled to the nearby air base to address Bundeswehr and U.S. soldiers as the last part of their scheduled visit.

Looking at Kohl's speech at the U.S. base gives us some insight into how, at this point, he interpreted the past to legitimate his particular policies and which terms he found ideologically important to emphasize. In his speech, Kohl walked a fine and contradictory line between a constant affirmation of the distinction between past and present but also the collapse of the two. As he stated in his opening sentence, "It is not often that the link between the past, present and future of our country reaches us as vividly as during these hours at Bitburg."[66] Linking and separating past and present required Kohl in his speech to dwell on comparisons of the distinction between the United States and Germany in the past as well as their contemporary synthesis, particularly in fighting the Soviet Bloc. Kohl stated: "Our visit to the soldiers' graves here in Bitburg was not an easy one. . . . For me it meant first and foremost deep sorrow and grief at the infinite suffering that the war and totalitarianism inflicted on nations, sorrow and grief that will never cease."[67] He mentioned soldiers but only as generic individuals, as potential victims, not as part of the functional support or willing participant in violent actions against ethnic groups in the east. Such a commonplace understanding of agency had been scrubbed from his speeches here and elsewhere. Further, his use of the past tense implicated Nazi terror's responsibility for the war dead, and his description of those killed emphasized the emotional need to mourn. But his shift into the future tense further indicated not only the ongoing effects of past Nazi totalitarianism but also those of the current version in the Communist east.

Further, while he identified the clear crimes of perpetrators in the Nazi past, his emphasis on mourning the dead as well as his stress throughout the speech on reconciliation defined what he saw as an essentially affirmative new position for West Germany in the world: "And the visit to the graves in Bitburg is also a reaffirmation and a widely visible and widely felt gesture of reconciliation between our peoples, the people of the United States of America and us Germans, reconciliation which does not dismiss the past but enables us to overcome it by acting together."[68] The overtly dualistic dynamics of past and present, opposition and synthesis, Nazi tyranny and NATO alliance, are clearly visible here. As Raul Hilberg wrote, "The deepest psychological conflict between the Germans and the Jews had become [at Bitburg] a contest of public relations in which only simple, visible cues could matter."[69] Such simple cues included references only to the most extreme fascists like Hitler while the true scale of victims could be safely recounted, without worrying too much about the imbalance such a presentation of the historical narrative implied. The soldier as victim as well as those killed by Nazi crimes were real, but the people who made and implemented these acts remained obscure in Kohl's narrative.

Kohl's rhetorical dynamic raised a polarization of past and present events or individuals only to collapse the real differentiation of historical actors by rendering the representation symbolic. He equally employed this strategy in discussing the victims of Nazism and the war. The key sentences read: "The town of Bitburg witnessed at first hand the collapse of the Third Reich. It suffered the year 1945. It was part of the reconstruction in the years of reconciliation. For 25 years now, Bitburg has been the site of joint ceremonies in which American, French and German soldiers and citizens of this town and region commemorate the victims of the war and time and again affirm their friendship and their determination to preserve peace jointly."[70] Kohl's historical slippage allowed for an acknowledgment of Nazi victims but simultaneously generalized the category of past victimization. In addition, he thoroughly abstracted the specific relationship between fascist policies of the past and the personal agency of German perpetrators and bystanders. Thus, his speech was a symbolic gesture that emphasized the important role of staged cultural events of mourning as it simultaneously legitimated contemporary militarist policies favorable to the neoconservative anti-Soviet agenda. He did not choose by chance the ceremonial value of a military cemetery and a military base. And he equally calculated his attempt to normalize the past and affirm the present by staging this in the presence of a U.S. president. Death implied finality, cemeteries invoked ceremonies of mourning, and military bases required the shoring up of contemporary coalitions. That Kohl ended by invoking God's blessing only further abstracted and universalized these tactics and ambitions.[71]

Conclusion

What comes out of an analysis of the particularly hyped symbolism of Bitburg is how the question of the agency of the perpetrator was at the core of the debate and that her or his invisibility was of central importance to Kohl.[72] As I have argued, different constituents variably acknowledged and nuanced their description or representation of the active role of individuals who pushed and legitimated policies during the Nazi period. Some cultural and political responses approached the past overtly as a matter of clear historical evidence while others approached it symbolically with strong and sometimes contentious polarization of terms and imagery. These different kinds of cultural and political responses participated mutually in this shared moment in a public debate in which the status of the National Socialist perpetrator was clearly up for grabs. Subsequently, West German academic culture took up the gauntlet with the *Historikerstreit* (the Historians' Debate) that followed on the tail of Bitburg and involved the entire historical community. In this round of disputes, issues of normalization, comparative totalitarian politics, individual culpability, and continued liability all clashed in the press and in the halls of the universities. As this extension of the public debate indicates, Kohl, like Kiefer, contributed his own narrative to a broad matrix of related positions on the Nazi past.[73] As such, he helped redefine for a new generation of conservatives the status of the perpetrator as an ideological abstraction.

I have tried to indicate how we can use a more precise understanding of the shift in Kiefer's paintings to help us better explain the contemporary artistic debates about the Nazi past and highlight specific tropes in the political reception of the perpetrator at Bitburg. By analyzing Kiefer's culturally conservative move from the specific subject positions of perpetrator and generational conflict toward the more symbolic and emotion-laden references to victims and monumental architecture, we can derive the key terms of this transformative moment: polarizing comparisons, cultural expression rather than political agency, memorialization, and the historical abstraction of symbolic rituals of mourning. Art criticism widely and hotly debated several of these terms in reference to art that related to the Nazi perpetrator, and the characteristics of the art world debate are useful in understanding aspects of Kohl's tactics at Bitburg. Hence, art history becomes an analytic tool to explore the specificities of state and party ideology and its intended effects.

Our understanding of the range of terms is all the more important precisely because of the need to analyze critically this initial moment of renewed conservative strength when Kohl and the CDU were attempting to formulate a policy of "normalization." Because of this attempt, certainly some contemporaries saw rhetorical strategies describing new concepts of the Nazi perpetrator as politically useful to Kohl and the NATO alliance. Jürgen Habermas, for example, in an article in *Die Zeit*, stated: "Kohl was able to drag the American president in front of the cemetery cameras with a clear conscience. After all, he was only insisting on a symbolic recompense. . . . As soon as one begins to replace purposive political rationality with a heavy-handed symbolism of destiny, one handshake follows the next."[74] In a broader sense, Habermas indicated the shift away from the earlier focus on the individual responsibility of perpetrators or the specific resistance of the sons and daughters of the second generation. This particular political moment had passed, and the debates concerning the Nazi period had moved into the realm of the symbolic. Such a move required "a purposefully selective presentation and integration of those valuable aspects of the past that would meet with an affirmative response from present generations,"[75] to quote Habermas further. Judicial policies and resistance in the street or the academy gave way to generalized public debate and ideology.

The relationship between Kiefer's art and Kohl's policies is not transparent. Kiefer's dualistic paintings changed their conceptual terms from the centrality of generational conflict toward an ideological debate on Nazi culture. Culture mediated between the perpetrator and the victim, and showcased both in symbolic terms that critics by 1984 greeted as an essentially affirmative comment on history. Concomitantly, Kohl and the CDU used an ideological interpretation of National Socialist society to legitimate their political interests and mystify their relation to the past or to the perpetrator. While Kiefer's works emphasized ambivalence, Kohl's policies searched for an absolute synthesis through the politics of reconciliation.

Each position, whether artistic or political, came to the fore based on the effectiveness of a political economy that propelled Kiefer's success and formed the backbone of conservative domestic and foreign policy. Using different concepts of what National Socialist history meant to contemporary West German society, conservative politics and Kiefer's painting both prospered in the flourishing wealth of multinational financial expansion. Further, they contributed to the density of a matrix of cultural and political reformulations of the Nazi perpetrator in the early 1980s that debated, contested, or denied the focal position of agency in previous discussions. The changing terms of the artist's practice and his reception shed significant light on the tactics of the politician, clarifying the groundedness of each in a particular cultural moment, an important lesson to be learned from analyzing the political reception of the Nazi perpetrator and postwar West German art.

 DANIEL LIBESKIND AND
THE NEO-NAZI SPECTER
THE RESURGENCE
OF THE PERPETRATOR

With some fanfare, the first Jewish Museum in Berlin opened its collection to the public in newly designed rooms in the Oranienburgerstrasse on January 24, 1933, six days before Hitler came to power. Plans for a Jewish Museum in Berlin go back to the art collection left to the Jewish community in 1907 by Albert Wohl, a Dresden jeweler. By 1917, the community had opened an "Art Collection of the Jewish Community in Berlin" in the Oranienburgerstrasse, near the main synagogue. During the Weimar Republic, the collection expanded from twenty to eighty paintings and included more Modernist Jewish artists, for example, Lesser Ury. In 1927, acting on the prewar idea of Salli Kirschstein, a Society for the Friends of the Jewish Museum was formed with Max Liebermann as its honorary president. During the Nazi period, the museum initially remained open and functioned as an important site for attempts by the community to continue its cultural existence, even though the developing Nazi purge of the civil service and cultural institutions increasingly excluded German Jews. Exhibitions included a retrospective of Liebermann after his death in 1936 and the 1937 show *100 Years of Jewish Art*. The museum was closed on November 10, 1938, after the so-called Kristallnacht pogrom, and the Reichskulturkammer confiscated the collection for its own planned museum meant to mark the end of Jewish influence on German life.[1]

When construction on a new Jewish Museum finally began after German reunification, the fate of the collection and its new building seemed far away from the earlier project's disastrous demise in the Nazi period. But the lingering influence of the war and the continued resonance of the Nazi past made any such thinking pure fantasy. While generational conflict or the continuity of the perpetrator in postwar West Germany seemed less urgent as themes, the cultural and ideological response to the past through state-sponsored memorialization of victims continued apace.[2] Still, at the moment of reunification, these established interests ceded ground to a new concern. The early 1990s began with the frightful specter of the reconstitution of radical right-wing parties and a concomitant resurgence in anti-semitic and racist attacks on German Jews, people perceived as Jews, foreign workers, and asylum seekers. Although such right-wing tendencies had existed prior to reunification (even making some headway in the authoritarian context of the German Democratic Republic in the eighties), the nationalist euphoria as well as the economic strain of the moment revealed new and deep fissures in sections of German society. From these fissures emerged a possibility that reunification had released both the political and social conditions that allowed the neo-Nazi revival of some National Socialist policies and beliefs. Right-wing movements could use the strategic alignment of their present positions with the Nazi past to take advantage of the changing conditions and concerns of this volatile social period. For those in charge of the Jewish Museum, this strategy signaled how the Nazi perpetrator seemed to be taking a very real if new form. Such a specter also haunted Helmut Kohl and the Christian Democratic Union's project of "normalization."

The volatile cocktail of an emergent contemporary racism that was constantly reflected off the Nazi past—embodied in a new kind of perpetrator—had a strong impact on major policy initiatives and ideological debates, particularly in the immediate post-reunification period. Racist attacks and right-wing electioneering both in the west and the east overlapped and intersected with a number of competing political–economic conditions and interests that had come to the fore with reunification. Culture was also subject to this dense matrix of ideological and material conditions and concerns, particularly in media such as architecture. A variety of interested parties could easily instrumentalize and manipulate architecture because of the political regulation of the built environment and its reliance on large-scale resources and labor. The high-profile construction projects of the once and future capital, Berlin, exemplified this process. Attempting to pull apart and analyze the interwoven skeins of architectural production, racism, economic growth, and government policy clarifies how the political debates concerning a resurgent Nazi perpetrator influenced cultural decisions in part or in whole in reunification Berlin.

Daniel Libeskind's Jewish Museum in the Berlin Municipal Museum embodies this interconnection of political and cultural conditions (see Plate 9). Perhaps no contemporary German building has been so thoroughly discussed as Libeskind's. From the competition design in 1989 to the opening of the permanent exhibition in 2001, Libeskind's project has generated endless public debate, architectural criticism, and philosophical speculation. Art and cultural historians have naturally focused on one of the most unique aspects of the plan, its central void (Figure 4.1), a space that can be seen but not entered, the absent axis to the zigzag structure.[3] And yet scholars have largely glossed over the relationship of national and local political debates concerning reunification and the rise of racist attacks to the internal and public discussions of Libeskind's project in the crucial years between its original design (1989) and the laying of the foundation stone (1992). Instead, the void and its phenomenological significance dominate all.

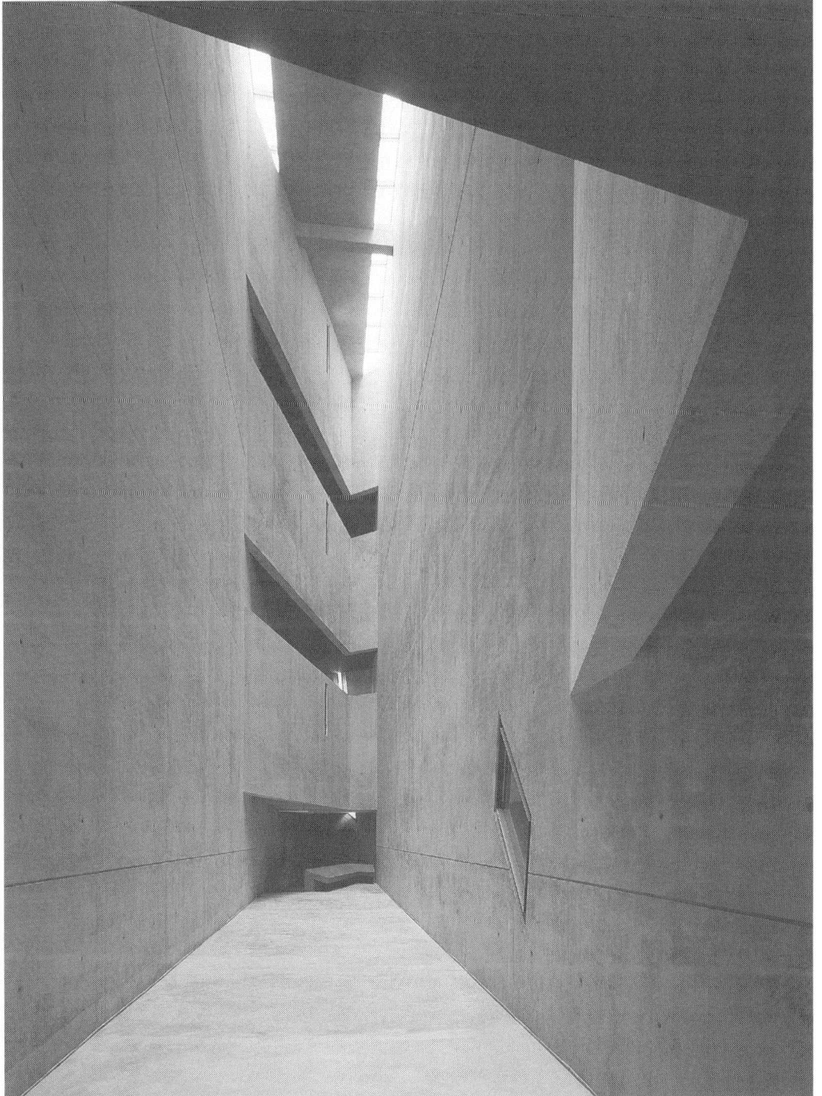

FIGURE 4.1. Daniel Libeskind, view of the central void, Jewish Museum in the Berlin Municipal Museum, Berlin, 1989–2001. Photograph copyright Bitter Bredt. Courtesy of Studio Daniel Libeskind.

Combined with its aesthetic innovations, Libeskind's design also became a focal point of bureaucratic debates concerning policy decisions as well as architectural developments in Berlin. Focusing on a broader analysis of its historical development and political conditions clarifies shifts in its interpretation and use.[4] Such a comprehensive approach relates the Cold War context before the fall of the Berlin Wall, as well as the rapidly shifting conditions that resulted from reunification, to the related aspects of the building's design and construction. After 1989, the particular constellation of people and events that responded to the rise of right-wing political groups and neo-Nazi violence influenced the interpretation and construction of the design more significantly than previously assumed. Indeed, as a result of right-wing pressures as well as other conditions of reunification, Libeskind's museum in these years became what Michael Omi and Howard Winant characterize, in a different context, as a racial project: "A racial project is simultaneously an interpretation, representation, or explanation of racial dynamics, and an effort to reorganize and redistribute resources along particular racial lines."[5] In this account, a racial project occurs when a variety of social, economic, and political factors converge to make a racial formation useful. I find this dynamic concept of the assertion of race helpful in thinking about how the Jewish Museum in the Berlin Municipal Museum became "Jewish," that is, a thoroughly and exclusively ethnic project.[6] As Daniel Bussenius has persuasively argued, public officials and the press had surprisingly unstable notions of what the museum was, what it was meant to hold, and who its historical subjects were.[7] This instability crystallized ideologically after 1989 in the important context of the new building economy of post-wall Berlin, the local political dynamics of the building bureaucracies and the particular context of the increased violence against foreigners and Jews in Germany. Museum personnel and the public press alike increasingly perceived the architecture as an antidote to any resurgence of the Nazi perpetrator in contemporary violence, tying the building to the larger ideological and policy goals of the state.

The changing interpretation of the building after reunification depended on the initial precompetition Cold War history of the project and its genesis within the physical and conceptual parameters of the International Building Exhibition (Internationale Bauausstellung, IBA). City officials thoroughly integrated the museum extension project with the local architectural debates in West Berlin as well as its developing competition with East Berlin.[8] Such integration contrasted strongly with the project's increasing exceptionalism after the fall of the wall. In this period, Libeskind's Jewish Museum became the sole new public building to continue planning and construction. Its concomitant symbolic importance grew accordingly.

The Jewish Museum architecturally maintained this balancing act between its integration with the local concerns of the IBA and its post-wall exceptional distance from these developments and interests. This balancing act, and the variable changes to the project and its meaning that inevitably resulted, allowed the building to become a racial project. From 1989 to 1992, Libeskind's museum existed at the nexus of fears of right-wing violence and the debates about whether such acts and others constituted a political revival of a new generation of Nazi perpetrators. We need to reestablish the political and architectural terms of the Jewish Museum's development to clarify the specific relationship of culture to the broader instrumentalization of the Nazi past and the fear of the perpetrator at this triumphant moment of a new Germany.

The History of the Jewish Museum within the Context of Pre-reunification Berlin

As Cilly Kugelmann reminds us, the Jewish Museum in the Berlin Municipal Museum began not as a symbolic manifestation of reunification but rather as a Cold War building.[9] It resulted from plans and interests that marked local Berlin politics as well as the developing relationship between West and East Germany since the 1960s up to the 1989 competition. During this period, officials were quite mindful of the violent end of the Berlin Jewish community during the genocide, enabled through an increasing political isolation of the Jews from German society. When the initiative to reconsider a Jewish Museum for West Berlin began to gain ground in the 1970s, Heinz Galinski (chair of the Central Council of Jews) and other active members also had the previous history in mind as they sought to avoid a museological repetition of this tragic isolation. By 1971, city museum officials began discussions with the remnants of the Jewish community. Both parties focused on opening a department within the municipal museum that combined Jewish history with that of the city as a whole. From these initial conversations, a plan developed that would eventually be formalized in 1987 as the "Integrative Model." It relied on the key concept that Berlin Jewish history and Berlin history in general must be represented as both distinct and integrally related simultaneously. On February 4, 1975, the Berlin Senate approved a plan to build a new structure as the Jewish Department within the Berlin Municipal Museum.[10]

Difficulty with financing and planning delayed further work on the project until the 1980s. Architecture in Berlin had already been well established at the center stage of national policy, given that the city was the symbolic outpost of the west in the face of the socialist GDR.[11] Since the constitution of the West German Federal Republic in 1949, Berlin had always maintained an artificial status reliant on federal funding from Bonn for culture and the support of its economic base. In the 1980s, architecturally speaking, funding concerns focused on reinvigorating residential construction as a means of reviving local economies and limiting political opposition from the urban core.[12] By 1979, the Social Democratic (SPD) administration in West Berlin appointed Josef Paul Kleihues to lead this architectural effort through the International Building Exhibition. The goal of the IBA was twofold: to restore usable turn-of-the century residential buildings, and to create mixed-use residential structures in poorer parts of West Berlin to stimulate growth and provide needed housing. With competitions beginning in 1980 and construction in 1984, the IBA brought together such well-known architects as Peter Eisenman, Aldo Rossi, and Zaha Hadid. They created attention-grabbing structures that nevertheless blended (through what was eventually called "critical reconstruction") with the character of specific parts of the city. Eisenman's dramatic project, for example, also included, in plan and elevation, relations to the contemporary and historical street grids of the neighborhood (Figure 4.2). Thus the building both gives a vibrant punctuation to the intersection and links the unusually fragmented form on the corner to the more traditional scale of

FIGURE 4.2. Peter Eisenman, IBA Social Housing, Berlin, 1981–85. Author's photograph.

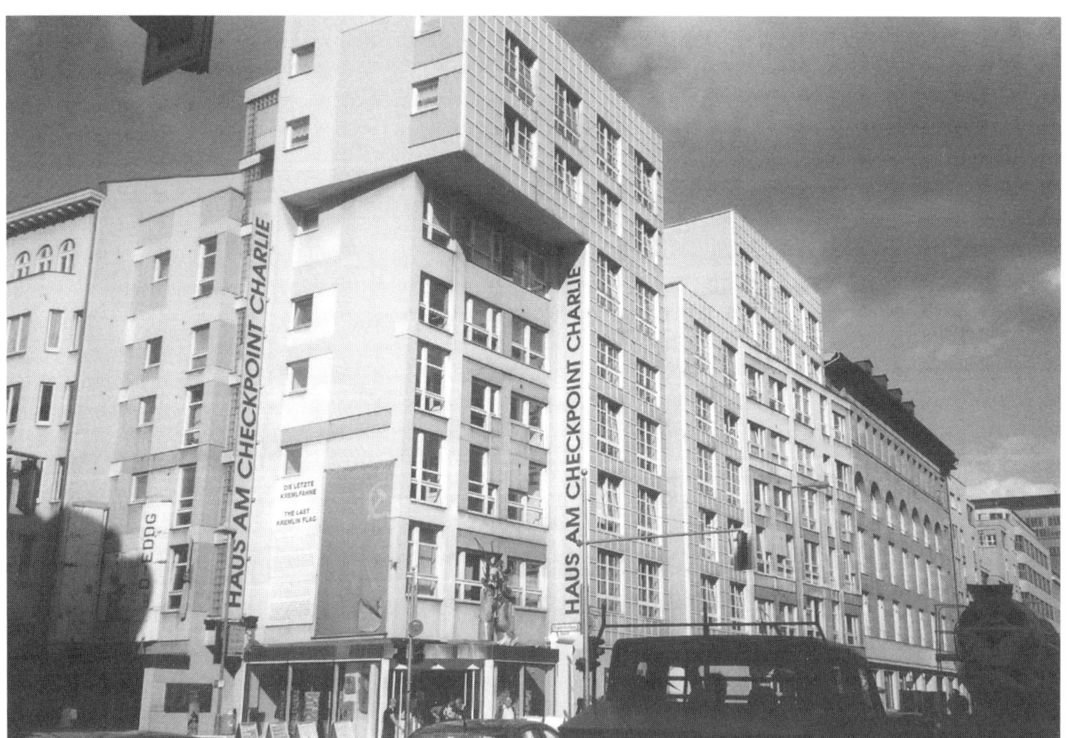

the older surrounding buildings that line the street. With these kinds of projects, the IBA focused on revitalizing the three areas of the southern Tiergarten, the Prager Platz, and the Friedrichstadt south of the Berlin Wall (part of Kreuzberg). The resulting new buildings showcased through their formal innovation the supposed glamour and success of Cold War West Berlin. They also attempted to fill the government's immediate local need for housing in areas that had seen violent confrontations between police and squatters as well as other autonomous groups in the early 1980s.[13]

In relation to the Jewish Museum, the IBA was more than mere architectural context. Rather, the IBA had targeted the Berlin Museum and many of its surrounding plots for a coordinated building campaign to restore the area's social and economic viability. Since 1969, the Berlin Municipal Museum had been located in the Baroque Kollegienhaus (Collegiate House), built in 1735 by the architect Philipp Gerlach in the southern Friedrichstadt on the Lindenstrasse (Figure 4.3). In addition, Gerlach designed the eighteenth-century extended plan of the area that included the formal axes of streets and the laying out of geometric plazas such as the Pariser Platz and Mehringplatz (the former Belle-Alliance-Platz, just south of the Kollegienhaus) (Figure 4.4). During the Nazi period, Friedrichstadt had contained many of the headquarters of the National Socialist

FIGURE 4.3. Philipp Gerlach, Kollegienhaus (Berlin Municipal Museum), Berlin, 1735. Author's photograph.

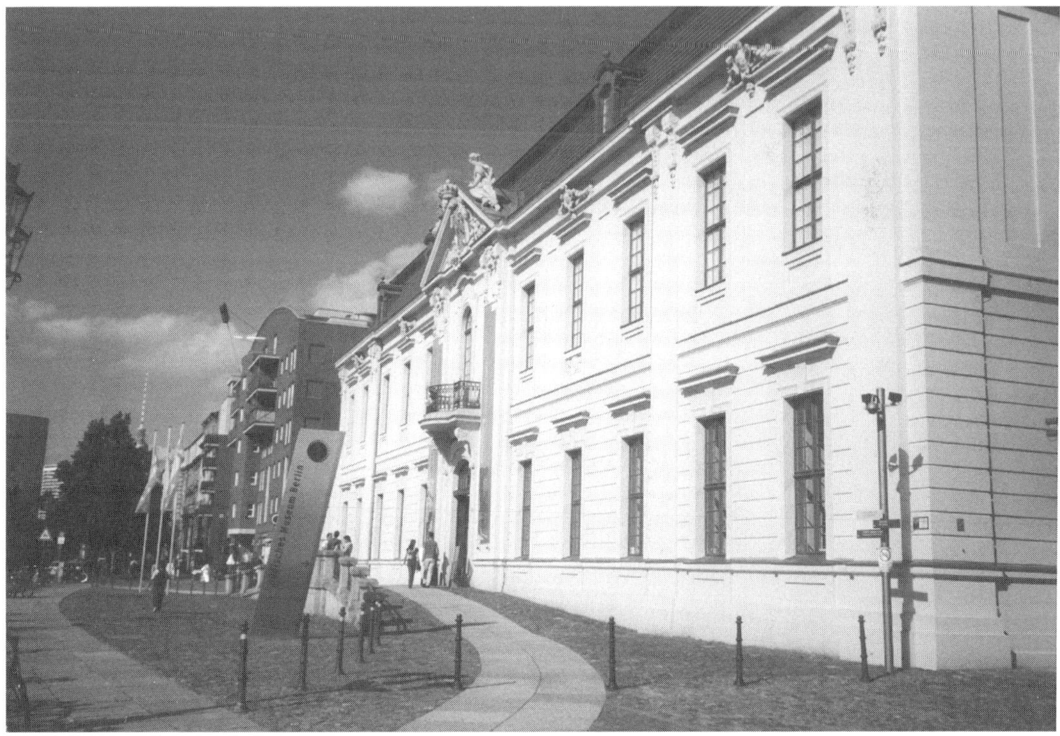

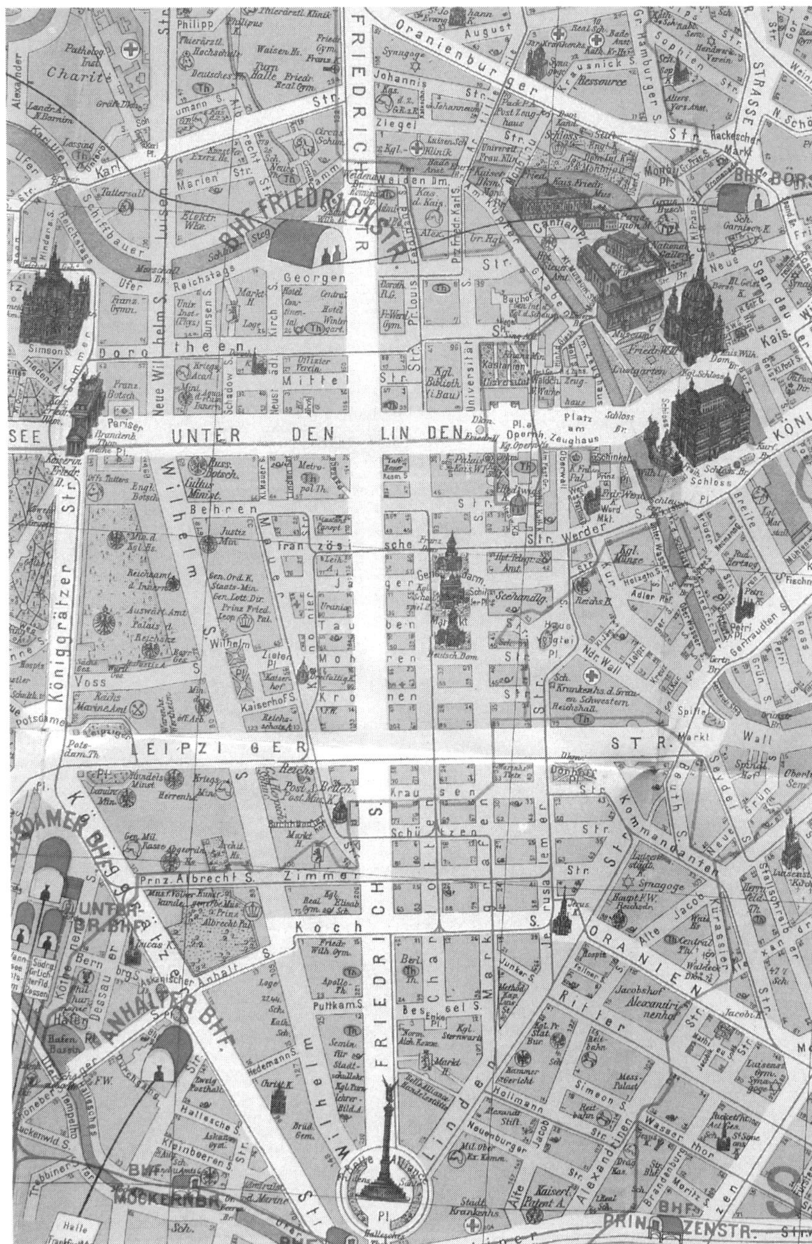

FIGURE 4.4. Area map of Berlin showing the grid of Friedrichstadt to the south, Berlin (Stadtplan Firma Pharus), circa 1903–14. Photograph courtesy of Zentralinstitut für Kunstgeschichte, Photothek.

bureaucracies, including the notorious Prinz-Albrecht-Strasse 8 and the Prince Albrecht Palace. These addresses had served as the headquarters of the Gestapo and the SS Reich Security Main Office (Reichssicherheitshauptamt), respectively, and are now demarcated at the site by the Topography of Terror (Topographie des Terrors) museum. As they did many areas of Berlin, but also as a result of this concentration of political power, the Allies thoroughly bombed the district during the war. Few traces of the eighteenth-century city remained, although the Kollegienhaus maintains some important reminders of the earlier building program. In particular, West Berlin urban planners preserved the sight line looking down the Markgrafenstrasse and concluding at its facade on the Lindenstrasse.[14]

With the construction of the wall in 1961 to the north, and the focus on housing and building at the Mehringplatz to the south, little active planning or coordination of building occurred in this period. Across the Lindenstrasse, a large hall was built and used for a wholesale flower market. The city curved the street itself in 1965 to improve the movement of traffic through the area, and planning officials proposed an east–west autobahn corridor since it appeared that, given the wall, there was not to be any north–south development. Obviously, this proposal was not approved, but it had an impact. When the city gave the plan up, local community officials took up the east–west corridor idea and pushed instead for the creation of a greenbelt on the site, as this area of Berlin lacked significant gardens and parks. The possible greenbelt became a major sticking point between the IBA plans and the museum's desire to use the land south of the Kollegienhaus, a debate that continued with the local Green/Alternative List representatives even after Libeskind won the competition. But with the founding of the IBA in 1978 and Kleihues's subsequent appointment, the architects and planners could use their authority to subordinate these concerns and previous proposals to their own designs. The IBA began to plan the area more systematically with mixed uses that included housing, cultural institutions, and workplaces. In addition, they decided to reemphasize the formal north–south orientation of the original eighteenth-century plat. They further proposed the expansion of the significance of the neighborhood by establishing institutions that had a larger regional importance, the maintenance of the historical height of the neighborhood fixed at a maximum of six stories, and the creation of a variety of visually differentiated spaces of parks, alleys, semiprivate courtyards, and the like. The IBA set the important formal criteria but also the functional variability that any new building had to contend with while also engaging the history of the site.[15] These criteria set the conditions for the extension to the museum and its grounds.

The Senate Administration for Cultural Affairs, represented by Reiner Güntzer, made the administrative link between the IBA and the museum operative on July 2, 1981, in a discussion with Rolf Bothe (the director of the Berlin Museum) and Kleihues. The attendees focused on selecting the location of the new Jewish Museum extension. They considered several suitable areas in Kreuzberg, including the site finally agreed upon south of the Kollegienhaus. Furthermore, they agreed on the need for the building to fit in formally with the historic character of the area and, in specific, to avoid marring the period facade of the existing eighteenth-century museum building. Clearly the planning for the extension leading up to the competition included working with the IBA and called for the political support of Kleihues. Kleihues would, as a result of this administrative link, also become a key member of the competition committee.[16]

Kleihues and the IBA had a significant amount of authority over the many projects in the Friedrichstadt that fell under their auspices.[17] For the area around the museum, they had proposals for several housing complexes, a number of gardens, and a school for the speech impaired. So, for example, with the massive housing project just to the north of the museum (Wohnpark am Berlin Museum, 1986) (Figure 4.5), one of the architectural teams of Kreis Schaad Schaad turned to Kleihues and his staff for design approval and for help with the necessary zoning variances and other bureaucratic issues. City officials in turn supported the IBA planners by endorsing not only their general goals but also such specific ideas as the interest in reconstructing the historical north–south orientation of the district.[18] Thus, the IBA could enliven the neighborhood with buildings and institutions as well as sustain the connection to the historical, even in buildings designed by a diverse set of international architects, including, eventually, Libeskind.

FIGURE 4.5. Kreis Schaad Schaad, Wohnpark am Berlin Museum (housing estate at the Berlin Museum), Berlin, 1986. Author's photograph.

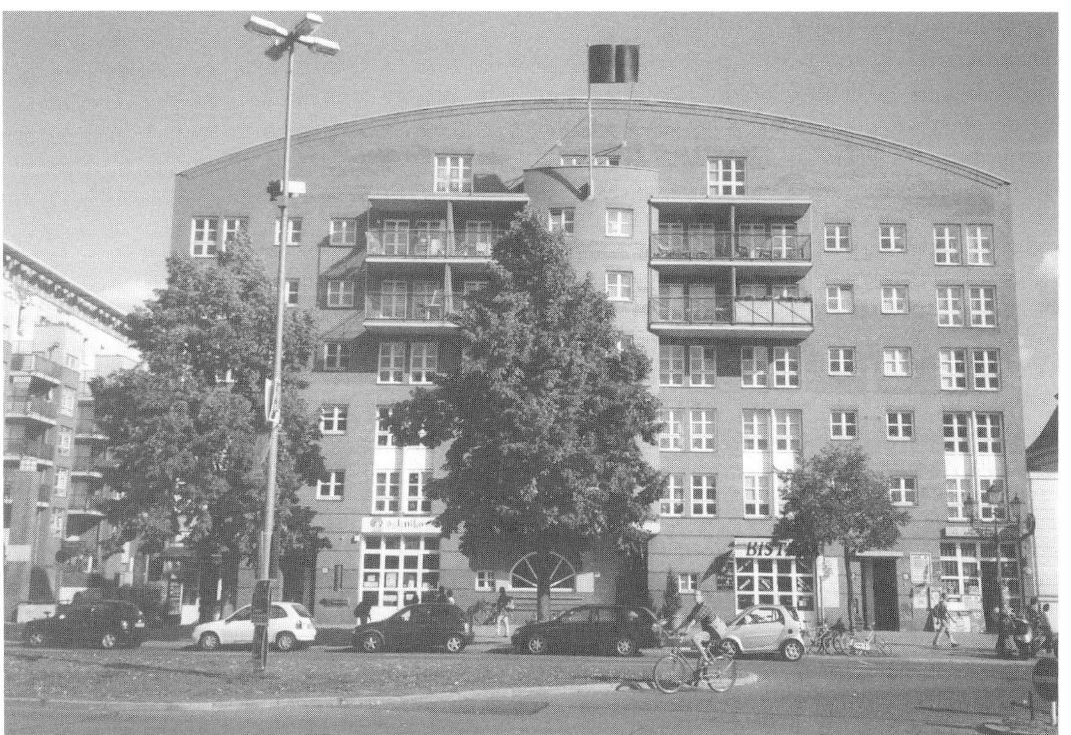

Tying the IBA to the proposal for the Extension of the Berlin Museum with the Jewish Museum Department (as the project was known in the competition call for entries)[19] secured the integration of local governmental planning with the new architectural project. But the Jewish extension was also not outside of the Cold War political competition between east and west that supported the IBA in the first place.[20] Most directly, the planning for the extension to the museum went in tandem and referenced East Berlin's actions to commemorate the former Jewish community. Historically, as we have seen, part of the founding mythology of East Germany had been that, as a socialist state, it had taken up the mantel of antifascism and the resistance to National Socialism. Yet coupled with the continued support of the western bloc for Israel in the postwar period, Stalin's anti-semitic campaign in 1952, and the Soviet alignment with the Palestinians, relatively little had been done at the official level. Party leaders did not recognize the culpability of perpetrators still living in the GDR or any remnant of the Jewish community.[21] In East Berlin, this situation changed in 1981. As part of the plan to rebuild the medieval Nikolai Quarter in preparation for the city's 750th anniversary celebration, the government announced that it was also going to rebuild the eighteenth-century Jewish residence of the Ephraim Palais as a symbol of the Jewish contribution to the city's history. Further, in 1987, Peter Kirchner, head of the Jewish Community in East Berlin, confirmed that the state had dedicated forty-five million marks to rebuild the Oranienburgerstrasse synagogue, the heart of the pre-Nazi community (Figure 4.6). Officials issued a decree in July 1988 that publicized the formation of a foundation for the "New Synagogue Berlin—Centrum Judaicum."[22]

In West Berlin, these initiatives became a leitmotif in the documents and meetings surrounding the Jewish extension to the Berlin Museum and spurred the West Berliners to action. For example, participants at the important Aspen Institute meeting of March 15, 1988, interested themselves in developments in East Berlin. At that meeting, the museum's director Rolf Bothe and Vera Bendt (director of the Jewish Department) presented the idea of the "Integrative Model," referring to an independent Jewish Museum that would be integrated and organized within the Berlin Museum as a whole. The assembled politicians and community members accepted this proposal as it avoided the isolation of the Jewish collections while also marking them as exceptional. But as Bussenius has pointed out, the proposal was open ended and still left a great deal of ambiguity as to how architects and curators could realize its goals. Yet, additionally, the Aspen Institute discussion referenced the plans in the east and how they provided a point of departure for key aspects of western decision making.[23] Within the city

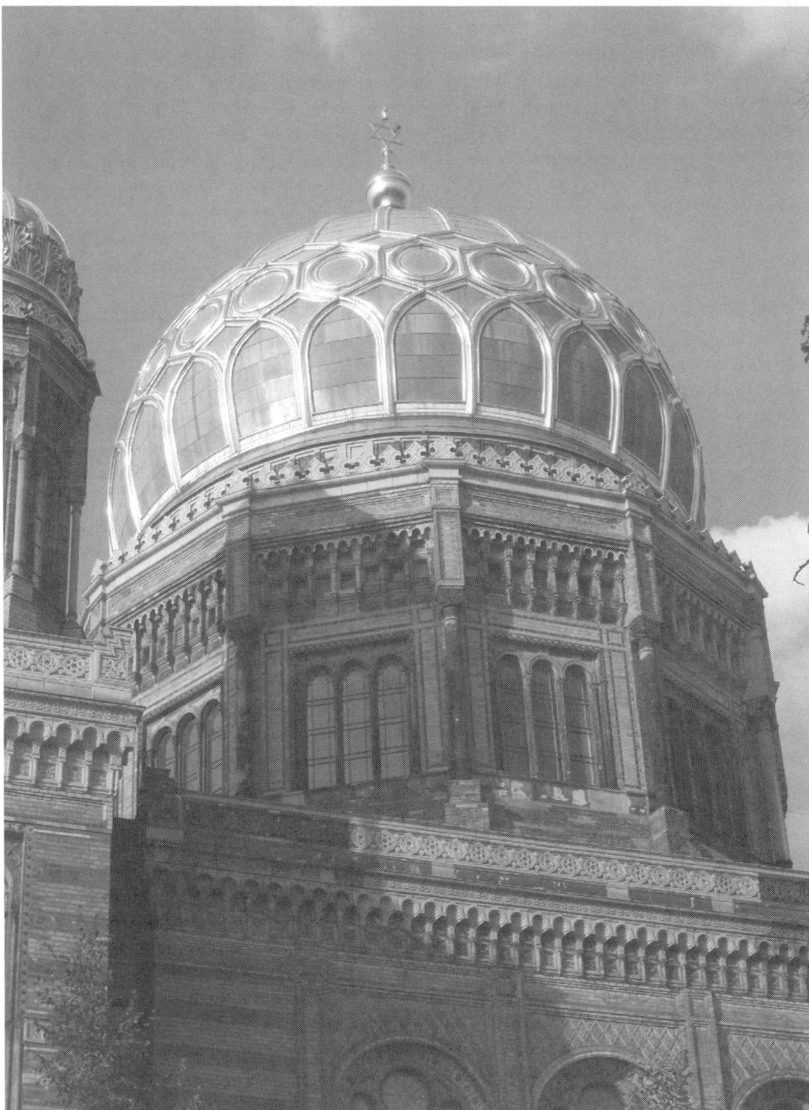

FIGURE 4.6. Carl Heinrich Eduard Knoblauch, New Synagogue (Oranien-burgerstrasse), Berlin, 1866. Photograph courtesy of Gerald P. Mulderig.

government, the cultural ministry carefully monitored eastern develop-ments, particularly in the jubilee year, for example, with a clippings file con-taining news of any exhibitions or plans for commemorating the Jewish community in East Berlin. Most specifically, as the CDU senator for cul-tural affairs, Volker Hassemer, prepared the communication for the archi-tectural competition, he and others emphasized in their internal exchanges how crucial it was to have a big announcement concerning commemoration on the fiftieth anniversary of the November 9, 1938, pogrom. While this was an important historical date, it also offered a possibility for West Ber-lin to compete with its neighbor. East Berlin city officials were going to announce plans to lay the cornerstone for the Centrum Judaicum on that same date. In addition, with the need to defend federal funds for West Berlin's subsidized economy, the city wanted an important project that could parallel Frankfurt in particular. The latter commemorated the pogrom anniversary with the opening of its own Jewish Museum. Ultimately, Hassemer could not maintain the November 9, 1988, date because of a conflict in CDU mayor Eberhard Diepgen's schedule. Still, they scooped the competition by announcing the architectural contest early with the mayor present on November 3. Hence, they introduced the week of commemoration but did not fall behind other West German city governments and maintained parity with the east.[24] The balancing act of West Berlin Cold War thinking spurred on the development of the Jewish Museum in the Berlin Municipal Museum.

By April 1989, architects had sent 165 entries from which the competition jury made its decision in June. The jury naturally considered the criteria and limitations that had conditioned the development of the idea for a Jewish Museum in the first place. City officials (since early 1989 under the SPD and Green/Alternative List coalition with SPD mayor Walter Momper) had approved the program. This centered on the "Integrative Model" in which the history of the Jews intersected with the broader history of Berlin. In addition, any project had to negotiate the site in relation to IBA housing policy standards and coordinate the structure with the Cold War politics of which many of the architectural decisions continued to be a flashpoint. As the overwhelming favorite with the jury, Libeskind's proposal addressed the concerns of the city administrators and urban politics particularly well (see Plate 10).[25]

Libeskind's proposal attempted to spatialize the integrative model by generating the form out of a complex geographic, historical, and conceptual matrix that combined rational criteria with seemingly random or irrational choices. Briefly, he set the project within the larger urban and historical context of Berlin, best exemplified by the Star of David Libeskind cut out of the city map, which in turn derived from the intersecting lines that connected the former residences of famous cultural and intellectual Jews and gentiles (e.g., Paul Celan and Mies van der Rohe) (Figure 4.7). By triangulating these lines, he formed the side of a kind of compressed star to make up the zigzag of the museum walls. He related this form to the yellow stars Berlin Jews had been forced to wear during World War II. The zigzag symbolizes the torturous but continuous history of the city that has no real beginning or end. The simple but broken element of the famous void down the middle interrupts this form, commemorating the disruption and absences of history created by the genocide.[26] While the shadow of the genocide hangs heavily over these designs, we should note that Libeskind has been clear from the beginning that he did not mean the museum to be a monument to the Holocaust. Indeed, in the original plans for the current empty tower of the Holocaust Memorial Void, he labeled it merely as the "Museum Department" in the basement plan and "temporary exhibits" on subsequent floors (Figure 4.8). He built a space for a memorial farther away from the museum, beyond the garden, although budget considerations would later force a cutback on any ancillary structures.[27]

Libeskind has long claimed that specific philosophical interests inspired his architectural thinking. As the architect has stated, Walter Benjamin's *One-Way Street* (1928) proved to be influential in the development of this specific form. Benjamin's text juxtaposed the varied addresses, shops, and attractions of a typical Berlin street with the fragmented observations of the author on time, space, and experience. Placing aphorisms on human experience in modern bourgeois society beside the built signs of that society, Benjamin sought to go beyond mere description and, hence, open up a critical debate on the subject in modern life. Like Benjamin's text, Libeskind's building developed from a static relation to the historical geography of Berlin that he then contrasted with the experiential and lively path of the individual moving through space. The concrete duality between stable built form and movement, continuity and rupture, structure and void, expands

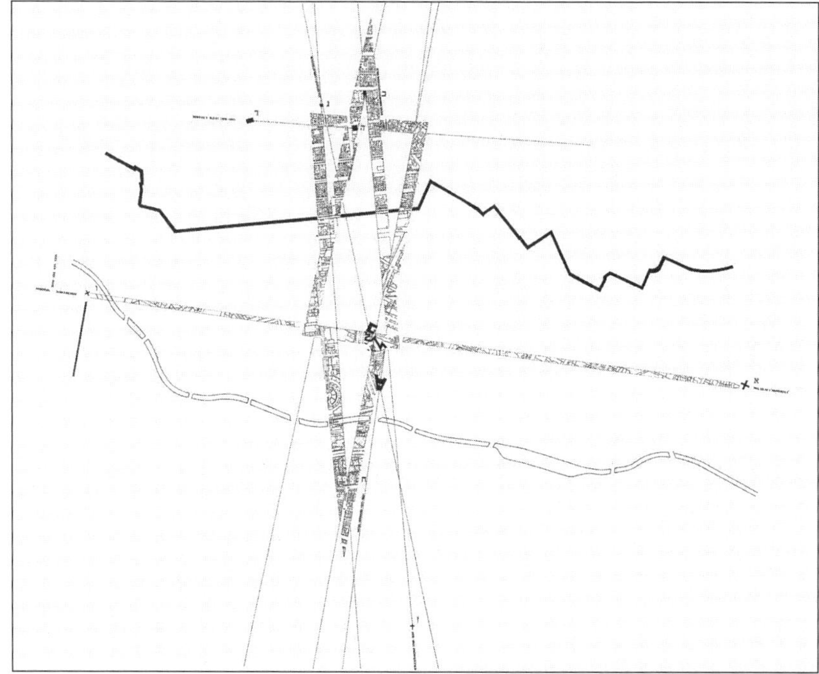

FIGURE 4.7. Daniel Libeskind, Star of David concept related to the Jewish Museum in the Berlin Municipal Museum, 1989. Photograph copyright Studio Daniel Libeskind.

into the conceptual dualities of history and experience. More broadly, Libeskind offers a diachronic and synchronic model for understanding the Jews in the development of Berlin. From this perspective, the physical disruptions created by the void as well as the scattered outer volumes are meant to shock one into the awareness of the fragmented individual spaces. On the other hand, the uninterrupted flow of the building through the zigzag form implies a meandering continuity. The complementary forms do not complete each other; rather the unified structure couples with the shifting experience of the space to hang together as a network of physical and, by extension, intellectual associations. In this sense, the building fulfills Libeskind's interest in construction as an expressive outcome of philosophy, something he has claimed for his previous unbuilt projects and subsequent work.[28]

But the building's success with a jury depended on making explicit the connection between this concept and the conditions of Cold War West Berlin. Libeskind's plan not only inscribed the building within the particular geographies of German Jewish cultural and intellectual life in Berlin but also, in specific details, related it to the site more broadly. In terms of the

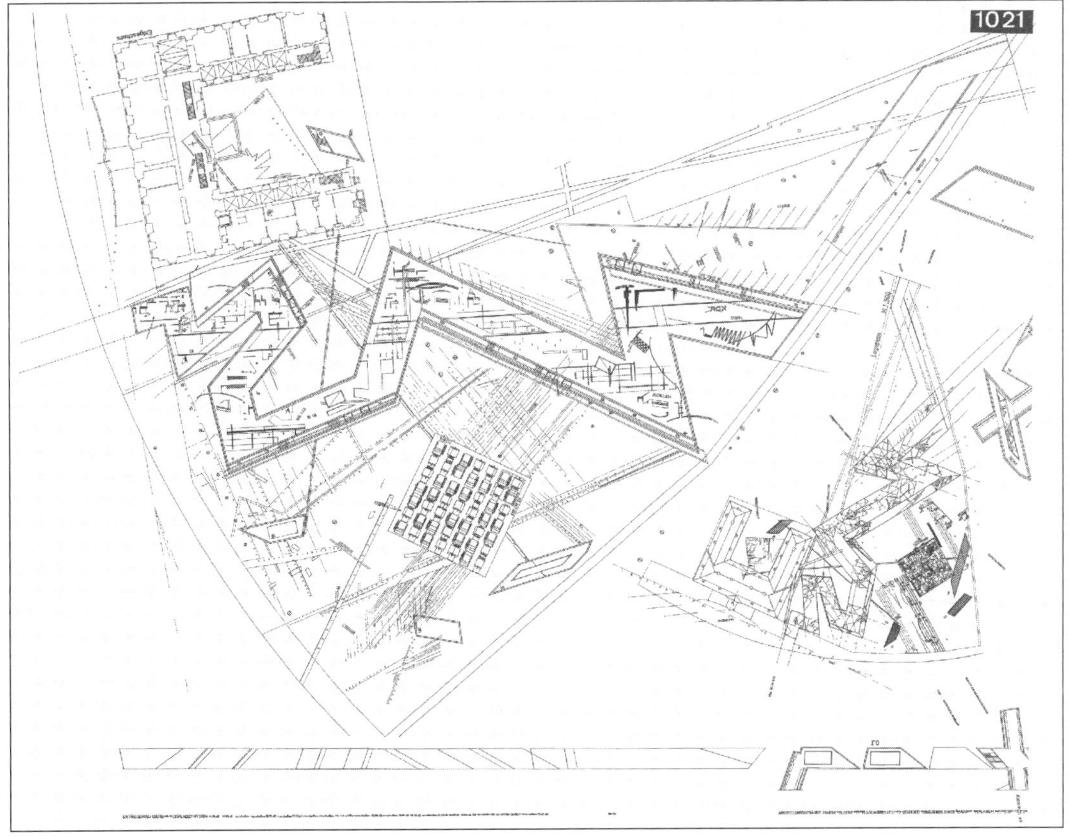

FIGURE 4.8. Daniel Libeskind, Jewish Museum in the Berlin Municipal Museum, first-floor plan, competition entry, 1989. Photograph copyright Studio Daniel Libeskind.

neighboring eighteenth-century building housing the main Berlin Municipal Museum, the zinc skin matches the window surrounds of the older building (as James Young has noted). More overtly, the bluish cast of the facade complements Gerlach's ocher facade (Figure 4.9). While the zigzag contrasts strongly with the staid plan of the older structures in the neighborhood, the line of the interior void is approximately aligned with Gerlach's building, a point further emphasized in subsequent construction drawings. It thus maintains the underlying integrity of the grid, something evident in the idealized proposal if a bit too abstract in the experience of the final building. Nevertheless, this contrasting and complementary form connects the building to other IBA projects that equally attempted to play off local buildings but also to create dynamic sculptural facades that enlivened the streetscape. As the architect himself put it, "In terms of the city, the idea is to give a new value to the existing context, the historical context, by transforming the urban field into an open and what I would call a hope-oriented matrix. The proposed expansion, therefore, is characterized by a series of real and implied transformations of the site. The compactness of

FIGURE 4.9. Contrast of Libeskind's Jewish Museum with Gerlach's Kollegienhaus, Berlin, after 2001. Photograph copyright Bitter Bredt. Courtesy of Studio Daniel Libeskind.

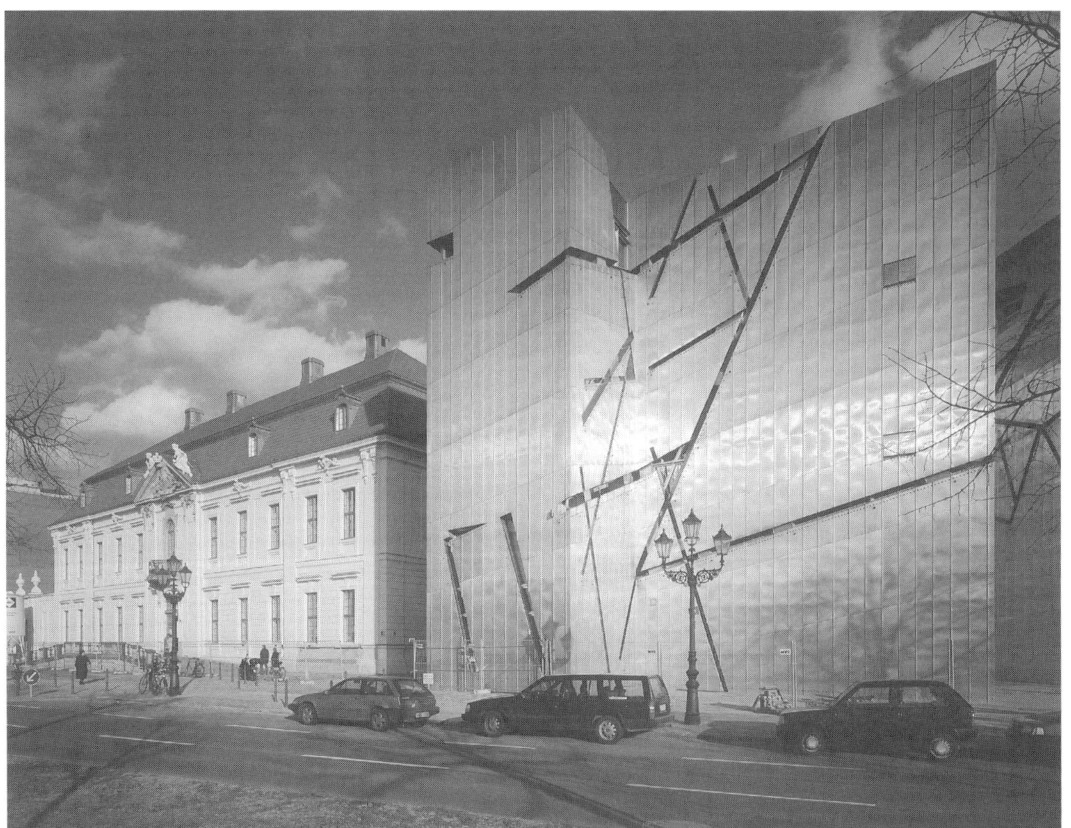

traditional street patterns is gradually dissolved from Baroque origins and then related diagonally across to the 1960s housing development and the new IBA projects."[29]

The architect made the connection of the plan to its site and the context of Berlin more explicit in discussions with the museum and the city bureaucracy. In an unpublished interview from July 26, 1989, Libeskind emphasized that the approximately sixteen-meter-high cornice line continued that of the Gerlach building. Further, the front western tip of the building went beyond the current property line of the Lindenstrasse, acting like a historic city gate. This protrusion emphasized the local interest in an east–west orientation while not hindering further designs for a stronger north–south connection to the Mehringplatz. On the inside of the plan, Libeskind described the staircase linking the two buildings as a reconstruction of the old central staircase of the Baroque building ("und zwar rekonstruiere ich die alte zentrale Treppe des Barockbaus"),[30] tying the older Berlin history to the modern city. The architect and his staff further elaborated such claims and connections in a discussion with museum officials and city landscape planners on January 22, 1990. The report summarizing the conversation noted that the plan incorporated not only the historic eighteenth-century city but also the plans of the 1960s, as well as addressed new needs such as those articulated by the IBA. So, for example, the use of the protruding form into the Lindenstrasse would mark the north–south traffic and emphasize the older axial street grid even while the east–west greenbelt proposed by local officials to replace the autobahn idea in the 1960s would be signaled with the directional orientation of the building's zigzag form. The front of the building bulging out into the street would act as a kind of tower on a city wall, pointing to the historical direction of traffic northward on Lindenstrasse, even while it was organically integrated with the structure of the new building. Such an accent also linked the extension to the IBA's model of city planning in the 1980s, with its emphasis on dramatic buildings that nevertheless bonded with their communities. In sum, "the architect suggested rather that the emphasis in this part of the city should be as a connecting point of three centuries of building traditions."[31] Libeskind also agreed in this meeting to shift the building farther south to make room for a playground and to allow the necessary space for fire trucks to pass between each structure. This shift had the added effect of bringing the central void more strictly parallel with the axis of the Gerlach building.

However idealized, such simultaneous claims for uniqueness and integration are also apparent in the interior plan. Libeskind's design articulates a complex interaction between the remnants of the Jewish community and the broader history of Berlin. He made the integrative model proposed by the competition itself clear through the arrangement of rooms. The two buildings connect only belowground through an off-axis stairwell. This stair descends to the basement floor and the rooms of the Jewish Museum. These comprised three exhibition spaces as well as two additional corridors that, with changes in 1990, terminate in the E. T. A. Hoffmann Garden and the Holocaust Memorial Void, respectively (Figure 4.10). Since this was meant as the area for the Jewish community material, Libeskind did not include the central axial void as part of the plan for this floor. Further-more, he skewed the alignment of the original ground plan of the basement story. Its outer walls did not correspond to the exterior walls of the floors above. Rather, he unified the building only by the void that opened from the basement ceiling to puncture the two floors above. On these upper floors, curators planned exhibition spaces for the theater collection of the Berlin Municipal Museum as well as the fashion collection, among other historical subjects not meant to be Jewish specific.[32] The viewer walked through these collections—which, like theater history, could include Jewish citizens who had contributed to these broader histories—crisscrossing the void and en-countering the awkward spaces that disrupt the idea of a linear history. As a result, the architecture indicates on the one hand the separate history of the Jewish community and its contemporary absence due to Nazi oppres-sion marked by the void. On the other, the continuous exhibitions inter-connect Berlin's broader history with Jewish contributions spatially and thematically. With this balancing act between the distinctive history of the Berlin Jews as well as their interrelationship with the zigzag path of Berlin

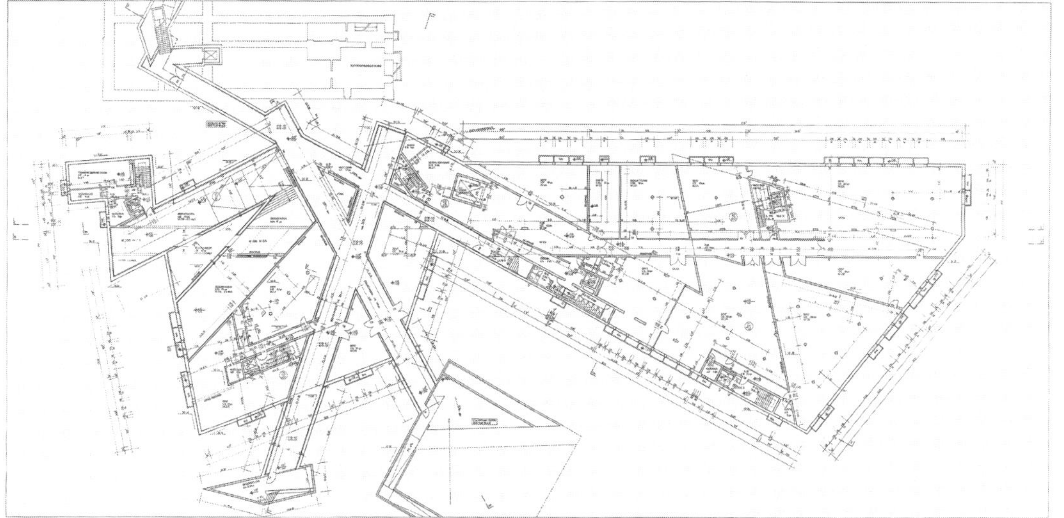

history as a whole, Libeskind attempted to visualize the "Integrative Model" that won over the jury. Such a balancing act complemented what the IBA asserted on the macro level. The design not only called for an integrated conceptual model on the interior but also, as we have seen, was thoroughly tied to the local and even regional world around it. Libeskind's design both integrated with its site and the city and, in formal terms, radically broke with previous built environments. As such, it was also an effective response to anything the East Berlin government would do to commemorate its Jewish community.

Reunification and Architecture in Berlin: The Isolation of the Jewish Museum

Of course, the very Cold War and local conditions that had influenced the development of the Jewish Museum within the Berlin Municipal Museum dramatically changed with the surprising fall of the Berlin Wall on November 9, 1989, and the equally speedy reunification of eastern and western Germany, completed by October 1, 1990. Although the complexities of reunification are not the topic here,[33] I want to highlight significant aspects of local and national developments in order to explain how Libeskind's building came to have an exceptional status quite different from the integration of building and site imagined earlier. The highly public nature of the building and debates about it contrasted with the prominent private initiatives of corporate construction, adding to its uniqueness and relative ideological isolation. This exceptional status within building in Berlin also connected the project, ultimately, to the shifting political debates about the Nazi perpetrator. In the process, the city perceived the need to reorient the building's goals as they developed beyond the specific requirements of the IBA and the Cold War.

Reunification had international, national, and local dimensions to its political development. At the level of international politics, U.S. and U.S.S.R. politicians drove concerns about the balance of global power as well as the potential interconnection of unified Germany with Europe. However, at the national level CDU politics developed a different if complementary set of ideological goals and economic constraints. Ideologically, the end of the collapse of the division between east and west led right-wing politicians to reassert national sovereignty, to affirm claims of a "normalized" Germany among other nations, and to declare victory over the antinationalist politics advanced particularly by the SPD and the Greens. Conservatives declared an end to World War II and the Cold War that also allowed them to proclaim an end to the inward-looking politics of contrition so powerfully mobilized by the left in the social and political struggles of the 1960s. These attitudes seemed to be affirmed by the strong vote for the CDU first in March 1990 in East Germany and then in the post-reunification national elections of December that reconfirmed the party's dominance in office.[34]

Economically, the CDU had more difficulty maintaining such confidence. The massive foreign debt of the GDR as well as its collapsing infrastructure caused Kohl to go back on his promise of a relatively painless transition into a unified state. The economic complexities of reunification also had a significant if variable impact on the local level, above all in the urban metropolis of Berlin. In June 1991, the Bundestag debated and confirmed Berlin's status as the capital if only by a margin of eighteen votes. The vote was crucial as the city was experiencing a marked economic change since the fall of the wall and needed all the federal support it could get. A brief post-reunification rise in the manufacturing and service sector quickly slowed and then stalled by 1993, when unemployment began to increase substantially and growth stopped. By 1997, unemployment was at 17 percent and manufacturing had fallen by over 41 percent from 1989 levels. The economic situation was exacerbated by national policies. Federal budget managers cut significantly the number of subsidies that had sustained Cold War West Berlin, in 1993 alone by 30 percent.[35]

Local and national policies that allowed for the influx of global capital in what supposedly were locally controlled economic issues further aggravated residents. Above all, the state sale of publicly owned real estate sparked a large debate on public versus private space. Globalization was a goal not only of the national CDU administration but, somewhat surprisingly, also of the short-lived Berlin government of the SPD/Green coalition. Taking charge in March 1989 after the January electoral victory, this coalition ended the eight-year rule of the CDU in Berlin. After the wall fell, the SPD mayor, Walter Momper, like Kohl on the international level, saw the advantage of giving Berlin a needed place in the globalized economy. He particularly worked to secure major corporate investments to give the city a clear symbolic and economic significance. So, on April 5, 1990, Momper famously overrode the authority of his urban development senator from the Green/Alternative List Party, Michaele Schreyer, who attempted to stop the sale and development of parts of Potsdamer Platz to Daimler-Benz for the headquarters of a new service division (Debis). Schreyer objected to the Daimler-Benz plan because it had been negotiated behind closed doors without public input. Further, the sale price of the land was well below market rate, thus not so subtly subsidizing Daimler-Benz's purchase and construction at a time when federal officials cut building subsidies for other projects of direct relevance to Berlin's citizens. Speaking about the city's future, SPD politicians defended the decision by citing the need to create jobs and investments and to participate in the post-reunification globalized economy. Much of the political debate in post-reunification Berlin stemmed from the sale and use of real estate as well as the international and local conflicts of interest that such sales inevitably generated.[36]

The scandal over Potsdamer Platz contributed to the breakdown in the red/green coalition and the loss of voter confidence in the SPD; in the December 1990 elections, the party fell to a historic low. Still, the newly constituted cabinet of the CDU/SPD black/red coalition that took control with the return of CDU mayor Diepgen in January 1991 expanded on Momper's efforts to globalize Berlin. In this context, Daimler-Benz and Sony announced their Potsdamer Platz buildings by Renzo Piano and Helmut Jahn, respectively, designed independently from a city planning competition that would otherwise have limited height and other distinctive details (Figure 4.11). With such aggressive tactics, public criticism boiled over about the Americanization and mallification of Berlin.[37] In spite of attempts to compromise with urban plans, the structures asserted the importance of the symbolic and spectacular corporate presence in the semiprivatized public spaces of Berlin, a crucial ideological goal of the flexible capital of globalization and both CDU and SPD leaders.

FIGURE 4.11. View of Potsdamer Platz, with Helmut Jahn's Sony Plaza (left) and Hans Kollhoff's Office and Commercial Building (right), Berlin, 2006. Not pictured is Renzo Piano's Debis Building (farther right). Author's photograph.

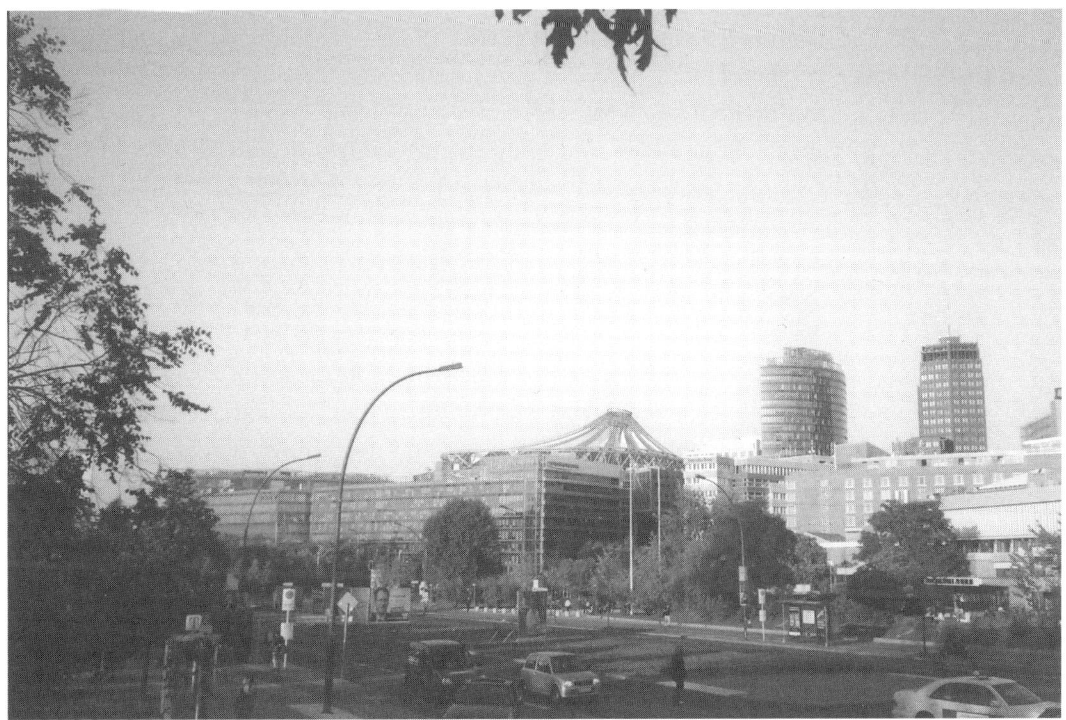

Hence, the period of reunification in Berlin saw the rise of specific political economic difficulties and debates that created particular conditions for building and for public policy. These conditions would also subsequently influence the development of the Libeskind design, particularly the local political debates focused on the question of how to balance private and public real estate. As the Potsdamer Platz case indicates, these difficulties allowed for the influence of major capitalist interests like Sony on the distribution of city resources (in this case, land). In addition, the SPD and the CDU accepted the glamorous corporate buildings as a necessary and desirable means of moving Berlin from a social welfare to a free-market economy. The expansive construction at Potsdamer Platz and other high-end sites in the city would be an ever-present and highly noticeable part of the unified Berlin. It would also starkly contrast with the collapse of the public building economy of which the Jewish Museum was a part.

After the wall fell, museum staff discussed the extension predominantly in pragmatic terms. Already by early 1990 a debate began within the museum itself as to whether reunification had made the extension to the Berlin Municipal Museum unnecessary. Their program duplicated aspects of eastern collections in the Märkisches Museum and the Centrum Judaicum. In particular, the latter was about to open in the renovated Oranienburgerstrasse synagogue in the heart of the pre-Nazi Jewish community. Under a unified city government and restricted funding structure, the prior east–west competitive concerns in the Cold War would clearly have to give way to some kind of shared or prioritized solution. As the issue of whether Berlin needed two Jewish collections picked up steam at the governmental level, Bothe called a meeting in July 1990 to negotiate areas of interest between the Centrum Judaicum and the Libeskind extension. Agreement was reached that the Centrum Judaicum would focus on the community as a whole while the extension would present specific problems and issues concerning the general history of Jews in Berlin (in addition to housing the theater and fashion collections).[38]

While substantial growth occurred in the private building economy, as the Potsdamer Platz case indicates, the political and economic difficulties of reunification did not bode so well for the continuation of public building campaigns, including Libeskind's Jewish Museum. The price of a unified Germany was becoming apparent to Kohl's government, leading to budget trimming throughout the country, including federal supports to Berlin. At the state level, the situation was exacerbated by the actions of the Treuhandanstalt (Trust Organization), originally established on March 1, 1990, by Prime Minister Hans Modrow, the last of the Socialist Unity Party (Sozialistische Einheitspartei Deutschland, SED) leaders in East Germany. After reunification in October, the Treuhand passed into the leadership of western business managers. By 1994, fourteen thousand businesses had been privatized under market principles and only 25 percent of the original workforces remained employed. Such a substantial transference of assets into the private sector favored the growth in real estate and in private construction; in Berlin, while manufacturing jobs fell 41.2 percent from 1989 to 1997, construction jobs increased slightly by 3.4 percent. As the private sector made use of this transfer of wealth and restructuring of former East German resources, the public sector was forced into austerity measures to pay for the rising social costs. Given this situation, after the December 1990 elections brought the CDU/SPD coalition to the Berlin Senate, members moved for large budget cuts and austerity measures in all departments and a postponement on specific new construction projects. Precisely at the moment in which privatization measures were advancing apace in the Potsdamer Platz and elsewhere, all public commissions were curtailed owing to other pressing priorities.[39]

Within this precarious financial situation, the Jewish Museum in the Berlin Municipal Museum saw the ebb and flow of the possibilities for its future. Complementing the highly discussed private growth exhibited at Potsdamer Platz, this public building site took on increased symbolic importance. On January 16, 1990, in the Berlin Senate's first initially optimistic deliberations on the building since the competition, it approved the plans with an official resolution and set DM 77 million as an approved estimate of costs with construction beginning in 1991. But the government commitment to the symbolic importance of the Libeskind extension in the face of increasingly dire economic conditions did not completely protect the building from the effects of reunification. Rather, the financial situation led to significant compromises in the plan and form. As the initial plans were finalized through 1990, the cost estimates for the building rose to DM 178.5 million. This proved to be too much for the Senate to swallow, and they asked Libeskind to reduce the project, which he did. By September his new plans had lowered the cost to DM 115.7 million. Among other changes, he raised the building to limit the depth of the foundation, straightened the inclination of the walls (which had leaned significantly east in the original plan), integrated rooms more cohesively into the plan, deleted several of the outlying towers that were meant to serve as the cafeteria and other functions, and compressed parts of the building to unify the exterior profile of the lower floor of the Jewish Museum with that of the upper building (see Plate 11). After Bausenator Wolfgang Nagel approved these changes in November, he noted that Libeskind had proposed them "*without* hurting the [original] idea or the architectural integrity of the building," a position that the senator for building would naturally want to project to the press.[40]

While the financial conditions changed the original form, the alterations nevertheless created a new status for the extension: it became the *only* public building funded by the Senate, allowing Libeskind to continue design and construction. City officials repeatedly emphasized this point in the first few years after reunification.[41] As such, its dynamic architectural form offered a social complement to the spectacular planning and design proposed for the financial center of the Potsdamer Platz down the road. Yet, in spite of Nagel's claim, the changes to the design also diminished the emphasis on the extreme fragmentation of the formal relationships of the parts of the interior to the whole. Originally, the shards of outlying volumes and the disjunction between the upper and lower floors of the museum circulated around and from the central void, emphasizing with the zigzag form and the tilted walls the concept of movement and destruction set dynamically at odds with the tectonic nature of building itself. Libeskind asserted these concepts to address not only the specific needs of the Jewish Museum that existed in the shadow of the Nazi genocide but also the continuity represented by the general institution of the Berlin Municipal Museum. Reducing these factors brought the building more clearly into line with more functional and prosaic exhibition spaces, even while, as Nagel stated, the changes preserved the essential conceptual contrast between continuous movement and formal disruption. Now, however, that contrast was reduced to its rather blunt aesthetic expression in the remaining void, the unusual line of the building that wrapped around it and the one separate volume of the Holocaust Memorial Void.

The simplification of the Libeskind design and the increased unity of its interior spaces resulted from the financial difficulties of reunification. These difficulties were in turn influenced by the economic priorities of the urban geography and real estate market of Berlin. The city continued to subsidize privatization projects at an alarming rate while cutting back on public investment. If this were all, though, then we could chalk up the changes to the inevitable constrictions imposed on public buildings through tightened budgets in capitalist economies, note the formal compromises, and move along. However, this history cannot be separated from the dynamic between public and private construction in post-reunification Berlin and the contingent broader political debates. The ongoing discussions of its budgets and the beehive of activity within government ministries concerned with the changes to the original design highlighted the Jewish Museum's increasing isolation as the only funded major public monument. The planning and

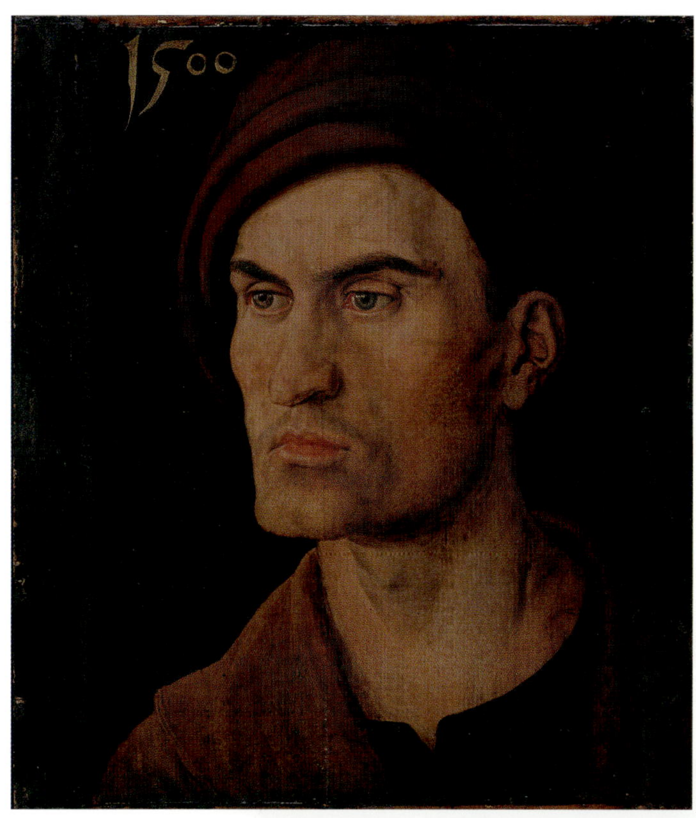

PLATE 1. Albrecht Dürer, *Portrait of a Man (Hans Dürer)*, 1500. Oil on limewood, 29 × 21 cm. Photograph courtesy of bpk, Berlin/ Bayerische Staatsgemäldesammlungen, Munich, Germany. Photograph by Alte Pinakothek. Art Resource, New York.

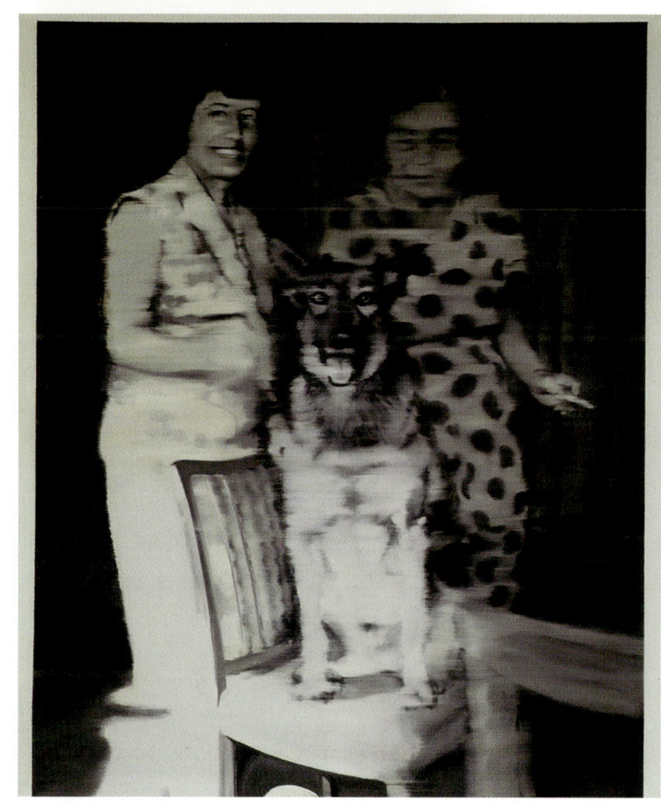

PLATE 2. Gerhard Richter, *Christa and Wolfi*, 1964. Oil on canvas, 59 × 51¼ inches (150 × 130 cm). Joseph Winterbotham Collection, 1987.276, The Art Institute of Chicago. Copyright Gerhard Richter, 2011.

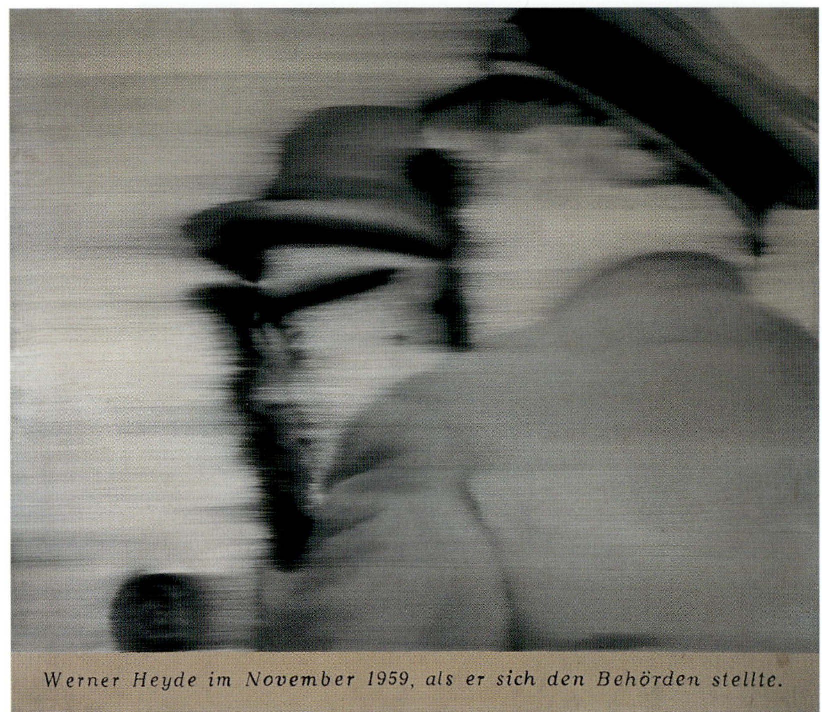

PLATE 3. Gerhard Richter, *Herr Heyde*, 1965. Acrylic on canvas, 21⅞ × 25⅝ inches (55 × 65 cm). Private collection. Copyright Gerhard Richter, 2011.

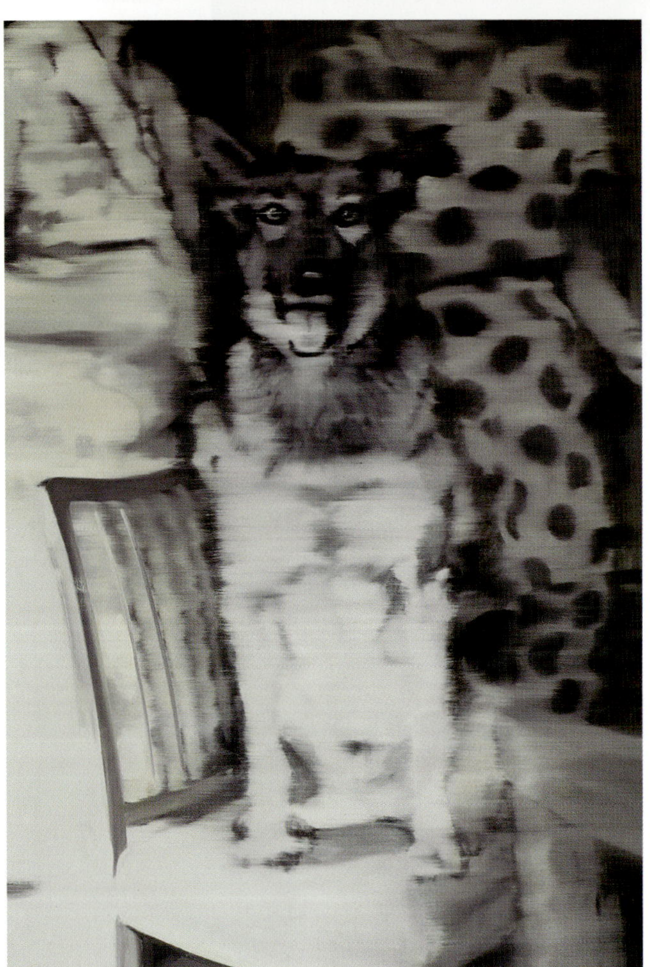

PLATE 4. Gerhard Richter, *Christa and Wolfi* (detail), 1964. Joseph Winterbotham Collection, 1987.276, The Art Institute of Chicago. Copyright Gerhard Richter, 2011.

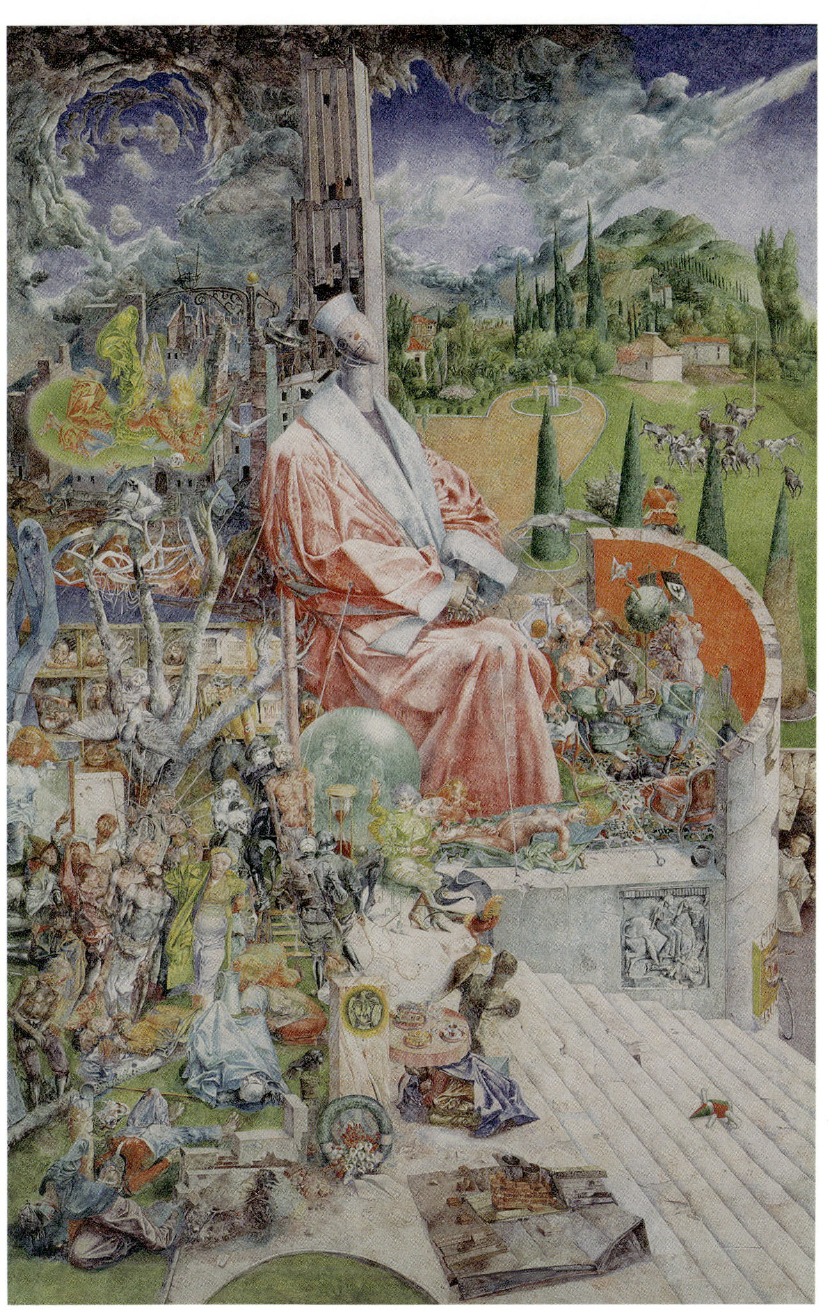

PLATE 5. Werner Tübke, *The Memoirs of the Honorable Schulze, J.D., III,* 1965. Tempera on canvas on wood, 188 × 121 cm. Photograph courtesy of bpk, Berlin/National-galerie, Staatliche Museen, Berlin. Photograph by Jorg P. Anders. Art Resource, New York. Copyright 2012 Artists Rights Society (ARS), New York/VG Bild-Kunst, Bonn.

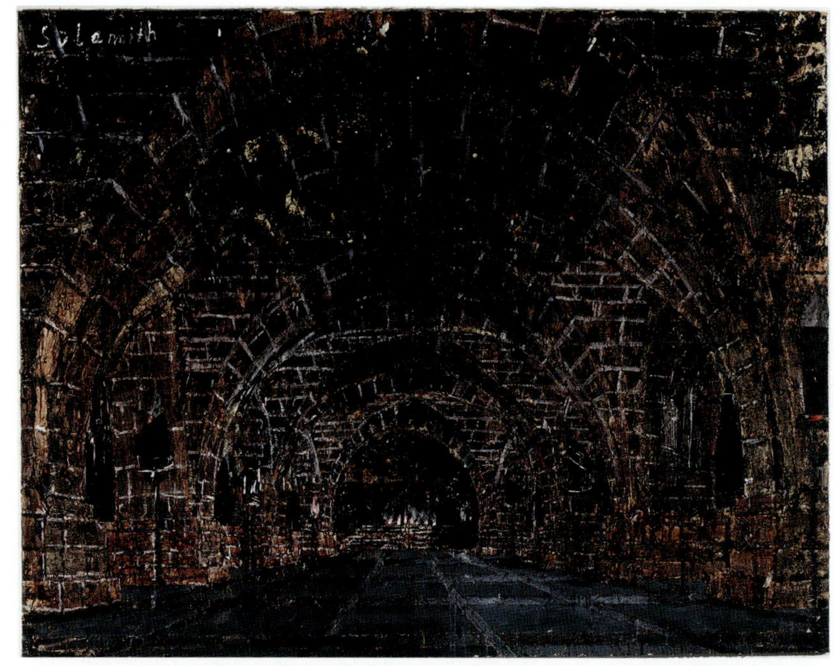

PLATE 6. Anselm Kiefer, *Sulamith*, 1983. Oil, acrylic, emulsion, shellac, and straw on canvas, with woodcut, 114³⁄₁₆ × 145¹¹⁄₁₆ inches (290 × 370 cm). Photograph courtesy of Saatchi Gallery. Copyright Anselm Kiefer.

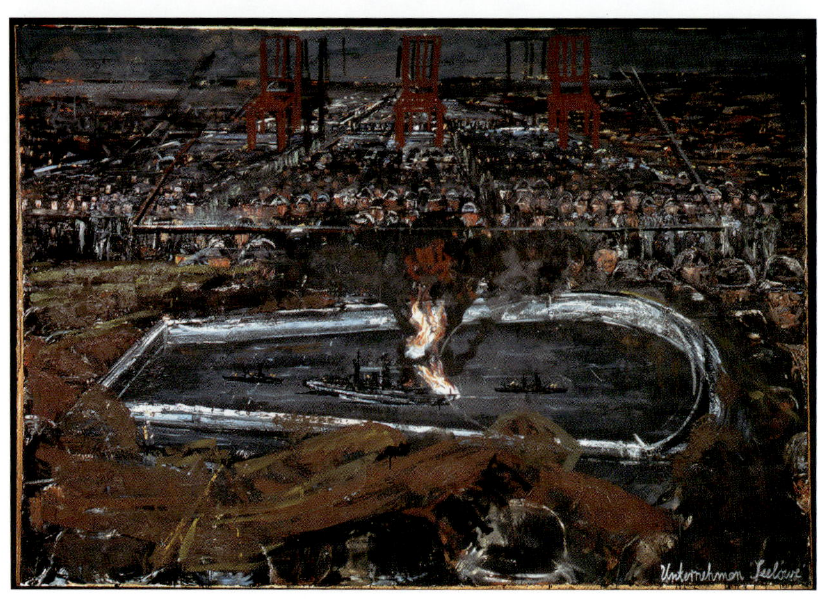

PLATE 7. Anselm Kiefer, *Operation Sea Lion I*, 1975. Oil on canvas, 86⅝ × 118⅛ inches (220 × 300 cm). Private collection. Copyright Anselm Kiefer.

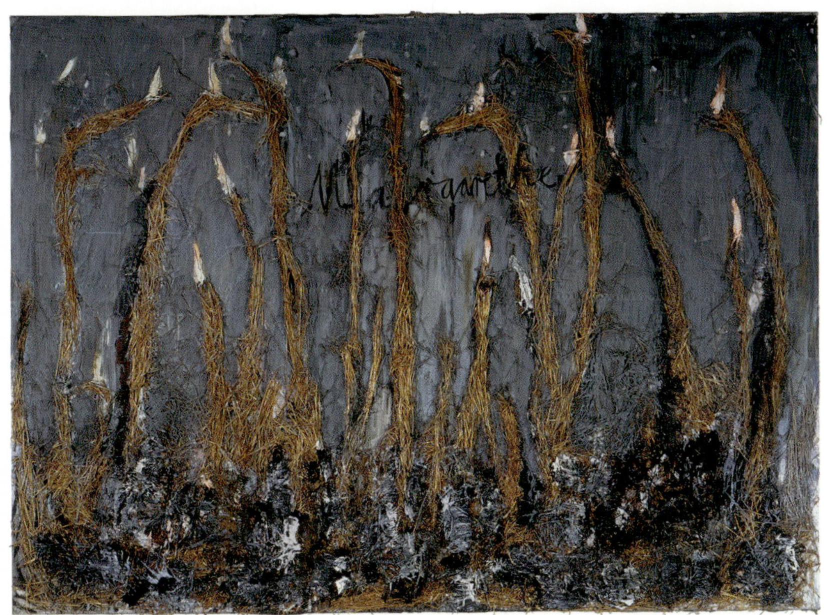

PLATE 8. Anselm Kiefer, *Margarete*, 1981. Oil and straw on canvas, 110 × 149⅝ inches (280 × 380 cm). Photograph courtesy of Saatchi Gallery. Copyright Anselm Kiefer.

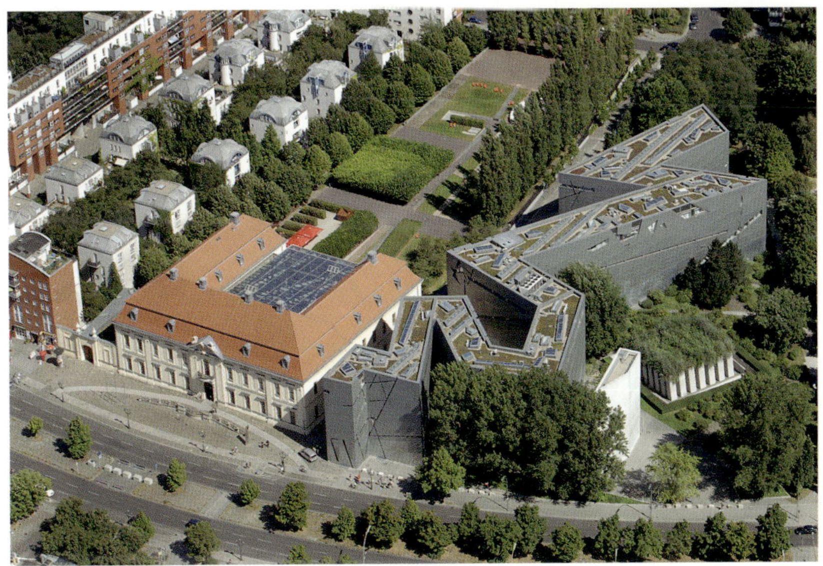

PLATE 9. Daniel Libeskind, Jewish Museum in the Berlin Municipal Museum, aerial view, Berlin, 1989–2001. Photograph copyright Guenter Schneider. Courtesy of Studio Daniel Libeskind.

PLATE 10. Daniel Libeskind, Jewish Museum in the Berlin Municipal Museum, competition entry model, Berlin, 1989. Photograph copyright Studio Daniel Libeskind.

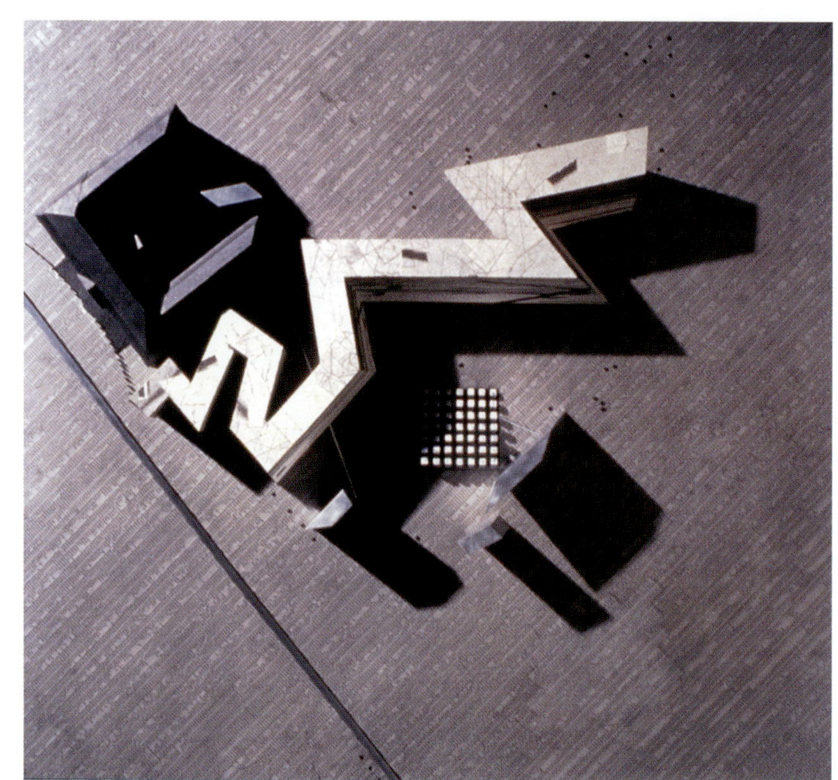

PLATE 11. Daniel Libeskind, Jewish Museum in the Berlin Municipal Museum, as built, Berlin, 1989–2001. Photograph copyright Bitter Bredt. Courtesy of Studio Daniel Libeskind.

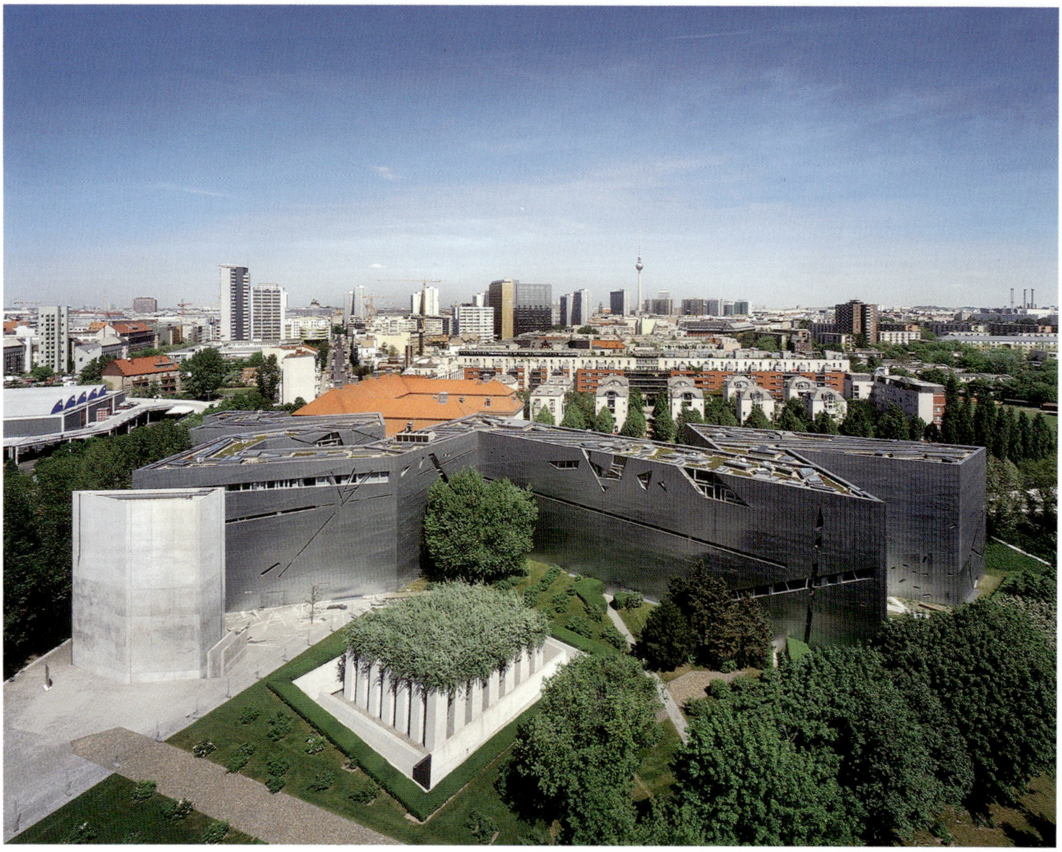

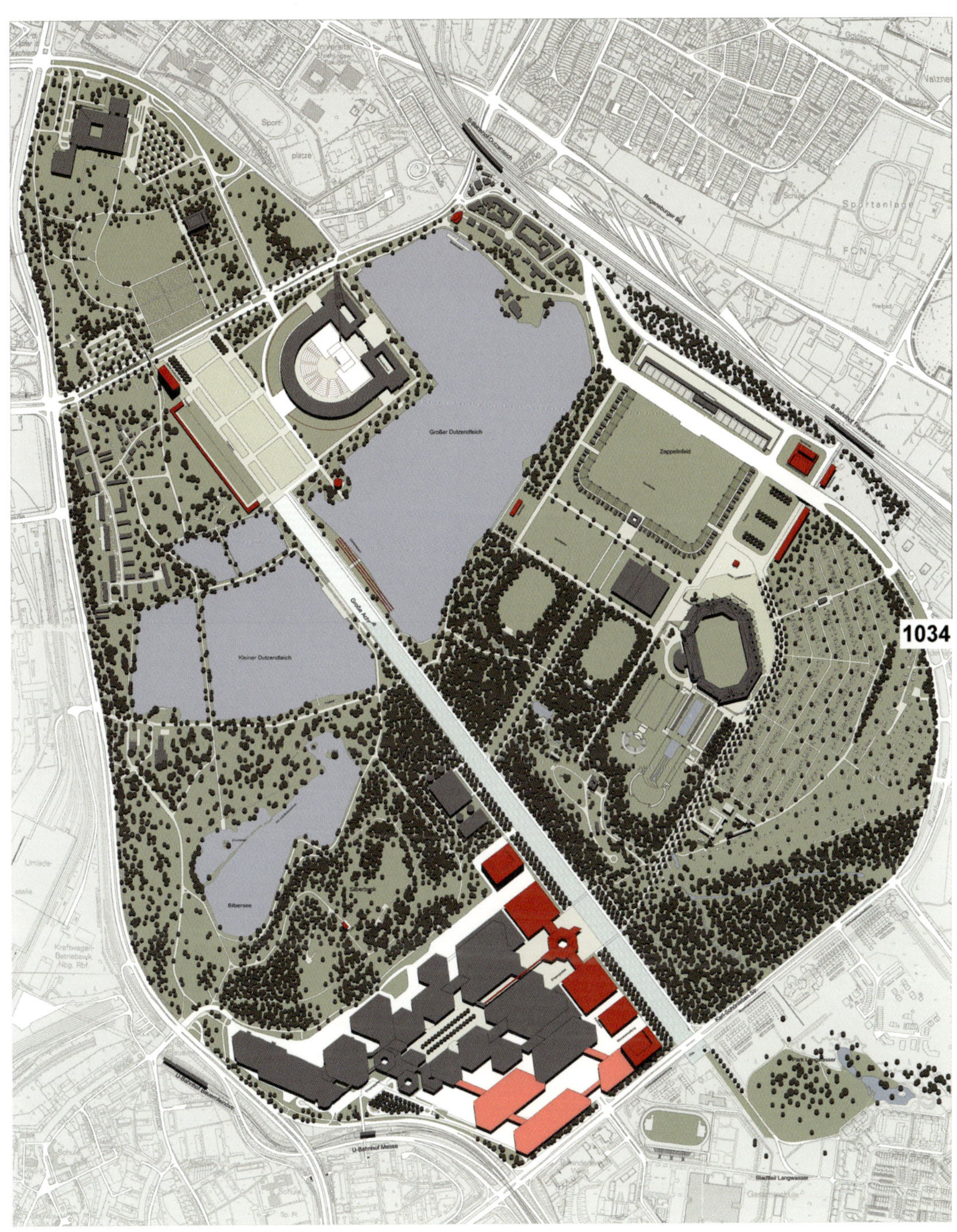

PLATE 12. Erik Meinertz and Harms Wulf,
entry for Reich Party Rally Grounds Design
Competition, second prize, Nuremberg, 2001.
Courtesy of Harms Wulf.

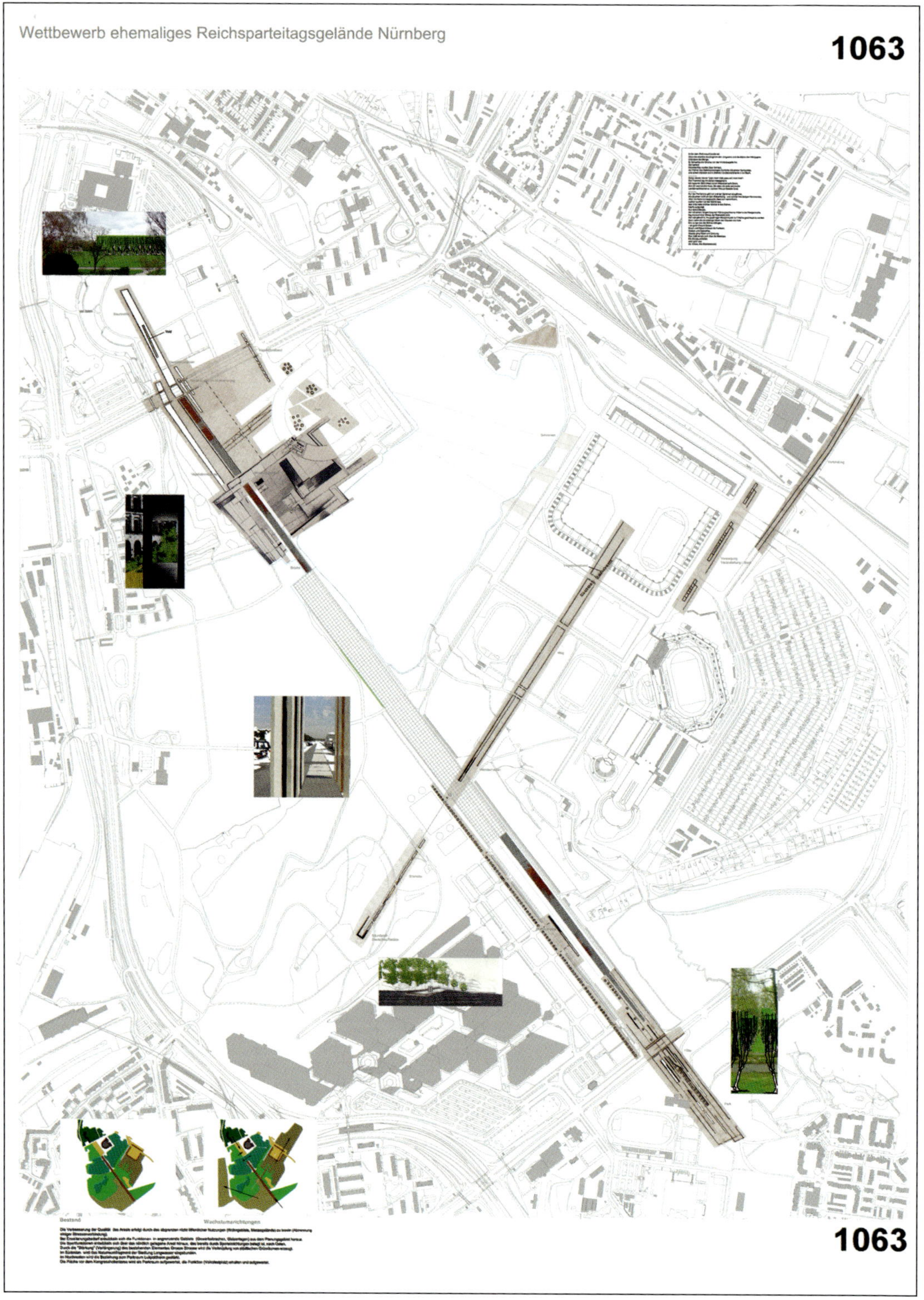

PLATE 13. Martina Erbs and Martin Stadtler, entry for Reich Party Rally Grounds Design Competition, second prize, Nuremberg, 2001. Courtesy of Martina Erbs.

construction process made the building the sole focal point of government patronage in comparison to the flurry of private construction. It thus became a natural target for ideological debates about the economic importance of culture and public construction in the moment of reunification. Certainly, after 1993, Libeskind's project was only one of many hotspots in the cultural conflicts regarding politics, architecture, and history in Berlin. That year saw the eruption of the controversy surrounding Kohl's conversion of Karl Friedrich Schinkel's Neue Wache to serve as the Central Memorial of the Federal Republic of Germany for the Victims of War and Tyranny, as well as the selection of Peter Zumthor as the architect for the Topography of Terror pavilion.[42] But before that date, Libeskind's building was the only active site, and hence it took on the singular role as the center of public and governmental debate. Further, its exceptional character due to its exuberant exterior form and the stark symbolic interior contrast of void and zigzag opened up the interpretation of the building with relative ease to other issues specifically influenced by post-wall society. These interpretations pushed the function of the building away from the original integrated exhibition strategy and obscured the physical relationships with the community so important to the IBA genesis of the plan. They also moved discussions of the building (outside the architectural press) far from the philosophical justifications Libeskind staked out for the competition design. In the initial stages of reunification up to the clear economic crisis marked by the recession of 1993, Libeskind's project needs to be understood as developing within a very particular conjunction of a variety of volatile new interests and needs, local and national. These interests included the changing political reception of the Nazi perpetrator.

The Jewish Museum and the Political Resurgence of the Nazi Perpetrator

The alterations of Libeskind's design after reunification partially limited the conceptual clarity of the original Cold War "Integrative Model" because of the economic compromises. In addition, the integration of the exterior with the neighboring structures and broader plans for West Berlin that had been so evident in the competition's genesis and defense as an expansion of IBA goals was superseded by a more abstract philosophical debate about the plan's formal origins in Jewish Berlin. That is, the balance between integration and exceptionalism, connectedness and fragmentation, began to give way as the interest in the exterior became more about its formal innovation while the organization of the interior started to become somewhat more unified. These developments in architectural form and interpretation happened simultaneously with a broader network of political and social changes, both in the capital and in the country as a whole.

In Berlin, the conflicts that influenced the museum's interpretation concentrated on one key issue that had both national and local ramifications: the rise of right-wing violence directed at German Jews, those perceived as Jewish, foreign laborers, and asylum seekers. Given that the program of the extension included the Jewish Museum as well as the obvious choice of an American Jewish architect, many press accounts and politicians had already connected the building to a partial mission of promoting ethnic identity. This mission, though, was one among many functions the extension was meant to serve. With right-wing violence, the ethnic focus became primary and integral in unanticipated ways. Right-wing electoral successes, heightening tensions concerning asylum policy in the wake of the Bosnian conflict, and the rise in foreign workers all generated extreme political heat. A variety of public and legislative initiatives of many sorts received renewed scrutiny under these conditions. It was in this context that the Jewish Museum within the Berlin Municipal Museum became a racial project.

An increase in racist violence stymied Kohl and other triumphant CDU politicians' arguments for "normalization," the idea that the reunified Germany could now be considered a normal nation free from the exceptional conditions of its compromised nation-state status that resulted from the Nazi debacle of the past. Chronologically, right-wing violence started to expand even before the wall fell in both West and East Germany. However, the public perceived it to be particularly intense in the early years after reunification, and 1991–95 saw a substantial increase in reported incidents. The attacks raised not only a massive political debate on German citizenship and immigration but also governmental discussions about National Socialist racial policies of the past and their potential resonance in the present. In addition, political parties such as the Republikaner (Republicans) were making electoral inroads in these years, further casting the specter of a right-wing insurgence over legitimate politics. Their party policy either overtly or indirectly took up nationalist and racist philosophies favored by the NSDAP. Germans did not express the fear that the past generations continued into the present; the real matter was whether Germany was seeing an entirely new population of ideologues and potentially criminal perpetrators who had found inspiration in Nazi goals. They could believably form an original and frighteningly effective strategy of political violence and electoral tactics in the present.

It is worth remembering that the process of reunification and its aftermath took place during the six-year cycle of commemorations marking the fiftieth anniversary of World War II, beginning in September 1989 and ending in May 1995, around the same time as the topping-out ceremony for the extension (May 5, 1995). In the shadow of this retrospective context, the process and aftermath of reunification led the public to debate Germany's status. Particular interest focused on whether the burden of the National Socialist past had been overcome and hence whether Germany could now claim an equal position to other nation-states in the world. Was the conclusion of World War II signaled by the final withdrawal of Allied and Soviet troops also a signal that Germany could be a nation with a productive nationalism and self-pride? As Konrad Jarausch has argued, the answer to this hotly debated question was politically divided:

> The Right generally seeks to use unification in order to escape the burden of past guilt, reduce the influx of foreigners, serve Western business interests, safeguard the existence of male privileges and promote greater international assertiveness. Conversely, the Left tries to cling to a sense of historical shame, create a multicultural society, support Eastern redistribution claims, advance affirmative action, and argue for circumspection abroad. Ironically, both sides represent different forms of traditionalism, since the former hopes to revive older national legacies, while the latter attempts to preserve the progressive heritage of [pre-reunification West Germany].[43]

With the CDU in power, Kohl and other conservative politicians in Berlin pushed the former position as a form of "normalization." They claimed that while the past needed to be mourned and remembered, reunified Germany was essentially a different state.[44] Such claims could be pursued in post-reunification moments of euphoria and national pride even while they were challenged by the economic and social disparities revealed in the process of bringing the Germanys together.

A policy of "normalization" was not monolithic or consistent, but it inflected many of the key public and private initiatives that Kohl and the CDU promoted in an attempt to reunify the country. Such assertions of a normal nation, however, occurred at the exact time as one of the strongest challenges to that very national unity in post-1989 Germany. In the initial years after the fall of the wall, politicians passionately debated who could or should be a German citizen, debates that arose in the face of the shocking rise in racist and antisemitic attacks as well as right-wing electoral victories. The analysis of this debate does not lead to an easy equation between violence and economic struggles in the east, nor were the patterns of political racism as clearly marked as has often been assumed.[45] Rather, looking at surveys, government data on racial violence, and some specifics on the political success of the extreme right gives a subtler picture of the nexus of events and beliefs. These external conditions and how they were linked to the Nazi perpetrator became crucial for internal and public debates about the developing project of the Jewish Museum.

Antisemitism and racist violence existed long before the wall fell, as we know. So, too, foreign labor had been part of German life throughout the postwar period. Foreign labor as a category could encompass the ethnic Germans escaping the developing Soviet Bloc in Eastern Europe after the war, Southern Europeans encouraged by the government in the 1960s to help with labor shortages, or the combination of workers and asylum seekers in the 1980s. Foreigners and German Jews specifically became targets in the 1980s due to particular situations. For example, in that decade, the number of asylum seekers from the loosening of borders in the Communist states of Eastern Europe rapidly increased, but also the presence of Jewish communities became visible with the memorializations surrounding the commemoration of Nazi oppression, such as the fiftieth anniversary of the November 9, 1938, pogrom. Simultaneously, new kinds of violence arose, such as attacks at soccer games on those perceived as non-German. Still, according to the FRG's Ministry of the Interior statistics, right-wing assaults on foreigners and against Jews peaked in 1982 (an election year) with a total of 2,510 incidents recorded. In 1986, this number dropped to 1,281. (Note that the state did not keep official totals on right-wing violence in the GDR, although there is evidence of the rise of some neo-Nazi affiliations within youth groups.)[46]

Right-wing violence steadily increased through reunification, briefly plateauing at around 1,850 incidents in 1989 and 1990. After that, the rise in attacks and reported incidents, including destruction of property, desecration of sites, or other kinds of violent actions against Jews and foreigners, exponentially increased, from 3,884 in 1991 to 7,684 in 1992, peaking at 10,561 incidents in 1993. During the same period, identifiable antisemitic incidents dropped from 350 in 1988 to 267 in 1989 and 208 in 1990, before rising again to 367 in 1991, 627 in 1992, 656 in 1993, and peaking at 1,366 in 1994. Hence, in the immediate period after the fall of the wall, violent incidents remained at a flat rate while antisemitic attacks actually decreased. A radical spike in the number of each ended this positive trend in 1991 after reunification had been complete. The dramatic increase in intolerance concerned many in German society, and news reports and public programming reflected this. However, the exaggerated fears expressed by the French and others in 1990 of a resurgent and even authoritarian German nationalism (such as speculations about a "Fourth Reich") remained unwarranted. The public reaction was strong and swift against this violence. Still, attacks began to increase after reunification in specific populations affected by economic destabilization. A rise in asylum seekers, the collapse of local authority, or the tactics of a resurgent right-wing political movement could all exacerbate the situation. These conditions affected particular communities in the west as well as the east. Thus, while violence increased, the fears that a new form of fascism would become a society-wide phenomenon played out more as an ideological reaction to the prospect of a unified Germany rather than as a reality even within the post-reunification rise in incidents. Violent behavior became more common, but it remained isolated and had no corresponding impact on a rise in society-wide antisemitic beliefs, as Werner Bergmann has convincingly shown.[47]

That said, two subgroups showed a marked increase in xenophobic and antisemitic attitudes: neo-Nazi adolescents and members of extreme right-wing political parties. The latter had already sparked great concern even before reunification. The right-wing political parties had long been a feature of West German society, although their influence had declined particularly in the 1970s. But the late 1980s saw renewed and surprising electoral successes, some of which continued after reunification. German public opinion expressed rising fears of another collapse of democracy into authoritarianism such as that which had accompanied the end of the Weimar Republic. Certainly, these were not Nazi groups, as attempts to re-create the NSDAP were and are illegal in Germany. But parties like the Republikaner believed in a strong nationalism, the inviolability of Germany's 1937 borders, a defense of a monolithic ethnic German culture, and a rejection particularly of liberal hand-wringing concerning the crimes of the Nazi past. Notably, neither these political parties nor most of the skinhead culture seemed to believe in the same kind of essential biological racism of Nazi ideologues like Rosenberg. Rather, post-wall racism focused less on pseudo-scientific explanations than on exclusionary tactics, aimed at ridding Germany of its "others." For right-wing groups, Jews, foreign laborers, asylum seekers (who were supposedly taking advantage of the law to steal jobs), and Muslims harmed local economies and seemed to garner a larger share of state resources. Within this view, the Nazi past could be selectively mobilized or made an implicit part of strategic politics to gather voters to their cause. The blurring of xenophobia and antisemitism effectively supported a broad policy aimed at reinforcing racialized notions of a core German culture.[48]

The year 1989 was particularly volatile in terms of right-wing political activity. In January, the Republikaner won 7.5 percent of the vote in Berlin local elections, followed in June by a surprising 7.1 percent of the votes of all West Germans for representatives to the European Parliament. During campaigning in April, party representatives advocated getting rid of the memorial at the former concentration camp at Dachau. In addition, the Ministry of the Interior banned Michael Kühnen's National Alliance (Nationale Sammlung) as a neo-Nazi organization that went against the constitutional prohibition on reviving Nazi positions. His followers would subsequently found the National List in Hamburg in March, a party that would again be banned in 1995. Also, in March, the National Democratic Party (Nationaldemokratische Partei Deutschlands, NPD) joined the city council in Frankfurt after winning 6.6 percent of the local elections. Such electoral successes even before the wall fell fueled speculation of a subsequent spread of right-wing support given the rising nationalist euphoria. Republikaner membership shot up from eighty-five hundred in 1988 to twenty-five thousand in 1989, and remained above twenty thousand through 1994. But, initially, their electoral support seemed to dwindle as they achieved only 2.1 percent in the federal elections in 1990. Its biggest success was yet to come, as the party achieved 10.9 percent in state elections for Baden-Württemberg in 1992. Most of the electoral victories of this and other right-wing parties were in western Germany, and the majority of voters were male and disproportionately young.[49]

Limited and concentrated or not, the image of electoral victory combined together both with high-profile antisemitic acts like the desecration of cemeteries and with the violence against perceived outsiders that occurred throughout Germany. The economic frustration of eastern German citizens as well as the breakdown in the official authority in specific communities led to an increase in antiforeigner sentiments overtly expressed in Hoyerswerda in September 1991, when neo-Nazis and skinheads attacked a housing unit for mostly Vietnamese and Mozambican foreign workers. Further attacks in the town led to the firebombing of other houses. In August 1992, the scene shifted to Rostock, where neo-Nazis again attacked a Vietnamese housing unit as onlookers cheered. While these were the most sensational of incidents, attacks occurred not only in the east but also in western Germany, especially Schleswig-Holstein and the Saarland. In 1991, registered attacks by right-wing extremists topped anticapitalist and antigovernment violence of the left wing for the first time since the 1960s. In 1992, seventeen victims were killed, the largest number of right-wing-affiliated deaths since the Allies and the Soviets forced the Nazis from power. This outpouring of racism (which also included a revival of antisemitism) occurred at the time in which Germany was also experiencing an influx of more than four hundred thousand Bosnian asylum seekers from the Balkan conflict. Further, the economy relied on foreign labor as 8 percent of its workforce.[50]

While it was clear that the vast majority of Germans roundly condemned such violence, politicians felt pressured to respond to the attacks and the inroads made by the Republikaners through conservative policies. As the CDU continued to state, Germany was not an immigrant land and the constitution limited citizenship even for second- or third-generation children born in the country. Those who could prove German ethnicity could also claim citizenship. Hence, politically, the CDU discussion of the attacks against perceived foreigners emphasized the failure of asylum policy and work permits rather than citizenship rights or structural racism. In fall 1992, Kohl began to try to restrict asylum with new laws in the face of right-wing pressure; while the opposition SPD initially pushed for a broader asylum policy after the attacks in Rostock, it too caved in and agreed to a stricter system in July 1993. In these debates, Kohl consistently relied on the traditional definition of German citizenship as ethnically based. Kohl countered the critical perception of a revived neo-Nazi movement by narrowing and "normalizing" the German population through restrictions in entrance and residence in the country.[51] Given these particular race-based policies and the violence on the street, the perception that contemporary Germany had made a definitive break with the past was difficult to maintain. Nevertheless, the electoral support of right-wing parties dropped considerably after the CDU passed the new asylum law.

The fear of nationalistic responses to reunification, the variable racist attitudes toward Jews and foreigners, the surprising victories in local and even national elections of the Republikaners, and the shocking right-wing violence after reunification were all factors that intersected with CDU attempts to maintain power nationally and locally in Berlin. Over all of this hung the shadow of the Nazi perpetrator that citizens and politicians alike could marshal to highlight the dangers of any moment in the development of these nationalist, antisemitic, or xenophobic events. This nexus of conditions and political actors formed a network of associations also mobilized to explain the necessity of Libeskind's museum proposal. Its formal singularity, the exceptional status as a public project, and the diminishing context of the IBA helped make the building an easy target for ideological projection. Internal developments within the museum contributed as well. By the laying of the foundation stone in 1992, the combined weight of these actions and conditions would strengthen the identity of the extension to the Berlin Municipal Museum as a purely "Jewish" museum. This exclusive ethnic association would subsequently become a reality in spite of the "Integrative Model" concept and its importance to the architectural design of the space.

Since the curatorial concept and space recognized that a variety of ethnic groups had always constituted Germany's citizenry, the political promotion of "normalization" as well as the rise in racist attacks rubbed against the basic idea of the museum. Architecturally, Libeskind's plan acknowledged the historical and ongoing conflict over ethnic diversity in a German nation by having intersecting historical developments and social groups marked in the experience of the zigzag plan around the void. This built-in diversity was, essentially, the opposite of Kohl's assertion in asylum law of the traditional definition of citizenship as a single group defined by blood. Given these contradictions, not only did the distinctive form and public status isolate the Jewish Museum in the Berlin Municipal Museum from private initiatives. Politicians and the press also increasingly interpreted it as an isolated monument that promoted a specific and singular ethnic history that responded to contemporary politics, both in Berlin and nationally. By being exceptional, it could function as a focal point for questions of ethnicity that could be historically and physically set apart from contemporary German society. In both plan and use, the building diverged from the original integrative model and moved toward a new function whereby the lessons of the recent Nazi perpetrator's victimization of the Jewish community resonated abstractly with contemporary problems. Libeskind's design in many ways became Omi and Winant's racial project, a nexus of intersecting historical factors in which definitions of race and ethnicity are both contested and constituted through public debate and government policy. Through this process, racial projects attempt to contain inherent social instability. Or, as they put it, "Racial projects connect what race *means* in a particular discursive practice and the ways in which both social structures and everyday experiences are racially *organized*, based upon that meaning."[52] The more the museum became an exceptional tool to be wielded against contemporary politics and racism, the more particular interests could associate the building with a specific ethnic agenda. It became exclusively a Jewish museum.

Much of this rather sudden shift of the museum to an ethnic-specific institution involved the internal development of all the Berlin museums as they became embroiled in Berlin politics as well as the external engagement of politicians with the contemporary fears of racism. Almost as soon as the wall had fallen, such an intersection of overlapping incidents occurred. For example, with design work beginning, the museum wanted to produce a small run of a thousand books documenting Libeskind's winning proposal, a standard practice for public competitions. The book would follow the opening exhibition of designs on December 7, 1989, one of several measures planned to get the word out about the museum extension. As the book came back from the publisher, though, an unknown member of the production team had put a cross after Libeskind's name when he was mentioned in the foreword by Senator for Cultural Affairs Anke Martiny. The cross seemed to indicate that he was deceased. The act led to intense debates and fears among the Berlin Municipal Museum staff that the extension had already become a target of antisemitism. Bothe noted, for example, in a letter to Bendt discussing some of the debates that up to that point no antisemitic acts had occurred at the museum since he had taken over. He favored letting the situation fade, as the public had not reacted in outrage, to avoid giving the person who had done it more attention. Bendt preferred a more overt response.[53] In addition, museum staff later in the year called a series of meetings particularly concerned with security in the new building, referencing the "growing antisemitic tendencies and the constant risk based on political motives."[54]

While internal discussions focused on a possible new antisemitism, Bausenator Nagel dealt with the public and political implications of the presumably racist act. In announcing the Senate's approval of the plans in January 1990, for example, Nagel informed the press that he and the other senators had thought that an official resolution to approve the plans had been needed, although it was not required by law. He told journalists that the Senate "wanted with the resolution to give an answer 'in public' to the resurgent right-wing tendencies" as well as confirm the museum's status as an exception to the financial savings rules.[55] Nagel repeated his emphasis on the Senate's resolution after the cross in the documentation had come to light in February. In this case, he claimed not only that the Senate was responding to the growth of the ultra right wing but also to neofascism. On February 22, he apologized publicly for the printing mistake and stated that he was deeply sorry. He was especially disturbed as he had just returned from a visit to Babi Yar where he had contemplated the death of thousands of Jews at the hands of "German fascism."[56] Nagel's public pronouncements and the Senate votes mark the ways in which the museum extension could function ideologically as a response to contemporary fears of right-wing political expansion and violence. As we have seen, these comments come at a time when antisemitic attacks had actually gone down but fears of a political resurgence of barely veiled Nazi policies were fueled by the pre-wall electoral victories of the Republikaner and other right-wing parties. In this sense, Nagel's use of the general term "fascism" to describe the political movement to the right was quite specific. The term unified his reflections on the destructive policies of Hitler's regime as well as linked the Nazi agents to their contemporary German political counterparts. At this stage, certainly, no one could predict how far the combination of German nationalism after the wall would push both reunification and a strengthened right wing.

As federal funding to Berlin became threatened, the economic pressures on the city, as well as the institutional situation of the seemingly redundant cultural institutions on each side of the former wall, weighed more heavily on staff discussions and governmental debates. Still, it appeared that voters eager to reject the perilous path of the late Weimar Republic were taking back most right-wing electoral victories. But violence against foreigners and attacks on Jewish property and persons were increasing, even if only isolated groups in specific locales perpetrated the acts. Against this backdrop, the Senate debated in July 1991 whether it should cut off funding to the museum project, given the huge needs for investment in, among others, infrastructure and housing now that the city had been chosen to be the capital. The CDU party whip, Klaus Landowsky, led this resolution and defended the decision. He noted as well the need for the city to save in order to have sufficient financial means to make its Olympic bid for the year 2000. Already by this time, Mayor Diepgen and even members of the Jewish Community had wondered aloud whether the collection might best be housed in an already standing structure such as the restored Ephraim Palais.[57] The museum extension seemed on the brink of cancellation.

The potential end to Libeskind's building proved to be a catalyst for the largest public debate surrounding the completion of the design. Defenders mounted the barricades in order to preserve the building and its unique funded status. In the process, the association of the building with an exclusively ethnic project became more pronounced as did the manner in which participants in the debate invoked the Nazi past to underscore the need for the museum in the present. Two parties proved crucial in defense of the museum extension: on the one hand, Bothe and Bendt from the museum; and on the other, Nina Libeskind, the manager of the project. The latter in particular was formidable, as Daniel Libeskind has stated. She mobilized the political support and international outcry necessary to push the Berlin Senate to maintain the building project. On the other side, Bothe worked the local constituencies as well as the network of Jewish museums to garner their support. Meanwhile, Nina Libeskind, who comes from a prominent family of socialist politicians in Canada, used these and other connections to rally an array of well-known supporters. To give some sense of the range of responses organized, letters were sent in protest to Mayor Diepgen from, among many others, Edward van Voolen, curator of the Joods Historisch Museum, Amsterdam; Andreas Huyssen, professor of German at Columbia University; Jack Lang, French minister of culture; Teddy Kollek, mayor of Jerusalem; former chancellor and former West Berlin mayor Willy Brandt; and Heinz Galinski, head of the Jewish Community in Berlin.[58]

But it was not merely prominent personalities who were mobilized to save the building. Rather, the press also highlighted the campaign and put the heat on the Berlin Senate in light of new violence and the circumstances of the city's application for the 2000 Olympics. In the letters of support, writers often mentioned the contemporary situation of the renewed anti-semitism as well as the rise of racist violence. Specifically, writers referenced the large neo-Nazi demonstration that took place on June 15 and involved followers of the murdered right-wing extremist Rainer Sonntag. In the middle of August, skinheads also desecrated the Jewish cemetery in Dresden.[59] But a more direct perceived connection to the Nazi past overshadowed even these incidents of violence in the letters and particularly in the press accounts. Reporters and letter writers consistently came back to the extremely problematic association of the decision to cut funding with the possible Olympic bid; unlike the right-wing violence, the Berlin senators had direct responsibility over this decision. In article after article, commentators pointed to the irony of the last Olympics in Berlin, those held in 1936 under Hitler's sponsorship. For them, the CDU's prioritization of the Olympic bid over the extension to the Berlin Municipal Museum showed a willingness to repeat the past by forgetting its lessons, caving in to potential financial and political gain by ignoring the responsibilities of education. This mixture of contemporary shame and right-wing violence, and especially the parallels with the past Berlin Olympics, placed the museum at the heart of post-reunification economic debates. The local CDU attempted to promote the new capital in the face of cuts in federal subsidies and the national party's desire to project a normalized nation-state. At this moment, as the senators and museum officials variably employed these factors to defend the building project or explain its cut in funding, the description of the building became completely unmoored from its official title as the Jewish Museum in the Berlin Municipal Museum. Instead, headline after headline repeated the phrase "Jewish Museum" or "Jewish Wing" (as the *New York Times* called it). Press accounts emphasized the ethnic orientation of the building. Journalists did not find explaining the integrative model a priority; rather, the overriding focus of the articles became saving the building as a Jewish building (which was, of course, only partially true) in the heart of contemporary Berlin. As Libeskind himself records in his response to Mayor Diepgen, "I came to build the Jewish Museum, and that's what I am going to do."[60] Within the museum administration, the integrative model concept would live on for several years. But other factors would assert a greater influence: the political landscape of the post-reunification period, the frequent reminders of racist violence, and the volatile political economy of public works in Berlin (as it was cast against the rapid successes of the private building economy). Faced with these conditions, the project took on further urgency as an ethnic project meant to respond to the criminal failures of the German Nazi past, to counteract a revived group of perpetrators, and to become the moral voice of the new Germany of the future.

In the inevitable Berlin Senate debate reconsidering its budget, senators weighed these positions. Landowsky maintained that there was a serious financial problem and the extension should be delayed at least until the late 1990s, while the senator for cultural affairs, Ulrich Roloff-Momin (SPD), argued that a different budget solution must be found. The Greens/Bundnis 90 talked about historical responsibility, while the left-wing PDS (Partei des Demokratischen Sozialismus [Party of Democratic Socialism]) hammered home the scandal of the hidden nationalism of reunification and the concomitant "growing radical right tendencies" of CDU political commentary.[61] Faced with the popular outcry and the letter-writing campaign, the CDU and the Senate finally reversed its decision at the end of August, approving once again work on the museum extension, with the compromise that construction would start only in 1992, slightly later than planned. They formalized this decision by agreeing to a proposal from the minority representatives from the local Greens/Bundnis 90. Roloff-Momin reversed the austerity measures for this specific project by the end of September 1991. Given this heightened drama, the Libeskind project became further isolated as an exceptional public work within the developing financial crisis of reunification. Its ethnic dimensions were also clearly overwhelming considerations for the public and political debate.[62]

The integrative model, though, remained viable. The museum produced another catalog in 1992 to accompany an exhibition of Libeskind's designs in tandem with the laying of the foundation stone on November 9. In the essays, the integrative model was still very much intact, particularly in the eloquent description of its complexity in a long essay by Bothe. As he put it, "The main exhibition rooms cannot be granted spatial sequence in a conventional fashion, as otherwise the 'voids' would lose their significance to the visitor and would be reduced to the status of dividing walls. The presentation in the exhibition halls [e.g., of the fashion and theater collections] must develop independently from the 'voids' to a large extent."[63] Notably, Bothe, like Mayor Diepgen and Senator Nagel in their introductions, refers only obliquely to the moral function of the museum as a response to contemporary intolerance while emphasizing instead the support of the city in spite of the difficult financial times. Conversely, Vera Bendt, the Jewish Museum department's curator, made the contemporary relevance of the original plan of the museum more explicit in terms of its comparative and integrative model: "To live with the many, the others, the strangers is no longer an emotive question of tolerance but one of survival in Europe at the end of the twentieth century. The solution is integration alongside one another, not supremacy or subordination to the demands of a powerful elite."[64] Her comments represent the idea of the museum as a sign of hope, a building in which the past and present continue to be healed by the recognition of both accomplishments and failures. The museum emphasized her position further in the brochure for the topping-out ceremony from May 1995, in which the museum was mentioned as a corrective to a new rise in antisemitism.[65] Still, even before the laying of the foundation stone in 1992, its contemporary relevance and its symbolic isolation within the ongoing politics of Germany and political economy of Berlin seemed sealed.

In spite of the intensive efforts of the museum staff to maintain the integrative model, by 1995, it collapsed with the arrival of the new chief curator, Amnon Barzel. Barzel argued that the layout for the building was not as fixed as previously assumed. He submitted his own ambitious plan for the room designs that separated more clearly the Jewish history from that of Berlin in general. Barzel planned to push the museum in the direction of an ethnic focus rather than a social history of the Jewish Community integrated with the rest of Berlin. His idea met with hefty criticism from within the staff of the Berlin Municipal Museum itself. The city released him from his position in 1998 and appointed Michael Blumenthal in his place.[66] Although Barzel was dismissed, ultimately the space of the museum became more and more congruent with his plans. Press reports and politicians maintained their 1991 perception that the extension was the Jewish Museum itself. They did not recognize the integrative concept in which the Jewish Museum was the ground floor of a larger and historically inclusive complex. Ideologically, the building continued to be mobilized as a bulwark against the rising tide of violence and harassment of foreigners, events that were either implicitly or explicitly consistently tied to the actions of former Nazi perpetrators. Subsequently, Peter Eisenman's Memorial to the Murdered Jews of Europe also functioned in this capacity after officials announced the first competition for the memorial's design in April 1994. For the museum, curatorial planning ultimately followed suit, resulting in the exhibition filling the entire museum with two thousand years of Jewish history that opened on September 20, 2001.[67] The point of the exhibition is clearly to relate this long history with German history. But, I would argue, the exhibition also embodies the culmination of the ethnic project in which public and official debates turned the museum itself away from its original plan as social history toward a focused and exceptional emphasis on ethnic history. The installation of photos, artifacts, and texts creates a consistent and unbroken historical narrative in direct conflict with the concept of the void and the question of fragmentation at the heart of the original proposal. Such a transformation process began during the early 1990s in the heat and conditions of reunification as a result of much internal and public debate. This shift also significantly changed the meaning of the design of the building, a Cold War project that had different goals and conditions.

Conclusion

The Jewish Museum within the Berlin Municipal Museum, like any public institution, is continuing to consolidate its public significance and its political function. Still, attending to the changes in planning objectives that resulted from reunification created a radically different context for the development and interpretation of the built environment of which Libeskind's design is a part. In the early days after reunification, we can identify an important isolation of the building and its intersection with contemporary political debates. Again, this building developed, in many ways, as a Cold War building. Yet its original Cold War function is naturally no longer necessary. Some of the influential factors that led to the rejection of the integrative model and the perception of the entire building as a Jewish museum included the internal needs of the Berlin Municipal Museum departments; the distribution of public resources; and the high-profile status the building extension took on in contrast to the private development schemes supported by the Berlin government. In addition, though, these specific conditions linked with the highly charged discussion of ethnicity in contemporary Germany, a discussion that always and by necessity went back to the National Socialist perpetrators of the past. Such a connecting project was a strategic goal of the neo-Nazi and right-wing political movements (even if they did not share the same biological concepts of antisemitism as their predecessors). But other politicians and cultural bureaucrats also described this possible connection as a fear articulated in their attempts to create an appropriate response to violence and extremist electoral successes. This context helps us evaluate the earlier planning and curatorial decisions that would result in the current structure and exhibition.

More broadly, we can see the Libeskind design and its manipulation as the latest manifestation of how the shifting sands of the political interpretation of the Nazi perpetrator further clarify postwar artistic and architectural choices, particularly in moments of intense debate and social upheaval. The conditions and events of 1989–92 set the building apart and, concomitantly, increased its symbolic importance. At times, its partial ethnic specificity stood in for a more complicated response to the fragmented but clearly present development of right-wing racist violence. Hence, the part of the project that was specifically ethnic—the Jewish Museum department on the basement floor of the plan—increasingly became recognized and acknowledged as the sole purpose of the building. This racialization of architecture and its function is even now an unstable and uneven process. At times different conditions and variable audiences make use of buildings just as definitions of race constantly shift as they are in need of being reasserted. The neo-Nazis of today are not the party members and perpetrators of Hitler's years. But attending to how contemporaries in post-reunification Berlin linked these two disparate moments helps clarify some of the instability of political debate at the end of the Cold War and after. Given this instability, state and local interests could mobilize the specific function of the museum extension and, at times, use the project to confront the contemporary resonance of the Nazi perpetrator. From there, the assumption that the building was solely about ethnicity was but a small step.

5 THE NUREMBERG PARTY RALLY GROUNDS AND LOCAL POLITICS
THE HISTORICIZED PERPETRATOR

By the end of the Weimar Republic, Nuremberg had already become a popular site for the rallies of the faithful of the National Socialist German Workers Party. Almost as soon as Hitler came to power, he chose the location as the permanent home of the annual rallies and began his plans for the monumental architecture that would famously frame these events. Throughout the mid-1930s into the early years of war, work continued on the architecture and urban plan, coordinated by Albert Speer. By war's end, the Reich Party Rally Grounds remained as the largest architectural remnant of the monumental state building of Nazi Germany (Figure 5.1). Approximately two kilometers wide and three kilometers long, the postwar site maintains the massive scale that was so much an integral part of the architectural and urban projects favored by Hitler and his architect, Speer. From the moment the war ended to the present day, this architectural complex has served as the backdrop for contemplating the propaganda of the Nazi past and its seductive effect. In response to this past, city officials and private interests have dramatically altered much of the landscape and added several new buildings to the site. Still, the Reich Party Rally Grounds have indelibly marked Nuremberg as the place where Nazi perpetrators were initially made, an association that continues today.[1]

An analysis of the political reception of the rally grounds indicates the long shadow of the Nazi perpetrator that hangs over German art in most of the twentieth century. As has been shown in these pages, postwar artists, architects, and audiences interested themselves in the shifting definition of who that perpetrator was and how he or she related to contemporary conservative politics in particular. In spite of Nuremberg's midsize population

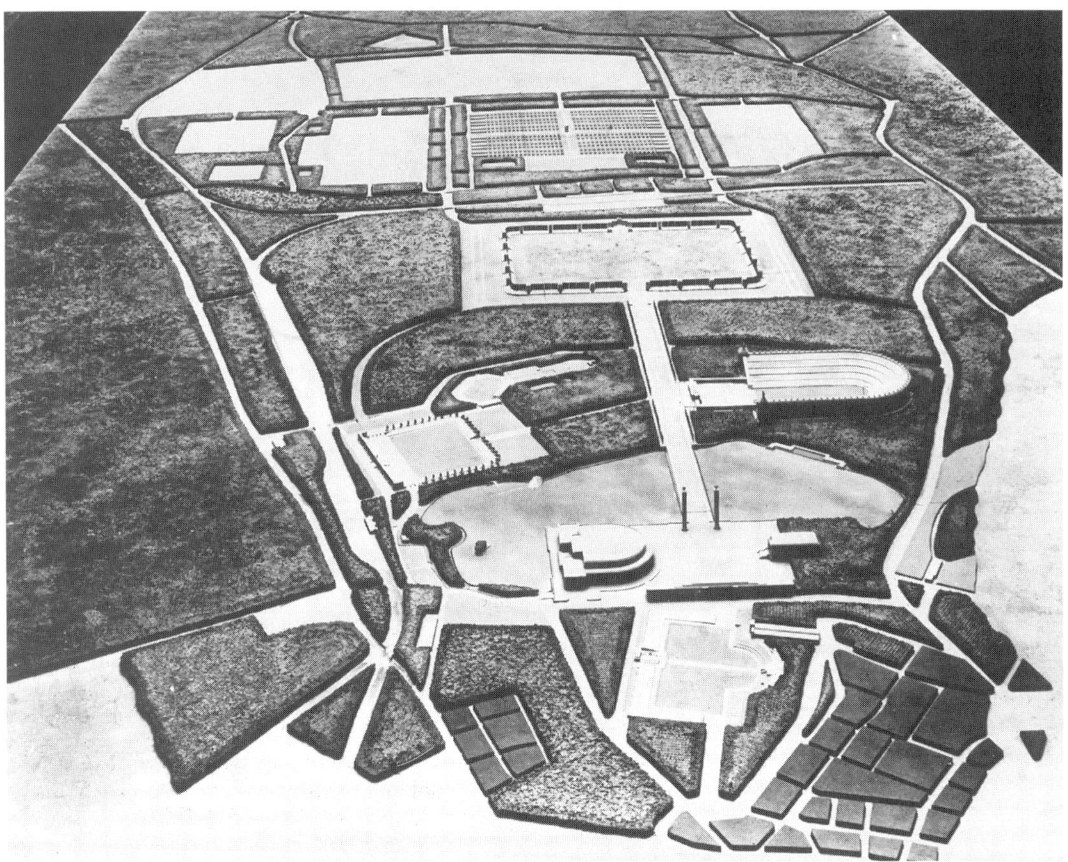

FIGURE 5.1. Albert Speer, Plan for the Reich Party Rally Grounds, Nuremberg, 1937. Photograph A76-RF-79-F1-17. Courtesy of Stadtarchiv Nürnberg.

and its secondary status to Munich, the capital of Bavaria, few cities other than possibly Berlin are more firmly fixed in the public consciousness as being so directly associated with Hitler, his policies, and his followers.[2] Whereas the other chapters of this book have focused on relatively discrete synchronic periods of debate, in the following, I wish to analyze changes to the built environment of the rally grounds diachronically. How one site architecturally transformed throughout the entire postwar period highlights the complex dynamics of ignoring or engaging the criminal past over time. Further, the brief and surprising rise in the 1990s of a conservative coalition in the city government led to a new way of thinking about the relationship of the present with the Nazi perpetrator. This new conception of the past projected an opposition between current Nuremberg residents and former perpetrators, a position strangely analogous to the general public attitude in the immediate postwar era.

Tracing the changes to the Reich Party Rally Grounds entails attention not only to alterations of the major National Socialist remnants but also new additions to the site, as well as housing estates and other vernacular structures that have received little scholarly attention. Such architectural additions shared thoroughly accepted aesthetic conventions with contemporaneous examples of West German design. But did the architects, officials, or the general public respond to these seemingly common design decisions differently because of the politically charged nature of their location and the historical built environment that surrounded them?[3] However much their Modernist gestures turned their back on Speer's neoclassicism, private and governmental decisions about the site still necessitated the recognition of the political significance of the Nazi past as a massive and unavoidable presence.

A more materially grounded account of the impact of Nuremberg's political and architectural past points to the general relevance of *Vergangenheitsbewältigung* (coming to terms with the past), a term historians have thoroughly discussed over the past several decades.[4] Still, the specific context of Nuremberg's past meant that Nazi history here had a particular impact on how citizens and officials used and interpreted the architectural remnants distinct from national trends, especially after reunification. In Nuremberg, a public debate emerged about the Rally Grounds that differed from more famous cases, such as Peter Eisenman's Memorial to the Murdered Jews of Europe (2004) in Berlin. Whereas Eisenman's design and its construction became a flashpoint of conflict, the post-reunification history of the Party Rally Grounds shows an unexpected degree of local political consensus during the same period. Both the conservative Christian Social Union (CSU) and the liberal Social Democratic Party (SPD) approached the problem of the Nazi monument with pragmatism, particularly through the 1990s with the upcoming 2006 World Cup soccer championship on the horizon (Nuremberg served as one of the host cities). Different politicians and party position papers still emphasized contrasting opinions, interpretations, and policies. However, a striking consensus politics developed within the Nuremberg city council (Stadtrat) that contrasts sharply with other high-profile centers such as Berlin and other examples highlighted in this book.[5] Ironically, the monumental scale of the site, a fundamental formal characteristic favored by Speer and Hitler, helped subsume the plurality of political views within an elastic practice of use. Hence, since the period of contentious debate over the perpetrators and the past in the 1980s and 1990s has faded away, we need to question the appropriateness of the term *Vergangenheitsbewältigung*. In post-reunification Nuremberg, the historical dynamic it is meant to describe no longer corresponds to a more analytic account of events on the ground.

I am not arguing that local constituencies have actually succeeded in coming to terms with the past because of consensus politics nor that they now ignore all influence of National Socialist perpetrators on their decisions. Rather, in Nuremberg, social and political groups have rejected the struggle inherent in *Vergangenheitsbewältigung* as the center of their attempts to deal with the past. They have embraced instead what we might characterize as a laissez-faire historicism that foregrounds other political economic concerns and allows for relative agreement on the preservation of the site. This approach is based on many often contradictory factors, such as the dying out of the wartime generation; the ability of conservatives to incorporate commemoration of the Nazi past into their politics; the interest of liberal politicians in getting beyond the generational politics of the 1960s; the acceptance of National Socialist architecture as part of the preservation landscape; and the increase in tourist interest in Nazi sites. Not surprisingly, a laissez-faire historicism that allows many perspectives to be incorporated occurs in a location where the ideological and symbolic debates are less loaded than in Berlin—the periphery distinctly leads the center. An interrogation of the postwar use of the Reich Party Rally Grounds at Nuremberg highlights a new regional variability to the political instrumentalization of the Nazi past. In the final instance, the relationship here of the built environment to a fading understanding of the perpetrator's crimes also parallels the perception of the relative disconnect of those crimes from contemporary conservative politics.[6]

From the Propaganda Spectacles of the Nazi Period to the Economic Goals of the "Miracle Years"

The site of the future Reich Party Rally Grounds along the waters of the Dutzendteich had great significance to the people and city of Nuremberg well before the Nazi era. In the early nineteenth century, citizens used the area around the water as the major park for the city, and boating, ice-skating, or promenading kept the location well populated. With the Bavarian Jubilee Exhibition of 1906, the city more formally organized the lands and established the landscaped area of the Luitpoldhain. The exhibition proved to be a huge success with over 2.5 million visitors celebrating the strength of Nuremberg as the largest industrial city in Bavaria. In 1930, the local government dedicated a war memorial (designed by Fritz Mayer) (Figure 5.2) in the Luitpoldhain to commemorate the World War I dead. Even before Hitler came to power, citizens had firmly established the function of the site for economic, recreational, and memorializing purposes.[7]

Construction on the site during the Nazi period was dramatic after Hitler chose Nuremberg as the permanent location for the Reich Party Rally Grounds. Between 1934 and 1937, Albert Speer completed the

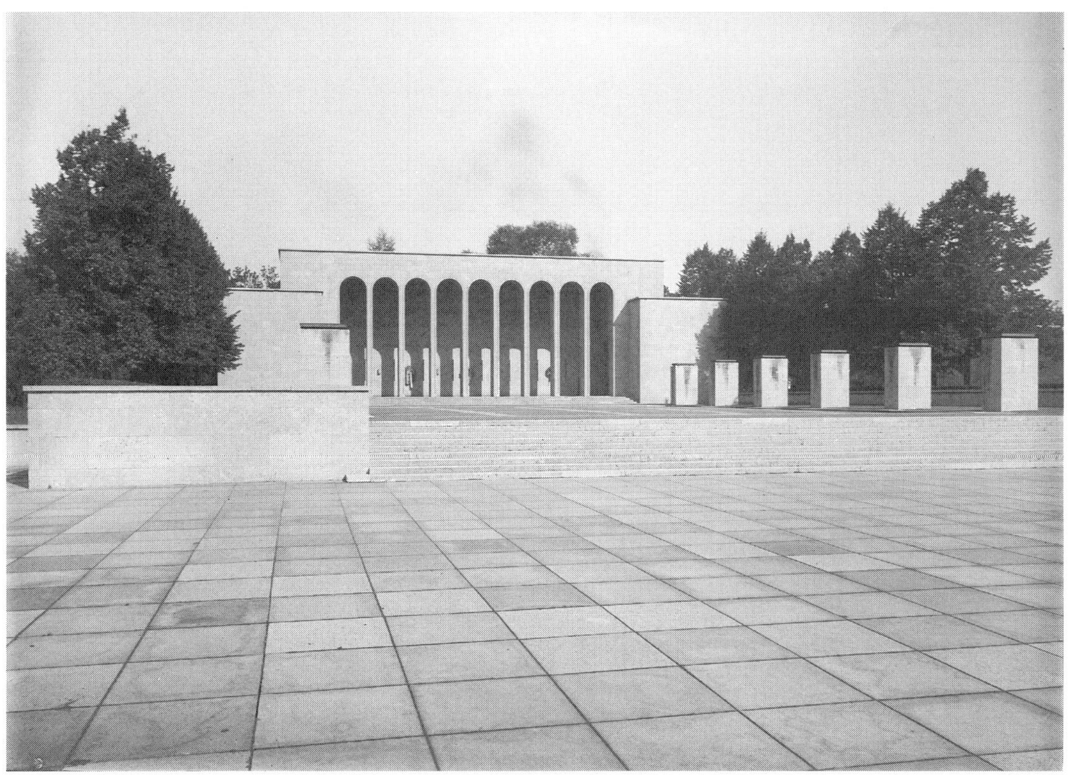

comprehensive plan as well as the design of all of the new buildings with
the exception of Ludwig and Franz Ruff's Kongresshalle (Congress Hall)
(Figure 5.3). The program followed the basic formal layout and ideological
projection Hitler favored in all the major state- and party-sponsored projects.
In terms of planning, Speer unified the buildings through the consistency
of materials (in this case, stone), a shared monumental scale, symmetry, and
a stripped-down neoclassicism, all arranged along the central axis of the
Grosse Strasse (Figure 5.4). Ideologically, the buildings combined elements
of various classical architectural traditions, which could be used to support both racial claims of the supposed Aryan connection of Germans to
ancient Greeks as well as interpretations of Germany as the new Roman
Empire. The buildings served as the backdrop for the announcement of key
National Socialist policies such as the Nuremberg Racial Laws in 1935 and
the Four-Year Plan in 1936. Combined with Hitler's keen interest in architecture, the development of the Rally Grounds formed a continuum with
the political and ideological goals of the state. As such, local and national
administrators privileged its construction well into the war. By 1942, however, the collecting of stone and work on various buildings on the site had
predominantly stopped.[8]

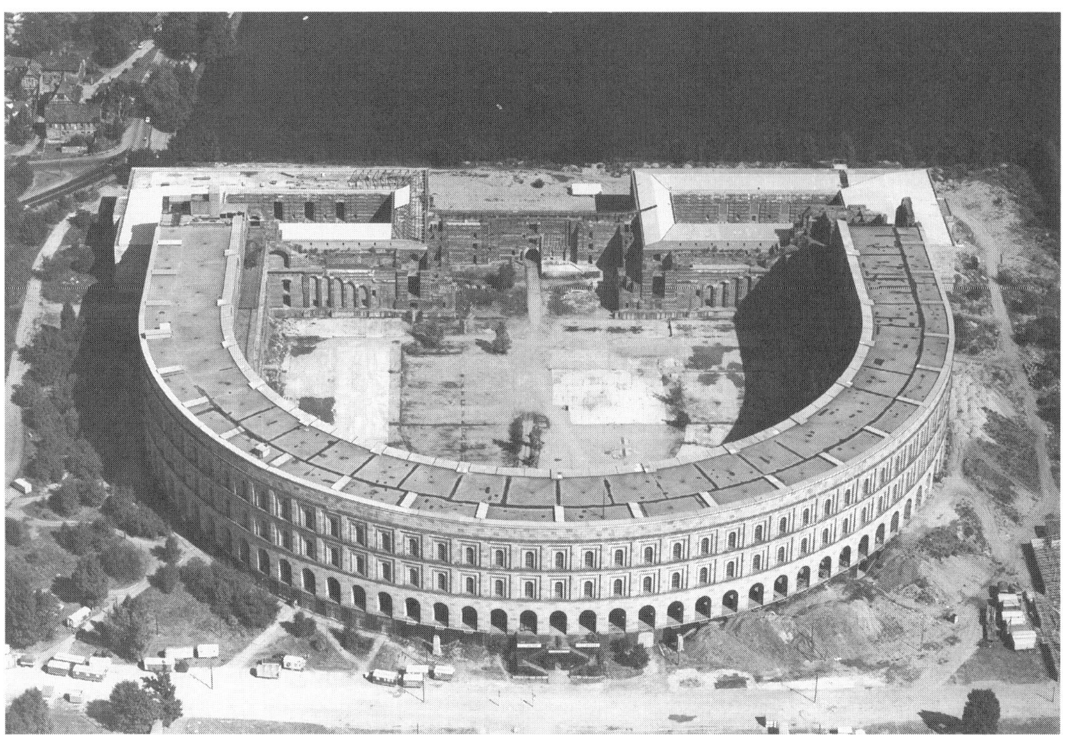

FIGURE 5.3. Franz and Ludwig Ruff, Kongresshalle, Nuremberg, 1935. Copyright Zentralinstitut für Kunstgeschichte, Photothek, Th 183689.

While construction on the monumental buildings had ceased, other changes to the site would have lasting consequences for postwar uses and construction. In addition to the monumental buildings of the grounds, the area called Langwasser south of the Märzfeld (March Field) served as a large camping site for SA (Sturmabteilung, Storm Troopers) and Hitler Youth visitors to the rallies, and during the war it was transformed into a prisoner of war camp (Stalag XIII and Oflag 73). Military authorities reemployed the basic streets laid out for the youth and Storm Troopers' camp, which had some infrastructure for water, sewage, and electricity. Here they built a large barracks complex to house as many as thirty thousand inmates at a time. The first prisoners were Polish, and after the Germans opened the Western Front, thousands more followed, including many French and Belgians. Soviet soldiers and Serbs came with the beginning of the eastern campaign, and Soviet prisoners were subject to particularly harsh treatment. While some of these prisoners worked in the end phase of foundation and construction activity for the monumental building, most were employed in local military–industrial installations as forced labor. In addition, the SS used the train station for the Märzfeld that lay between the rally grounds and the POW camp as a gathering point for local and regional German Jews who were shipped from here to the death camps

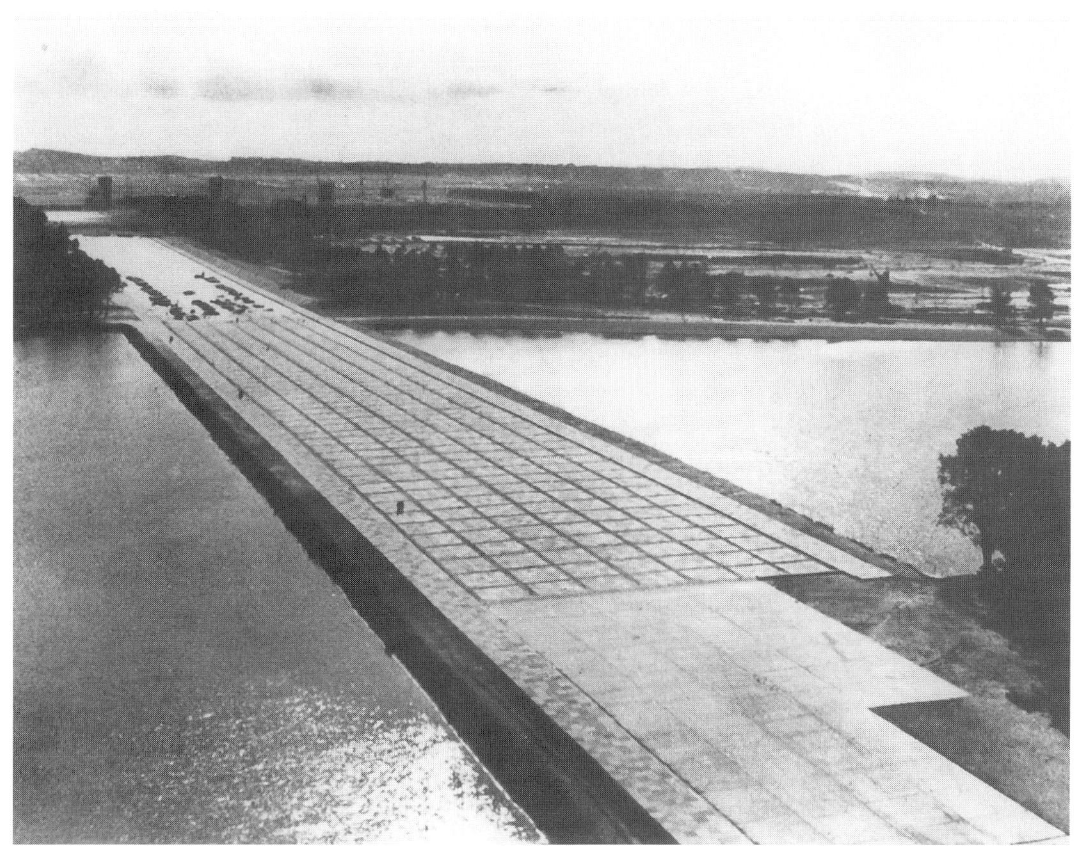

in the east.[9] Thus, the symbolic and ideologically driven architecture to the north grotesquely complemented its functional and political corollary of the train station and the camp to the south. Together, they formed a dense agglomeration in miniature of the worlds of perpetrator and victim as imagined and constructed by the brutality of Nazi architects and administrators.

The planners meant such architectural bombast and policies of oppression to strengthen the German resolve and carry out the racist goals of the National Socialist war of aggression in Europe and elsewhere. This political and ideological agenda became increasingly difficult to sustain after the turn in World War II at the Battle of Stalingrad. On the local level the January 2, 1945, attack by the British air force that subjected the city to massive destruction with twenty-three hundred tons of bombs, further dispelled any illusions of victory. The British reduced the historic town of Albrecht Dürer and its famous inner city to rubble, although remarkably the painter's house and his statue survived unscathed. As they had with other cities in Germany, the Allies had used the firebombing to target specific military outposts but also to wreak havoc on the German population

FIGURE 5.4. Albert Speer, Grosse Strasse, Nuremberg, circa 1938. Copyright Dokumentationszentrum Reichsparteitagsgelände.

through the destruction of, for example, medieval centers, a goal of dubious legitimacy or strategic value at that stage of the war and one that resulted in the deaths of thousands. The Rally Grounds, which lay outside the city center, received minimal damage, although they became the site of some of the street-by-street combat that occurred when the U.S. Army made its push into Nuremberg in April. The city fell on Hitler's birthday, April 20, 1945, and became part of the American Zone of occupation.[10]

The bombing of the city and the U.S. military presence led almost immediately to the first postwar architectural transformation of the site. By May 1945, U.S. officials already had changes to the Rally Grounds in the works because of the choice of Nuremberg as the site for hosting the International Military Tribunal (IMT) of the major war criminals. The United States led the effort to have a trial for the surviving leaders of the military and Nazi state as a means of propagating the concept that subjecting state authorities to a higher rule of law would have a lasting impact on international human rights law and the waging of war. As we have seen, it established the first fundamental definition of the ideologically driven, extremist perpetrator. Many legal minds inside and outside the United States debated the legitimacy of this potential victor's justice (and at the time the Soviets thought the leaders should simply be shot, an opinion shared by, among others, Winston Churchill). Still, the attempt to judge the war criminals in the city of their most high-profile hubris, one which happened to be in the American Zone, proved to have long-lasting ramifications for the image of the city in Germany and abroad.[11]

Nuremberg became the choice for the IMT when U.S. General Lucius Clay took Associate Supreme Court Justice Robert Jackson to the city to view one of the few surviving buildings, the Palace of Justice. This structure along with its attached prison, as well as the relatively undamaged Grand Hotel, meant that the number of indicted criminals as well as the prosecutorial staff and reporters could be housed conveniently. Jackson, though, as the chief American prosecutor, worried about the damage to the city and the inability to get around conveniently. In response, within a few weeks, Clay had General Patton mobilize fifteen thousand German POWs, who cleared the rubble to create the thoroughfares necessary to convince the other Allies that Nuremberg was an acceptable choice. The rubble was moved to the former Rally Grounds and dumped at the site of the foundations for the Deutsches Stadion (German Stadium). Here it would form the core of the hill of the city's ruins, which would become the Silberbuck, now a lightly forested area with paths and a lookout over the grounds. The necessary improvements to the city streets proved successful, and the IMT began in November 1945. The architectural site of the grounds and the city as a whole, naturally, formed an important backdrop to the trial. As Stephen Brockmann has put it, "The twenty-three defendants represented Nazism itself, and the destroyed city in which the trial took place represented the Germany that they had led into defeat and ruin."[12] The trial marked the city symbolically as the site of international human rights law and the first attempt to establish a coherent definition of the perpetrator. It also provoked the first real physical changes to the Rally Grounds with the Silberbuck, a site that would signal the direction of future transformations of other Nazi construction zones converted to largely recreational purposes.

In the shadow of both the IMT and subsequent U.S.-led trials for various National Socialist groups, the city began to come to terms with its postwar reconstruction. For the historic center, debate started immediately about how and what to rebuild. To focus these discussions, the city sponsored a planning competition in 1948, and 188 competitors submitted proposals. The entries represented a wide range of responses to the wartime destruction but generally fell broadly into variations on two approaches. They tended to cluster into Modernist, rationalized plans that would give Nuremberg a completely new profile, or traditionalist models that imagined rebuilding the historical core more or less as it had once been. City officials decided on the more traditionalist approach, not surprisingly, particularly given the importance of potential U.S. tourist dollars to be spent in the city. For reconstruction, any remaining relatively intact prewar fabric had to be kept and repaired, although architects and planners could build new structures where buildings had been completely destroyed. In these cases, they did not need to copy the ruined structure, but they did have to follow certain historic parameters of design, particularly in terms of scale. While destroyed German cities formulated postwar design in various ways, Nuremberg's approach echoed that of Munich and the Bavarian emphasis on preserving the historic fabric, a conservative tendency that was evident already by the nineteenth century.[13] This stood in contrast to other rebuilding efforts such as that in Cologne or Dresden.

In relation to the monumental architecture of the former Rally Grounds, the occupying forces of the U.S. Army also strongly influenced the initial development of the area. Beyond blowing up the swastika on top of the Zeppelinfeld (Figure 5.5), the army at first changed little of the architectural remnants other than their use. For example, the Märzfeld and its eleven completed towers remained but became depots for munitions and fuel for the American military. Soldiers used the field itself (like the Zeppelinfeld) either as a recreational site or for military exercises. That said, the Cold War context of the U.S. presence in Nuremberg did not preclude the continuity of multiple interest groups expressing their desire to use the

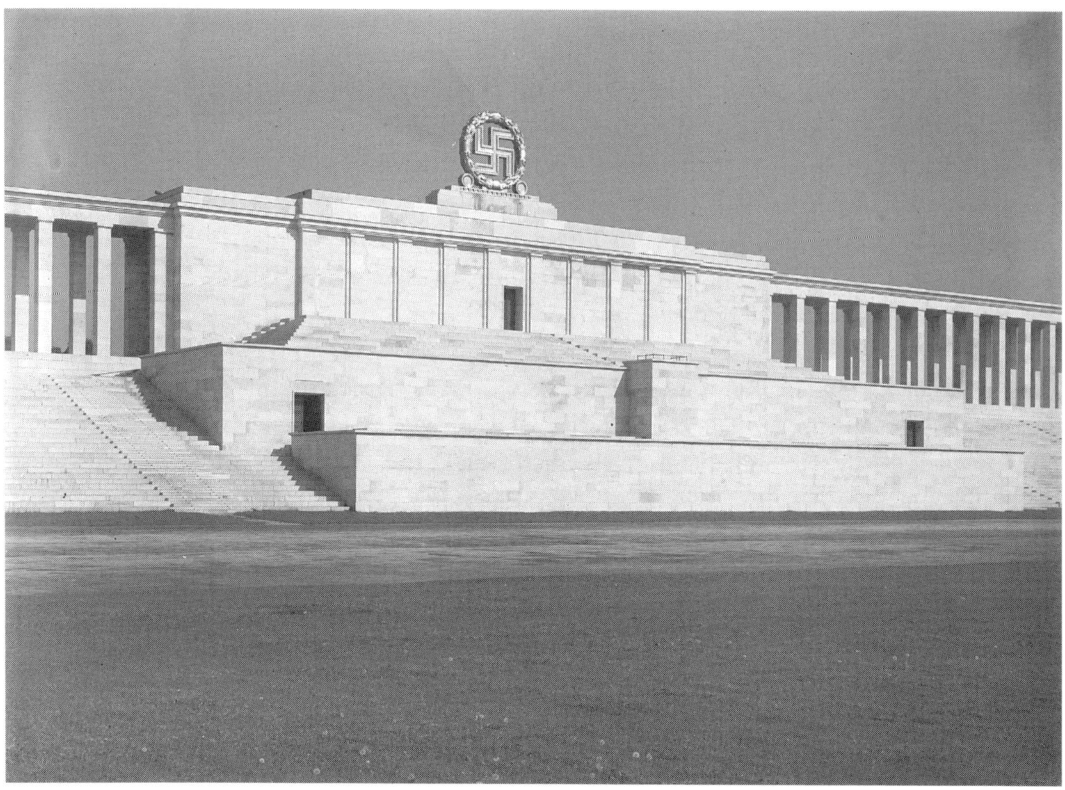

FIGURE 5.5. Albert Speer, Zeppelinfeld, Nuremberg (detail of central podium and Swastika standard), 1934. Courtesy of Bayerisches Landesamt für Denkmalpflege. Photograph Dr. Arthur Schlegel.

area. Nuremberg citizens enjoyed the Dutzendteich and park areas as sites for recreation, and the U.S. forces allowed the Zeppelinfeld to serve as a grandstand for concerts and other events. By 1961, they also gave the soccer stadium back to the control of the city. Hence, the patterns of use from the Nazi and pre–National Socialist era continued to assert themselves, and several high-profile aspects of the grounds such as the Zeppelinfeld were incorporated into those recreational purposes with no reflection on their problematic political heritage.[14] Since the perpetrators had been identified in the trials as the extreme leaders of National Socialism associated particularly with crimes in the east, everyday local discussions of former Nazi architects, forced-labor brigades, or the enthusiasm of a mass audience for its Führer remained outside public debate about the site.

More pragmatic concerns governed the immediate postwar use and adaptation of Langwasser, the large camping grounds south of the Märzfeld train station. While here too the criminal significance of the site seemed to fade from discussion after the war, nevertheless the architectural response to Speer's scale and stripped-down classicism became more marked than in the recreational areas. In 1946, U.S. forces first adapted the former POW camp to use as a holding center for captured Waffen-SS members, which they maintained until 1949. The United Nations used another part of the camp as a site to house displaced persons. At its high point, it held up to forty-five hundred persons from thirty nations making it the largest camp for exiles in Bavaria. As with the German POWs, the structures used were refurbished and repaired wooden barracks, followed in 1950 by somewhat more permanent but still provisional masonry structures. Into this camp streamed those fleeing the consolidating Soviet Bloc in the east, ethnic Germans driven out of Silesia and the Sudetenland, German and Central European Jewish survivors waiting for visas to the United States or Australia, and others. The first exiles to enter the camp had been from Estonia and Latvia and, apparently, had given the camp the nickname of the Valka Lager after their shared border city of Valka. The name stuck until the camp was dissolved in 1960 to make way for the expansion of housing (Figure 5.6). From 1954 to 1960, it had served as the central entrance point (*Anlaufstelle*) for asylum seekers in Germany. The great variety of ethnic groups as well as ethnically German migrants to and through the camps would mark this area of the former Rally Grounds to this day both negatively and positively in the local imagination as an area of foreigners and

FIGURE 5.6. Valka Lager barracks, Langwasser, Nuremberg, circa 1950. Photograph A39-Fi-L-577. Courtesy of Stadtarchiv Nürnberg.

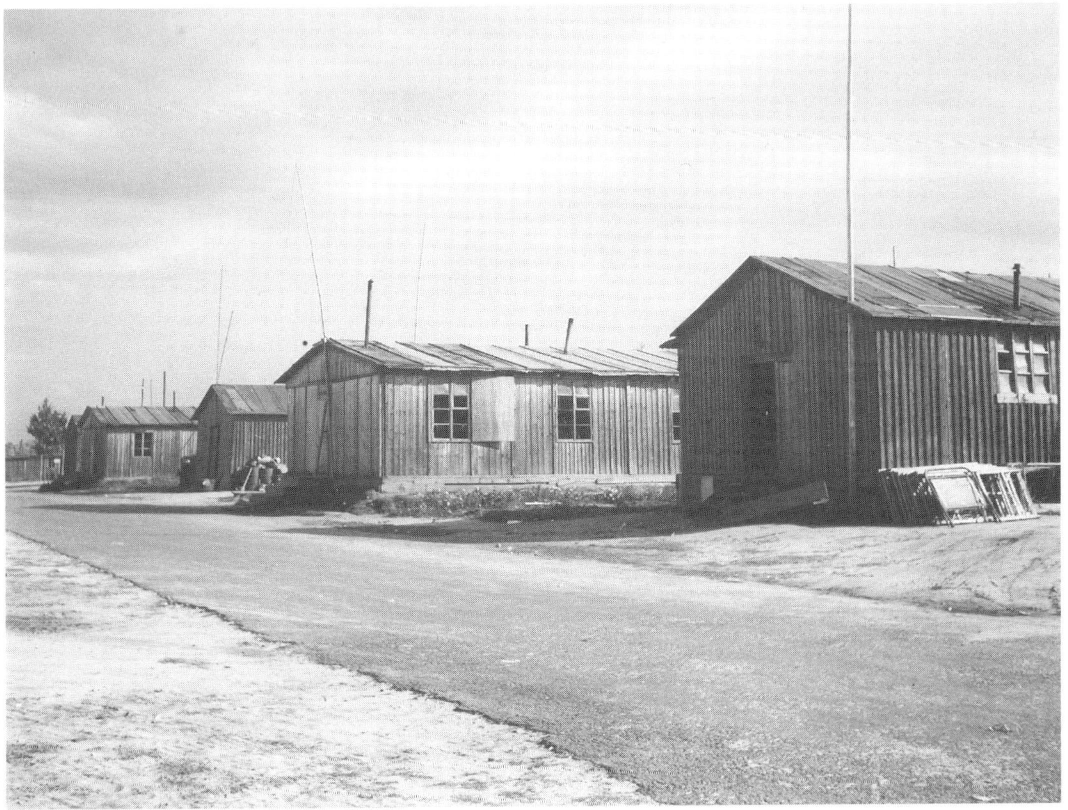

internationalism.[15] At the local level, who exactly was dangerous in the post-war era became exceedingly blurry.

At the same time that Langwasser consolidated its reputation as an area for migrants, it was also being transformed into an experiment in postwar Modernist town planning that countered Speer's intentions. Beginning with plans from 1948, the city constructed a series of permanent housing estates in the area for German refugees from the east and, in the 1950s, for foreign so-called guest workers. Under the patronage of the city, labor organizations, Christian groups, and other charitable or public sources, Langwasser grew and expanded to become an exemplary satellite city that addressed the urgent need for housing in postwar Nuremberg. By 1952, two significant and large estates had been completed, the Werkvolksiedlung (Figures 5.7 and 5.8) and the housing on the Dr.-Linnert-Ring (Figure 5.9), both on the northwestern part of the land and within sight of the remaining towers of the Märzfeld. The Catholic community sponsored the Werkvolksiedlung, planned in particular for German refugees. The Dr.-Linnert-Ring estates resulted from Marshall Plan funding through the Economic Cooperation Administration (ECA), which provided support for housing in many parts

FIGURE 5.7.
Werkvolksiedlung,
Langwasser,
Nuremberg, 1952.
Photograph A39-
Fi-L-506. Courtesy
of Stadtarchiv
Nürnberg.

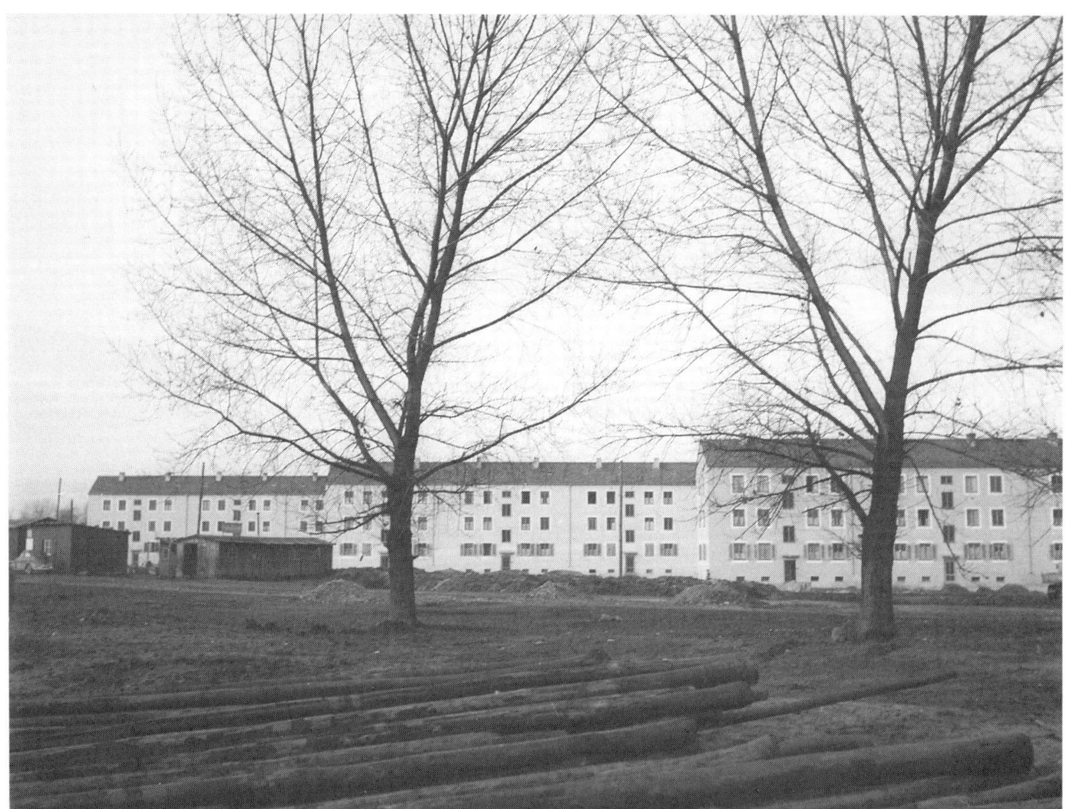

of Germany. Construction cost DM 2.7 million, consisted of 288 dwellings for fifty-six hundred people, and was the first of fifteen ECA estates to be completed in the Federal Republic. Local architect Franz Reichel designed the buildings and Hermann Thiele the landscape, both beginning their many years of activity on projects in the area. By 1955, other estates such as the Idealsiedlung were completed and the first major business, Maul & Co. printers, had opened to help the employment situation for the settlers. In 1967, after many years of delay, the U.S. authorities blew up the towers of the Märzfeld and gave the rest of the site over to the city for more expansion of the housing estates.[16] At this time, no attempt was made to commemorate forced labor at the site or consider the site's historical significance for the perpetrators. The early years of postwar Langwasser marked a decided architectural and conceptual turning away from the previous use and significance of the historical location.

The architecture of these early estates also rejected the immediate past with a tepid combination of Modernist functionality and construction that used some regional vernacular details. In the Werkvolksiedlung housing, for example, the modularity of the units is evident in the repetition of forms, window treatments, and the parallel layout of the buildings at an angle to the street (Trebnitzerstrasse). As with Mies van der Rohe's apartment building

FIGURE 5.8. Werkvolksiedlung, Nuremberg, 1952. Author's photograph.

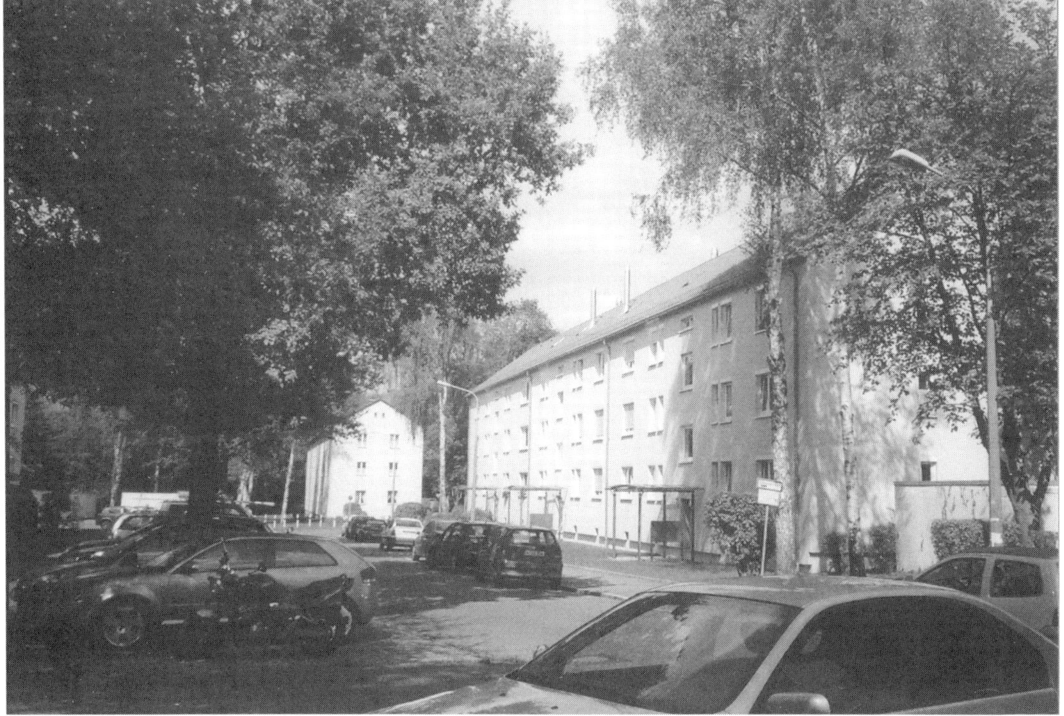

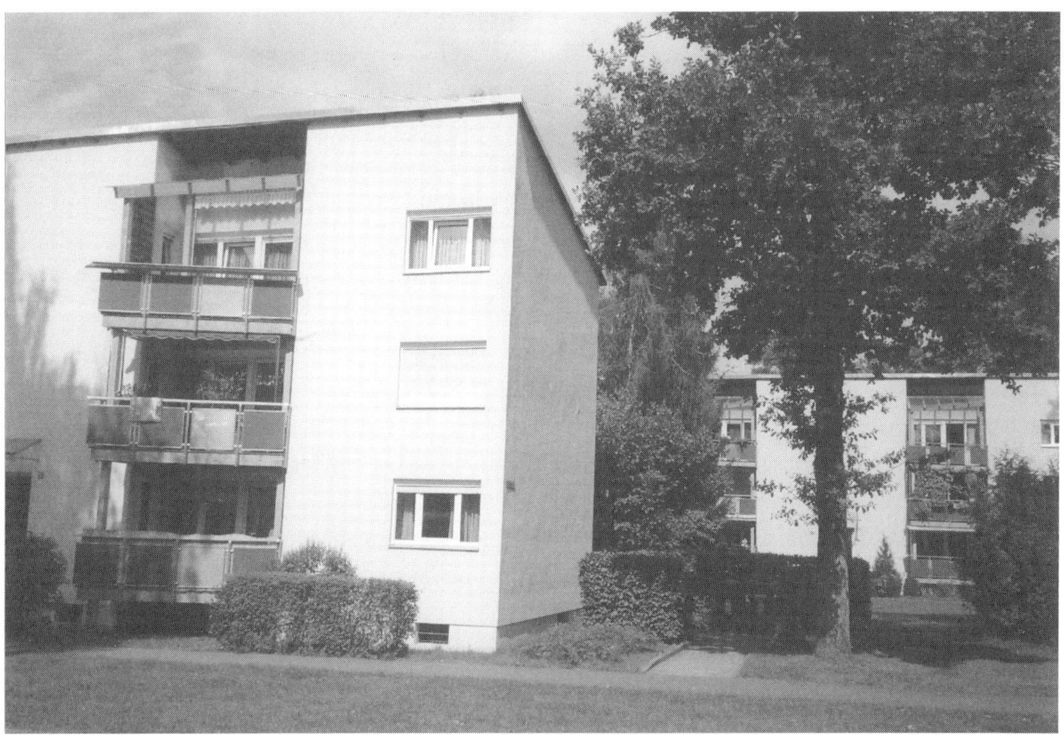

FIGURE 5.9. Franz Reichel, Dr.-Linnert-Ring, Nuremberg, 1952. Author's photograph.

for the Weissenhofsiedlung (1927) and other pre–National Socialist Modernist estates, the functionality of the private versus public spaces is also clearly articulated in the distinctive forms. The windows and the door of the centrally placed shared entrance and stairwells rhythmically punctuate the facades with their vertical emphasis. This accent breaks up the larger unified and repetitious pattern of the buildings into relatively more intimately scaled component segments. But in contrast to these institutionalized Modernist features, the architects applied paint around the windows reminiscent of stone surrounds, and included hipped roofs and the hard-to-miss shutters on the lower floors. These tactics are variations less on Mies than on local building traditions established before and continuing through the Nazi period.

Reichel also employs this balance of aesthetic choices in the more ambitious ECA estate, just to the west of the Werkvolksiedlung. In addition to the repetition of forms, the articulation of public spaces, and the concrete walls, the roofs are slightly slanted (without a hipped attic) and more in line with conventional Modernism. Nevertheless, here as well Reichel evidences vernacular traditions, as he extends the roofline beyond the wall to form a small eave supported by articulated wooden beams. He thus combined an ever-more popular international aesthetic for democratic capitalist states with a return to the regional residential type. This strategy marked a fitting rejection of and local response to the public and ideologically motivated classicism and monumental planning of the Party Rally Grounds.[17] The transformation of function and the influx of immigrant residents gave the space new meaning. The architecture also allowed for the beginning of the erasure, consciously or not, of the previous presence of the Nazi perpetrators and propagandistic uses of the site.[18]

As these estates were going up, it had became clear to the City Planning Office (Stadtplanungsamt) that the development of the former southern lands of the Rally Grounds required a more systematic plan and should not be left up to the variety of public and private patrons most likely to sponsor housing estates. By 1954, the city's Wiederaufbaureferent (reconstruction expert), Andreas Urschlechter (SPD; mayor 1957–87), charged the Wohnungsbaugesellschaft (Residential Building Society; WBG), a public building society, with creating a plan for the area, with the potential for 25,000–30,000 residents. The WBG ran a limited competition in 1956 of nine architectural teams that had experience in postwar Modernist town planning, the dominant trend in planning departments in New York, Chicago, and elsewhere in the United States.[19] The WBG required entrants to create a functional plan that clearly divided work from residential zones. Further, 50 percent of the plan should deal with larger residences of multiple stories with the rest divided among small-scale structures, including single-family houses.

The team of Reichel, Thiele, and Hermann Scherzer won the competition with a proposal that spread the various kinds of housing into separate communities along the current Oppeliner Strasse and Otto-Bärnreutherstrasse, that is, the main route into the historic center from Langwasser (Figure 5.10). Reichel, Thiele, and Scherzer's plan in particular imagined the main concentration of large building blocks at the southern end of the site around the already constructed ECA estate and Werkvolksiedlung with another set of buildings along the main road to the north. The smaller single-family housing would mostly be sprinkled around rambling roads on the former Märzfeld land controlled by the U.S. Army with other romantic garden-city extensions to the west of that land. Each of the plan's clusters of housing had separate entrance roads, and Thiele made use of plenty of green space to make the functional distinctions between residential areas clear. The combination of the Modernist housing blocks with the garden-city-inspired segments, like the earlier housing estates, indicated that the comprehensive plan would both engage in the functionalist planning process and maintain a nostalgic concept of *Gemeinschaft* (community) and comfort. The plan would guide the further extension of Langwasser, with some variations, through the years.[20] While the planning concept was not unique to Nuremberg, such strategies signaled a specific local agenda: not only urbanistically looking backward before the Nazi era but also embracing postwar practices that avoided and implicitly rejected the large-scale, visually unified, and classical academic planning so evident in Speer's designs.

Indeed, what is notable in this period of the *Wirtschaftswunder* (economic miracle) is the total lack of interest in general in the Rally Grounds'

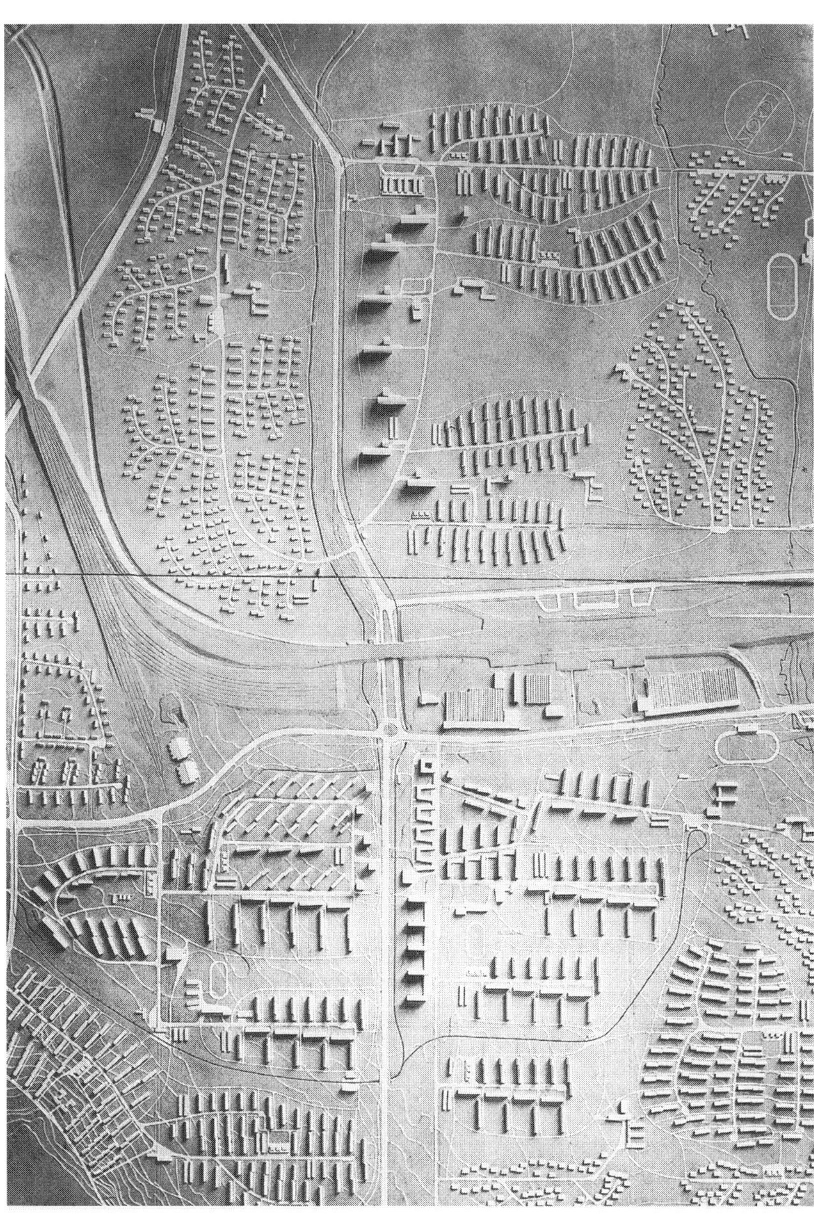

FIGURE 5.10. Franz Reichel, Thiele and Scherzer, Plan of Langwasser, Nuremberg, 1956. Courtesy of WBG Nürnberg GmbH.

historical and ideological significance or the presence of local perpetrators. Naturally, this pattern follows the treatment of other sites in West Germany, such as the Tempelhof Airport (1936) constructed in Berlin by Ernst Sagebiel or the CDU's attempt to downplay the continuity of perpetrators in prominent positions that arose, as we have seen, following the Eichmann trial. Representatives from across the political spectrum perpetuated a notion of what Neil Gregor characterizes as the "city as victim," a position meant to bracket the past and distance it from any association with the present citizens of Nuremberg. Such a strategy became noticeable when, in the mid-1960s, the three prominent parties in the city council—the CSU, SPD, and FDP—united against the rising influence of the National Democratic Party (NPD), a right-wing party committed to continuing specific policies from the Nazi platform. The NPD achieved particular success in the Bavarian state elections of November 1966, including 13.1 percent of the vote in Nuremberg. As Gregor highlights, the election and the immediate years following led the NPD to attempt to occupy key Nazi spaces within the Rally Grounds for their meetings, including the old Messehalle and the new Meistersingerhalle. The city council was only variably successful at stopping these meetings, particularly since they were completely legal. Nevertheless, the process of targeting the NPD and its use of the Rally Grounds constituted another way in which politicians and activists attempted to form a local citizenry distinct from the perpetrators of the past or the present. Neither group could be claimed to be related to contemporary citizens, city goals, or for that matter city architecture and planning.[21] In these debates here and elsewhere, the biographical and human perpetrator took center stage, not the spaces and buildings of his or her crimes. Not surprisingly, the response in the 1960s of painters who depict these individuals would be more in tune with contemporary political debates, unlike their architectural brethren marching through the fields of postwar international Modernism.

However much the aesthetic and conceptual design principles and political function evidenced at Langwasser rejected past practices, the scale of the site and its variable use made any real avoidance of the historical burden of the land almost impossible. In addition to the example of the NPD's awareness of the site's usefulness, two important architectural additions to the grounds during this period emphasize this point: the Meistersingerhalle (1963) and the Convention Center (Messezentrum, 1973). Nuremberg politicians and business leaders used these buildings to focus on expanding the economic ambitions of the city and securing its position within the competitive capitalist environment of the Cold War. The Meistersingerhalle, a large cultural facility, and the new Convention Center would serve to modernize Nuremberg's buildings and image. They transformed key areas of the Party Rally Grounds with a seemingly neutral and international Modernist rationality. Such wished-for neutrality, however, would have a hard time given the Nazi ruins all around that continued to spark questions about who the local perpetrators might be who planned these areas in the first place.

Across the Bayernstrasse north of the Kongresshalle, the Luitpold-hain, the famous set for central scenes in Leni Riefenstahl's *Triumph des Willens* (1934), was broken up in the postwar period and became again a grassy field surrounded by flowers and trees. As the city transformed this area in April 1958, a building commission approved the clearing of part of the northern end of the site for a new concert hall (the last remaining ruins in the area were blown up in August). After winning the design competition that same year, the thirty-six-year-old Nuremberg architect Harald Loebermann took over the construction of the hall, which was completed along with the landscaping in 1963 (Figures 5.11 and 5.12). At the Luit-poldhain, the outline of Speer's field remained under the new plantings (as did some of his light fixtures) and the older Weimar era war memorial by Fritz Mayer was maintained. But the meandering circuit of the garden paths along with the expressly Modernist facade of the Meistersingerhalle sig-naled a very different ethos, one that was brought into the public dialogue distancing the city from its criminal past. As one local paper put it at the opening of the hall with now-Mayor Urschlechter, "Hitler's torso [of the Kongresshalle beyond the field to the south] could present to the eyes of the younger generation the destructive violence of megalomania. The new hall will [by contrast] prove to them that even a city like Nuremberg can distinguish itself with such an imposing building (through its artistic form as well as its dimensions) from much larger cities."[22] This author referred to the clear stacked volumes of the building, as well as the combination of vertical and horizontal linear elements. In addition, like Mies's Barcelona Pavilion (1929), the use of notable textures in the materials, such as the polish of the steel as well as the slate wall facing the park, went beyond the sober Modernism of public housing to signal the cultural pretensions of the hall. While not as innovative as its contemporary, Hans Scharoun's Philharmonie (1963) near the Berlin Wall, it was certainly meant, like its counterpart, to revive an area with difficult associations and brighten Nurem-berg's international architectural and cultural reputation.[23]

More ambitious were the plans for the Convention Center, which began to gather steam in 1968. During the Cold War, West German fed-eral policy dictated absolute support of the western powers, even though this monolithic focus was breaking down and would be balanced by the

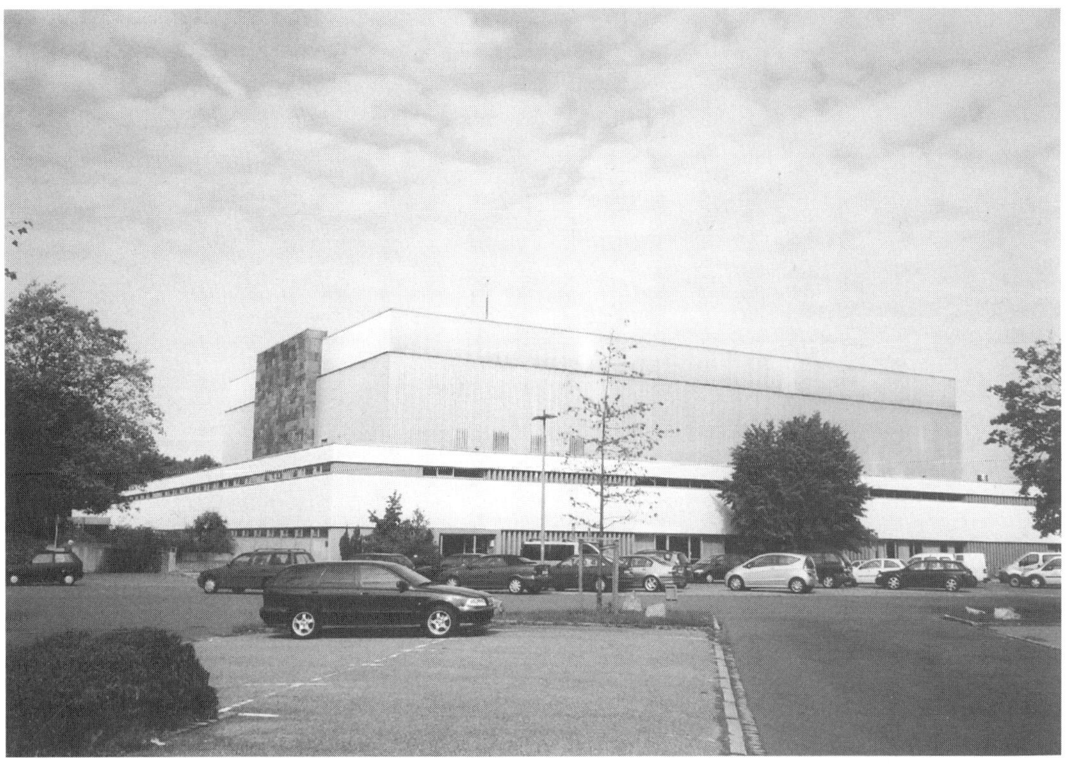

FIGURE 5.11. Harald Loebermann, Meistersingerhalle, Nuremberg, 1963. Author's photograph.

"Ostpolitik" of SPD chancellor Willy Brandt. To foreign observers, however, West Germany's prestige was clearly located in its economic dynamism, the export of a wide range of German products, and the ability to compete internationally.[24] Since Nuremberg was not the industrial production center it once was, such competition increasingly relied on tourism and the local engine of the trade fairs, including the famous Toy Fair held every year. By September 1968, confidential city memos indicated that the more than one hundred displays expected at the next fair would push the limits of the provisional building they had been using in the Berliner Platz. If the city was to compete in drawing international exhibitors (who were beginning to boycott Nuremberg in favor of Paris), it would need a new fairgrounds. It should be built close in to the historic center and big enough to also serve for the increasing popularity of ice-skating revues and other events. Discussions continued and in March 1969, Urschlechter announced that the city would be looking to build a new center "in the modern standard" to maintain Nuremberg's economic competitiveness.[25] In these initial conversations, the Toy Fair organization (Spielwarenmesse GmbH) made it clear that anywhere outside the city center (such as on the Dutzendteich) could not possibly be considered.[26]

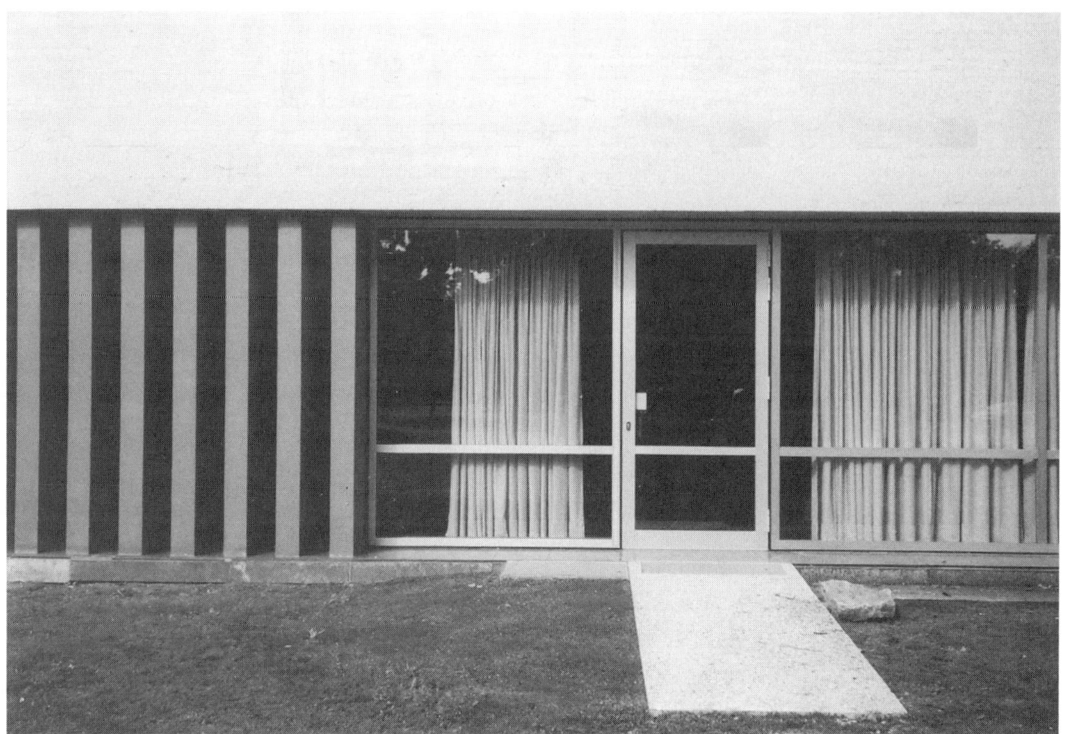

FIGURE 5.12. Harald Loebermann, Meistersingerhalle (detail, side entrance), Nuremberg, 1963. Author's photograph.

Within the month, however, city officials would indeed go forward with plans to put the center on land they controlled at the Reich Party Rally Grounds, in spite of the objections of the powerful Toy Fair lobby. A decision needed to be made in the wake of a political back-and-forth on the project between the city SPD and the state CSU. The political dustup occurred in response to a statement by Franz Sackmann, head of the Bavarian State Ministry of Economic Affairs, who noted that the state would not participate in any shared costs, as the only industrial fair of any significance to come to Nuremberg was the Toy Fair. For Sackmann, the provincial interests of the city were of little concern to the more ambitious goals of the state. Fritz Drescher, from the Toy Fair organization, immediately decried Sackmann's comments, noting that they appeared to be merely an ideological pronouncement meant to promote the political posturing of the CSU, which governed the state. Drescher suspected Sackmann's tactic was meant to counter the powerful Bavarian SPD–controlled cities such as Munich and Nuremberg. While the political rivalry was clearly at issue in these debates, it is important to emphasize that the political past of the Nazi era that potentially burdened the fair and its location was not in the least a topic of any relevance. By the end of March, the Nuremberg economic expert (*Wirtschaftsreferent*) Wilhelm Doni suggested that a relatively inexpensive solution for the location of the new fairgrounds would be in the area north of Langwasser along the Grosse Strasse. Doni's choice raised no comment from local SPD officials and was met with indifference from the CSU state politicians.[27]

The political debates ignored the historical significance of the location even while taking advantage of the large property at the Rally Grounds under their control. So too did the design and construction decisions for the convention center explicitly avoid and implicitly reject the neoclassical concept of the Speer plan and neighboring buildings. Yet within the ultimately Modernist rejection of the recent past (à la the Meistersingerhalle), specific features of the Nazi grounds still influenced planning and construction. The preliminary design of the center was initially put in the hands of Loebermann, following his previous experience with the city. At a meeting with the architect at the Baureferat (building department) in September 1969, city officials and fair representatives noted that the best design from their perspective would be a large hall with several smaller halls attached. This would allow either one large-scale event or several smaller gatherings that could be kept relatively distinct, to maximize the use of the center and its profits. As recorded in the protocol, unnamed participants suggested, for example, that perhaps the building could be laid out in a U shape with two wings of pavilions and an attractive courtyard in between. In Loebermann's follow-up conversation with Doni, the architect expanded on the advantages of this idea: the potential interconnection of rooms; the function of the interior courtyard as a large space that would allow visitors to walk between the pavilions; the use of the exterior walls as a secondary space marked out for deliveries easily accessible to trucks from the exhibitors; and center patrons' easy access to the subway then under construction. In spite of the amount of work and the forced time line that Loebermann complained about, by summer 1970 the architect had developed a basic layout and plan of six pavilions arranged along a central axis leading to a large hall.[28]

This preliminary design showed only a boxlike, simple Modernist structure with no clear orientation to the surrounding area. But the city decided on a limited architectural competition for the final design, with five invited teams identified to take Loebermann's idea and make it a reality. Plan GmbH, a group of architects and engineers from Munich led by Ernst Denk, Herbert Groethuysen, and Wolfgang Uebe, won the competition in September, a result approved by the Stadtrat on October 15, 1970 (Figures 5.13 and 5.14). Their original proposal included a variation on Loebermann's plan with octagonal pavilions arranged in two wings expanding out to the north and south from a central courtyard connected to a large meeting hall next to the subway station to the west. In terms of the location on the Rally Grounds, the Plan design turned its back on the Grosse Strasse, placed the parking facility west of the southern wing (separate from the view to the rest of the Party Rally Grounds), and oriented the courtyard and main building toward the subway station. The official city chronicle declared gleefully that the pavilion system would result in a revolutionary building form that would be decisive for improving Nuremberg's trade significance ("handelspolitische Bedeutung"), particularly in reference to the expanding opportunities to the east that were then opening up with Brandt's Ostpolitik. All in all, this project used its geometrically innovative design and functionalist layout as architecture aligned with federal and local economic policy with no hint of an interest in the historical significance of the site.[29]

The Plan GmbH group finalized the design of the center by February 1972, and construction continued until the grand opening on January 10, 1973, in time for that year's Toy Fair. The finished structure followed the basic original idea laid out by Loebermann, but there were several important alterations that contributed to its final form. As with the preliminary proposal, the Convention Center had a central meeting hall from which two wings extended around a courtyard. Unlike Loebermann's proposal, however, the meeting hall was actually modest in scale, unified in its cornice line

FIGURE 5.13. Plan GmbH, Messezentrum, Nuremberg, 1973. Photograph A39-L-1602A-45. Courtesy of Stadtarchiv Nürnberg.

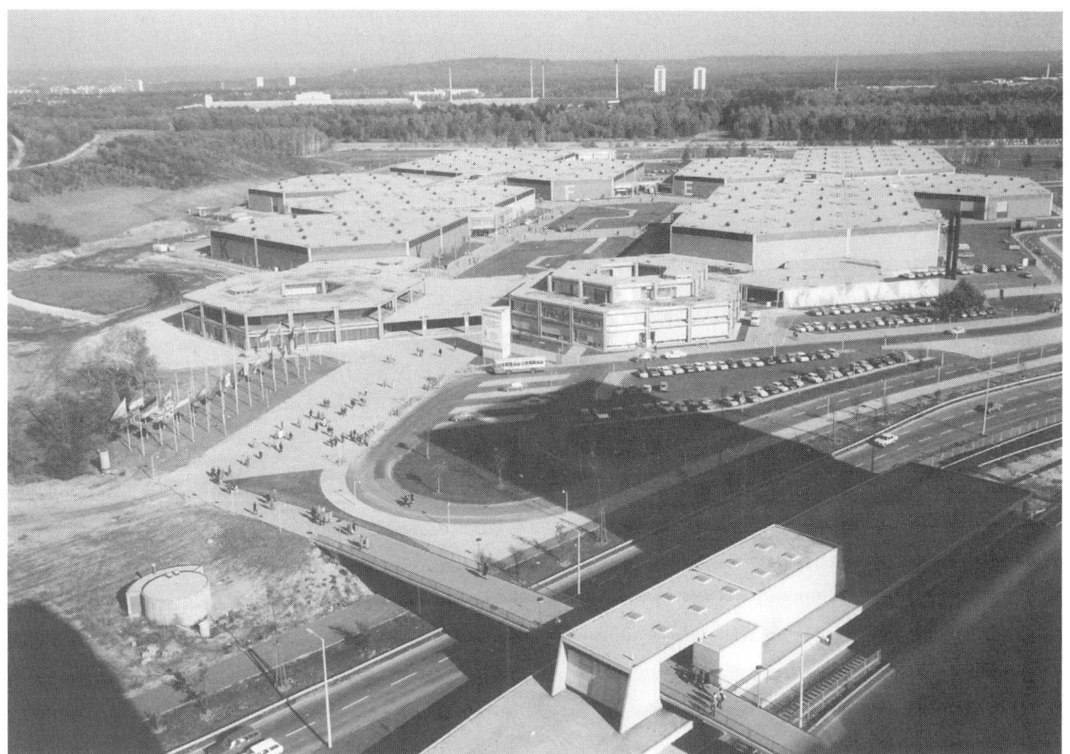

with the attached pavilion structures so that there was a greater visual consistency among the buildings as a whole. To make the parts functionally clear, Plan GmbH used the by-then conventional Modernist device of pulling the curtain wall glass infill back to assert the tectonic expression of the structural concrete elements around the two main courtyard entrances, thus distinguishing the hall and the important transitional spaces of the doors. In contrast, the pavilions were covered in simple flat metal plates that hid the structural core. Furthermore, instead of Plan GmbH's original idea of octagons, the basic unit of the final center was the more fundamental form of the triangle, combined in the pavilions and the main hall into regular hexagonal profiles. The triangular units were revealed in the forms of the reinforced concrete as well as in the patterns in the pavement and interior layout of rooms, a device typical, for example, in Mies's large-scale urban ensembles during the same period.[30] And finally, the architects more clearly oriented the expansive courtyard that formed the core of the pavilions from west to east in the constructed design, coming from the entrance near the subway station and opening out to the Grosse Strasse at the other end. Hence, its physical orientation more overtly engaged with the main features of the Party Rally Grounds.

FIGURE 5.14. Plan GmbH, Messezentrum (detail, courtyard entrance), Nuremberg, 1973. Author's photograph.

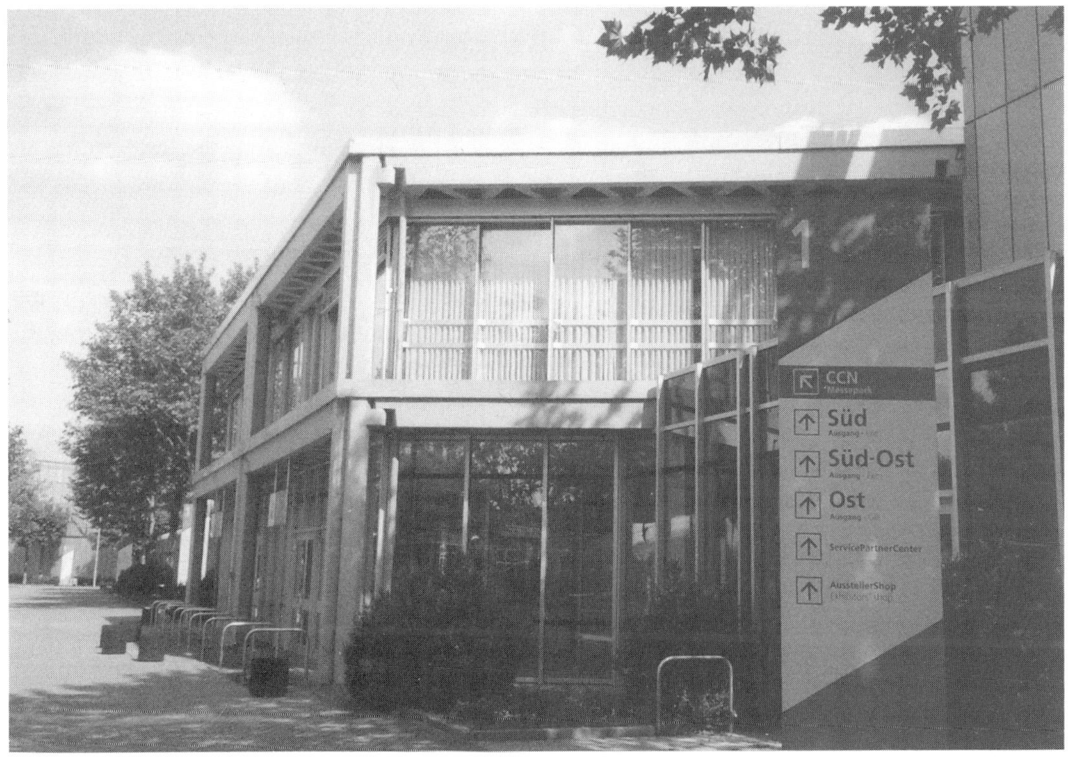

The Modernist and tectonic form was a conventional denial of the aesthetic principles of Speer's project, and even the orientation to the Grosse Strasse seems to have been nothing more than a matter of convenience to take advantage of the open site for parking. Indeed, the center depended on the massive scale of Speer's plan since it needed a large open site, but the historical use by Nazi politicians and architects of this area between the Deutsches Stadion and the Märzfeld was literally ignored. The economic confidence asserted in the up-to-date architecture of the Convention Center at the southwestern edge of the Rally Grounds mirrored the cultural aspirations embodied in Loebermann's elegant Meistersingerhalle on the northern end. Both projected an image consistent with the international architectural philosophy of most democratic capitalist public buildings emanating from the United States. They also served the specific West German postwar agenda of subsuming the militarist policies of aggression into dreams of playing an important role as an economic center of industrial production.[31]

In spite of the occasional flare-up of NPD activity or local controversy, these Modernist insertions into the Rally Grounds and the inclusion of new residential functions effectively stifled real debate about the historical significance of the site or a clear connection to specific concepts of the perpetrator. In terms of the Nazi architectural remnants on the land, the planning and building of residential, cultural, and commercial structures seemed to barely affect them. There were as yet no individual perpetrators other than Speer associated with the buildings, and he after all had been tried and was still imprisoned for his crimes. While an avant-garde artist like Alexander Kluge could choose the stands of the Zeppelinfeld as the location for his exploration of fascism in his film, *Brutalität in Stein* (1960), city officials and the U.S. Army treated the site as little more than a convenient set of bleachers. Further, the city designated the Deutsches Stadion's former foundation as a dumping ground that produced a lake (the Silbersee) of poisoned runoff full of chemicals. An additional lack of official attention necessitated the removal in 1967 of the colonnade atop the Zeppelinfeld due to its imminent structural collapse (Figure 5.15). The historical significance of the architecture was not as yet socially or politically useful on a local or national level. It was thus with some annoyance that city bureaucrats took on the problem of maintaining and restoring key parts of the site (in particular the remains of the Zeppelinfeld and the Kongresshalle) after the entire Party Rally Grounds were classified as a historical monument in the 1973 revision of the Bavarian Denkmalschutzgesetz (Historic Preservation Law).[32] Still, in the same year, the city did not hesitate to cut a large parcel of land out of the southern quadrant around the area of the Deutsches Stadion with no consideration of its historical significance for use by the new Convention

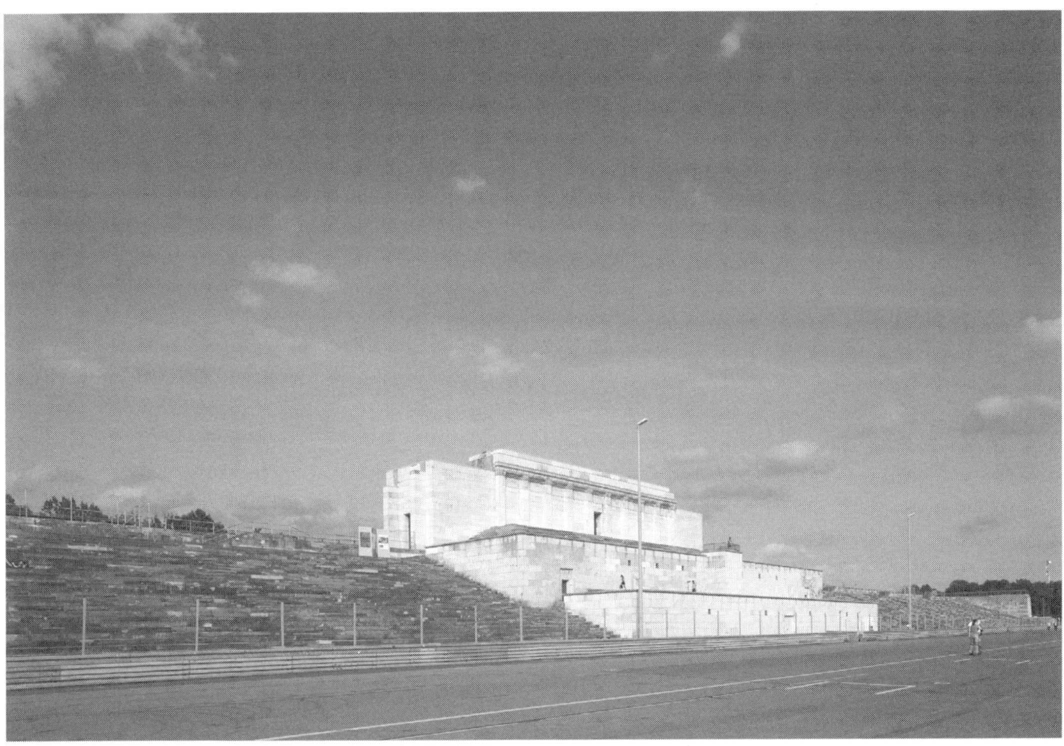

Center. Nazi perpetrators and the Nazi past were someone else's problem and other people's heritage, to be explored in photographs and paintings perhaps, but not codified in specific geographies of place.

The Reich Party Rally Grounds through Reunification and the Political Shift in their Interpretation and Use

Thus, by the time the Bavarian state began to recognize the Nazi site as a significant object of historical interest, commercial, recreational, and military uses had already asserted themselves. With initiatives of the city and the U.S. Army, as well as the return of the land as a leisure ground for the local population, the multiple interests limited any monolithic interpretation or preservation of its historical import. This pattern remained firmly entrenched, even after the site became a locus of ideological confrontation in the 1980s as a result of the commemorative events leading up to the fortieth anniversary of the end of World War II. Throughout this era (the high point of *Vergangenheitsbewältigung*), Speer's and Hitler's preference for monumental scale significantly contributed to the site's ability to absorb an unfocused plurality of uses, even after its designation as a historical monument

FIGURE 5.15. Albert Speer, Zeppelinfeld (after removal of colonnade), Nuremberg, 2010. Copyright Dokumentationszentrum Reichsparteitagsgelände.

and politicization by various constituencies. As with Helmut Kohl's ceremonies at Bitburg, with the general cultural turn in the debates about the
ideological perpetrator came also what we might call a spatial turn of these
discussions as Nuremberg citizens began to recognize their own Nazi past
hiding in plain sight.

The development of marking the historical plans for the grounds
paralleled other efforts in Germany, particularly the spate of commemorative monuments and countermonuments that increased dramatically after
the rise of Kohl to power in 1982. Kohl and his CDU government became
quickly embroiled in the ideological debates of commemoration politics
because of the multiple plans to mark the fortieth anniversary of World
War II. The SPD opposition at the national level excoriated Kohl for his
bungled attempts to use various sites for conservative advantage and Cold
War politics. SPD criticism paralleled the unprecedented organization of
independent liberal-left citizen initiatives at the local level, which confronted
the attempts of the CDU to bracket the activity of Nazi perpetrators at
such sites as Berlin's Topography of Terror. Control and debate over the
architectural and urban remains of the Nazi past encountered a new and
high-profile area around which the political confrontation between Kohl's
conservative agenda and the varied opposition positions crystallized.[33]

These national debates were not lost at the local level, but their politicization was significantly different. In Nuremberg, the SPD had dominated
the Stadtrat for over thirty years. As in other Bavarian cities such as
Munich, the entrenched power of the SPD at the municipal level countered
the equally strong control of the CSU at the state level. Such a splintering limited the ability of preservationists to garner needed state and local
funds for major commemorative interests, as each dominant party wanted
the other to pay for specific plans. This situation left the door open for a
variety of attempts to use private industry to develop the Rally Grounds,
in particular the fantastically bungled idea put forth in 1987 to turn the
Kongresshalle into a multipurpose site encompassing a senior center, pent-
house condominiums, and a shopping mall.[34] But the political impasse related to funding also meant that, when specific attempts at historicization
did succeed in moving forward, the will had to come from independent initiatives outside public institutions. These struggles and debates, both within
established institutions as well as from the outside, would form the very
basis of *Vergangenheitsbewältigung* at the local level.

The work of independent groups in Berlin and elsewhere and the
commemorations of World War II spurred on Nuremberg citizens interested in memorializing the Nazi past.[35] For example, an initial attempt in
1983 by the city's Kulturreferent (cultural director) Hermann Glaser to

create an exhibition in conjunction with the fiftieth anniversary of Hitler's coming to power failed. Glaser did show, though, that at least some bureaucrats were interested in focusing on the prominent Nazi perpetrators who had populated and made use of Nuremberg. But more effectively in the same year, local historians consolidated a plan for an educational exhibition about the importance of the Nazi rallies and grounds. By 1985, this left-liberal group had successfully lobbied for the use of the unheated mosaic hall within the Zeppelinfeld for its installation of *Faszination und Gewalt* (*Fascination and Terror*). The exhibition featured rough wooden boards covered in text that documented the Rally Grounds, an aesthetic choice meant to counteract the monumentality and prestigious masonry materials of the site. The exhibition addressed how the ideology of the Nazi Party was formed in Nuremberg and used for violent ends. The pressure of the group as well as the popularity of the exhibition pushed the SPD and the minority party of the CSU in the Stadtrat to agree that the site should be commemorated; but equally they agreed that the National Socialist past was a national heritage and thus had to be funded at the national level. Given this conception of the past, the agency of former possibly criminal individuals at the local level, a portion of whom were still alive, would not be acknowledged. The Nuremberg SPD/Green coalition, however, received no support from Kohl's national government, even for this more limited agenda.[36]

The political struggle inherent in the funding situation changed dramatically in the 1990s. At the national level (and above all in Berlin), Kohl reversed his Cold War resistance to expanding commemoration sites by proposing a centralized location for mourning the victims of fascism, communism, and war at Schinkel's Neue Wache and embracing plans for Peter Eisenman's Holocaust Memorial. As the generation of both victims and perpetrators was fading away, Kohl could promote these abstract sites as generally positive signs that his government took the past seriously but also as a way of marking the past as distinct from post-reunification institutions. That is, the architectural sites became ideologically useful as the continuity between wartime and postwar generations seemed more and more ruptured.[37]

While these trends naturally affected Nuremberg, the shift in national policy paralleled an institutional change that played out very differently at the regional level, particularly around the political consensus of the parties in the Stadtrat. On the one hand, the city had begun to be more confident about its postwar role, particularly with the continued American interest in the history and legal significance of the Nuremberg Tribunals. For example, along with the expansion of the important Germanic National Museum, the city held a design competition in 1988 for the Kartäusergasse, a small alley adjacent to the museum. Dani Karavan, an Israeli artist who won the competition, proposed a "Street of Human Rights" (Strasse der Menschenrechte) on which large concrete pillars would be engraved with the thirty articles of the Universal Declaration of Human Rights (Figure 5.16). The texts were in German as well as twenty-nine other languages. With this project, the city showed its ability to actively engage the Nazi past through its commemoration of the aftermath localized in the tribunals. Two years after its construction, the city sponsored a new award for international human rights work, now used to focus attention on Nuremberg not as a site of Nazi oppression but as a place where a positive postwar response to the National Socialist past was worth celebrating.[38] Perpetrators were punished, not created, in Nuremberg.

On the other hand, the city government also began to address more directly the architecture of the grounds as historic criminal sites in need of pedagogic information and orientation for locals and tourists alike. In 1994, the city appointed Franz Sonnenberger to head all local museums and set him the task of creating a unified plan for the nine relatively disparate collections. By this time, the exhibition *Fascination and Terror* had also become the responsibility of the city museums. Sonnenberger proposed the creation of a permanent facility on the site for this installation, an

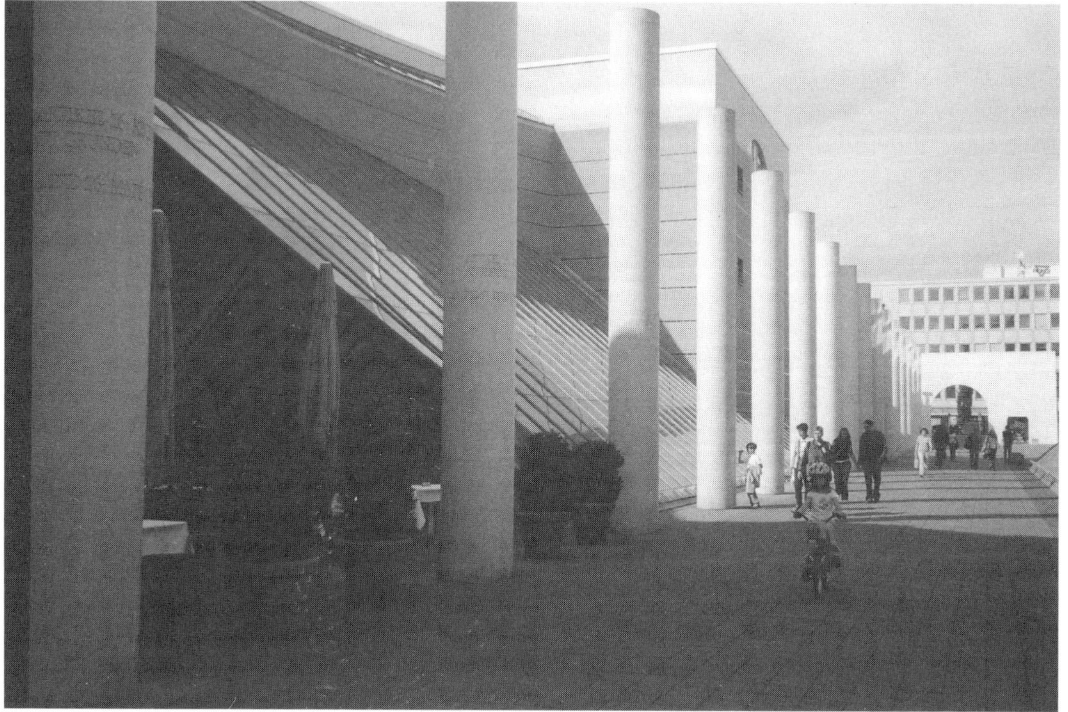

FIGURE 5.16. Dani Karavan, Street of Human Rights (Strasse der Menschenrechte), Nuremberg, 1993. Author's photograph.

idea that paralleled similar thoughts coming from the citizens' initiatives of the past decade. He pushed for a contemporary building that would recall the lighthouse on the Dutzendteich removed by the Nazi government in 1933, a form that aesthetically and conceptually broke with the monumental neoclassicism of Speer's architecture as well as literally signaled the "enlightenment" of the postwar years. Even before he came to office, local historians and curators had proposed architectural interventions that would preserve the site while aesthetically complicating its fascist message. Nevertheless, it would be Sonnenberger's institutional authority that would make these proposals a reality. His idea would become the basis for the creation of the Documentation Center of the Reich Party Rally Grounds (Dokumentationszentrum Reichsparteitagsgelände).[39]

But to achieve such plans, Sonnenberger still faced the challenge of funding, which was complicated by the CDU/CSU resistance to the local SPD government. Such resistance could only be overcome after the surprising CSU victory in the communal vote of 1996, displacing the forty-year SPD dominance of the Rathaus. The new mayor, Ludwig Scholz, like other conservative regional politicians, always downplayed the question of any real local postwar biographical or spatial connection to the Nazi past (while happy to play up the city's role in hosting the tribunals). He emphasized that the history of the site was not specific to Nuremberg but remained a national heritage:

> The question of how I handle the past is certainly a political topic and there I am of a somewhat different opinion than my mayoral predecessor. I acknowledge the past and I don't hide it. I don't find it pretty, I don't turn it inside out or distort it. But past is past, it is no present. Our political actions today must be oriented forward. . . . But the belief that the Third Reich should be a continual theme with us, that we must take a continual position to it, is a position that I at least would not want to propagate. I say we are a city like all others.[40]

Furthermore, Scholz denied that the new building was part of a plan to take advantage of the increased popularity of tourists fascinated by fascism, implying a mercenary motive for promoting a new museum. For Scholz, as for Kohl, the perpetrator was an unmentioned or at best opaque category, while cultural commemoration correctly handled could be an appropriate response to the past.

Nevertheless, in spite of Scholz's aligning himself with clear CSU positions, the various parties involved (including the independent citizens groups) came together to approve the new Dokumentationszentrum. Under Scholz, Nuremberg achieved an almost unique position in commemorating the Nazi past at that time: political and local consensus. Relatively quickly, leaders of the two dominant political parties, who had been tending in this direction for years, agreed to Sonnenberger's suggestions and began to support the idea of a permanent exhibition pavilion.[41] With this decision, city politicians made the first serious attempt to prioritize the broad history of the Nazi perpetrators above other interests at the site. Notably, however, politicians did not achieve consensus on how to historicize the Rally Grounds as a whole, only on how to use one part of the site for the (now-national) memorialization agenda. The new pedagogic and historical functions followed the dominant tendency of earlier local governments to promote pragmatic solutions rather than any systematic attempt to grapple with the National Socialist heritage embodied by the site in its entirety. Noticeable again was the absence from the debates of any sustained discussion of specific local perpetrators.

In 1998, the city sponsored an architectural competition for the Dokumentationszentrum. The Austrian Günther Domenig won with a plan for a museum that slashed through one corner of the Kongresshalle (Figure 5.17). His design, while rejecting Sonnenberger's lighthouse proposal, remained true to the original suggestion by emphasizing the disparity between the fragmented steel and glass museum and Ludwig and Franz Ruff's monumental stone Kongresshalle. Such a disparity not only asserted a Modernist counteraesthetic, as in the Meistersingerhalle and Convention Center, but also attempted to draw attention to the forms of the National Socialist buildings by explicitly reacting to them. Reporters and politicians widely commented on the new structure's asymmetrical cut into the side of the Kongresshalle as a symbolic rejection of the Nazi past by a democratic present.[42] In this sense, the Dokumentationszentrum continued the pattern established by the self-reflective *Fascination and Terror* exhibition as well as the implicit message behind the Modernism of the Convention Center, but on a much grander scale and with explicit critical engagement. Officials proclaimed that the aesthetic choices antithetical to the monumental masonry and axial plans at the site were transparent to historical critique. In the process of drawing a line between the past and present, the building asserted the agency of contemporary Nuremberg citizens as distinct from and opposed to the criminal activities of the past. While the federal government initially dismissed the plans (citing the need to channel any cultural funds to the new states in the east), by 1999 it had agreed to help support the project.[43]

The city building administration under Walter Anderle used the consensus surrounding the development of the Dokumentationszentrum as a reason to call for a real comprehensive plan for the Party Rally Grounds site

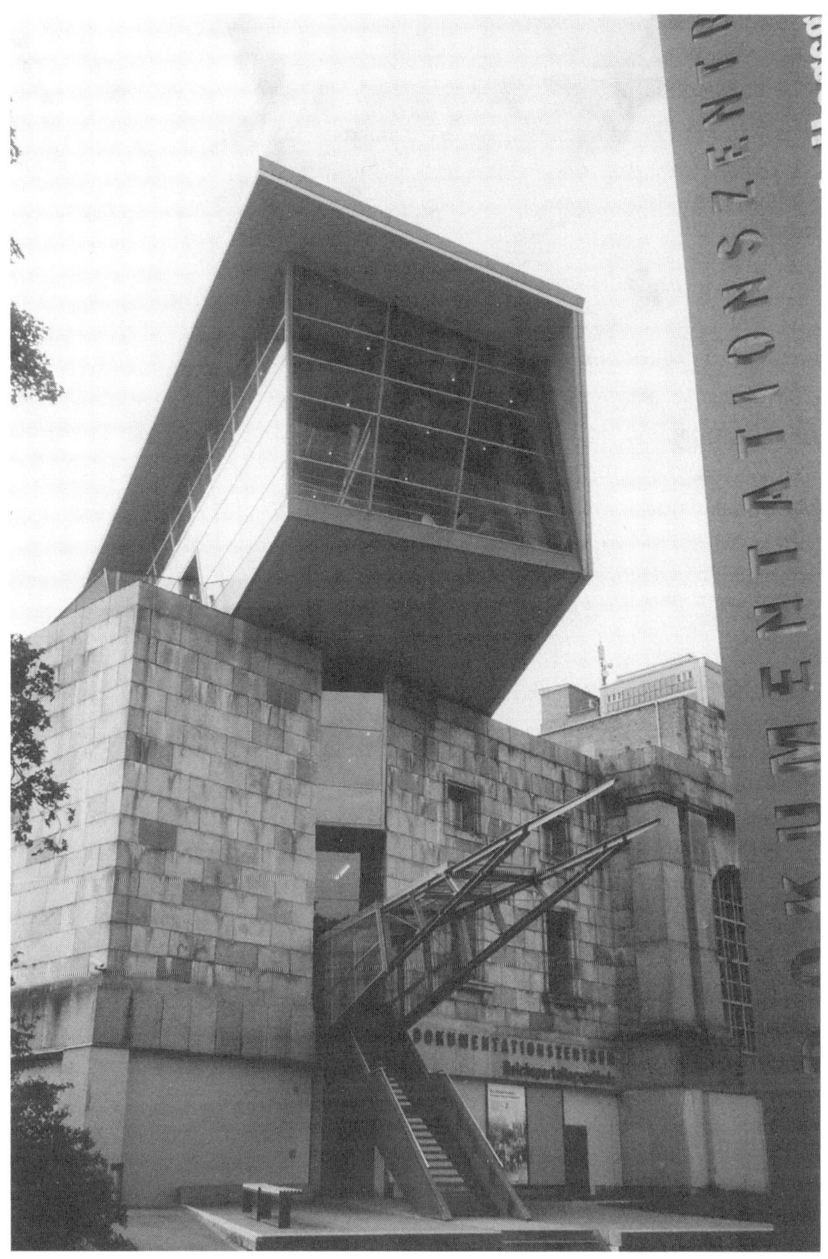

FIGURE 5.17. Günther Domenig, Dokumentationszentrum Reichsparteitagsgelände, Nuremberg, 2001. Author's photograph.

as a whole, something that had been ignored in the hodgepodge construction of the postwar years. The competition called for a unified planning approach as well as a clearer presentation of historical information compatible with the goals of the Dokumentationszentrum. Entries should respond to the multiplication of uses that resulted in a cacophony of architectural forms and alterations to the landscape. For example, the Convention Center continued to lobby for more use of the land regardless of its historical import while local citizens expanded the recreational activities with a variety of new functions. Anderle emphasized that such random development of uses could not be sustained. The city needed to have a comprehensive strategy respectful of the various interests (economic, social, historical) that nevertheless somehow made sense of the monumental scale and history of the site. While ultimately limited in architectural scope, his agenda, like that of the Dokumentationszentrum, found consensus in the fragile coalition of the CSU city council. The council approved an international architectural competition of ideas in May 2000.[44]

The competition took place in 2001. The task of the participants was a difficult one, as it involved integrating the varied uses of the site without significantly changing the architectural remnants under historical protection. Preservation, however, was hardly the number one local priority in all aspects of the program. For example, the Convention Center planned to expand its parking facilities (approved before the competition) on the site of Speer's Deutsches Stadion. The new structure required the removal of the one historically significant remnant of the Nazi building, the corner stone laid by Hitler in 1937. That is to say, while Anderle achieved consensus around the need for a comprehensive plan, the variety of interests at stake led to multiple contradictions and limitations for the participating architects. The competition revealed to a much greater degree than the Dokumentationszentrum the emphasis on the site's instrumental use for goals other than historical or historicist ones.[45] Such had been the fate, after all, of most perpetrator sites in urban centers throughout Germany at least up to the 1980s. Given the massive scale of the site, the multiple users and group interests could push for control over bits and pieces of the grounds without seeming to damage the unity of the whole. In the process, however, the ability to achieve a consensus among all the diverse stakeholders necessary to implement any comprehensive design strategy became increasingly remote.

Although the entries were naturally diverse, clear patterns and points of emphasis frequently emerged. For example, due to the vast size of the grounds, multiple entries proposed large-scale unifying devices, such as a separate transportation system or, most commonly, a series of visually related pavilions dotting the entire area. Others gave up on a unified system and, instead, proposed distinct zones of activity, most commonly historical and museological in the north, sport and leisure in the southeast, and economic around the Convention Center. Many entries tended to use a scheme of formally fragmenting the site to signal the violence of the Nazi past, and another large group of entries proposed subtle changes that affirmed and preserved the clarity of Speer's layout. The majority of proposals that suggested strong alterations to the architecture or historical plan focused in particular on the Kongresshalle, taking their cues from the Dokumentationszentrum architecture but also recognizing the open space around the building as a possible zone to be manipulated. The prize winners (three honorable mentions, three fourth-place prizes, one third place, and two second place) tended to either put forth radical transformations of the grounds through disruptions, morphed landscapes, lighting systems, and the like, or proposed only subtle alterations that preserved the historical framework.

The results of the competition confirmed that any unified historical or architectural plan would be sacrificed to the multiple interests at stake. More specifically, the jury members' competing ideas about how to subsume National Socialist history within the demands of variable recreational and economic uses strongly influenced the results. The jury, half of whom were architects, planners, and historians, and half of whom were city representatives, did not reach a consensus for a first prize. Rather, it split between those who favored doing as little as possible to change the grounds or mark their historical significance and those who wanted a more aggressive architectural solution. As a result, it awarded two second prizes. The proposal of Erik Meinertz and Harms Wulf won one of these prizes because of its minimal changes to the site (see Plate 12). Their proposal rested in particular on changes to the landscape that more firmly linked the historical structures visually as well as some smaller built alterations around the land. This plan seemed to emphasize Speer's original intention by adding a structure across from the Kongresshalle and another in front of the Convention Center buildings that exaggerated the symmetry and hence the monumentality of the grounds. On the other hand, it became a focal point for those who were disgusted with any acknowledgment of the architectural merit of the site as well as those who wanted its historical resonance to fade into the background in favor of other uses. In addition, preservationists argued that it did the least damage to the historic fabric.

Those jury members who favored a dramatic architectural solution awarded the other second prize to the plans of Martina Erbs and Martin Stadtler, who proposed a series of incisions and ruptures that cut across and partially fractured the unity of the whole (Daniel Libeskind's Jewish Museum design seems influential in this regard, as was Domenig's Dokumentationszentrum, under construction at the time) (Plate 13). The intersecting axes visually linked the important components of Speer's plan but also emphasized the historical confrontation with fascism. Erbs and Stadtler planned for specific points that disrupted the unity of the whole, particularly evident in the interruption, for example, of the Grosse Strasse as that axis crosses the Dutzendteich. This solution extended and exaggerated the more public and apparently critical aesthetic engagements with the land that had produced such exhibition spaces as *Fascination and Terror.*

Yet while the aesthetic rejection of Speer's monumentality may have been fine for one corner of the Kongresshalle for city representatives of many political stripes, the nonarchitectural representatives on the jury in particular found the strategy too disruptive of the many interests at stake, both historical and pragmatic. Thus in spite of the original political consensus around the need for a comprehensive plan, the diverse jury itself could not get beyond the contradictions inherent in the call for participants. They could not agree on a formal or historical solution, only a fragmentary response that allowed for the most flexible of pragmatic uses.[46] As a counterweight to such lack of consensus, the Dokumentationszentrum opened to great fanfare on November 4, 2001, with an exhibition that aimed for a popular audience. As Sonnenberger has stated, it specifically related to the conceptual and museological strategies of the U.S. Holocaust Memorial Museum, an acceptable language of commemoration.[47] The Dokumentationszentrum could tie Nuremberg to the (American) Allies firmly, while the question of how to historicize the sites of perpetrator activity remained unresolved.

The competition's results implicitly sacrificed any attempt to create a coherent historical experience in favor of pragmatic pluralism. This fractured approach ironically reflected a more accurate expression of the reigning political and social (if not aesthetic) consensus. With the communal vote of 2002, the SPD won back the mayor's office and the city council, with Ulrich Maly as mayor. In a February 2003 letter directed to a wide range of local constituents, Maly rejected the original intention of the competition with its attempt to achieve a total architectural solution for the site. Indeed, by this point, the competition had become a prominent symbol in administrative memos of what to avoid. Instead, his cultural department came up with a position paper that proposed a series of discussions to be held over time that allowed the functional use of the land to develop organically as befits a "democratic pluralistic" society. In essence, the new plan was to have no plan, or at least no fixed plan, and Maly explicitly rejected a single architectural solution to the site. While the mayor intended to provide flexibility and an ongoing debate concerning the historical significance of the area, in practice his plan avoided any serious critical reckoning with the grounds beyond the central facility of the Dokumentationszentrum. As a result, however, it also avoided the local contradictions that surfaced when architectural and historical solutions faced off against the narrow protection of variable uses that had doomed the 2001 competition. The one architectural gesture that Maly's new plan made to deal with this past was the proposed development of some kind of small-scale system of informa-tion panels. Scattered around the grounds, these panels expanded the his-torical message beyond the Dokumentationszentrum in time for the 2006 soccer championships, for which the city hosted qualifying matches.[48]

The panels as completed relate to the other proposals in the 2001 competition that laid out a series of informational pavilions to unify the site (Figure 5.18). Smaller in scale, the twenty-three panels cover not only the

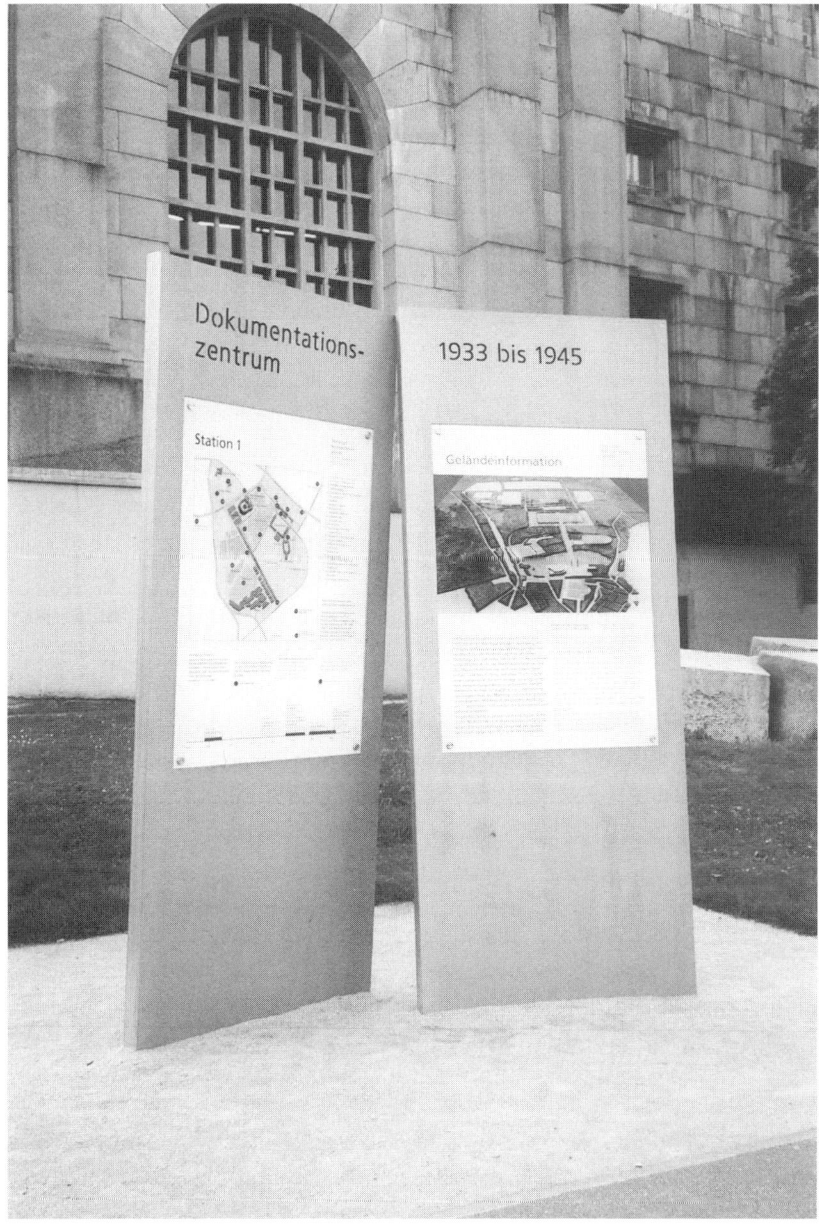

FIGURE 5.18. City of Nuremberg, infor-mation panels for the Reich Party Rally Grounds, Nuremberg, 2006. Author's photograph.

remnants of the current site but also those no longer associated with the Party Rally Grounds, such as the former SS Barracks on the Bayernstrasse and the now inaccessible former Märzfeld train station. They consist of two steel plates, set against each other at a canted angle, again conjuring up the concept of visual disjunction as a metaphor for historical violence. On one side, the panels display photos, maps, and text related to the use of the location in the Nazi period; on the other, they talk about its use since 2001, including narratives on the variety of social groups that enjoy the grounds. Given the grand scale of the site, from a distance the relatively small panels blend into the surrounding environment. Nevertheless, they are a regular part of the landscape and, owing to their numbers, hard to avoid. History and historical clarification exist side by side with the other functions of the site undisturbed.

CONCLUSION

If Nuremberg were Berlin or even Munich, one would perhaps have expected that, with a shift from CSU to SPD, as well as the stakes of the World Cup, more explicit ideological allegiances would have been formed as the various perspectives clashed over the proper way to emphasize the city's historical Nazi burden. Intensification of struggle is a key component of *Vergangenheitsbewältigung*, after all. But such was not the case. Rather, after some initial debates in the 1980s when emphasizing the National Socialist past became a national project, Nuremberg entered a phase of political consensus in which each side could find what it needed in the site. For the left-liberal independent initiatives, that meant an institutionalization of the grassroots effort to confront the Nazi past through tours and through the historical displays in the Dokumentationszentrum. For the liberal SPD, that meant emphasizing the pluralistic uses of the site, particularly as this favored its own position on guest workers, youth, and other groups within its policy interests who used the area recreationally. And for the CSU, the site was not going to be excessively documented, the economic engine of the Convention Center was to be undisturbed, and the state and federal government were to acknowledge through funding that, after all, it really was not a local history with specific perpetrators that needed to be particularized but rather a national history that needed to be generalized.

Given these conditions, it is no wonder that the 2001 competition was the exception that proved the rule. As in the other moments we have studied, it took a turn in conservative politics with the CSU victory to move the discussion forward with the competition. But in this case, namely, issues surrounding possible perpetrators still active in CSU circles, the ideological positions of different perpetrators that overlapped with conservative politics or the potential strategic use of the site by current neo-Nazis played a minimal role in debates or in defining clear positions. Instead, the competition, sparked by the chain of events following the CSU victory in the Rathaus, revealed how many constituencies accepted that the question of the perpetrator was a thing of the past with little relevance in the present. The competition failed to propose a comprehensive historical solution as that would have contradicted the necessity for a pluralistic contemporary solution acceptable to all. The city demanded multiple architectural and urbanistic responses that could colonize and make use of bits and pieces of the massive Nazi site to match a larger matrix of competing interests and concerns. Maly learned this lesson and proposed instead letting the site develop organically. The Stadtrat unanimously approved Maly's position on May 19, 2004. This vote confirmed that the historical significance of the site and its scale—the latter, a distinctive contribution of Speer's original plan—could be easily subsumed into a variety of uses. Hence, each stakeholder could rest assured that his or her vision of the site would be actualized to some degree.[49]

This overview of the contemporary use of the Nuremberg Party Rally Grounds leads us to several conclusions. Initially, with the construction of the housing estates in Langwasser as well as the splashy Modernism of the Meistersingerhalle and the Convention Center, politicians and planners followed national trends evident particularly in bombed-out areas of West Berlin in which housing and up-to-date cultural institutions fit the *Wirtschaftswunder* ethos, adapted to local constituencies. The development of the site continued to adhere to national trends with the ideological conflict between left and right in the 1980s over perpetrators and the past. But the debates about the use of the rally grounds achieved an exceptional state of consensus in the late 1990s not seen at the national level, at least in terms of the general goals for the land. Such consensus rested on a complicated series of factors involving the regional and national interests and local coalition politics. But the consensus itself managed to avoid, surprisingly, the particularly contentious debates in Berlin that centered on the questions of whether the Nazi criminal activities or victims should be commemorated at a particular site and who should control that ritualization of historical memory. Clearly, a variety of interests was and still is at stake in how the architecture and land are used. Still, the smaller scale of regional politics, as well as the centralized authority of the city administration in the development process (and the key role of consensus builders such as museum director Sonnenberger), made a difference. In many ways, these conditions forced the dominant parties to push through a series of initiatives that would not be possible in the higher-stakes national centers of Berlin or Munich.

The city's latest proposal makes clear that the local consensus of the last decade is as much subject to change as any other. Still, it nevertheless indicates that the supposed burden of the past is much more variably handled than art historians have previously assumed, a point that has naturally been a central thesis of this book. Contrasting with the debates concerning perpetrators that helped explain Richter's work, the silence of architectural neglect may be the dominant tone of the first postwar decades in Nuremberg. But complementary to the discussion of Kiefer and Kohl, the struggles and debates characterized by *Vergangenheitsbewältigung* may very well suffice to describe the situation of Nuremberg in the seventies and eighties. But these terms are insufficient to account for the past decade of policy concerning the Party Rally Grounds. The ideologically driven debates about commemorating the Nazi past have been subsumed by a pragmatism whereby specific interests dominate symbolic considerations, a trend that is increasingly visible elsewhere. Such laissez-faire historicism of the site positions current citizens and uses as distinct from and opposed to the perpetrators of the past. At the Party Rally Grounds, the variable postwar political uses of Nazi architecture could not be more concretely demonstrated. Through consensus and pragmatic interests, local constituencies have relegated questions of symbolic import and the ideological significance of the National Socialist perpetrator to a secondary concern. Hitler's aesthetic interest in monumentally scaled sites allows this attitude to play itself out particularly well in Nuremberg.

The variable interests that came together at Nuremberg challenge the fundamental abstraction of debates about architecture and memory in much of the art historical literature, particularly on Berlin. Far from a generalized notion of mourning and melancholia, the instrumentalization of former sites of perpetrators and victims requires a closer look at the agency of individuals and institutions. Local constituencies in turn reinterpreted and repurposed decisions and ideological confrontations that occurred at the national level. Such instrumentalization is, of course, much more often about contemporary conditions than it is about any coherent "politics of memory." The complexity and contradictions of these conditions are critical factors for explaining the social significance of the built environment. Analyzing the postwar history of the Reich Party Rally Grounds indicates how less hyperbolic examples of key local debates clarify the political function of architecture. At Nuremberg, that political role contributed to and highlights the fading resonance of the National Socialist perpetrator as a category of urgent contemporary debate.

THE NAZI PAST IN POSTWAR GERMANY'S CULTURAL HISTORY

But we can also say that the long life of the Holocaust (including its so-called recent resurrection) is a complex phenomenon. It shows us that some of the prejudices, dangers, misconceptions, and triggers of violence that were present then are still with us today. They may look different, come from other sources, beliefs, and politics, but they share some similarities. The notion that one learns from an atrocity should not be discarded. But one of the most important lessons must be that learning about atrocities does not prevent their recurrence. On the contrary, as the number and scale of atrocities, genocides, and destructive impulses multiply, and as our belief in progress, modernization, education, and social mobility diminishes, we must think of this leitmotif not only as a key to understanding the past but also as a warning about the future.

—Omer Bartov, "The Holocaust as Leitmotif of the Twentieth Century"

In spite of the distance of more than half a century and the beginning of a new millennium, it is hard to say that we have left the effects of World War II and the Holocaust behind in our society. The latter is still the litmus test with which we subsequently judge all unfortunate other genocides.[1] The war itself was obviously fundamental for the ascension of the military and economic dominance of the United States, a position that continues to affect us with the conflicts and competitions of a global world. In Germany itself, the impact of the period led to a divided nation that became a premier ideological and geographic battleground for the Cold War. Even with unification and the removal of the stigma of occupation, the war and particularly the Holocaust are reference points for debating contemporary culture and society on issues of central importance. By now, the period and its grotesque outcome have become ubiquitous, known the world over in films and novels. Politicians use its leader as a cudgel to compare him to their worst international enemies, and the trial of its top officials still functions as an important basis of international human rights law.[2] The world of the National Socialist perpetrator continues to be felt in Germany and elsewhere, even while the concept of who exactly that perpetrator was morphs and changes with the political and cultural conditions of a given place and time.

But if we all recognize the significance of that impact, why has this period been either bracketed or its changing reception only partially treated by historians of modern art and architecture? Art historians, along with scholars from many disciplines, have done important work in understanding the cultural and social significance of memorialization of victims and the critical debates about the philosophical import of representing the Holocaust. But other aspects of the past also have cultural relevance. Too often art historical debate is limited to works of aesthetic or conceptual complexity or cultural production that affirm market norms. Banal architecture, more intellectually obvious visual culture, aesthetic decisions against the grain of the dominant market trends, or cultural works that are compromised by their overt right-wing connections play little to no role in postwar art history, in Germany or elsewhere. The result is a canonical art history that concomitantly narrows the intricate range of relevant political questions. This art history leaves the entire cultural significance of right-wing politics at best firmly confined to the fascist era and, at worse, completely outside consideration.

Such an isolation or marginalization gives a distorted view of German art and architecture. By looking at the long-term influence on conservative politics of the Nazi Party and the significance of postwar debates about the perpetrator, I have indicated how these political debates lead us to more comprehensive and critical interpretations of West German architecture and art, from the best-known examples to those that are relatively obscure. As a primary or secondary condition, the developing impact of the policies, practices, and perpetrators of the Nazi state, as well as the defining influence of its greatest crime of the genocide, shaped the cultural production of artists and architects. Such an analysis cannot be limited to the importance of memorialization of the victims any more than it can be sidestepped by referencing only the ethical challenge of the genocide's destructive logic, however important this research is. Other categories of evidence and kinds of knowledge need to be brought to bear so that the reception of the Nazi past can be more thoroughly integrated into the history of modern German art.

This is a materialist project that is sensitive to chronology, geography, and specific conditions as much as it relies on more traditional art historical tactics of visual analysis. It also draws its examples from the significance of the political debates, not from the standard artistic categories or media. So the paintings by Richter and Kiefer are of more relevance in the earlier period of my study because of their thematization of the personal or generational connections to the perpetrator, the main political concern in the immediate postwar period. On the other hand, the ideological projections and major policy shifts connected to the Nazi past after Kohl solidified his hold on the chancellor's office are better clarified by the architectural examples of Libeskind and the Reich Party Rally Grounds. Attending to these factors and distinctions sheds a very different light on the relationship of these cultural cases to the NSDAP, its policies, and former personnel. Ultimately, political history helps us ask different kinds of art historical questions.

For Holocaust studies, an attention to the visual when investigating the reception of the Nazi perpetrator is a matter of increasing urgency. While the policy debates and analysis of ideological positions will always be important to understanding the enactment of the Jewish genocide, its postwar impact is more and more mediated by questions of representation. Film studies has been on the forefront of contributing to this analysis, but art history also could have much more to say.[3] Too often, visual imagery has been used by historians and others as mere background to a broader argument about memory and memorialization. It serves only to illustrate a particular political position or point. Art history offers a way of seeing the visual not as ancillary but as essential to the wide nexus of ideological and cultural conditions that have been wielded in political debates instrumentalizing the Nazi perpetrator. Weighing art and architecture with other kinds of evidence means carefully calibrating the relative impact, which is sometimes fundamental and sometimes incidental to other kinds of visual, textual, or verbal responses. Through a more comprehensive analysis of this evidence, we also gain a more precise understanding of how the typology of the perpetrator shifted in the postwar period up to the current trend visible in Nuremberg, where the individual actors from the Nazi past are consigned to the historical realm. The social field of debate and division, the particular struggles concerning representations to which art history can speak, come more clearly to the fore as fundamental problems in need of analysis for the scholarship as a whole.

In this regard, debates about the perpetrator, like those concerning Holocaust victims or other historical groups and events, change and vary in the post-Nazi era and can be either central or only secondary to explaining specific works of art or architecture, depending on the circumstances. But in highlighting the perpetrator, I have argued that art history has missed the very multiplicity of political positions and questions that help explain the total social function of culture. Take, for example, a building in Berlin that is known for its tortured and seemingly impossible history through the political minefields of twentieth-century German society. Ernst Sagebiel's Air Force Ministry (1936) (Figure A.1), built to house Hermann Göring's expanding military bureaucracy, was one of the first large-scale buildings sponsored by the Nazi state completed in Berlin.[4] The stripped-down neoclassicism, emphasis on large volumes, and especially its travertine facade all became familiar markers of the aesthetic preferences for most official state and party building. Here is a building that Germans in the west and east should have associated with the brutal conquering ambitions of Hitler, the genocidal project that buttressed these goals, and the way in which cultural production served these ends.

To the contrary, though, its postwar history did not intersect with any major discussion of the Nazi perpetrator or criminal activity of the past; rather, GDR citizens created associations based on new political events and policies. After surviving the battle for Berlin relatively intact, the building served as the headquarters for the Soviet military until the foundation of the GDR in 1949. At that time, it became the House of Ministries, encasing a variety of diverse bureaucracies within the East German state (as with so many Nazi buildings, its scale made the multiple uses almost inevitable). In June 1953, antigovernment protesters rose up and took to the streets, demonstrating outside this building. These protests were subsequently suppressed, although West Berliners tried to keep the memory of them alive in typical Cold War style by renaming part of Unter den Linden the Street of the 17th of June (Strasse des 17. Juni). The socialists ruled until the renewed demonstrations preceding the fall of the Berlin Wall. Part of the

FIGURE A.1. Ernst Sagebiel, Air Force Ministry, Berlin, 1936. Author's photograph.

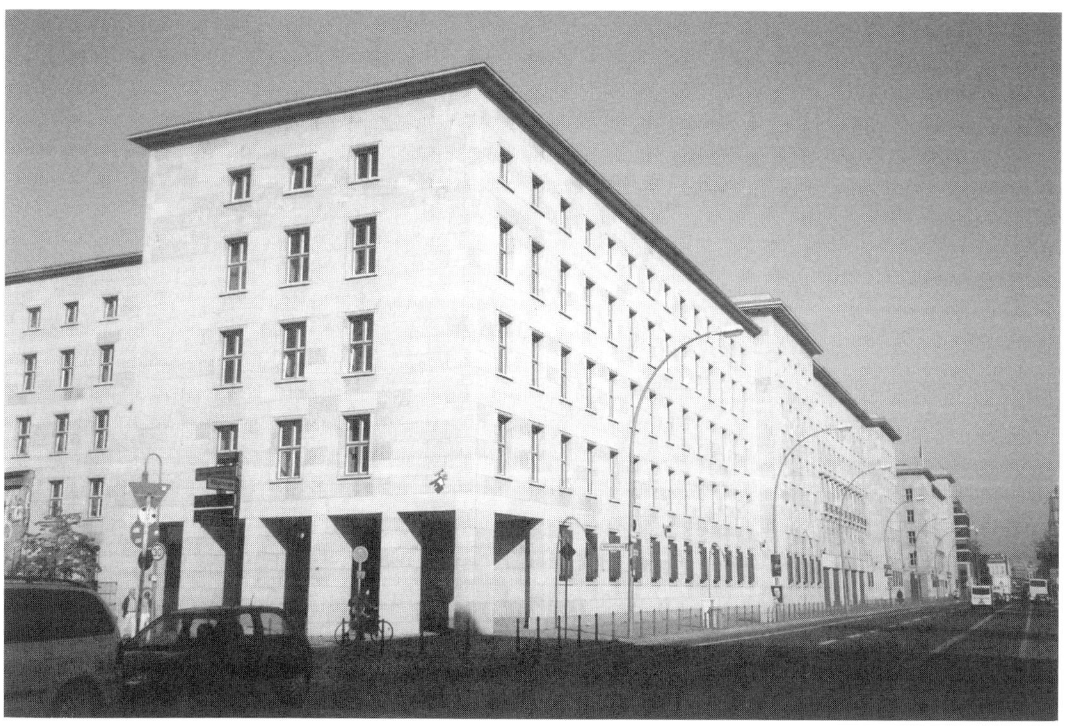

wall ran beside the building. For a brief moment (1991–95) after reunification the building housed the much-hated Treuhandanstalt, the oversight organization coordinating the privatization and distribution of East German state assets. Today, it houses the Finance Ministry, and it serves equally as the remarkable backdrop to the somber *Topography of Terror* exhibition just across the Niederkirchnerstrasse (the former Prinz-Albrecht-Strasse) to the south.[5] And yet the discussion of the Nazi perpetrator as the clear historical agent in the displays at the *Topography of Terror* seems to have barely touched the meaning or use of the ministry across the street. At the former site, the SS tortured victims, a subject that we need to memorialize; in the latter, though, Nazi military officials planned aspects of the domination of Europe, a topic seemingly outside postwar cultural interests in commemoration or historicization. The more complex relation to the politics of both Nazi Germany and all subsequent regimes has generated little response in the art historical record.

This brief history raises a number of relevant questions for my study. Clearly, at one level the building has been little more than a convenient site, an empty box to be filled and used by the changing bureaucracies of German state power in the twentieth century. Just as clearly, we know that Göring saw the prominence and prestige of the building as a sign of his own rise and the permanence of Hitler's state that he served. The Allies tried Göring at the International Military Tribunal, which made him the most immediate postwar personification of the extreme, ideologically driven perpetrator, and the building remains as a way of explaining his ambition, actions, and identity. But is that the end of its ideological import or its political instrumentalization? How did the Soviets interpret their use of this building? What did this perpetrator site mean, if anything, to the building workers demonstrating against the socialist government in 1953? How were the two eras linked again and reinterpreted after 1989 by the triumphant West German bureaucrats in charge of disposing of the assets of both regimes? What is its purpose now in relation to official tourist policies that, benevolently or not, cater to those of us who come to explore the Nazi past in the *Topography of Terror* and other sites in the once and current capital? Bits and pieces of these questions have been explored for many sites in Berlin and in other places in Germany, as well as in relation to specific works of art that overtly engage the past, particularly in the literature surrounding memorialization. But as I have argued, a sporadic interest in political history for an analysis of postwar art and architecture woefully underplays the cultural engagement with the variable debates of real consequence concerning the Nazi past and the changing understanding of the perpetrator. A consistent and comprehensive political history of art responds to that lacuna. The focus on the Nazi perpetrator helps highlight a variety of different political debates and issues previously unanalyzed in art history.

Like any period, however atrocious, National Socialist Germany will eventually fade from public memory and its contours will be blurred as it is supplanted by other moments in time, other tragedies of state violence. We will not forget this history, but it will be seen as less urgent to the problem of defining who we are in contemporary society, a process I have argued we can begin to see with the current reception of the buildings in Nuremberg. Artists will turn to other events of resistance or oppression to engage their critical visions, and architectural patrons will have debates about preservation of structures or sites of commemoration from different moments in time and place. But scholarship has goals distinct from the documentary films on television, paintings in galleries, or political speeches at commemorative sites. For scholars, a more comprehensive, nuanced, and analytic understanding of the past serves to argue for recognizing and comprehending the fundamental conditions of modern life. In this case, the integration of Nazi history with art history helps clarify the extreme and destructive relationship of culture and politics in modern industrial society. Conversely, it shows that art history has important work to do in charting the ins and outs, the conflicts, and contradictions of that relationship. What is perhaps most fascinating with the political reception of the Nazi perpetrator in postwar Germany is its variability and its chameleon nature, changing with every new contemporary crisis and being used by new and surprising individuals throughout the postwar period. Charting this variability has been essential to understanding how art historical questions were at times woven into these political moments and events. The study of the Nazi perpetrator in art history exposes the depth and texture of the relationship between politics and art as well as its potential limits.

By focusing on political history, my project attempts to argue for a different emphasis than exists in the current analysis of the postwar German art and architecture of the Federal Republic. My argument takes its cues not from internal aesthetic or philosophical debates within critical artistic practice but rather from the events and conditions of modern society. Concentrating on buildings and artworks of intense public and ideological scrutiny indicates the possibilities or impossibilities of art to engage with historical change. Importantly, it also raises the question of how a history of the function of art can clarify the complexities of the historical development of a given society. The political debates about the Nazi perpetrator engaged postwar German art at many levels. The analysis of this fraught engagement moves us from a more complete account of art to a more compelling understanding of the potential for using art history to critique the circumstances that demarcate moments of political struggle and debate in any society.

ACKNOWLEDGMENTS

The arc of this book has a long trajectory. It began with the History of Art Department at University College London, which invited me to give the Tomás Harris Memorial Lectures in 2003. Those talks were the genesis of this book, and I am grateful for the kind invitation as well as the reception of my colleagues at UCL. In particular, I thank Warren Carter, Tamar Garb, Tom Gretton, and Helen Weston. Fred Schwartz, as always, provided me with the critical feedback and support then and at subsequent stages of the project. I express my gratitude for the UCL faculty's generous time, critical comments, and encouragement.

Subsequent individuals and audiences contributed important commentary at key moments in the development of the book. Many editors and readers were involved with the various manifestations of this project, and I am indebted to all the anonymous readers, in particular the careful attention of Matthew Biro, Geoff Eley, Stephanie Fay, and Jonathan Wiener. I am grateful to the many audiences that stimulated my thinking. Specifically, I thank the organizers of the Jean and Harold Gossett Lectures at the University of Chicago, where crucial parts of the opening chapters were presented. At the University of Chicago, I am indebted to ongoing conversations with Christine Mehring and Rebecca Zorach and their efforts to keep the Chicago community of art historians lively. Other friends and colleagues in Chicago helped in multiple conversations, small and large, and I especially thank Jill Bugajski, Jay Clarke, Holly Clayson, Stephanie d'Alessandro, Hannah Feldman, Christina Kiaer, Jeannette Trembley, and David Van Zanten. Stephen Eisenman offered particular support as a friend and a critical voice.

Debra Mancoff has been there to help every step of the way. At DePaul University, I am grateful for my colleagues and friends, especially Joanna Gardner-Huggett, Matthew Girson, Trish Kelly, and Liz Lillehoj for their comments on specific parts of the argument as well as the advice and patience of Anne Bartlett, Tom Donley, Steve Harp, Louise Lincoln, Jerry Mulderig, Darrell Moore, Kevin Stevens, and Julia Woesthoff. Susan Solway always managed to find the right stipend or the right word at the right time, which was more help than she knows. I thank Dean Charles Suchar and the College of Liberal Arts and Sciences for the frequent summer grants that funded many of my research trips.

At a crucial stage of my research, this project was supported by a research leave sponsored by DePaul's University Research Council as well as by a grant from the U.S. Holocaust Memorial Museum Center for Advanced Holocaust Studies. The staff and many colleagues there went above and beyond to assist my work. Special thanks to Lisa Yavnai and Traci Rucker for solving all problems, as well as to Martin Dean, Jürgen Matthäus, Marc Masurovsky, and Suzanne Brown-Flemming for discussions. The team around the geographies of the Holocaust project, while not directly involved with the arguments in this book, nevertheless gave constant intellectual stimulus and friendship during the past few years. My thanks to Robert Ehrenreich and his indefatigable efforts on our behalf and, especially, the leaders Tim Cole, Alberto Giordano, and Anne Kelly Knowles. Other fellows at the Center for Advanced Holocaust Studies (CAHS) were also of crucial help, notably Daniella Doron, Jennifer Geddes, and Jonathan Judaken. Special thanks to Noah Shenker and Eran Neuman for helping make the CAHS dialogue a decidedly cultural one. Finally, my time in Washington, D.C., would have been impossible without the extraordinary kindness of my hosts, Sheila Jaskot and Bill Wax, who, through it all, somehow kept a smile.

I am further indebted to the College Art Association's Millard Meiss Publication Fund and its selection committee for the generous grant that helped support the reproduction of images. Further support was also given by DePaul's University Research Council.

Much of this research was done in archives in Berlin, Munich, and Nuremberg. The staff at the Senatsverwaltung für Wissenschaft, Forschung und Kultur, Berlin, were extraordinarily generous in opening files and space to me, and I am also grateful to the fine work of the Berlin Landesarchiv. The Stadtarchiv Nürnberg became a crucial site for research with its ever-friendly staff, and I appreciate the continued interest in my work from colleagues at the Dokumentationszentrum des Reichsparteitagsgelände, especially Eckart Dietzfelbinger, Martina Christmeier, and Hans-Christian Täubrich. My understanding of Nuremberg was greatly aided by the generous time given to me by the former director of the city museums, Franz Sonnenberger.

Munich, and especially the Zentralinstitut für Kunstgeschichte, holds a particular pride of place in importance for this book. The staff there was generous and interested, and the visiting colleagues a positive challenge to the development of key ideas. To Wolf Tegethoff I will always be indebted, and I am thankful for the continued support of Iris Lauterbach. Stephan Klingen made heroic efforts to find specific photographs as well as engaged intellectually (along with Helga Puhlmann) with the thrust of my project. Christian and Sabine Fuhrmeister went to extraordinary lengths to make their home mine while I was there, and I am deeply grateful for their friendship. Christian's work, from which I am still learning, provides a model of how art history needs to think about Nazi Germany. I am grateful for the many conversations with fellow visitors to the Zentralinstitut, above all Jonathan Petropoulos and Evonne Levy: they both read important passages of the book and made patient corrections that added immeasurably to the argument.

This book comes out of the wide fields of art history, German studies, and Holocaust studies. I received critical feedback on aspects of the project from Doris Bergen, Stephen Brockmann, Jean-Louis Cohen, Guillaume de Syon, Jeffry Diefendorf, Carol Duncan, Sabine Eckmann, April Eisman, Fred Evans, Hartmut Frank, Sabine Hake, Peter Hayes, Elizabeth Heineman, Dagmar Herzog, Keith Holz, Kathleen James-Chakraborty, Annie Kellogg-Krieg, Sherry Lindquist, Maria Mitchell, Kevin Murphy, Olaf Peters, Emily Pugh, Michael Rothberg, Terry Smith, and James Young. Despina Stratigakos and James Van Dyke both exemplified what engaged colleagues and friends can do to shape one's work, and I cannot thank them enough: their work takes German art history to new levels. Nancy Troy has always been there to encourage and advise on all things art historical, which helped me along on countless occasions. Gavriel Rosenfeld also was a great defender at a crucial time, and our work together on a related anthology sustained my thoughts in many ways. Alan Steinweis generously invited me to present several chapters of this book as the Miller Visiting Professor at the University of Vermont; his attention to my work, as well as the comments and friendship of Jonathan Huener, Frank Nicosia, and Susanna Schrafstetter, made my time in Vermont a truly meaningful experience. Outside this specific academic network, many years of this project overlapped with my involvement with the College Art Association. Linda Downs and her extraordinary staff made many a difficult time easy, which helped my writing in countless ways. I am particularly grateful for the engaged interest in my work of board colleagues and friends Nicola Courtright, Jeffrey Cunard, and Jack Hyland.

No book can reach its full potential without the patience and guidance of its editor and publishing staff. I appreciate the commitment of the University of Minnesota Press, the engaged advice and support of Pieter Martin, and the indefatigable work of Kristian Tvedten. In addition, I am grateful for the work of Mary Byers, Rachel Moeller, and Laura Westlund in improving the quality of the manuscript.

Finally, five people went above and beyond. One was my mother, Georgia Bourquin Jaskot, who sadly passed away before seeing the completion of this book. Her tireless efforts to take us to every possible art museum in our childhood travels sparked my lifelong interest in art; she is dearly missed. My other four friends read more of the manuscript than they probably care to admit. Andrew Hemingway has been an unfailing advocate of a critical Marxist art history that he models in his work as well as in his support of other scholars' work. From the first lectures at UCL to the most recent versions of this manuscript, he has not shied from giving advice or maintaining an active engagement. I cannot thank him enough. Barbara McCloskey has been a defender of my work since the beginning. She does not pull any punches when she addresses the form and content of an art historical argument, and I can only be grateful that she continues to make time to read almost every word that I have written. I hope this book at least approaches her high standards. Roshanna Sylvester gave me the outside eye of a Russian historian, showing that true collegiality can also involve intense intellectual connections across disciplinary divides. I cannot overstate the importance and friendship of all three, who have carried me through many a thorny patch.

And, at last, Robert Buerglener. Rob suffered the difficult times with his distinctive sangfroid, lived with the manuscript through all its twists and turns, and listened to every possible variation of ideas from the most banal to those that showed promise. Along with these great acts of patience and kindness, he has been a constant reader of texts, both the draftiest and the most polished, never stinting on the best of his advice. He has shown an intellectual interest in my progress and always helped me to focus on the necessities of the moment, whether it meant long periods of travel or equally long moments of silence and concentration. He provided me with the kind of stability and support that I need most, and I don't know where this book or I would be without him.

NOTES

INTRODUCTION

1. The following biographical information is based on Backes and Jesse, *Politischer Extremismus in der Bundesrepublik Deutschland*, 343–44, and his obituary in David Childs, "Franz Schönhuber: SS Officer Turned Right-wing Politician," *Independent*, November 30, 2005, online edition. http://www.independent.co.uk/news/obituaries/franz-schonhuber-517501.html.

2. For a brief discussion of the "new populism" in Europe, see Judt, *Postwar*, 736–48.

3. See, for example, the interesting essays in Ray, *Joseph Beuys*.

4. "Ausstellung Paul Mathias Padua."

5. For a canonical approach to this question, see Young, *The Texture of Memory*, and more recently, the fascinating overview of Marcuse, "Holocaust Memorials." For an analysis of the historiography on this topic, see Jaskot and Rosenfeld, "Introduction," in Rosenfeld and Jaskot, *Beyond Berlin*, 1–21.

6. Hilberg, *Perpetrators Victims Bystanders*, ix.

7. Waller, *Becoming Evil*, 175–235.

8. Ibid., xi.

9. Although I began with Hilberg, his typology of perpetrator, victim, and bystander has been generally acknowledged as too neat. Indeed, of importance in this book is how loosely the term can be applied. Famously, the blurring of victim and perpetrator status has been convincingly and starkly highlighted in Gross, *Neighbors*.

10. Herf, *Divided Memory*, 111.

11. Castillo, *Cold War on the Home Front*, 98–99.

12. Much important art historical work, for example, has been done on the political debates on the right and left in the Weimar Republic. Most recently, see van Dyke, *Franz Radziwill and the Contradictions of German Art History, 1919–45*.

13. See, e.g., the classic text on architectural continuity, Durth, *Deutsche Architekten*, or the recent essays and bibliography in Doll et al., *Kunstgeschichte nach 1945*.

14. Foundational texts on this subject include Reichel, *Politik mit der Erinnerung*, and Young, *The Texture of Memory*.

15. I discuss specific elements of this scholarship in the subsequent chapters on the individual artists. For an excellent example, though, see Biro, *Anselm Kiefer and the Philosophy of Martin Heidegger*.

16. The best in scholarship that dovetails with this trend can be found in the important catalog Barron and Eckmann, *Art of Two Germanys*. I refer to particularly useful essays from this volume later in the book.

1. National Socialists and Art

1. My project here parallels James Waller's attempt to characterize the social-psychological attributes of individuals who commit genocide. However, while Waller is looking for shared psychic and contextual patterns among individuals in general, my concern is more with how specific actions or moments in the implementation of oppressive policies in Nazi Germany became particularly recognizable to a postwar audience. The postwar temporal variability of *what* was recognized and *when* is, of course, the realm of the historian, which complements Waller's work but leads to a somewhat different typology. Waller, *Becoming Evil*.

2. For examples of the integration of art, architecture, and art history into Nazi political goals, see, among others, Doll, Fuhrmeister, and Sprenger, eds., *Kunstgeschichte im Nationalsozialismus*; Jaskot, "Architecture and the Destruction of the European Jews"; and Peters, *Neue Sachlichkeit und Nationalsozialismus*.

3. Art and art history of the Nazi period have always been somewhat overlooked in the general triumphal march of modern art. Important surveys discuss the period, if at all, as background for exiled Modernists or with a few examples of propagandistic art that contrast with nonfascist examples. In the past few decades, important critical work has been done, particularly in Germany, including early scholarship by Berthold Hinz, Hartmut Frank, and Kathrin Hoffman-Curtius. More recently, art history under National Socialism has been of increasing interest in the work of, for example, Nikola Doll, Christian Fuhrmeister, and Olaf Peters. Still, while the earlier literature explored the ideological content of art and the more recent literature has begun to look at institutional contexts, a systematic and sustained account of National Socialist art, art policy, and the dynamics of the art world remains to be written. For an approach to a comprehensive analysis, see Spotts, *Hitler and the Aesthetics of Power*, or Backes, *Hitler und die bildenden Künste*.

4. By comparison, see, for example, the philosophically complex introduction to Brett Ashley Kaplan's analysis of postwar aesthetics and the Holocaust. In spite of its title, "politics" is an intellectual claim with no historical specificity. Kaplan, "The Politics of Aesthetic Pleasure in Holocaust Representation," in *Unwanted Beauty*.

5. For a classic analysis of the involvement of individuals in the early years of the Nazi Party, see Merkl, *Political Violence under the Swastika.*

6. "Der Eheskandal Charlie Chaplins," *Völkischer Beobachter,* February 15, 1927, 2. The Garbo advertisement can be found in *Völkischer Beobachter* (supplement), January 18/19, 1931, 2.

7. See, e.g., one of the rare examples of a major cultural article on the front page, which includes a report on a cultural day held in Munich as well as a speech by Hitler exhorting his colleagues to see criticism of the degeneracy and "Jewification" of art as a necessary component of their political struggle: "Nationalsozialismus und Kunstpolitik," *Völkischer Beobachter,* January 28, 1928, 1.

8. Mühlenberger, *Hitler's Voice,* 17–22. As Mühlenberger notes, while the *VB* has been a well-known source for its articles, relatively little scholarly attention has been paid to the newspaper itself. His study is an attempt to remedy this and includes chapters on the various phases of activity (focusing on the *Kampfzeit*) as well as translations of key articles. While there are several studies of art magazines produced during the Nazi period, to my knowledge, there is no art historical analysis of the art criticism and cultural reporting in the *VB,* a rather stunning absence in the field. Once again, Barbara Miller Lane's excellent text comes closest, with her attention to Nazi attitudes toward Modernist architecture for which she uses many sources from the *VB.* See Miller Lane, *Architecture and Politics in Germany, 1918–1945,* 147–67.

9. For discussion of Wölfflin and his early development, see Lurz, *Heinrich Wölfflin,* 53–120. More recently, see the important work by Evonne Levy, including Levy, "The Political Project of Wölfflin's Early Formalism." I am indebted to Levy for her deep knowledge of the art historian. For a summary of his ways of viewing style as a schema or conceptual strategy influenced by Kant, see Hart, "Heinrich Wölfflin," 425ff. The Wölfflin literature is vast. For the context of this discussion, see also Holly, *Past Looking,* 91–111, as well as the standard biographical entry in Betthausen, Feist, and Fork, *Metzler Kunsthistoriker Lexikon,* 483–88. More recent interpretations of his philosophical influence include, among others, Adler, "Painterly Politics"; and Koss, "On the Limits of Empathy."

10. Wölfflin was certainly not alone in this period for attempting to classify social production in racialized terms. Needless to say, many art historians have pointed out this issue, and it has become a particular leitmotif in recent work, although not the central subject of analysis. For two excellent examples, see Kaufmann, *Toward a Geography of Art;* and Schwartz, *Blind Spots.* See also Levy, "The Political Project of Wölfflin's Early Formalism." Martin Warnke's important essay "On Heinrich Wölfflin" was the first to argue for a political interpretation of the art historian. He asserted that *Principles* represented an antinationalist point of view, given its refusal to assert a particular German nationalism while being written during World War I. However, he does not address the racialized vocabulary in this and other Wölfflin texts. Notably, whatever the value of much of the recent literature on art history under National Socialism, this scholarship has focused on how Nazi ideas and policies developed outside art history are reflected in scholarship or

implemented in university institutional contexts. They do not talk about the reverse, which is how art historical ideas were politically appropriated. For a related discussion of the criminal culpability of art historians as they became part of the looting bureaucracy during the war, see Petropoulos, *The Faustian Bargain*, 165–214.

11. Peukert, *The Weimar Republic*, 247–72.

12. Notably, by the late twenties, Wölfflin was already removed from the major debates within art history, which at this time had shifted to questions such as epistemology and phenomenology with the work of younger art historians like Ernst Panofsky, Wilhelm Pinder, and Hans Sedlmayr. For a set of useful intellectual biographies, see Dilly, ed., *Altmeister moderner Kunstgeschichte*. More recently, Fred Schwartz has done us a great service by investigating the relationship of early-twentieth-century German art history, including Wölfflin, and critical theory in much greater depth, resulting in a more nuanced understanding of intellectual debates than has previously been assumed. See, in particular, Schwartz, *Blind Spots*, 146–51. For art history during the Nazi period, see in particular the articles and bibliography in Doll, Fuhrmeister, and Sprenger, eds., *Kunstgeschichte im Nationalsozialismus*.

13. Meinhold Lurz's exegesis of Wölfflin's writing is the most detailed. But he analyzes this text only in relation to the specific thought of Wölfflin himself, not in terms of the politics of the time: Lurz, *Heinrich Wölfflin*, 199–209. For the reference to the *völkisch* see 42–45 and 259 n. 369. Predominantly for Lurz, while there are essentializing elements in Wölfflin, he sees the *völkisch* as a direction drawn from his work by others (e.g., Hans Günther) rather than as a crucial part of the art historian's own writing. Although *Heinrich Wölfflin* is an excellent intellectual biography, Lurz's interest in Günther and other Nazi intellectuals who may have used his writing is limited.

14. Wölfflin, *Italien und das deutsche Formgefühl*, 145–46.

15. Ibid., 142–43. All translations throughout are mine, unless otherwise noted.

16. Ibid., 80. For the broader intellectual context, see the still-foundational work of Mosse, *The Crisis of German Ideology* as well as *Toward the Final Solution*.

17. One of the classic texts on the usefulness of culture to political debates in the late Weimar remains Miller Lane, *Architecture and Politics in Germany, 1918–1945*, 147–67. My account parallels and expands on Miller Lane's fascinating analysis of the usefulness of architecture and Schultze-Naumburg for Nazi propaganda. See also Eric Michaud's discussion of the central role of art and ritual for the NSDAP in *The Cult of Art in Nazi Germany*.

18. For an excellent interpretation of Günther, see Steinweis, *Studying the Jew*. See also the overview of Schultze-Naumburg's career during the Weimar and Nazi eras in Borrmann, *Paul Schultze-Naumburg, 1869–1949*, 141–220.

19. For Frick's concepts on art and politics, see Mathieu, *Kunstauffassungen und Kulturpolitik im Nationalsozialismus*, 282–84. See also Zuschlag, "*Entartete Kunst*," 32–37. The first solid overview of the importance of cultural politics in Thuringia, particularly of debates concerning Modernist architecture, is Miller Lane, *Architecture and Politics in Germany, 1918–1945*, 156–57.

20. Josef Stolzing-Czerny, "Die Dürer-Ausstellung in Alten Pinakothek," *Völkischer Beobachter* (supplement), March 30, 1928, 1; "Die Nürnberger Dürertage," *Völkischer Beobachter* (supplement), April 13, 1928, 1. See also the biography and articles gathered on the full-page spread under the title "Albrecht Dürer—Zu seinem 400. Todestage," *Völkischer Beobachter* (supplement), April 7, 1928, 2.

21. "Die Albrecht Dürer-Feier," *Völkischer Beobachter* (Munich supplement), April 12, 1928, 1.

22. Ibid., summarizing Wölfflin.

23. Ibid., 2. Dürer, not surprisingly, would become even a more popular figure within art history during the Nazi years. In a fascinating statistical analysis of university lectures from 1933 to 1945, Martin Papenbrock has shown that the most popular single artist to be the subject of a university lecture was Dürer, with Rembrandt a distant second. Papenbrock, "Kunstgeschichtliche Forschung und Lehre im Nationalsozialismus," 30–35.

24. Rosenberg, *The Myth of the Twentieth Century*, 173–290. For reference to Wölfflin, see 187. Note that this edition by the Noontide Press clearly attempts a revisionist position and the preface by Peter Peel is pro-Rosenberg. See also the analysis of Rosenberg's thought in Mathieu, *Kunstauffassungen und Kulturpolitik im Nationalsozialismus*, 164–243.

25. Piper, *Alfred Rosenberg*, 259. Piper has the most detailed analysis of the complexities of Rosenberg and his administration of the KdfK. See also, though, the first systemic study in Bollmus, *Das Amt Rosenberg und seine Gegner*, 27–39, as well as the important institutional analysis by Steinweis, "Weimar Culture and the Rise of National Socialism." Although frequently referenced, the KdfK has received remarkably little serious study in art history. Many authors continue to cite the first early analyses in Brenner, *Die Kunstpolitik des Nationalsozialismus*, and Miller Lane, *Architecture and Politics in Germany, 1918–1945*.

26. For an excellent overview of this period, see Peukert, *The Weimar Republic*, 236–67.

27. Piper, *Alfred Rosenberg*, 262–74.

28. "Ein 'Kampfbund für deutsche Kultur,'" *Völkischer Beobachter*, January 11, 1929, 1.

29. See the excellent overview in Bechstedt, Deutsch, and Stöppel, "Der Verlag F. Bruckmann im Nationalsozialismus." For citations of Wölfflin's letters to Elsa Bruckmann, see 289–90. I am very grateful to Evonne Levy for her critical comments and for first pointing out to me that Wölfflin's association with the group was not voluntary.

30. Piper, *Alfred Rosenberg*, 259. Wölfflin's two earliest books, *Renaissance und Barock* (1888) and *Die klassische Kunst* (1898), as *Principles of Art History*, were also published in later editions by the F. Bruckmann publishing house. In her analysis of art history in Munich in the early twentieth century, Sybille Dürr also briefly mentions Wölfflin's visits to the Bruckmann household and the possibility that he met Hitler there, although she gives no source for this observation. Dürr, "Wölfflin, Hauttmann, Pinder," 271. The Bruckmanns' role in promoting social connections

between members of the NSDAP and other right-wing ideologues is well established (see, for example, Borrmann, *Paul Schultze-Naumburg, 1869–1949*, 198–99). Note that Wölfflin's appearance as a cosigner is the cause for mentioning him in passing in Brenner's original 1963 text, which summarizes the activities of the KfdK.

31. Franz Hofmann, "Die Kunst der Renaissance: Heinrich Wölfflins neuestes Buch," *Völkischer Beobachter* (supplement), October 11/12, 1931, 2.

32. The best account of the early dynamics of the Nazi state's cultural policy remains Steinweis, *Art, Ideology, and Economics in Nazi Germany*.

33. Sudhalter, "14 Years Bauhaus," 337. For a typical example of propaganda criticizing the Bauhaus during the late Weimar Republic, see "Das Bauhaus in Weimar: 'Kunstpolitik' in Thüringen," *Völkischer Beobachter*, March 14, 1930, 2.

34. Although Miller Lane was the first to go into detail about how National Socialists attacked the Bauhaus, the now classic essay on the topic remains Nerdinger, "Bauhaus Architecture in the Third Reich."

35. Van Dyke, "Franz Radziwill."

36. Zuschlag, "An 'Educational Exhibition.'" The best interpretation of the *Degenerate Art* exhibition remains the important work of Zuschlag. See also Fuhrmeister, "Adolf Ziegler (1892–1959), ein nationalsozialistischer Künstler und Funktionär."

37. For a subtle analysis of changes within the regime and popular responses, see the reprint of Kershaw, "The 'Everyday' and the 'Exceptional,'" in *Hitler, the Germans, and the Final Solution*, 119–38.

38. Zuschlag, "An 'Educational Exhibition,'" 85–87.

39. See the reproduction of the catalog in Barron, ed., "*Degenerate Art*," 357–90.

40. Schultze-Naumburg, *Kunst und Rasse*. See also the overview of Schultze-Naumburg's career in Borrmann, *Paul Schultze-Naumburg, 1869–1949*. Schultze-Naumburg used a strategy of comparing photographs to construct typological similarities and differences in his important set of earlier writings on the connection of "good" architecture to regional traditions and peoples, for example, Schultze-Naumburg, *Dörfer und Kolonien*. See the excellent analysis of the significance of this work in Gutschow, "The Anti-Mediterranean in the Literature of Modern Architecture." What is at stake in his 1928 book, though, is the distinct and separate use of two different visual presentations, one based on connoisseurship and the other popularly identified with Wölfflin. The contrast of design styles in the same book makes the more overt racial point of the later work clear. I am grateful for discussions with Christian Fuhrmeister on this topic.

41. Barron, ed., "*Degenerate Art*," 365.

42. Ibid., 376–90.

43. Ibid., 61.

44. For an exceptional critical analysis of Hitler's developing use and interest in art, see Werckmeister, "Hitler the Artist."

45. Most recently on this theme, see Herf, *The Jewish Enemy*. See also my essay on the topic, "'Realism'?" (forthcoming).

46. I use the term "functional" to draw on the large literature that discusses how bureaucratic institutions and decision making radicalized and enabled the implementation of genocide in particular. This is often contrasted with an "intentionalist" stance in which decisions are meant to be ideologically rather than structurally driven. While scholars no longer maintain the extreme dichotomy of the earlier debates, I would argue that a modified functionalist position was operative in the architectural bureaucracy of Auschwitz. For a thorough analysis of these issues, see Browning, "Beyond 'Intentionalism' and 'Functionalism.'" For the intersection of imperialist and genocidal goals, see the broad-ranging analysis of Tooze, *The Wages of Destruction.*

47. Exceptions to this trend are two important volumes on Auschwitz: Dwork and van Pelt, *Auschwitz;* and Gutschow, *Ordnungswahn.* My work here, partially supported by National Science Foundation grant 0820501, has developed from the more extensive analysis of Auschwitz in Paul B. Jaskot, Anne Kelly Knowles, and Chester Harvey, "Visualizing the Archive" (forthcoming). I am particular indebted to Knowles's discussion of questions of space at Auschwitz.

48. For an overview of the development of concentration camp architecture and productivity, see Jaskot, *The Architecture of Oppression,* 114–39.

49. For SS Zentralbauleitung building records, including the saunas, see U.S. Holocaust Memorial Museum, Center for Advanced Holocaust Studies (CAHS), RG 11.001M.03, reel 59. On planning, consult Gutschow, *Ordnungswahn.* Most recently, David Bertolini has argued that the ideological and the functional intersect in the architecture of Auschwitz. His provocative essay, though, is driven by a theoretical construct untethered from the complexity of the material reality of the buildings and the history of the site, which makes his conclusions speculative. Bertolini, "The Architecture of Auschwitz-Birkenau and the Nazi Fantasy."

50. See the administrative orders including the daily commands issued by Höss in CAHS, RG 11.001M.03, reel 21. For the Zentralbauleitung library and copy of Neufert, see CAHS, RG 11.001M.03, reels 62 and 63.

51. See Tooze, *The Wages of Destruction.* Most recently, Jean-Louis Cohen has also argued for a larger view particularly with respect to the inextricability of architecture from war. See his exceptional catalog, Cohen, *Architecture in Uniform.*

52. I am following here Adorno, *In Search of Wagner,* who was developing Marx's ideas on the commodity in terms of the cultural expression in Wagner.

53. Heineman, "The Hour of the Woman," 33–34; Moeller, "Remembering the War in a Nation of Victims," 83–84.

54. Diefendorf, *In the Wake of War;* Durth, *Deutsche Architekten,* 247–77; Marrus, "History and the Holocaust in the Courtroom." See also my assessment of the Allied treatment of Speer's architectural career in Jaskot, *The Architecture of Oppression,* 140–44.

55. Mitchell, "Materialism and Secularism."

56. Doll, "Der Erste Deutsche Kunsthistorikertag 1948"; Fastert, "Pluralismus statt Einheit," 53–57. See also the activity of art historians involved in looting in Petropoulos, *The Faustian Bargain.*

57. Castillo, "The Bauhaus in Cold War Germany," 172–78; Frommhold, "Hans Grundig—Rektor und Lehrer, 1946–1949"; Kaes, *From Hitler to Heimat,* 11–12; and Eckmann, "Ruptures and Continuities." See also Gillen, "Images around 1945." While the essays are relatively short, Gillen's edited volume *German Art from Beckmann to Richter* is one of the few that attempts to show that the Nazi past was consistently relevant to postwar German artists. He also cocurated the important show *Art of Two Germanys: Cold War Cultures.*

58. Moeller, *War Stories,* 2–3.

59. Moeller's *War Stories* is comprehensive on these points. For an overview, however, see Moeller, "Remembering the War in a Nation of Victims." For the GDR, see Herf, *Divided Memory,* 162–200.

60. For the GDR, see McCloskey, "Dialectic at a Standstill."

61. Much excellent work has been done in the past decade on the relationship of West German design, art, and architecture to Cold War politics, including the important Barron and Eckmann catalog. See, in addition, Betts, *The Authority of Everyday Objects;* Gillen, ed., *German Art from Beckmann to Richter,* 84–99; and James-Chakraborty, *German Architecture for a Mass Audience.* See also Fehrenbach, *Cinema in Democratizing Germany,* 148–68; Moeller, *War Stories,* 123–70; and Wiener, *West German Industry and the Challenge of the Nazi Past, 1945–1955,* 157–78.

62. Michael Meng gives an excellent assessment of how the dynamics of victim memorialization intersected with the politics of the DDR. See Meng, "The Politics of Antifascism."

2. Gerhard Richter and the Advent of the Nazi Past

1. Elger, *Gerhard Richter, Maler,* 9–15.

2. Küper, "Gerhard Richter." See also Elger, *Gerhard Richter, Maler,* esp. 161–205.

3. Schreiber, *Ein Maler aus Deutschland,* 57–117, 228–33. Schreiber takes a very literary approach to his subject, with the result that his text can at times be quite lyrical whereas elsewhere it tends toward the oversentimental. For a brief account of how women were affected in a variety of ways by sterilization policies, see Heineman, *What Difference Does a Husband Make?,* 21–31.

4. John Curley offers a recent exception to this standard interpretation, with a very strong piece on how *Uncle Rudi* in particular functions as a sign of the specific political strategies of the use of photography in both East and West Germany. Curley, "Gerhard Richter's Cold War Vision." Still, the Nazi past, while important, is not the central concern in Curley's argument about Cold War politics. He does not, for example, discuss the other overt work concerning the Nazi past and Richter's family, the portrait of his aunt.

5. Even such careful critics of the period as Stefan Germer tend to treat the pre-1980s West German art scene in these psychological terms: "[Richter] encounters history within the materials that he uses for his pictures. He discovers the

historical in the sites into which one had displaced it after the end of the Third Reich. What had disappeared from the public sphere has kept its place in the private [world], in the photo albums and memories of war." Germer, "Die Wiederkehr des Verdrängten," 44.

6. Moeller, "Remembering the War in a Nation of Victims," 83.

7. While brief in their discussion, important exceptions to this general avoidance of the systematic relationship between the artist and the National Socialist past are Curley, "Gerhard Richter's Cold War Vision"; Küper, "Gerhard Richter"; Schreiber, *Ein Maler aus Deutschland*; and Storr, *Gerhard Richter*, 40–42. See also Jaskot, "Gerhard Richter and Adolf Eichmann," 457–78. Benjamin Buchloh, one of the most prominent critics of Richter's work, addresses the artist's attempts to deal with the Nazi past, although he finds Richter's particular historical conditions to be much less relevant for the questions he asks. See his important essay, Buchloh, "Gerhard Richter's *Atlas*." In addition, see the analysis of the continuities in the artist's early career in Nugent, "Family Album and Shadow Archive." My work builds off this important literature. Still, in the current chapter I argue that the Nazi perpetrator as he or she reappeared in conservative political scandals concerning Adenauer was much more of an influence on a large number of Richter's choices than has been recognized in previous scholarship. The history of conservative politics has played no significant role in the literature on the artist.

8. In a trenchant overview of Nazi historical questions in postwar German culture, Andreas Huyssen also argues for the importance of the trials as a turning point for analysis. Huyssen, "Figures of Memory in the Course of Time," 230–31.

9. Note that in the historical literature on the Adenauer period, there is by now almost universal agreement that the notion of the repression of the Nazi past is more scholarly ideology than historical reality. See, for example, Peter Reichel's comments to that effect in Reichel, *Vergangenheitsbewältigung in Deutschland*, 9–12. In addition, see the important works: Frei, *Vergangenheitspolitik*; and Herf, *Divided Memory*. A corresponding correction of the art historical account is a main goal of my book.

10. Nesbit, "Crash Course."

11. Kramer, "Art Nourishes Life—Joseph Beuys," 261–71; Ray, "Joseph Beuys and the After-Auschwitz Sublime." For an excellent history of postwar Auschwitz, including the IAC, see Huener, *Auschwitz, Poland, and the Politics of Commemoration, 1945–1979*, esp. 150–69.

12. See the discussion of Vostell's *Auschwitz Floodlight* (1958) and his related later work in Gillen, "Wolf Vostell."

13. Jaskot, "Gerhard Richter and Adolf Eichmann," 461–62.

14. For Adenauer's speech and discussion of the "Gesetz gegen Volksverhetzung," see Reichel, *Vergangenheitsbewältigung in Deutschland*, 152–57.

15. Note that the re-creation in 1991 of the *Entartete Kunst* exhibition organized by the Los Angeles County Museum of Art has no systematic discussion in the catalog of this previous (and first) reconstruction of works of art featured in the notorious 1937 show. Reference to the 1962 show comes up only at the very end of

the catalog, in a one-page overview of the past literature. See Barron, ed., *"Degenerate Art,"* 405. There has been no analysis of this 1962 re-creation in the art historical scholarship.

16. Schrag, "Entartete Kunst," 59.

17. Müller-Mehlis, "Entartete Kunst"; Müller-Mehlis, ". . . und Schämten sich nicht!" See also the discussion of art critics, their participation in art plundering during the Third Reich, and their exoneration after the war in Petropoulos, *The Faustian Bargain,* 111–64.

18. Wellensiek, "Bildersturm und Busse."

19. Petropoulos discusses this tendency to demonize the few leaders in order to excuse the many in great detail in relation to the art professions in the postwar period. Petropoulos, *The Faustian Bargain.*

20. Küper, "Gerhard Richter," 233. On the question of euthanasia policies and their centrality to the National Socialist state, see Friedlander, *The Origins of Nazi Genocide.*

21. Almost every art historian working on this period of his paintings makes this point, supported by Richter's own claims of detachment and neutrality (for example, see the article with quotations from a Richter interview of van Bruggen, "Gerhard Richter"). In addition, see Curley for his interpretation that the ambiguity in many of these images constitutes a commentary on the use of photography on both sides of the Cold War wall.

22. Nugent, "Overcoming Ideology," 86–89. See also McCloskey, "Dialectic at a Standstill."

23. See the discussion of these years in the biographical essay in the retrospective catalog: Harten, ed., *Gerhard Richter,* 9–18.

24. The crisis in the direction of abstraction as well as the rise of Pop Art and the conceptual strategies of Fluxus were widely perceived developments in the German art press from 1962 to 1966. For typical points of debate, see Klapcheck, "Kunstausstellungen in Westdeutschland 1964/65"; Müller-Mehlis, "Zeit der Umwertung"; and Neugass, "Pop-Art Epidemie." For a systematic analysis of Richter in relation to the western avant-gardes, see Nugent, "Family Album and Shadow Archive," 150–205.

25. Certainly the best discussion of Richter's relationship to the historical and contemporary avant-garde remains the many articles on Richter by Benjamin Buchloh. See, for example, his article on photography and painting in Buchloh, *Neo-Avantgarde and Culture Industry,* 365–403. For a solid summary of the West German art scene during this period, see Damus, *Kunst in der BRD, 1945–1990,* 136–252. See also Mehring, "The Art of a Miracle."

26. A strong exception to this trend with Richter is the discussion of his painting series of the Baader–Meinhof group titled *October 18, 1977.* For monographs on these works in relation to their historical import, see Henatsch, *Gerhard Richter;* Storr, *Gerhard Richter: October 18, 1977.*

27. Buchloh, "Interview with Gerhard Richter," 20.

28. Moeller, "Remembering the War in a Nation of Victims."

29. Herf, *Divided Memory*, 289–94; Reichel, *Vergangenheitsbewältigung*, 20–29.

30. Herf, *Divided Memory*, 296. See also the analysis of Earl, *The Nuremberg SS-Einsatzgruppen Trial, 1945–1958*.

31. For a discussion of the defacement of the Cologne synagogue and the beginnings of the Auschwitz Trials, see Reichel, *Vergangenheitsbewältigung*, 125–29, 138–52, 158–81.

32. Arendt, *Eichmann in Jerusalem*. See, in particular, Arendt's discussion of moral judgment and individual agency in relation to Eichmann, 83–111. Note as well that Arendt's book was quickly translated and available in the Federal Republic in 1964. Thus at the moment when Richter was painting *Christa and Wolfi* and other works derived from the *Atlas*, her analysis of the Eichmann trial was widely discussed and debated. An overview of historical issues raised by the multiple trials related to the genocide can be found in Marrus, "History and the Holocaust in the Courtroom."

33. Arendt, *Eichmann in Jerusalem*, 16–17.

34. For a revealing text that offers some correction of Arendt's account, see Lang ed., *Eichmann Interrogated*. See also the biographical account of Eichmann in Safrian, "Adolf Eichmann—Organisator der Judendeportation."

35. Wittmann, *Beyond Justice*, 1–14. See also the classic Buchheim et al., *Anatomie des SS-Staates*.

36. Schreiber, *Ein Maler aus Deutschland*, 233–34.

37. Ibid., 7.

38. Ibid., 174–90. See also the in-depth study of how perpetrators thought of their actions at the time in Browning, *Ordinary Men*.

39. For an excellent statistical breakdown of specific themes and issues in the West German and Israeli press during postwar trials, including Eichmann and the Auschwitz process, see Wilke et al., *Holocaust und NS-Prozesse*, 81–97. Devin Pendas discusses the disjunction between press reports and public ambivalence toward the Auschwitz process in Pendas, "'I Didn't Know What Auschwitz Was.'"

40. Richter, *Gerhard Richter*. Volume 3 of this work includes the catalogue raisonné. See, as well, Friedel, ed., *Gerhard Richter*. Although as stated seven paintings can be identified with this theme, nevertheless, this must be seen as the base number for what appears to be more work, subsequently edited out of the catalogue raisonné for unknown reasons. For example, the 1985 retrospective includes several illustrations (such as the interrogation piece, a subject completely misidentified by the editor) not reprinted in the catalogue raisonné (Harten, ed., *Gerhard Richter*). In a public lecture at the Art Institute of Chicago (June 25, 2002), Robert Storr also noted that the back of *Hirsch* (1963) includes a playing card portrait of Hitler. In addition, see the brief discussion of Nazi-era themes in relationship to the varied representational strategies of 1960s art in Nugent, "Family Album and Shadow Archive," 236–40, as well as Curley's interpretation of *Execution by Firing Squad* (1962; edited out of the catalogue raisonné) as it relates to the ambiguity of the use of photography during the Cold War. Curley, "Gerhard Richter's Cold War Vision," 24–28.

41. Buchloh, "Gerhard Richter's *Altas.*"

42. Schreiber, *Ein Maler aus Deutschland*, 233–34.

43. Checking with the catalogue raisonné, there are at least three paintings and a print derived from the first four panels of the *Atlas*.

44. Heineman, *What Difference Does a Husband Make?*, 8–9 and 108–75.

45. The presence of German shepherds (or police dogs) for the SS and other branches of the Nazi policing institutions is a recurring motif in the postwar descriptions of brutality. See, for examples, Wiesel, *Night*, 37, as well as the documentary footage in Alan Resnais's *Night and Fog* (1958). Wiesel's account was originally published in 1960 and translated and widely discussed in Germany in 1962.

46. Storr, *Gerhard Richter: Forty Years of Painting*, 294.

47. April A. Eisman, "Fighting Fascism in East German Art: The Case of Bernhard Heisig," unpublished manuscript (2009). I am grateful to Eisman for sharing her work on this subject, including her compelling contextualization of the famous East German artist within the specific political and artistic world of the GDR. See also Eckhart Gillen's contributions to this debate, especially Gillen, "Die Kriegsgeneration und der Antifaschismus." In relation to his discussion of Richter, Gillen's text relies predominantly on a short essay by Schreiber that appeared in *Der Tagesspiegel* (August 22, 2004). His main point of comparison rests on the skeptical and, hence, distancing approach he sees in each artist's work.

48. Note that Staudte's film comedy *Roses for the Prosecutor* (1959) dealt explicitly with West Germany's compromised judiciary, and it was shown to some public success. Such examples once again debunk any concept of the "repression" of the Nazi past in postwar German society. See Hake, *German National Cinema*, 92–93.

49. Meissner, "Um die Vertiefung realistischer Aussage." More generally on the paintings in relation to other works by Tübke, see Beaucamp, "Werner Tübke."

50. Beaucamp, "Werner Tübke," 219.

51. Meissner, "Die Bildfolge *Lebenserinnerungen des Dr. jur. Schulze* im Schaffen Werner Tübke," 13–14. In this essay, Meissner argues that Tübke's personal experiences at the end of the war (he was arrested and tortured by the Soviets) are also signaled in this painting. While that may well be, critics made no biographical connection in the 1960s.

52. Ministerium für Kultur in Galleria del Levante, *Werner Tübke*, n.p. While Tübke's work was clearly dissident in form and content in relation to more mainstream artistic production in the GDR, it is hard to maintain an emphasis on this point, as scholars have done, given that the state seems to have found little difficulty here in embracing his paintings.

53. In spite of how his work complements the state's position, Tübke's critical and nonaffirmative stance in these works remained relatively exceptional compared to the vast majority of GRD artistic production.

54. See the most recent discussion of these early images as a group in Moorhouse, *Gerhard Richter Portraits*. Moorhouse's text is an excellent summary of current

analyses of Richter's techniques and subjects. Still, he pays little attention to the question of the Nazi past.

55. See also Nugent's discussion of the formal and iconographical complexities of the nurse paintings in Nugent, "Family Album and Shadow Archive," 263–68.

56. Visual artists were, of course, by no means alone in this interest. See, e.g., Peter Weiss's scandalous 1965 play based on the transcripts of the Auschwitz Trial: Weiss, *Die Ermittlung.* See also Huyssen, "Figures of Memory in the Course of Time," 231–32.

57. Kershaw, *Hitler,* 518–19. See also Block, "Not a Monument but Rather Food for Thought."

58. The terms by which scholars render Richter and other artists "avant-garde" are in some obvious need of critical expansion. It is here that the question of autonomy is relevant, as expanding the field of reference with political history and other materially driven questions makes the study of art or an artist not a matter of a hermetic analysis that focuses on the unique contribution of an individual career, but rather of how art helps us to understand the complexity and depth of central social struggles and formations of a period. For a historicization of how the question of aesthetic autonomy was a relevant posture variably employed for the avant-garde in this period, see Potts, "Autonomy in Post-war Art, Quasi-heroic and Casual."

59. For an analysis of work that falls outside most art historical assessments (either because of historical market conditions or critical elisions), see Sholette, "Heart of Darkness."

3. Anselm Kiefer and the Ascendance of Helmut Kohl

1. Kiefer, *In Kriegs- und Friedenszeiten.*

2. For an analysis of this moment in the German art world that is decidedly more critical, see Buchloh, "Figures of Authority, Ciphers of Regression."

3. There have indeed been a few exceptions in the literature that have bucked the dominant intellectual trend, especially in how they analyze Kiefer's crucial shift to using Nazi architecture and his figuration of Nazi victims in the early 1980s. The most significant works that take this moment seriously as a historical and artistic problem are two texts that appeared in 1999 (Lisa Saltzman and Sabine Schütz), as well as the oft-cited and still-canonical 1989 essay by Andreas Huyssen. In addition, Matthew Biro provides perhaps the closest and most careful reading of the philosophical and ontological claims of Kiefer's painting. I will certainly rely on important aspects of some of the trenchant work of these authors. Saltzman's analysis of particular aspects of Kiefer's critical reception, read through her interpretation of Adorno, is important, as is the comprehensive research on specific phases of Kiefer's career evident in Schütz, a text to my knowledge still little known to English-language critics. And, of course, when dealing with paintings like *Sulamith,* the analytical conclusions of Huyssen remain crucial for any investigation. Biro makes an important argument about the undecidability at the heart of Kiefer's project and discusses generally the relation of his early 1980s works to issues of

individual responsibility concerning the Nazi past and rising nationalism. Biro, *Anselm Kiefer and the Philosophy of Martin Heidegger*; Huyssen, "Anselm Kiefer"; Saltzman, *Anselm Kiefer and Art After Auschwitz*; and Schütz, *Anselm Kiefer—Geschichte als Material*. Still, the specificities of the political context and the status of the perpetrator that form the heart of my concerns remain at best on the edges of the discussion in these texts.

4. For a general assessment of the "New Realism" in Europe, see Judt, *Postwar*, esp. 535–47.

5. For an early and outstanding account of the significance of the *Historikerstreit*, see Maier, *The Unmasterable Past*.

6. For an analysis that provides a framework for discussing how the changes in Cold War society intersected with art related to the Nazi past, see Huyssen, "Figures of Memory in the Course of Time." Notably, Huyssen's is one of only two essays in this volume that even briefly mentions Kohl.

7. Backes and Jesse, *Politischer Extremismus in der Bundesrepublik Deutschland*, 159–69, 326–27. See also the helpful overview of this period in Berghahn, *Modern Germany*, 246–58. Dutschke would die a decade later from the aftereffects of the attempt on his life.

8. See Judt, *Postwar*, 390–421.

9. NPD Program, as cited in Backes and Jesse, *Politischer Extremismus in der Bundesrepublik Deutschland*, 86.

10. Ibid., 83–94; Herf, *Divided Memory*, 334–41.

11. Berghahn, *Modern Germany*, 248–52, 302–3. See also the discussion of the postwar commemorations at the Warsaw Ghetto memorial, including that of Brandt, in Young, "The Biography of a Memorial Icon."

12. See the overview of the response to fascism within art history in Held, "New Left Art History and Fascism in Germany." Among several key early texts that formed the basis of much later thinking (including my own initial research into the field) are Hinz, *Die Malerei im deutschen Faschismus*, and Miller Lane, *Architecture and Politics in Germany, 1918–1945*. Hinz's book was later published in an English translation titled *Art in the Third Reich*.

13. Hinz, "Der 'Bamberger Reiter.'" See also Warnke's introduction to the volume, where he notes that art historians were following the generational revolt against fascism that had begun in other disciplines such as literature in the mid-1960s in Germany.

14. "Diskussionsbericht," in Warnke, ed., *Das Kunstwerk zwischen Wissenschaft und Weltanschauung*, 45–47. I am indebted as well to the trenchant analysis of this session in a different context by Werckmeister, "Radical Art History."

15. See Schütz's perceptive comments on this and several other 1974 Kiefer works that take up the scorched-earth metaphor, in Schütz, *Anselm Kiefer—Geschichte als Material*, 258–67.

16. Saltzman, *Anselm Kiefer and Art After Auschwitz*, 48–74. On the social history of the generation of perpetrators, see the collection of essays in Schissler, ed., *The Miracle Years*.

17. Albert Kiefer, *In Kriegs- und Friedenszeiten.*

18. For a comparative model that asserts similar positions about the military, see Buchheim, *Eines Lebenslauf.* In addition to authoring *Das Boot,* Buchheim also was a wartime artist who did many large-scale naturalistic images of heroicized naval officers.

19. Albert Kiefer, *In Kriegs- und Friedenszeiten,* 27.

20. Albert Kiefer makes evident in his autobiography that he has good relations with his son. Indeed, the text is clearly written from the point of view of connecting his own life to that of his more famous progeny. In this regard, he illustrates many of his son's works and articulates as well the important market position of his son's works as the first to break the postwar taboo on the National Socialist past: "He [Anselm] dared to be one of the first German artists who turned to the taboo past and took up a differentiated position regarding the worst events of German history" (ibid., 270).

21. For an analysis of the series, see Arasse, *Anselm Kiefer,* 26–45.

22. For the military, see in particular Bartov, *Hitler's Army.*

23. Albert Kiefer, *In Kriegs- und Friedenszeiten,* 240–43. See also the discussion of the scandal that erupted with the 1975 publication of these images in the avant-garde journal *Interfunktionen* by then editor Benjamin Buchloh in Mehring, "Continental Schrift." David Hughes also does a close reading of many of these early book projects: Hughes, "Playing It by the Book—the Early Work of Anselm Kiefer." Notably, Hughes, like others in the Kiefer literature, thinks the uniform is a mock uniform and, hence, does not explore the relationship to the father.

24. Schütz, *Anselm Kiefer—Geschichte als Material,* 269–74. The information on the bathtub is cited from an interview in Arasse, *Anselm Kiefer,* 79. Arasse argues that Kiefer's work is essentially Nietzschean in its approach.

25. Huyssen, "Anselm Kiefer," 36.

26. For a complex overview of Kiefer's work in the 1980s, see Biro, "Representation and Event." Biro's work here, as elsewhere, is a strong interpretation of the formal and philosophical implications of Kiefer's art in relation to other debates of *Vergangenheitsbewältigung,* including the *Historikerstreit.* However, he does not elaborate on the political import or instrumentalization of these debates in relation to Kiefer's art.

27. Celan, *Gedichte,* vol. 1, 40–42. See also Felstiner, *Paul Celan,* 22–41, 70–72. I am following Felstiner's translation here (31–32).

28. For a compelling interpretation of the *Margarete* series as conceptually ambivalent, as well as the paintings' relationship to Kiefer's interest in Abstract Expressionism see Biro, *Anselm Kiefer and the Philosophy of Martin Heidegger,* 182–91. Refer also to Arasse's summary of Kiefer's career, which follows much of Biro, Saltzman, and Huyssen. Michael Auping brings together many of these same points of reference in relation to Kiefer's interest in various spiritual traditions in Auping, *Anselm Kiefer.*

29. Cordulak, "Anselm Kiefer," 171. For the history of the Soldiers' Hall, see Jaskot, *The Architecture of Oppression,* 88–113.

30. See, for example, Mark Rosenthal's analysis in *Anselm Kiefer*, 115–19.

31. After World War II, the high-profile architectural commissions favored by Hitler were either destroyed or appropriated by the occupying powers to be used for supposedly neutral activities (Speer's Zepplinfeld at Nuremberg, for example, has been used for a variety of events, including auto racing and as a football field for U.S. military personnel). While the specificities of particular monuments were all but forgotten, these buildings were discussed in relation to a general scholarly and public interest in National Socialist architecture as a propaganda tool. With historians and critics (from the left and the right) focusing on Nazi architecture as an embodiment of the manipulation of power, the architecture became a focus of debates about the ideological continuity or discontinuity of the present with the past (depending on the political interests of the author). Kiefer's interests are consistent with this view of architecture. Huyssen and Saltzman generally see the work as one of contesting strategies rather than ambivalences, the latter being a key theme of Biro's work, albeit more in relation to Kiefer's equally famous work *Interior* (1981). See, in particular, Biro, *Anselm Kiefer and the Philosophy of Martin Heidegger*, 102–7. For an encyclopedic study of the sources for the imagery, see Schütz, *Anselm Kiefer—Geschichte als Material*, 285–359.

32. Saltzman, *Anselm Kiefer and Art After Auschwitz*, 97–123. Here, as elsewhere, Saltzman's interest is in the question of national identity formation in relation to the representation of repression. The shifting and changing political meanings of that past are outside her study.

33. By comparison, see Buchloh's discussion of the turn to figuration in these years as a more general phenomenon that evokes disturbing nationalist sentiments in Buchloh, "Figures of Authority, Ciphers of Regresssion."

34. Kipphoff, "Die Lust an der Angst—der deutsche Holzweg."

35. Kipphoff, "Verbrannte Erde und gestuerzter Trommler."

36. Hecht was an enthusiastic supporter of the German contribution to the Biennale. See Hecht, "Venedig 1980." In the same issue, Hecht's editorial deals with art and politics as part of the history of the German contribution to the Biennale, including the use of the pavilion originally designed by Speer (3).

37. Presler, "Ein famoser Kerl"; Vieten, "Fälscher," 117.

38. The Buchheim controversy would prove to be significant for shaking up the arts bureaucracy in Bavaria. See Hecht's original interview with Buchheim, which sets off the controversy (Hecht, "München ist nun wirklich keine Kunststadt"), as well as the discussion of Buchheim's comments and his biography as a war artist in the November 1980 issue of *Art*.

39. The series began with Nicolaus, "Verfolgt, verfemt, entartet," and continued through September of that year.

40. Welti, "Den Stein von innen her begreifen"; Hüllenkremer, "George Segals Holocaust-Denkmal." See also Young's discussion of the 1980s and commemoration in Germany and the United States in Young, *The Texture of Memory*, 27–48, 287–322.

41. Schulze, "Der stete Stachel der Teilung."

42. For example, Hübl, "Denk ich an Deutschland in der Kunst."

43. Monjau, "Am 17. Mai ging der Transport nach Auschwitz—niemand kehrte zurück"; Engelbert and auf der Lake, "Den Betrachter zwingen, daß er anfängt Fragen zu stellen."

44. "Zu diesem Heft" (January/March 1983); Antoni, "Der Faschismus will im Bild bleiben." Antoni's text picks up on issues surrounding the sudden fascination with Nazi imagery and history. While not alluding to Susan Sontag on this point, his insights parallel some of her observations as articulated in her groundbreaking essay "Fascinating Fascism." Sontag's essay was first published in 1975 and translated into German in 1981. For authors who connect NATO military policies, the German right, and the specter of the Nazi past, see, for example, the series of articles in *Tendenzen* 21, no. 131 (July/September 1980). For a helpful overview, see Rattinger, "Change versus Continuity in West German Public Attitudes on National Security and Nuclear Weapons in the Early 1980s."

45. Friedländer, *Reflections of Nazism*. The French original was published in 1982. See also Rosenfeld, "The Normalization of Memory."

46. Saltzman, for example, cites only one other text by Friedländer, his book *History and Psychoanalysis*.

47. Friedländer, *Reflections of Nazism*, 21–22.

48. Ibid., 39.

49. Ibid., 136.

50. See Habermas's discussion of this period "marked by the interaction of opposing tendencies" in Habermas, "On How Postwar Germany Has Faced Its Recent Past."

51. Friedländer, *Reflections of Nazism*, 128–29.

52. Schmidt, *Mahnung und Verpflichtung*, 24.

53. Ibid., 29.

54. Ibid., 35.

55. Rattinger, "Change versus Continuity in West German Public Attitudes on National Security and Nuclear Weapons in the Early 1980s." For an art historical assessment of the conflicts over nuclear weapons debates, see Werckmeister, "Radical Art History."

56. Kaes, *From Hitler to Heimat*, 30–34.

57. Merhav, "Honouring Evil," 197–98.

58. Kohl, *History's Inescapable Impact on the Present*, 22. German original in Kohl, *Die Unentrinnbare Gegenwart der Geschichte*, 19–27.

59. Kohl, *Reden, 1982–1984*, 113.

60. Ibid., 111.

61. Kohl, *Die Unentrinnbare Gegenwart der Geschichte*, 6–7.

62. Ibid., 10.

63. For the European geopolitical context of the commemorations in these years and the popular support of these policies in West Germany, see Hilberg, "Bitburg as Symbol," 16–17. For an overview of the internal politics of Bitburg and its significance to Kohl, see Herf, *Divided Memory*, 350–54.

64. "Remarks of President Reagan to Regional Editors, White House, April 18, 1985," excerpted in Hartman, ed., *Bitburg in Moral and Political Perspective*, 240.

65. A summary of the day's event can be gleaned from the reprint of the *New York Times* article by Bernard Weinraub, "Reagan Joins Kohl in Brief Memorial at Bitburg Graves," reprinted in Hartman, ed., *Bitburg in Moral and Political Perspective*.

66. Kohl, "Address by Chancellor Helmut Kohl to German and American Soldiers and Their Families at Bitburg, May 5, 1985," 256.

67. Ibid.

68. Ibid.

69. Hilberg, "Bitburg as Symbol," 21.

70. Kohl, "Address by Chancellor Helmut Kohl to German and American Soldiers and Their Families at Bitburg, May 5, 1985," 256–57.

71. In blunt terms, Kohl would describe in 1988 the contemporary need to relate to the past as follows: "The truth is that Germans became guilty as individuals, but the injustice perpetrated under the National Socialist tyranny is part of our common history. This history has been entrusted to us in its entirety." Kohl, *History's Inescapable Impact on the Present*, 52.

72. Kohl's speech contrasted famously with that of the president of the Federal Republic, Richard von Weizsäcker, delivered to the Bundestag on May 8, 1985, to commemorate the end of World War II. Weizsäcker's talk does not descend into easy polarities and attempts to differentiate, like Helmut Schmidt, the various kinds of guilt and relations to the past. Such a differentiation begins with the victims, including of course the Jews but also among others the Soviets (both military and civilian populations), people in Poland, the Sinti and Roma, homosexuals, and also the German who died as a result of the war brought on by Nazi policies. Furthermore, when he discussed guilt, he did not separate perpetrator from postwar generations, noting that while the former acted during the period the latter was "liable" for those actions. Weizsäcker, "Speech by Richard von Weizsäcker, President of the Federal Republic of Germany, in the Bundestag during the Ceremony Commemorating the 40th Anniversary of the End of the War in Europe and of National Socialist Tyranny, May 8, 1985," in Hartmann, ed., *Bitburg in Moral and Political Perspective*, 265. See also the discussion of the political polarization of debates surrounding the potential construction of an appropriate national monument to honor victims in Moller, *Die Entkontretisierung der NS-Herrschaft in der Ära Kohl*, 28–31.

73. See Maier, *The Unmasterable Past*.

74. Habermas, "Defusing the Past," 44.

75. Habermas, "On How Postwar Germany Has Faced Its Recent Past," 8.

4. Daniel Libeskind and the Neo-Nazi Specter

1. Weinland and Winkler, *Das Jüdische Museum im Stadtmuseum Berlin* (published simultaneously in English as *The Jewish Museum in the Berlin Municipal Museum*), 7–10 (documents reprinted are in German only). See also Steinweis, *Art, Ideology, and Economics in Nazi Germany*, 123–24.

2. For a longer view of the recurrence of the German past in the modern period, see Koshar, *From Monuments to Traces.*

3. One of the most influential interpretations, with its introduction of Heidegger's concept of the uncanny, remains Vidler, "Building in Empty Spaces," in Vidler, *Warped Space.* While I disagree with the metaphoric weight Vidler assigns to built forms, his analysis is both typical and exemplary in terms of the philosophical tendency to interpret the building. For a historical account that has expanded on the concept of the uncanny and become standard, see Young, "Daniel Libeskind's Jewish Museum in Berlin," in Young, *At Memory's Edge.* Andreas Huyssen discusses more historical and literary contexts for the void itself in Huyssen, "The Voids of Berlin." More recently, the building and its void have been compared to other projects, for example, the Reichstag dome (Chametzky, "Rebuilding the Nation"), as well as within the context of post–September 11, 2001, architectural debates (Smith, *The Architecture of Aftermath,* 67–94).

4. This research project has surprisingly been of little interest to previous interpreters of the site. Most analyses summarize the prehistory of the Jewish Museum as well as the institutional development of the current project from information gleaned from the introductions to several volumes produced in conjunction with its construction and opening. See, most important, Weinland and Winkler, *Das Jüdische Museum im Stadtmuseum Berlin,* 7–75. In addition, Daniel Bussenius is completing an institutional history of the current museum. While the architectural design is not his focus, I am grateful to Bussenius for our discussions on other shared interests. See also the impressive recent work of Pieper, *Die Musealisierung des Holocaust,* a well-researched and -argued book. Pieper's thesis complements my own and our research at times overlaps. My work, though, analyzes in more detail the political significance of the past within the local dynamics of Berlin and its impact on the architecture and urban plan around the building. Pieper is particularly strong on the history and significance of the installations.

5. Omi and Winant, *Racial Formation in the United States,* 56.

6. See also Pieper's formulation of how the multifunctional building became "Jewish" in Pieper, *Die Musealisierung des Holocaust,* 253.

7. Daniel Bussenius, "Die Anfänge des Jüdischen Museums Berlin."

8. Jaskot, "Daniel Libeskind's Jewish Museum in Berlin as a Cold War Project."

9. Kugelmann, "Bringschuld, Erbe und Besitz."

10. See citation of approval in the construction plan of the Senatsverwaltung für Wissenschaft und Kunst, July 17, 1975, reprinted in Weinland and Winkler, *Das Jüdische Museum im Stadtmuseum Berlin,* 104–5. For the early history of the "Integrative Model," see Bussenius, "Die Anfänge des Jüdischen Museums Berlin," 345–48. For the broader context, see Kugelmann, "Bringschuld, Erbe und Besitz."

11. See the important work of Greg Castillo on this point, e.g., Castillo, "Socialist Realism and Built Nationalism in the Cold War 'Battle of the Styles.'" Castillo expands on his argument that aesthetic decisions and policies interacted with each other across the divide of the Iron Curtain in *Cold War on the Home Front.*

12. See the summary of financial support of Berlin from the Cold War through reunification in Strom, *Building the New Berlin*, 79–87. Strom's political economy of the city is largely ignored in the art historical literature.

13. Ladd, *The Ghosts of Berlin*, 106–7, 228–35. See also Kleihues's brief discussion of IBA in relation to the history of Berlin in the official city publication for the 750th anniversary: Kleihues, "Von Großstadtträumen zur Stadterneuerung." More recently, see Pugh, "The Berlin Wall and the Urban Space and Experience of East and West Berlin, 1961–1989."

14. For a recent overview of the history and postwar significance of the *Topographie des Terrors* site, see Till, *The New Berlin*, 120–52. The best overview of the development of this area and its Nazi past remains Ladd, *The Ghosts of Berlin*, 127–73.

15. See Wolfgang Engel, "Berlin-Südliche Friedrichstadt," preparatory report, March 15, 1989, in Landesarchiv Berlin (LA Berlin), B Rep 009 Nr. 4577. For debates about green space, see, e.g., the 1989 exchange of Bezirksstadträtin Franziska Eichstädt-Bohlig with the office of Bausenator Wolfgang Nagel in Senatsverwaltung für Wissenschaft, Forschung und Kultur, Berlin Museum Documents (SenKult), File Nr. 327: Berlin Museum, Erweiterungsbau, 2/88–90. For a general overview of the IBA influence on the site planning, consult Schäche, "Städtebauliche Entwicklung vor der IBA."

16. Protocol for discussion reprinted in Weinland and Winkler, *Das Jüdische Museum im Stadtmuseum Berlin*, 137–38. See also related IBA documents in ibid., 153–57, 262–63. The site on the Hollmanstrasse was finalized by 1985.

17. For Kleihues's role in the IBA, see Nerdinger, "Foreword."

18. Requests from Kreis Schaad Schaad for their project for the Wohnpark am Berlin Museum in LA Berlin, B Rep 009 Nr. 4576, Südliche Friedrichstadt. This file also contains a report from Wolfgang Engel, Senator für Stadtentwicklung und Umweltschutz, from June 21, 1982, stating that he thought the overall plan by Hans Kollhoff and Arthur Ovaska for the housing complex was too starkly oriented to the east–west and that this should be corrected.

19. Note that Libeskind's description of his competition invitation states that he was told it would be a "Jüdische Abteilung" or "Jewish Department," a term that was also used in the Nazi period within the SS and other bureaucracies for offices concerned with the implementation of antisemitic policies. However, at least since the Aspen Institute meeting in December 1987, internal and public documents most often refer to the project as "Abteilung Jüdisches Museum" or "Jüdisches Museum im Berlin Museum," although this is not completely consistent. Libeskind, *Breaking Ground*, 78–81; cf. Senatsverwaltung für Bau- und Wohnungswesen, ed., *Realisierungswettbewerb Erweiterung Berlin Museum mit Abteilung Jüdisches Museum*, and Weinland and Winkler, *Das Jüdische Museum im Stadtmuseum Berlin*, 247.

20. See Jaskot, "Daniel Libeskind's Jewish Museum as a Cold War Project," and, more generally, Pugh, "The Berlin Wall and the Urban Space and Experience of East and West Berlin, 1961–1989."

21. Cohn, *The Jews in Germany, 1945–1993*, 71–80; Jarausch, Seeba, and Conradt, "The Presence of the Past," 50–52. See also the discussion of architecture and commemorating the former Jewish communities in East Germany in Dresden and Potsdam by Susanne Vees-Gulani ("The Politics of New Beginnings") and Michael Meng ("The Politics of Antifascism"), respectively, in Rosenfeld and Jaskot, eds., *Beyond Berlin*.

22. Weinland and Winkler, *Das Jüdische Museum im Stadtmuseum Berlin*, 21, 27–30, 36.

23. Bussenius, "Die Anfänge des Jüdischen Museums Berlin," 350–52. Bothe and Bendt's proposal from December 14, 1987, in Weinland and Winkler, *Das Jüdische Museum im Stadtmuseum Berlin*, 226–33. Protocol of the Aspen Institute meeting from March 15, 1988, in ibid., 234–52.

24. Clippings file concerning progress in East Berlin, in SenKult, File Nr. 331, Berlin-Museum, Jüdische Abteilung, Sonderakte, 9/88–12/90; Hassemer and plans for the announcement of the competition in SenKult, File Nr. 329, folder 19, Berlin-Museum, Erweiterungsbau. See also the October 5, 1988, letter from Reiner Güntzer (Senatsverwaltung für Wissenschaft, Forschung und Kultur) reporting that November 3 was a possible date for Diepgen in SenKult, File Nr. 320, Berlin-Museum 9/88–93.

25. Press release from June 26, 1989, Senator für Bau- und Wohnungswesen, Pressestelle, announcing results of competition in SenKult, File Nr. 329, folder 20, Berlin-Museum, Erweiterungsbau. See also Senatsverwaltung für Bau- und Wohnungswesen, ed., *Realisierungswettbewerb Erweiterung Berlin Museum mit Abteilung Jüdisches Museum*. For an excellent overview of the dynamics of the Red/Green coalition, see Raschke, *Die Grünen*, 809–22.

26. Libeskind articulated the goals of his design in a lecture first given in Hannover, December 1989, titled "Between the Lines," his preferred title for the proposal. Reprinted in a variety of publications ever since, the talk has become his best-known statement on the building. See, e.g., Libeskind, "Between the Lines."

27. See the plans dated August 4, 1989, in SenKult, File Nr. 327, folder 22, Berlin-Museum, Erweiterungsbau, 2/88–90. Bothe, "The Berlin Museum and Its Extension," 47.

28. E.g., Libeskind, *Radix Matrix*.

29. Libeskind, "Between the Lines," 63. See also selective jurors' comments that support this interpretation reprinted in Weinland and Winkler, *Das Jüdische Museum im Stadtmuseum Berlin*, 43–45.

30. SenKult, Nr. 397, Berlin-Museum Jüdische Abteilung Libeskind (1980–89), interview, 18. The interview, translated into German, appears to be part of a collection of documents meant to help explain the building to the office of the Bausenator.

31. Meeting report, January 22, 1990, in SenKult, File Nr. 327, Berlin-Museum, Erweiterungsbau, 2/88–90.

32. Art historians have been extraordinarily inattentive to the layout of the original space. The one systematic description of the original interior I have found

is Bothe, "The Berlin Museum and Its Extension," 44–48, although his account separates the building from other considerations such as the IBA. For a detailed description of the functional distribution of the original space within the new extension for the varied departments of the Berlin Museum, including the Jewish Museum, see the list of needs approved by the Senator für Finanzen and the Senator für Bau- und Wohnungswesen from October 11, 1988, reprinted in Weinland and Winkler, *Das Jüdische Museum im Stadtmuseum Berlin*, 282–86. Note that the Jewish Museum makes up 1,300 square meters of space of the 9,986 square meters needed.

33. The literature on reunification is expansive and interdisciplinary. For an effective introduction to and analysis of the national political developments, see Maier, *Dissolution*. See also Judt, *Postwar*, 637–64.

34. Jarusch, Seeba, and Conradt, "The Presence of the Past," 55–60; Maier, *Dissolution*, 236, 297.

35. Strom, *Building the New Berlin*, 79–94, 160–63.

36. Caygill, "The Futures of Berlin's Potsdamer Platz," 38–42. While Caygill is a useful introduction, he makes several historical errors by relying on poor secondary sources and, for his political history, mostly summarizes information available elsewhere. For a broader analysis of the coalition, see Raschke, *Die Grünen*.

37. Strom, *Building the New Berlin*, 194–98. For a typical critical assessment, see Michael Mönninger, "Stadtplatz im Windkanal: Der Potsdamer Platz in Berlin wird zur amerikanischen Plaza," *Frankfurter Allgemeine Zeitung*, August 19, 1992.

38. Letter from Bothe, July 17, 1990, to the Senatsverwaltung für Kulturelle Angelegenheiten, reprinted in Weinland and Winkler, *Das Jüdische Museum im Stadtmuseum Berlin*, 294–97. See also the initial conversation (Mitarbeiterbesprechung, January 17, 1990) between the Berlin and the Märkisches Museums in SenKult, File Nr. 320: Berlin-Museum 9/88–93.

39. Maier, *Dissolution*, 293–303; Strom, *Building the New Berlin*, 60–63, 83–84.

40. Press release, January 16, 1990, SenKult, File Nr. 327, Berlin-Museum, Erweiterungsbau, 2/88–90, emphasis in the original; Bausenator Nagel to Senatorin für Kulturelle Angelegenheiten Martiny, November 13, 1990, File Nr. 328, Berlin-Museum, Erweiterungsbau, 5/90–4/91. See also Libeskind's description of gaining Nagel's approval in Libeskind, *Breaking Ground*, 96–99, as well as Pieper, *Die Musealisierung des Holocaust*, 250–51.

41. All the politicians who wrote the forewords to the 1992 published version of the drawings mention its exceptional status as a funded project. See Feireiss, ed., *Daniel Libeskind*.

42. Reichel, *Politik mit der Erinnerung*, 196–209; Till, *The New Berlin*, 102–5; and Ladd, *The Ghosts of Berlin*, 160–69, 217–24.

43. Jarausch, *After Unity*, 18.

44. See the vehement critique of this position in Habermas, "Wir sind wieder 'normal' geworden."

45. Anthropologist Uli Linke takes up the question of how concepts of the racialized body formulated and used in the Nazi period are contiguous with the West German and unified German attitude toward the German body as well as violence against the foreign body. In this argument, she follows Klaus Theweleit, who analyzed the continuity of discourse from World War I and after, and interprets from that national patterns of thought. While useful in identifying a variety of vernacular sources on everyday discussions of the body, I find the analysis overdrawn, and, in particular, its discussion of racial violence after reunification asserts a connection to the Nazi past without really analyzing how that past was mobilized for very different purposes and by distinctly specific populations. See, especially, Linke, *German Bodies,* 153–216.

46. See the overview of German immigration since 1871 as well as analysis of some of the particularities of immigration and racism in the 1980s in Panayi, "Racial Exclusionism in the New Germany," 130–34. Most analyses rely on statistics from the Ministry of the Interior. See the very helpful summary chart in Kurthen, Bergmann, and Erb, eds., *Antisemitism and Xenophobia in Germany after Unification,* 8.

47. Kurthen, Bergmann and Erb, eds., *Antisemitism and Xenophobia in Germany after Unification,* 8. Bergmann, "Antisemitism and Xenophobia in Germany since Unification," 27–35.

48. Bergmann, "Antisemitism and Xenophobia in Germany since Unification," 34–35; Panayi, "Racial Exclusionism in the New Germany," 140–41. Note that before the debates on asylum following the Balkan conflict in the 1990s, Germany's asylum laws were particularly liberal and defended in relation to the racist NSDAP policies of the past.

49. Erb and Kurthen, "Chronology of Antisemitic and Extreme Right-Wing Events in Germany during and after Unification, 1989–1994," 263–65; Kurthen, Bergmann, and Erb, eds., *Antisemitism and Xenophobia in Germany after Unification,* 8; Panayi, "Racial Exclusionism in the New Germany," 141–42.

50. Backes and Jesse, *Politischer Extremismus in der Bundesrepublik Deutschland,* 126–27; Peck, Ash, and Lemke, "Natives, Strangers, and Foreigners," 78–83.

51. Peck, Ash, and Lemke, "Natives, Strangers, and Foreigners," 79–85.

52. Omi and Winant, *Racial Formation in the United States,* 56.

53. SenKult, File Nr. 320, Berlin-Museum 9/88–93: Bothe to Bendt, February 28, 1990.

54. SenKult, File Nr. 328, folder 27: Berlin-Museum, Erweiterungsbau 5/90–4/91: Bendt to Kirchner, September 3, 1990.

55. SenKult, File Nr. 320, Berlin-Museum 9/88–93: press release, January 16, 1990.

56. February 21, 1990, wire service news summary, and press clipping (no source) February 22, 1990, SenKult, File Nr. 327, Berlin-Museum, Erweiterungsbau, 2/88–90.

57. "Kultursenator: Jüdisches Museum so bald wie möglich bauen," *Tagesspiegel,* August 6, 1991, n.p. This and subsequent articles are from an extensive

clippings file in SenKult, File Nr. 386, Berlin-Museum, Erweiterungsbau 1991. See also, e.g., Ernst Cramer's resignation from the board of directors of the Society for a Jewish Museum, March 4, 1991, in which he states that with the fall of the wall, another museum is not required; in Weinland and Winkler, *Das Jüdische Museum im Stadtmuseum Berlin*, 300–304.

58. Daniel Libeskind describes this mobilization campaign in Libeskind, *Breaking Ground*, 140–46. See also the collection of letters and supporting documents in SenKult, File Nr. 386, Berlin-Museum, Erweiterungsbau 1991. Pieper also briefly discusses this moment and the ethnic identification of the museum in *Die Musealisierung des Holocaust*, 253–54.

59. Erb and Kurthen, "Chronology of Antisemitic and Extreme Right-Wing Events in Germany during and after Unification, 1989–1994," 268.

60. Libeskind, *Breaking Ground*, 144. See also the many clippings in SenKult, File Nr. 386, Berlin-Museum, Erweiterungsbau 1991. These include, e.g., the *New York Times*, July 8, 1991, "Jewish Wing for Berlin Museum in Jeopardy"; *Tagesspiegel*, August 6, 1991, "Kultursenator: Jüdisches Museum so bald wie möglich bauen"; *Neue OZ*, August 29, 1991, "Entscheidung für Jüdisches Museum."

61. "Kultursenator: Jüdisches Museum so bald wie möglich bauen," *Tagesspiegel*, August 6, 1991, n.p., in SenKult, File Nr. 386, Berlin-Museum, Erweiterungsbau 1991.

62. As Roloff-Momin made clear in a speech accepting a gift of paintings from Israeli collections, "I can assure you that the Senate has not stopped the planning for the Jewish Museum, unlike with most building plans for the western portion of the city." Roloff-Momin, September 25, 1991, speech, reprinted in Weinland and Winkler, *Das Jüdische Museum im Stadtmuseum Berlin*, 313. See also the draft of the resolution by the Greens/Bundnis 90 and entered by the SPD and CDU in ibid., 315.

63. Bothe, "The Berlin Museum and Its Extension," 52.

64. Bendt, "The Model of Integration," 30.

65. Weinland and Winkler, *Das Jüdische Museum im Stadtmuseum Berlin*, 51, 62.

66. See the summary of Barzel's activity in 1995 and documents related to his change in the plan of the museum in ibid., 53–60, 67–72, 416–39.

67. T. J. Reed, "Unplayable History," *TLS*, October 5, 2001, 21. See also Jüdisches Museum Berlin, *Geschichten einer Ausstellung*. Pieper gives an extensive analysis of the installation, but the reader should also consult the interesting analysis of its public reception in Chametsky, "Not What We Expected."

5. THE NUREMBERG PARTY RALLY GROUNDS AND LOCAL POLITICS

1. Zelnhefer, *Die Reichsparteitage der NSDAP*. See also Jaskot, *The Architecture of Oppression*, 47–79.

2. All scholars who have worked on postwar Nuremberg have taken Nuremberg's unique status as a starting point. I am particularly indebted to the excellent

recent work of Brockmann, *Nuremberg*; Gregor, *Haunted City*; and Macdonald, *Difficult Heritage*. Brockmann's work emphasizes the reception of Nuremberg as a whole in literary and social discourse; Gregor focused on the immediate postwar period and the changes to the city; and Macdonald reveals how the Nazi past at the site and in Nuremberg in general is perceived by different local constituencies. My work, though, focuses more specifically on the architecture of the Party Rally Grounds, as well as additions to the site beyond just the Dokumentationszentrum, and how their shifting interpretation was influenced by local political debates. In addition, see my articles "The Reich Party Rally Grounds Revisited" and "Introduction," both in Rosenfeld and Jaskot, eds., *Beyond Berlin*.

3. Although less interested in the more vernacular architectural examples at the site, Macdonald addresses this question well in relation to the specific example of the Zeppelinfeld. In addition to her book, *Difficult Heritage*, see also Macdonald, "Words in Stone?"

4. Herf, *Divided Memory*. For the built environment, see Diefendorf, *In the Wake of War*.

5. Reichel, *Politik mit der Erinnerung*, 209–17.

6. Other scholars have begun to examine how the built environment outside Berlin had a different relationship to the history of National Socialist Germany. See, for example, the essays in Rosenfeld and Jaskot, eds., *Beyond Berlin*, and the case studies in Neumann, *Shifting Memories*.

7. Dietzfelbinger and Liedtke, *Nürnberg—Ort der Massen*, 11–22. As any scholar working on the Rally Grounds must admit, the work of local historian Dietzfelbinger remains unparalleled in its depth. My account is also indebted to his work and our discussions.

8. Jaskot, *The Architecture of Oppression*, 47–79; Scobie, *Hitler's State Architecture*, 69–92. See also the indispensible overview in Zelnhefer, *Die Reichsparteitage der NSDAP*.

9. Dietzfelbinger and Liedtke, *Nürnberg—Ort der Massen*, 85–87; Geschichte für Alle, ed., *Langwasser*, 9–10. Geschichte für Alle is a local citizens' initiative that formed to provide a bottom–up view of history, particularly with regard to confronting the Nazi past in Nuremberg.

10. Brockmann, *Nuremberg*, 205–6. See also the useful and anecdotal short volume by Heigl, *The U.S. Army in Nuremberg*. For the firebombing of German cities, see the book that helped redefine the debate: Sebald, *On the Natural History of Destruction*, as well as the evocative first-person account of Hamburg a few days after the Allied attacks in Nossack, *The End*.

11. Brockmann, *Nuremberg*, 237. See also the comparative legal perspective offered in Ball, *Prosecuting War Crimes and Genocide*.

12. Brockmann, *Nuremberg*, 237–56 (quotation on 249). Brockmann's text is a sweeping and highly compelling analysis of how Nuremberg's development from the time of Dürer was imaged and imagined in texts as diverse as poetry, travelers' accounts, films, and other media.

13. Mack-Phillip, "Stadtplanung und Stadtentwicklung prägen das Gesicht der Stadt." See also the comparison to Munich in Rosenfeld, *Munich and Memory*.

14. Dietzfelbinger and Liedtke, *Nürnberg—Ort der Massen*, 97–105; Heigl, *The U.S. Army in Nuremberg*, 52–57.

15. Geschichte für Alle, ed., *Langwasser*, 11–13, 25–33. In relation to more contemporary uses, see the interview with Wolfgang Lang, immigrant adviser (*Aussiedlerbeirat*) for the city in ibid., 34–35. In addition, see Gregor's strong discussion of refugees, evacuees, and returning veterans in Gregor, *Haunted City*, 37–74.

16. Geschichte für Alle, ed., *Langwasser*, 13–14; Dietzfelbinger and Liedtke, *Nürnberg—Ort der Massen*, 94–96. The Ministry of the Interior changed the name of the site to Langwasser in 1951. See Stadtchronik (F2), vol. 49, 367, Stadtarchiv Nürnberg.

17. Modernist architecture as an expression of unity among the western capitalist states is a well-known trope in the literature. For an excellent example, see Wharton, *Building the Cold War*.

18. Dietzfelbinger notes that, as early as 1948, a proposal had been made by a group formed to give German youth vocational training to set up workshops just south of the Märzfeld as a symbolic rejection of the previous purposes of the land. See Dietzfelbinger and Liedtke, *Nürnberg—Ort der Massen*, 151 n. 7.

19. See, for example, Ballon and Jackson, eds., *Robert Moses and the Modern City*.

20. For the discussion of the WBG competition, see Geschichte für Alle, ed., *Langwasser*, 14–16, and Stadtchronik (F2), vol. 51, 428; vol. 52, 75, Stadtarchiv Nürnberg.

21. Gregor, *Haunted City*, 19, 368–73.

22. Wilhelm Westecker, "Der schlichte und lichte Musikpalast," *Nürnberger Zeitung*, September 7, 1963.

23. Ironically, the Meistersingerhalle would find itself embroiled in the return of the Nazi past with a gift of a tapestry from the Bavarian state, commissioned from Hermann Kaspar in 1966. Kaspar had worked earlier in his career on many Nazi commissions, including the Neue Reichskanzlei. This compromised past sparked hefty protests from Nuremberg citizens. The city at first rejected the work but then was persuaded to accept it. At the installation in January 1970, the Bavarian minister Theodor Heuss (CSU) spoke of how the gift helped overcome the past, which struck many in the audience as a painful analogy. Mayor Urschlechter merely thanked the state and the cultural representatives, dispensing with his usual remarks, and left the building reception early. See the multiple articles on this affair in Stadtarchiv Nürnberg, Press Collections, Meistersingerhalle (F7/I, nr. 782). On Scharoun's Philharmonie, see James-Chakraborty, *German Architecture for a Mass Audience*, 103–4.

24. Greg Castillo has a very compelling analysis of how product and interior design interacted with Cold War economic policy on both sides of the wall in Castillo, *Cold War on the Home Front*. Notably, in spite of the Convention Center's

clear importance to postwar Nuremberg, scholarship on the Party Rally Grounds has not analyzed its history or significance.

25. "Erweiterung des Messe-Komplexes" (September 11, 1968), Referat VI, and Amtsblatt der Stadt Nürnberg (March 12, 1969), in Archivbestand Baureferat, C 75, Nr. 831, Stadtarchiv Nürnberg.

26. Protocol Stadtratsitzung (February 16, 1969), in Archivbestand Baureferat, C 75, Nr. 831, Stadtarchiv Nürnberg.

27. Press Report (March 13, 1969) and Press Report (March 26, 1969) in Archivbestand Baureferat, C 75, Nr. 831, Stadtarchiv Nürnberg. Note that the City Council did not officially approve the site until February 4, 1970. Other sites were considered at the Rally Grounds, such as refurbishing the Kongresshalle as a new facility.

28. Baureferat Protocol (September 5, 1969) and meeting between Loebermann and Doni (September 15, 1969) in Archivbestand Baureferat, C 75, Nr. 831, Stadtarchiv Nürnberg. See also Doni's article on the planned center with an illustration of Loebermann's initial design in Doni, "Die Messe strebt zu neuen Ufern," 4–8.

29. Stadtchronik (F2), vol. 62, 303, Stadtarchiv Nürnberg. See also the Beschluss des Stadtrates (October 15, 1970) and the exchange between the city's Office of Landscape Planning and the Baureferat (November 1971) in Archivbestand Baureferat, C75/835 Messehalle, 1970–71, Stadtarchiv Nürnberg. The original design is illustrated in a photo from a clipping from the *Nürnberger Zeitung* (February 10, 1971) in Press Collections, F7/I, No. 785, Stadtarchiv Nürnberg.

30. See, for example, the discussion of Mies's IIT plan as well as the Federal Center in Chicago in Cohen, *Mies van der Rohe*, 99–109, 146–59.

31. It is worth thinking of the economic agenda of the postwar years in relation to the foreign policy initiatives of Gustav Stresemann in the Weimar Republic. Stresemann also faced international pressure after World War I to maintain a nonmilitarist state and, thus, the lowering of German influence and status. For him, pursuing a dominant economic role became a way of supporting Germany's international influence even while it stayed nominally true to the terms of the Treaty of Versailles. For an excellent analysis of this position and its collapse with the coming of the Nazi state, see the introduction to Tooze, *The Wages of Destruction*, 1–33.

32. Dietzfelbinger and Liedtke, *Nürnberg—Ort der Massen*, 97, 102–3, 110–12. See also Macdonald, *Difficult Heritage*.

33. Ladd, *Ghosts of Berlin*, 217–35.

34. Dietzfelbinger and Liedtke, *Nürnberg—Ort der Massen*, 112–13; cf. Peter Reichel, *Politik mit der Erinnerung*, 31–42.

35. Remarkable in this period are the number of variable approaches to the Nazi past that sprang up in both West and East Germany. For an analysis of local case studies or comparative actions taken by a variety of cities during this period, see, respectively, Neumann, *Shifting Memories*, and Rosenfeld and Jaskot, eds., *Beyond Berlin*. Note, though, as I stated in the introduction, the East German commemorations rarely discussed the presence of perpetrators in contemporary GDR

society, focusing instead on Communists and increasingly Jews as victim groups. Perpetrator sites were not preserved as such in the GDR.

36. Dietzfelbinger and Liedtke, *Nürnberg—Ort der Massen,* 120–23; Volker Probst, "Was bleibt vom Gedenken?" *Plärrer* 7 (July 1995), n.p.; Peter Schmitt, "Hitlers Aufmarschplatz als Dokumentationszentrum," *Süddeutsche Zeitung,* February 17, 1998, n.p. Unless otherwise noted, all subsequent newspaper citations in the chapter with "n.p." are taken from the Presseberichte, Dokumentationszentrum Reichsparteitagsgelände (Collection of Museen der Stadt Nürnberg). My thanks to Franz Sonnenberger for providing me with this collection. See also the catalog for the *Fascination and Terror* exhibition: Dietzfelbinger, *Faszination und Gewalt/ Fascination and Terror,* as well as Macdonald's comprehensive analysis of the exhibition (Macdonald, *Difficult Heritage*). Note that the city museum's preferred translation is "Fascination and Terror," although it is more literally "Fascination and Violence." I have kept the museum's preference. For Glaser's important local role, see in particular Brockmann, *Nuremberg,* 259–69.

37. See the numerous publications on this subject by Peter Reichel.

38. Brockmann, *Nuremberg,* 261–64.

39. Annekathrin Fries, "Aus der Geschichte lernen," *Nürnberg Heute,* December 1996, n.p. See also Brockmann's discussion of the 1992 proposals, in Brockmann, *Nuremberg,* 270–71.

40. Scholz, as cited in Schürgers, "Argument der Bürger ernst nehmen."

41. Raimond Kirch, "Wir haben nur etwas die Phantasien beflügelt," *Nürnberger Zeitung,* July 16, 1997, 3.

42. Compare this with the discussion of the zigzag form of Libeskind's Jewish Museum in chapter 4.

43. "Bund zahlt für Doku-Zentrum," *Abendzeitung,* December 17, 1999, n.p. See also the overview of the competition in Dietzfelbinger and Liedtke, *Nürnberg—Ort der Massen,* 123–28. For architecture as a countermonument to Nazi monumental building, see, for example, Barnstone, *The Transparent State,* as well as Fischer, "Invoking the Past in Recent German Exhibition Design."

44. Stadt Nürnberg, *Dokumentation,* 4; Siegfried Zelnhefer, "Ludwig Scholz nimmt Bund und Land in die Pflicht," *Nürnberger Nachrichten,* July 16, 1997, 13.

45. Stadt Nürnberg, *Auslobungstext,* 30–31; Protokoll des Kolloquiums zum Wettbewerb ehemaliges Reichsparteitagsgelände am 19.03.2001 (Ingo Schlick, Baureferat, Stadt Nürnberg [author's collection]). In the interest of full disclosure, it should be noted that I participated in this process as a nonvoting historical adviser to the jury.

46. Stadt Nürnberg, *Dokumentation,* 6–9; Siegfried Zelnhefer, "Ideen für NS-Areal," *Nürnberger Nachrichten,* August 2, 2001, 1, 11.

47. André Fischer, "Finanzierung muss schnell geklärt werden," *Nürnberger Zeitung,* June 14/15, 1997, n.p.; Verlag Hans Müller, *Nürnberger Facetten,* 256–59. For responses to the rally grounds by local constituents, see the sociological analysis by Sharon Macdonald in *Difficult Heritage.*

48. Stadt Nürnberg, "Ein Diskussionsbeitrag über den Umgang mit dem ehemaligen Reichsparteitagsgelände in Nürnberg," February 2003 (author's collection). A digital version can also be found at http://www.kubiss.de/kulturreferat/reichs parteitagsgelaende/downloads/Obm-rpg.pdf (referenced July 21, 2011). See also Brockmann's discussion of this memorandum in Brockmann, *Nuremberg*, 275–76.

49. "Beschluss des Stadtrates vom 19.05.2004: Nutzung des ehemaligen Reichsparteitagsgeländes," http://www.kubiss.de/kulturreferat/reichsparteitagsge laende/downloads/Beschluss.pdf (referenced July 21, 2011).

Afterword

1. For issues related to comparative genocide, see Waller, *Becoming Evil*.

2. Ball, *Prosecuting War Crimes and Genocide*.

3. An important recent counterexample is Didi-Huberman, *Images in Spite of All*.

4. Miller Lane, *Architecture and Politics in Germany, 1918–1945*, 200–202. Miller Lane argues that the building is much more closely connected to Modernist aesthetics than most examples of Nazi state architecture.

5. See the solid summary of the building's transformation in Wise, *Capital Dilemma*, 102–7.

BIBLIOGRAPHY

Adler, Daniel. "Painterly Politics: Wölfflin, Formalism and German Academic Culture, 1885–1915." *Art History* 27, no. 3 (June 2004): 431–56.

Adorno, Theodor. *In Search of Wagner.* Translated by Rodney Livingstone. London: Verso, 2005.

Antoni, Ernst. "Der Faschismus will im Bild bleiben." *Tendenzen* 24, no. 141 (January/March 1983): 5–14.

Arasse, Daniel. *Anselm Kiefer.* Munich: Schirmer/Mosel, 2001.

Arendt, Hannah. *Eichmann in Jerusalem: A Report on the Banality of Evil.* New York: Viking Press, 1964.

Auping, Michael. *Anselm Kiefer: Heaven and Earth.* Fort Worth, Tex.: Modern Art Museum of Fort Worth, 2005.

"Ausstellung Paul Mathias Padua." *Weltkunst,* September 15, 1965, 779.

Backes, Klaus. *Hitler und die bildenden Künste: Kulturverständnis und Kunstpolitik im Dritten Reich.* Cologne: DuMont, 1988.

Backes, Uwe, and Eckhard Jesse. *Politischer Extremismus in der Bundesrepublik Deutschland.* Bonn: Bundeszentrale für Politische Bildung, 1996.

Ball, Howard. *Prosecuting War Crimes and Genocide: The Twentieth-Century Experience.* Lawrence: University Press of Kansas, 1999.

Ballon, Hilary, and Kenneth T. Jackson, eds. *Robert Moses and the Modern City: The Transformation of New York.* New York: W. W. Norton, 2007.

Barnstone, Deborah Ascher. *The Transparent State: Architecture and Politics in Postwar Germany.* London: Routledge, 2005.

Barron, Stephanie, ed. *"Degenerate Art": The Fate of the Avant-Garde in Nazi Germany.* New York: Abrams, 1991.

Barron, Stephanie, and Sabine Eckmann, eds. *Art of Two Germanys: Cold War Cultures.* New York: Abrams, 2009.

Bartov, Omer. *Hitler's Army: Soldiers, Nazis, and War in the Third Reich.* Oxford: Oxford University Press, 1992.

———. "The Holocaust as Leitmotif of the Twentieth Century." In *The Holocaust in International Perspective,* edited by Dagmar Herzog, 3–25. Lessons and Legacies, vol. 7. Evanston: Northwestern University Press, 2006.

———. *Mirrors of Destruction: War, Genocide, and Modern Identity.* Oxford: Oxford University Press, 2000.

Beaucamp, Eduard. "Werner Tübke: Lebenserinnerungen des Dr. jur. Schulze III (1965)." In *Kunst gegen Krieg und Faschismus,* edited by Gabriele Saure and Gisela Schirmer, 219–24. Weimar: Verlag und Datenbank für Geisteswissen-schaften, 1999.

Bechstedt, Anne, Anja Deutsch, and Daniela Stöppel. "Der Verlag F. Bruckmann im Nationalsozialismus." In *Kunstgeschichte im "Dritten Reich": Theorien, Methoden, Praktiken,* edited by Ruth Heftrig, Olaf Peters, and Barbara Maria Schellewald, 280–311. Berlin: Akademie Verlag, 2008.

Bendt, Vera. "The Model of Integration." In Feireiss, *Daniel Libeskind,* 24–30.

Benjamin, Andrew. *Kiefer's Approaches.* London: Institute of Contemporary Art, 1991.

———. *Object, Painting.* London: Academy Edition, 1994.

Benjamin, Walter. "*One-Way Street* (Selections)." In *Reflections,* edited by Peter Demetz, 61–94. New York: Schocken Books, 1986.

Bergdoll, Barry, and Leah Dickerman, eds. *Bauhaus: Workshops for Modernity.* New York: Museum of Modern Art, 2009.

Berghahn, V. R. *Modern Germany.* 2nd ed. Cambridge: Cambridge University Press, 1987.

Bergmann, Walther. "Antisemitism and Xenophobia in Germany since Unifica-tion." In *Antisemitism and Xenophobia in Germany after Unification,* edited by Hermann Kurthen, Werner Bergmann, and Rainer Erb, 21–38. New York: Oxford University Press, 1997.

Bertolini, David. "The Architecture of Auschwitz-Birkenau and the Nazi Fantasy." *Holocaust Studies: A Journal of Culture and History* 14, no. 3 (Winter 2008): 25–60.

Betthausen, Peter, Peter H. Feist, and Christiane Fork. *Metzler Kunsthistoriker Lexikon.* Stuttgart: Metzler, 1999.

Betts, Paul. *The Authority of Everyday Objects: A Cultural History of West German Industrial Design.* Berkeley: University of California Press, 2004.

Biro, Matthew. *Anselm Kiefer and the Philosophy of Martin Heidegger.* Cambridge: Cambridge University Press, 1998.

———. "Representation and Event: Anselm Kiefer, Joseph Beuys, and the Memory of the Holocaust." *Yale Journal of Criticism* 16, no. 1 (2003): 113–46.

Block, René. "Not a Monument but Rather Food for Thought." In Gillen, *German Art from Beckmann to Richter,* 214–17.

Bollmus, Reinhard. *Das Amt Rosenberg und seine Gegner.* 2nd ed. Stuttgart: Deutsche Verlags Anstalt, 2006.

Borrmann, Norbert. *Paul Schultze-Naumburg, 1869–1949.* Essen: R. Bacht, 1989.

Bothe, Rolf. "The Berlin Museum and Its Extension." In Feireiss, *Daniel Libeskind,* 32–52.

Brenner, Hildegard. *Die Kunstpolitik des Nationalsozialismus.* Reinbeck bei Hamburg: Rowohlt, 1963.

Brockmann, Stephen. *Nuremberg: The Imaginary Capital.* Rochester: Camden House, 2006.

Browning, Christopher. "Beyond 'Intentionalism' and 'Functionalism': A Reassessment of Nazi Jewish Policy from 1939 to 1941." In *Reevaluating the Third Reich,* edited by Thomas Childers and Jane Caplan, 211–33. New York: Holmes and Meier, 1993.

———. *Ordinary Men: Reserve Police Battalion 101 and the Final Solution in Poland.* New York: HarperCollins, 1992.

Brunkhorst, H., G. Koch, and H.-J. Lissmann. *"Holocaust"—Impulse, Reaktionen, Konsequenzen.* Frankfurt am Main: Didaktischen Zemtrums der Johann-Wolfgang-Goethe-Universität, 1980.

Buchheim, Hans, Martin Broszat, Hans-Adolf Jacobsen, and Helmut Krausnick. *Anatomie des SS-Staates.* 2 vols. Munich: Deutscher Taschenbuch, 1967.

Buchheim, Lothar-Günther. *Eines Lebenslauf.* Feldafing: Buchheim, 2006.

Buchloh, Benjamin H. D. "Divided Memory and Post-Traditional Identity: Gerhard Richter's Work of Mourning." *October* 75 (Winter 1996): 60–82.

———. "Figures of Authority, Ciphers of Regression: Notes on the Return of Representation in European Painting." *October* 16 (Spring 1981): 39–68.

———. "Gerhard Richter's *Atlas*: The Anomic Archive." *October* 88 (Spring 1999): 117–45.

———. "Interview with Gerhard Richter." Translated by Stephen P. Duffy. In *Gerhard Richter: Paintings,* edited by Roald Nasgaard, 15–29. London: Thames and Hudson, 1988.

———. *Neo-Avantgarde and Culture Industry: Essays on European and American Art from 1955 to 1975.* Cambridge, Mass.: MIT Press, 2000.

Bussenius, Daniel. "Die Anfänge des Jüdischen Museums Berlin: Zur Entstehung des 'integrativen Konzepts' vor der Wiedervereinigung." *Mitteilungen des Vereins für die Geschichte Berlins* 102, no. 2 (April 2006): 345–52.

Castillo, Greg. "The Bauhaus in Cold War Germany." In James-Chakraborty, *Bauhaus Culture,* 171–93.

———. *Cold War on the Home Front: The Soft Power of Midcentury Design.* Minneapolis: University of Minnesota Press, 2010.

———. "Socialist Realism and Built Nationalism in the Cold War 'Battle of the Styles.'" *Centropa* 1, no. 2 (May 2001): 84–93.

Caygill, Howard. "The Futures of Berlin's Potsdamer Platz." In *The Limits of Globalization: Cases and Arguments,* edited by Alan Scott, 25–54. London: Routledge, 1997.

Celan, Paul. *Gedichte.* 2 vols. Frankfurt am Main: Suhrkamp, 1995.

Chamberlain, Houston Stewart. *Foundations of the Nineteenth Century.* New York: H. Fertig, 1968.

Chametzky, Peter. "Not What We Expected: The Jewish Museum Berlin in Practice." *Museum and Society* 6, no. 3 (November 2008): 216–45.

———. "Rebuilding the Nation: Norman Foster's Reichstag Renovation and Daniel Libeskind's Jewish Museum, Berlin." *Centropa* 1, no. 3 (September 2001): 245–64.

Cohen, Jean-Louis. *Architecture in Uniform: Designing and Building for the Second World War.* Montreal: Canadian Centre for Architecture, 2011.

———. *Mies van der Rohe.* 2nd ed. Basel: Birkhäuser, 2007.

Cohn, Michael. *The Jews in Germany, 1945–1993.* Westport, Conn.: Praeger, 1994.

Cole, Tim. *Selling the Holocaust: From Auschwitz to Schindler; How History Is Bought, Packaged, and Sold.* New York: Routledge, 1999.

Cordulack, Shelley. "Anselm Kiefer: Art, Work and Vocation in the Third Reich." *Buckmann's Pantheon* 57 (1999): 169–77.

Curley, John J. "Gerhard Richter's Cold War Vision." In *Gerhard Richter: Early Work, 1951–1972,* edited by Christine Mehring, Jeanne Anne Nugent, and Jon L. Seydl, 11–35. Los Angeles: J. Paul Getty Museum, 2010.

Damus, Martin. *Kunst in der BRD, 1945–1990.* Reinbeck bei Hamburg: Rowohlts, 1995.

Dickel, Hans. "Der Fall Kiefer." *Kritische Berichte* 28, no. 1 (2000): 87–92.

Didi-Huberman, Georges. *Images in Spite of All: Four Photographs from Auschwitz.* Chicago: University of Chicago Press, 2008.

Diefendorf, Jeffry M. *In the Wake of War: The Reconstruction of German Cities after World War II.* Oxford: Oxford University Press, 1993.

Dietzfelbinger, Eckart. *Faszination und Gewalt/Fascination and Terror.* Nuremberg: Museen der Stadt Nürnberg, 1996.

Dietzfelbinger, Eckart, and Gerhard Liedtke. *Nürnberg—Ort der Massen.* Berlin: Ch. Links Verlag, 2004.

Dilly, Heinrich, ed. *Altmeister moderner Kunstgeschichte.* Berlin: Reimer, 1990.

Doll, Nikola. "Der Erste Deutsche Kunsthistorikertag 1948." In Doll, Fuhrmeister, and Sprenger, *Kunstgeschichte im Nationalsozialismus,* 325–37.

Doll, Nikola, Christian Fuhrmeister, and Michael H. Sprenger, eds. *Kunstgeschichte im Nationalsozialismus: Beiträge zur Geschichte einer Wissenschaft zwischen 1930 und 1950.* Weimar: VDG, 2005.

Doll, Nikola, Ruth Heftrig, Olaf Peters, and Ulrich Rehm, eds. *Kunstgeschichte nach 1945: Kontinuität und Neubeginn in Deutschland.* Cologne: Böhlau, 2006.

Doni, Wilhelm. "Die Messe strebt zu neuen Ufern." *Nürnberg Heute* 10 (July 1970): 4–8.

Dorner, Elke. *Daniel Libeskind: Jüdisches Museum Berlin.* Berlin: Mann, 1999.

Dürr, Sybille. "Wölfflin, Hauttmann, Pinder: Das Kunsthistorische Institut der Universität München." In *Münchner Moderne,* edited by Felix Billeter, Antje Günther, and Steffan Krämer, 268–77. Munich: Deutscher Kunstverlag, 2002.

Durth, Werner. *Deutsche Architekten: Biographische Verflechtungen.* Braunschweig: Vieweg, 1987.

Dwork, Deborah, and Robert Jan van Pelt. *Auschwitz: 1270 to the Present*. New York: W. W. Norton, 1996.

Earl, Hilary. *The Nuremberg SS-Einsatzgruppen Trial, 1945–1958*. Cambridge: Cambridge University Press, 2009.

Eckmann, Sabine. "Ruptures and Continuities: Modern German Art in between the Third Reich and the Cold War." In Barron and Eckmann, *Art of Two Germanys*, 48–63.

Ehrenfried, Susanne. *Ohne Eigenschaften: Das Portrait bei Gerhard Richter*. Vienna: Springer, 1997.

Elger, Dietmar. *Gerhard Richter, Maler*. Cologne: DuMont, 2002.

Engelbert, Arthur, and Hans auf der Lake. "Den Betrachter zwingen, daß er anfängt Fragen zu stellen: Ein Gespräch mit Fritz Cremer." *Tendenzen* 22, no. 134 (January/March 1981): 52–56.

Erb, Rainer, and Hermann Kurthen. "Chronology of Antisemitic and Extreme Right-Wing Events in Germany during and after Unification, 1989–1994." In *Antisemitism and Xenophobia in Germany after Unification*, edited by Hermann Kurthen, Werner Bergmann, and Rainer Erb, 263–86. New York: Oxford University Press, 1997.

Fastert, Sabine. "Pluralismus statt Einheit: Die Rezeption von Wilhelm Pinders Generationenmodell nach 1945." In *Kunstgeschichte nach 1945: Kontinuität und Neubeginn in Deutschland*, edited by Nikola Doll, Ruth Heftrig, Olaf Peters, and Ulrich Rehm, 51–65. Cologne: Böhlau, 2006.

Fehrenbach, Heide. *Cinema in Democratizing Germany: Reconstructing National Identity after Hitler*. Chapel Hill: University of North Carolina Press, 1995.

Feireiss, Kristin, ed. *Daniel Libeskind: Erweiterung des Berlin Museums mit Abteilung Jüdisches Museum/Extension to the Berlin Museum with Jewish Museum Department*. Berlin: Ernst, 1992.

Felstiner, John. *Paul Celan: Poet, Survivor, Jew*. New Haven, Conn.: Yale University Press, 1995.

Fischer, Jan Otakar. "Invoking the Past in Recent German Exhibition Design." *Harvard Design Magazine* 19 (Fall 2003/Winter 2004): online edition.

Forster, Kurt W. "Monstrum Mirabile et Audax." In Feireiss, *Daniel Libeskind*, 17–23.

Frei, Norbert. *Vergangenheitspolitik: Die Anfänge der Bundesrepublik und die NS-Vergangenheit*. Munich: Deutscher Taschenbuch Verlag, 1999.

Friedel, Helmut, ed. *Gerhard Richter: Atlas der Fotos, Collagen und Skizzen*. Cologne: Oktagon, 1997.

Friedlander, Henry. *The Origins of Nazi Genocide: From Euthanasia to the Final Solution*. Chapel Hill: University of North Carolina Press, 1995.

Friedländer, Saul. *History and Psychoanalysis: An Inquiry into the Possibilities and Limits of Psychohistory*. New York: Holmes and Meier, 1978.

———. *Reflections of Nazism: An Essay on Kitsch and Death*. New York: Harper and Row, 1984.

Frommhold, Erhard. "Hans Grundig—Rektor und Lehrer 1946–1949." In *Trotzdem: Neuanfang 1947; Zur Wiedereröffnung der Akademie der bildenden Künste*

Dresden, edited by Rainer Beck and Natalia Kardinar, 141–52. Dresden: Verlag der Kunst, 1997.

Fuchs, R. H. "Kiefer schildert." *Museumsjournal* 25 (1980): 302–9.

Fuhrmeister, Christian. "Adolf Ziegler (1892–1959), ein nationalsozialistischer Künstler und Funktionär." In *200 Jahre Akademie der Bildenden Künste München*, edited by Nikolaus Gerhart, Walter Grasskamp, and Florian Matzner, 88–95. Munich: Hirmer, 2008.

Galleria del Levante. *Werner Tübke*. Milan: Gallera del Levante, 1971.

Gantner, Joseph, ed. *Heinrich Wölfflin, 1864–1945: Autobiographie, Tagebücher und Briefe*. Basel: Schwabe, 1984.

Germer, Stefan. "Familienanschluß: Zur Thematisierung des privaten in neueren Bildern Gerhard Richters." *Texte zur Kunst*, no. 26 (June 1997): 108–16.

———. "Die Wiederkehr des Verdrängten: Zum Umgang mit deutscher Geschichte bei Georg Baselitz, Anselm Kiefer, Jörg Immendorf und Gerhard Richter." *Jahresring* 46 (1999): 38–55.

Geschichte für Alle, ed. *Langwasser: Heimisch warden in Nürnbergs jüngstem Stadtteil*. Nuremberg: Sandberg-Verlag, 2001.

Gillen, Eckhart, ed. *German Art from Beckmann to Richter: Images of a Divided Country*. Cologne: DuMont Buchverlag, 1997.

———. "Images around 1945: Felix Nussbaum, Karl Hoffer, Werner Heldt, Otto Dix, Hans Grundig, Horst Strempel." In Gillen, *German Art from Beckmann to Richter*, 68–70.

———. "Die Kriegsgeneration und der Antifaschismus: Franz Fühmann und Gerhard Richter im Vergleich mit Bernhard Heisig." In *Bernhard Heisig: Die Wut der Bilder*, edited by Eckhart Gillen, 330–59. Leipzig: Museum der bildenden Künste Leipzig, 2005.

———. "Wolf Vostell: German View." In Gillen, *German Art from Beckmann to Richter*, 208–13.

Gregor, Neil. *Haunted City: Nuremberg and the Nazi Past*. New Haven, Conn.: Yale University Press, 2008.

Gross, Jan T. *Neighbors: The Destruction of the Jewish Community in Jedwabne, Poland*. Princeton, N.J.: Princeton University Press, 2001.

Günther, Hans. *Rasse und Stil*. Munich: J. F. Lehmanns Verlag, 1927.

Gutschow, Kai K. "The Anti-Mediterranean in the Literature of Modern Architecture." In *Modern Architecture and the Mediterranean Ideal: Vernacular Dialogues and Contested Identities*, edited by J. F. Lejeune and M. Sabatino, 161–85. London: Routledge, 2009.

Gutschow, Niels. *Ordnungswahn: Architekten planen im "eingedeutschten Osten," 1939–1945*. Basel: Birkhäuser, 2001.

Habermas, Jürgen. "Defusing the Past: A Politico-Cultural Tract." In Hartman, *Bitburg in Moral and Political Perspective*, 43–51.

———. "On How Postwar Germany Has Faced Its Recent Past." *Common Knowledge* 5, no. 2 (1996): 7–8.

———. "Wir sind wieder 'normal' geworden." *Die Zeit*, December 18, 1992, 48.

Hake, Sabine. *German National Cinema*. London: Routledge, 2002.

Hall, James. "Anselm Kiefer: The Generalized Image of Authority." *Apollo* 130 (1989): 269–70.

Hart, Joan. "Heinrich Wölfflin: An Intellectual Biography." PhD diss., University of California, Berkeley, 1981.

———. "Reinterpreting Wölfflin—Neo-Kantianism and Hermeneutics." *Art Journal* 42 (1982): 292–300.

Harten, Jürgen, ed. *Gerhard Richter: Bilder, 1962–1985*. Cologne: DuMont, 1986.

Harten, Jürgen, and Ulrich Krempel. *Jörg Immendorf: Café Deutschland*. Düsseldorf: Städtische Kunsthalle, 1982.

Hartman, Geoffrey H., ed. *Bitburg in Moral and Political Perspective*. Bloomington: Indiana University Press, 1986.

Haxthausen, Charles Werner. "Kiefer in America: Reflections on a Retrospective." *Kunstchronik* 42 (1989): 1–16.

Hecht, Axel. "München ist nun wirklich keine Kunststadt." *Art*, no. 9 (September 1980): 76–78.

———. "Venedig 1980: Aktuelle Kunst Made in Germany." *Art*, no. 6 (June 1980): 40–53.

Heigl, Peter. *The U.S. Army in Nuremberg on Hitler's Nazi Party Rally Grounds*. 2nd ed. Nuremberg: P. Heigl, 2005.

Heineman, Elizabeth. "The Hour of the Woman: Memories of Germany's 'Crisis Years' and West German National Identity." In Schissler, *The Miracle Years*, 21–56.

———. *What Difference Does a Husband Make? Women and Marital Status in Nazi and Postwar Germany*. Berkeley: University of California Press, 1999.

Held, Jutta. "New Left Art History and Fascism in Germany." In *Marxism and the History of Art: From William Morris to the New Left*, edited by Andrew Hemingway, 196–212. London: Pluto Press, 2006.

Henatsch, Martin. *Gerhard Richter: 18. Oktober 1977*. Frankfurt: Fischer Taschenbuch, 1998.

Herbert, Ulrich. "Der Holocaust in der Geschichtsschreibung der Bundesrepublik Deutschland." In *Zweierlei Bewältigung: Vier Beiträge über den Umgang mit der NS-Vergangenheit in den beiden deutschen Staaten*, edited by Ulrich Herbert and Olag Groehler, 7–27. Hamburg: Ergebnisse, 1992.

———. "Rückkehr in die Bürgerlichkeit? NS-Eliten in der Bundesrepublik." In *Rechtsradikalismus in der politischen Kultur der Nachkriegszeit: Die verzögerte Normalisierung in Niedersachsen*, edited by Bernd Weisbrod, 157–73. Hannover: Hahn, 1995.

Herf, Jeffrey. *Divided Memory: The Nazi Past in the Two Germanys*. Cambridge, Mass.: Harvard University Press, 1999.

———. *The Jewish Enemy: Nazi Propaganda during World War II and the Holocaust*. Cambridge, Mass.: Harvard University Press, 2006.

Hilberg, Raul. "Bitburg as Symbol." In Hartman, *Bitburg in Moral and Political Perspective*, 15–26.

———. *Perpetrators Victims Bystanders: The Jewish Catastrophe, 1933–1945*. New York: Aaron Asher Books, 1992.

Hinz, Berthold. "Der 'Bamberger Reiter.'" In *Das Kunstwerk zwischen Wissenschaft und Weltanschauung*, edited by Martin Warnke, 26–44. Gütersloh: Bertelsmann, 1970.

———. *Die Malerei im deutschen Faschismus*. Munich: Hanser, 1974.

Holly, Michael Ann. *Panofsky and the Foundations of Art History*. Ithaca, N.Y.: Cornell University Press, 1984.

———. *Past Looking: Historical Imagination and the Rhetoric of the Image*. Ithaca, N.Y.: Cornell University Press, 1996.

Hübl, Michael. "Denk ich an Deutschland in der Kunst." *Kunstforum International* 70, no. 2 (March 1984): 199–201.

Huener, Jonathan. *Auschwitz, Poland, and the Politics of Commemoration, 1945–1979*. Athens: Ohio University Press, 2003.

Hughes, David A. "Playing It by the Book—the Early Work of Anselm Kiefer." *Tel Aviver Jahrbuch für deutsche Geschichte* 34 (2006): 232–53.

Hüllenkremer, Marie. "George Segals Holocaust-Denkmal." *Art*, no. 6 (June 1983): 13.

Huyssen, Andreas. "Anselm Kiefer: The Terror of History, the Temptation of Myth." In *Twilight Memories: Marking Time in a Culture of Amnesia*, 209–47. New York: Routledge, 1995.

———. "Figures of Memory in the Course of Time." In Barron and Eckmann, *Art of Two Germanys*, 224–39.

———. "The Voids of Berlin." *Critical Inquiry* 24, no. 1 (Autumn 1997): 57–81.

James-Chakraborty, Kathleen, ed. *Bauhaus Culture: From Weimar to the Cold War*. Minneapolis: University of Minnesota Press, 2006.

———. *German Architecture for a Mass Audience*. New York: Routledge, 2000.

Jarausch, Konrad H., ed. *After Unity: Reconfiguring German Identities*. Providence, R.I.: Berghahn Books, 1997.

Jarausch, Konrad H., Hinrich C. Seeba, and David P. Conradt. "The Presence of the Past: Culture, Opinion, and Identity in Germany." In Jarausch, *After Unity*, 25–60.

Jaskot, Paul B. "Architecture and the Destruction of the European Jews." In *The Holocaust's Ghost: Writings on Art, Politics, Law and Education*, edited by F. C. DeCoste and Bernard Schwartz, 145–64. Edmonton: University of Alberta Press, 2000.

———. *The Architecture of Oppression: The SS, Forced Labor and the Nazi Monumental Building Economy*. London: Routledge, 2000.

———. "Daniel Libeskind's Jewish Museum in Berlin as a Cold War Project." In *Berlin: Divided City, 1945–1989*, edited by Philip Broadbent and Sabine Hake, 145–55. New York: Berghahn Books, 2010.

———. "Gerhard Richter and Adolf Eichmann." *Oxford Art Journal* 28, no. 3 (2005): 457–78.

———. "'Realism'? The Place of Images in Holocaust Studies." In *Reexamining Perpetrators, Victims, and Bystanders,* edited by Sara Horowitz. Lessons and Legacies, vol. 10. Evanston, Ill.: Northwestern University Press, forthcoming.

———. "The Reich Party Rally Grounds Revisited: The Political Resonance of the Nazi Past in Postwar Nuremberg." In Rosenfeld and Jaskot, *Beyond Berlin,* 143–62.

Jaskot, Paul B., Anne Kelly Knowles, and Chester Harvey. "Visualizing the Archive: Building at Auschwitz as a Geographic Problem." In *Geography and the Holocaust,* edited by Tim Cole, Alberto Giordano, and Anne Kelly Knowles. Bloomington: Indiana University Press, forthcoming.

Jüdisches Museum Berlin. *Geschichten einer Ausstellung: Zwei Jahrtausende deutsch-jüdische Geschichte.* Berlin: Stiftung Jüdisches Museum Berlin, 2001.

Judt, Tony. *Postwar: A History of Europe Since 1945.* New York: Penguin, 2005.

Kaes, Anton. *From Hitler to Heimat: The Return of History as Film.* Cambridge, Mass.: Harvard University Press, 1989.

Kaplan, Brett Ashley. *Unwanted Beauty: Aesthetic Pleasure in Holocaust Representation.* Urbana: University of Illinois Press, 2007.

Kaufmann, Thomas DaCosta. *Toward a Geography of Art.* Chicago: University of Chicago Press, 2004.

Kershaw, Ian. *Hitler, 1936–1945: Nemesis.* New York: Longman, 2000.

———. *Hitler, the Germans, and the Final Solution.* New Haven, Conn.: Yale University Press, 2008.

———. *The Nazi Dictatorship: Problems and Perspectives of Interpretation.* London: Edward Arnold, 1985.

Kiefer, Albert. *In Kriegs- und Friedenszeiten: Ästhetische Erziehung als Lebensaufgabe.* Hamburg: Verlag Dr. Kovač, 2003.

Kiefer, Anselm. *Über Raume und Völker: Ein Gespräch mit Anselm Kiefer.* Frankfurt am Main: Suhrkamp Taschenbuch, 1990.

Kipphoff, Petra. "Die Lust an der Angst—der deutsche Holzweg." *Die Zeit,* June 6, 1980, 42.

———. "Verbrannte Erde und gestuerzter Trommler." *Die Zeit,* April 13, 1984, 43–44.

Klapcheck, Anna. "Kunstausstellungen in Westdeutschland 1964/65." *Jahresring* 65/66 (1966): 405–10.

Kleihues, Josef Paul. "Von Großstadtträumen zur Stadterneuerung: Architektur und Städtebau in Berlin." In *750 Jahre Berlin: Stadt der Gegenwart,* edited by Ulrich Eckhardt, 170–79. Frankfurt am Main: Ullstein, 1986.

Kohl, Helmut. "Address by Chancellor Helmut Kohl to German and American Soldiers and Their Families at Bitburg, May 5, 1985." In Hartman, *Bitburg in Moral and Political Perspective,* 256–57.

———. *History's Inescapable Impact on the Present.* Bonn: Presse- und Informationsamt der Bundesregierung, 1988.

———. *Reden, 1982–1984.* Bonn: Presse- und Informationsamt der Bundesregierung, 1984.

———. *Die unentrinnbare Gegenwart der Geschichte*. Bonn: Presse- und Informationsamt der Bundesregierung, 1988.

Koshar, Rudy. *From Monuments to Traces: Artifacts of German Memory, 1870–1990*. Berkeley: University of California Press, 2000.

Koss, Juliet. "On the Limits of Empathy." *Art Bulletin* 88, no. 1 (March 2006): 139–57.

Kramer, Mario. "Art Nourishes Life—Joseph Beuys: Auschwitz Demonstration, 1956–1964." In Gillen, *German Art from Beckmann to Richter*, 261–71.

Krens, Thomas, Michael Govan, and Joseph Thompson, eds. *Refigured Painting: The German Image, 1960–1988*. Munich: Prestel, 1988.

Kugelmann, Cilly. "Bringschuld, Erbe und Besitz: Jüdischen Museen nach 1945." In *Erinnerung als Gegenwart: Jüdische Gedenkkulturen*, edited by Sabine Hödl and Eleonore Lappin, 173–92. Berlin: Philo, 2000.

Küper, Susanne. "Gerhard Richter: Capitalist Realism and His Painting from Photographs, 1962–1966." In Gillen, *German Art from Beckmann to Richter*, 233–36.

Kurthen, Hermann, Werner Bergmann, and Rainer Erb, eds. *Antisemitism and Xenophobia in Germany after Unification*. New York: Oxford University Press, 1997.

Kuspit, Donald. *The New Subjectivism: Art in the 1980s*. New York: Da Capo, 1993.

Ladd, Brian. *The Ghosts of Berlin: Confronting German History in the Urban Landscape*. Chicago: University of Chicago Press, 1997.

Lang, Jochen von, ed. *Eichmann Interrogated: Transcripts from the Archives of the Israeli Police*. In collaboration with Claus Sibyll. New York: Da Capo Press, 1999.

Levy, Evonne. "The Political Project of Wölfflin's Early Formalism." *October* 139 (Winter 2012): 39–58.

Libeskind, Daniel. "Between the Lines." *Architectural Design* 67, nos. 9/10 (September/October 1997): 58–63.

———. *Breaking Ground: Adventures in Life and Architecture*. New York: Riverhead Books, 2004.

———. *Countersign*. London: Academy Editions, 1991.

———. *Daniel Libeskind: One to the Other*. Berlin: Aedes Galerie für Architektur und Raum, 1987.

———. *Kein Ort an seiner Stelle: Schriften zur Architektur, Visionen für Berlin*. Dresden: Verlag der Kunst, 1995.

———. *Radix Matrix*. New York: Prestel, 1997.

Libeskind, Daniel, and Anne Wagner. "Resisting the Erasure of History: Daniel Libeskind Interviewed by Anne Wagner." In *Architecture and Revolution*, edited by Neil Leach, 130–38. London: Routledge, 1999.

Liebman, Lisa. "Anselm Kiefer at Marian Goodman New York." *Art in America* 35, no. 1 (1982): 60.

Linke, Uli. *German Bodies: Race and Representation after Hitler*. New York: Routledge, 1999.

Lurz, Meinhold. *Heinrich Wölfflin: Biographie einer Kunsttheorie.* Worms: Wernersche Verlagsgesellschaft, 1981.

Macdonald, Sharon. *Difficult Heritage: Negotiating the Nazi Past in Nuremberg and Beyond.* London: Routledge, 2008.

———. "Words in Stone? Agency and Identity in a Nazi Landscape." *Journal of Material Culture* 11 (2006): 105–26.

Mack-Phillip, Andrea. "Stadtplanung und Stadtentwicklung prägen das Gesicht der Stadt." *Nürnberg Heute* 68 (May 2000): 6.

Maier, Charles S. *Dissolution: The Crisis of Communism and the End of East Germany.* Princeton, N.J.: Princeton University Press, 1997.

———. *The Unmasterable Past: History, Holocaust, and German National Identity.* Cambridge, Mass.: Harvard University Press, 1988.

Marcuse, Harold. "Holocaust Memorials: The Emergence of a Genre." *American Historical Review* 115, no. 1 (February 2010): 53–89.

Marrus, Michael R. "History and the Holocaust in the Courtroom." In *The Holocaust and Justice,* edited by Ronald Smelser, 215–39. Lessons and Legacies, vol. 5. Evanston, Ill.: Northwestern University Press, 2002.

Mathieu, Thomas. *Kunstauffassungen und Kulturpolitik im Nationalsozialismus.* Saarbrücken: PFAU, 1997.

Matuštik, Martin Beck. "The Critical Theorist as Witness: Habermas and the Holocaust." In *Perspectives on Habermas,* edited by Lewis E. Hahn, 339–66. Chicago: Open Court, 2000.

McCloskey, Barbara. "Dialectic at a Standstill: East German Socialist Realism in the Stalin Era." In Barron and Eckmann, *Art of Two Germanys,* 104–17.

Mehring, Christine. "The Art of a Miracle: Toward a History of German Pop, 1955–1972." In Barron and Eckmann, *Art of Two Germanys,* 152–69.

———. "Continental Schrift." *Artforum* 42, no. 9 (2004): 178–83, 233.

Meier, Nikolaus. "Heinrich Wölfflin, 1864–1945." In *Altmeister moderne Kunstgeschichte,* edited by Heinrich Dilly, 61–79. Berlin: Reimer, 1999.

Meissner, Günter. "Die Bildfolge *Lebenserinnerungen des Dr. jur. Schulze* im Schaffen Werner Tübke." In *Werner Tübke: Die Retrospektive zum 80. Geburtstag,* edited by Hans-Werner Schmidt, 10–17. Leipzig: Museum der bildenden Künste, 2009.

———. "Um die Vertiefung realistischer Aussage." *Bildende Kunst* 2 (1966): 74.

Meng, Michael. "The Politics of Antifascism: Historic Preservation, Jewish Sites, and the Rebuilding of Potsdam's Altstadt." In Rosenfeld and Jaskot, *Beyond Berlin,* 231–50.

Merhav, Meir. "Honouring Evil." In Hartman, *Bitburg in Moral and Political Perspective,* 194–98.

Merkl, Peter H. *Political Violence under the Swastika.* Princeton, N.J.: Princeton University Press, 1975.

Michaud, Eric. *The Cult of Art in Nazi Germany.* Translated by Janet Lloyd. Stanford, Calif.: Stanford University Press, 2004.

Miller Lane, Barbara. *Architecture and Politics in Germany, 1918–1945*. Cambridge, Mass.: Harvard University Press, 1968.

Mitchell, Maria. "Materialism and Secularism: CDU Politicians and National Socialism, 1945–1949." *Journal of Modern History* 67, no. 2 (June 1995): 278–308.

Moeller, Robert G. "Remembering the War in a Nation of Victims: West German Pasts in the 1950s." In Schissler, *The Miracle Years*, 83–109.

———. *War Stories: The Search for a Usable Past in the Federal Republic of Germany*. Berkeley: University of California Press, 2001.

Moller, Sabine. *Die Entkontretisierung der NS-Herrschaft in der Ära Kohl*. Hannover: Offizin, 1998.

Monjau, Mieke. "Am 17. Mai ging der Transport nach Auschwitz—niemand kehrte zurück." *Tendenzen* 20, no. 128 (November/December 1979): 45–49.

Moorhouse, Paul. *Gerhard Richter Portraits: Painting Appearances*. New Haven, Conn.: Yale University Press, 2009.

Mosse, George L. *The Crisis of German Ideology: Intellectual Origins of the Third Reich*. New York: Grossett and Dunlap, 1964.

———. *Toward the Final Solution: A History of European Racism*. 2nd ed. Madison: University of Wisconsin Press, 1985.

Mühlenberger, Detlef. *Hitler's Voice: The Völkischer Beobachter, 1920–1933*. Oxford: Peter Lang, 2004.

Müller-Mehlis, Reinhard. "Entartete Kunst." *Tendenzen*, nos. 17–18 (December 1962).

———. "…und Schämten sich nicht! Vom Vorleben unserer Kunstkritiker in grosser deutscher Zeit." *Tendenzen*, nos. 17–18 (December 1962).

———. "Zeit der Umwertung." *Tendenzen*, no. 28 (August 1964).

Museo d'Art Contemporani. *Photography and Painting in the Work of Gerhard Richter*. Barcelona: Museo d'Art Contemporani, 1999.

Nerdinger, Winfried. "Bauhaus Architecture in the Third Reich." In James-Chakraborty, *Bauhaus Culture*, 139–52.

———. "Foreword." In *Josef Paul Kleihues: Themes and Projects*, edited by Thorsten Scheer, 9–12. Basel: Birkhäuser, 1996.

Nesbit, Peter. "Crash Course: Remarks on a Beuys Story." In Ray, *Joseph Beuys*, 5–17.

Neugass, Fritz. "Pop-Art Epidemie." *Weltkunst* 33, no. 18 (September 15, 1963): 12.

Neumann, Klaus. *Shifting Memories: The Nazi Past in the New Germany*. Ann Arbor: University of Michigan Press, 2000.

Nicolaus, Frank. "Verfolgt, verfemt, entartet: Künstler unter Hakenkreuz." *Art*, no. 3 (March 1982): 84–104.

Nora, Pierre. "Between Memory and History: Les Lieux de Mémoire." *Representations*, no. 26 (Spring 1989): 7–24.

Nossack, Hans Erich. *The End: Hamburg 1943*. Translated by Joel Agee. Chicago: University of Chicago Press, 2004.

Nugent, Jeanne Anne. "Family Album and Shadow Archive: Gerhard Richter's East, West, and All German Painting, 1949–1966." PhD diss., University of Pennsylvania, 2005.

———. "Overcoming Ideology: Gerhard Richter in Dresden, the Early Years." In *From Caspar David Friedrich to Gerhard Richter: German Paintings from Dresden*, edited by Heike Biedermann, Ulrich Bischoff, and Birgit Dalbajewa, 79–94. Los Angeles: J. Paul Getty Museum, 2006.

Omi, Michael, and Howard Winant. *Racial Formation in the United States*. 2nd ed. New York: Routledge, 1994.

Panayi, Panikos. "Racial Exclusionism in the New Germany." In *Germany Since Unification*, edited by Klaus Larres, 129–48. New York: St. Martin's Press, 1998.

Papenbrock, Martin. "Kunstgeschichtliche Forschung und Lehre im Nationalsozialismus: Studienprojekt, Dokumentation, Analyse." In Doll, Fuhrmeister, and Sprenger, *Kunstgeschichte im Nationalsozialismus*, 27–36.

Peck, Jeffrey, Mitchell Ash, and Christiane Lemke. "Natives, Strangers, and Foreigners." In *After Unity: Reconfiguring German Identities*, edited by Konrad H. Jarausch, 61–102. Providence, R.I.: Berghahn Books, 1997.

Pendas, Devin O. "'I Didn't Know What Auschwitz Was': The Frankfurt Auschwitz Trial and the German Press, 1963–1965." *Yale Journal of Law and the Humanities* 12, no. 2 (Summer 2000): 397–446.

Peters, Olaf. *Neue Sachlichkeit und Nationalsozialismus: Affirmation und Kritik, 1931–1947*. Berlin: Reimer, 1998.

Petropoulos, Jonathan. *The Faustian Bargain: The Art World in Nazi Germany*. Oxford: Oxford University Press, 2000.

Peukert, Detlev. *The Weimar Republic: The Crisis of Classical Modernity*. New York: Hill and Wang, 1993.

Pieper, Katrin. *Die Musealisierung des Holocaust: Das Jüdische Museum Berlin und das U.S. Holocaust Memorial Museum in Washington, D.C.* Cologne: Böhlau, 2006.

Pinder, Wilhelm. "Architektur als Moral." In *Festschrift Heinrich Wölfflin zum siebzigsten Geburtstage*, 145–51. Dresden: Wolfgang Jess Verlag, 1935.

Piper, Ernst. *Alfred Rosenberg: Hitlers Chefideologe*. Munich: Blessing, 2005.

Potts, Alex. "Autonomy in Post-war Art, Quasi-heroic and Casual." *Oxford Art Journal* 27, no. 1 (2004): 43–59.

Presler, Gerd. "Ein famoser Kerl." *Art*, no. 1 (January 1980): 104–13.

Pugh, Emily. "The Berlin Wall and the Urban Space and Experience of East and West Berlin, 1961–1989." PhD diss., City University of New York, 2008.

Rampley, Matthew. "In Search of Cultural History: Anselm Kiefer and the Ambivalence of Modernism." *Oxford Art Journal* 23, no. 1 (2000): 73–96.

Raschke, Joachim. *Die Grünen: Wie sie wurden, was sie sind*. Cologne: Bund-Verlag, 1993.

Rattinger, Hans. "Change versus Continuity in West German Public Attitudes on National Security and Nuclear Weapons in the Early 1980s." *Public Opinion Quarterly* 51, no. 4 (Winter 1987): 495–521.

Ray, Gene, ed. *Joseph Beuys: Mapping the Legacy*. Sarasota, Fla.: The John and Mable Ringling Museum of Art, 2001.

———. "Joseph Beuys and the After-Auschwitz Sublime." In Ray, *Joseph Beuys*, 55–74.

Reichel, Peter. *Politik mit der Erinnerung: Gedächtnisorte im Streit um die national-sozialistische Vergangenheit*. Munich: Hanser, 1995.

———. *Vergangenheitsbewältigung in Deutschland: Die Auseinandersetzung mit der NS-Diktatur von 1945 bis Heute*. Munich: C. H. Beck, 2001.

Richter, Gerhard. *Altas der Fotos, Collagen und Skizzen*. Munich: Städtische Galerie im Lenbachhaus, 1997.

———. *Gerhard Richter: Catalogue Raisonné, 1962–1993*. Ostfildern: Hatje Cantz Verlag, 1997.

———. *Gerhard Richter, Text: Schriften und Interviews*. Frankfurt/Main: Hans-Ulrich Obrist, 1993.

Rosenberg, Alfred. *The Myth of the Twentieth Century: An Evaluation of the Spiritual-Intellectual Confrontations of Our Age*. Translated by Vivian Bird. Newport Beach, Calif.: Noontide Press, 1982.

Rosenfeld, Gavriel D. *Munich and Memory: Architecture, Monuments, and the Legacy of the Third Reich*. Berkeley: University of California Press, 2000.

———. "The Normalization of Memory: Saul Friedländer's *Reflections of Nazism* Twenty Years Later." In *The Holocaust in International Perspective*, edited by Dagmar Herzog, 400–410. Lessons and Legacies, vol. 7. Evanston, Ill.: Northwestern University Press, 2006.

Rosenfeld, Gavriel D., and Paul B. Jaskot, eds. *Beyond Berlin: Twelve German Cities Confront the Nazi Past*. Ann Arbor: University of Michigan Press, 2008.

Rosenthal, Mark. *Anselm Kiefer*. Chicago: Art Institute of Chicago, 1987.

Safrian, Hans. "Adolf Eichmann—Organisator der Judendeportation." In *Die SS. Elite unter dem Totenkopf*, edited by Ronald Smelser and Enrico Syring, 134–46. Paderborn: F. Schöningh, 2000.

Sager, Peter. "Gespräch mit Gerhard Richter." *Kunstwerk* 25, no. 4 (1972): 16–27.

Saltzman, Lisa. *Anselm Kiefer and Art After Auschwitz*. Cambridge: Cambridge University Press, 1999.

Santner, Eric. "The Trouble with Hitler: Postwar German Aesthetics and the Legacy of Fascism." *New German Critique* 57 (1992): 5–24.

Schäche, Wolfgang. "Städtebauliche Entwicklung vor der IBA." In *Realisierungs-wettbewerb Erweiterung Berlin Museum mit Abteilung Jüdisches Museum*, edited by Senator für Bau- und Wohnungswesen, 49–52. Berlin: Senator für Bau- und Wohnungswesen, 1988.

Schissler, Hanna, ed. *The Miracle Years: A Cultural History of West Germany, 1949–1968*. Princeton, N.J.: Princeton University Press, 2001.

Schmidt, Helmut. *Mahnung und Verpflichtung*. Bonn: Presse- und Informationsamt der Bundesregierung, 1978.

Schneider, Bernhard. *Daniel Libeskind: Jüdisches Museum Berlin*. Munich: Prestel 1999.

Schönhuber, Franz. *Ich war dabei*. Munich: Langen Müller, 1981.

Schrag, Otto. "Entartete Kunst: Haus der Kunst, München." *Kunstwerk* 16, nos. 5–6 (November/December 1962): 59.

Schreiber, Jürgen. *Ein Maler aus Deutschland: Gerhard Richter; Das Drama einer Familie*. Munich: Pendo, 2005.

Schultze-Naumburg, Paul. *Dörfer und Kolonien*. Kulturarbeiten, vol. 3. Munich: Callwey, 1908.

———. *Kunst und Rasse*. Munich: J. F. Lehmanns Verlag, 1928.

Schulze, Bernhard. "Der stete Stachel der Teilung." *Weltkunst*, no. 10 (May 15, 1985): 1440–41.

Schürgers, Norbert. "Argument der Bürger ernst nehmen." *Nürnberg Heute* 60 (July 1996): 14–15.

Schütz, Sabine. *Anselm Kiefer—Geschichte als Material: Arbeiten, 1969–1983*. Cologne: Dumont, 1999.

Schwartz, Frederic J. *Blind Spots: Critical Theory and the History of Art in Twentieth-Century Germany*. New Haven, Conn.: Yale University Press, 2005.

Scobie, Alex. *Hitler's State Architecture*. University Park: Pennsylvania State University Press, 1990.

Sebald, W. G. *On the Natural History of Destruction*. New York: Modern Library, 1999.

Senatsverwaltung für Bau- und Wohnungswesen, ed. *Realisierungswettbewerb Erweiterung Berlin Museum mit Abteilung Jüdisches Museum: Voraussetzung, Verfahren, Ergebnisse*. Berlin: Senatsverwaltung für Bau- und Wohnungswesen, 1990.

Sholette, Gregory. "Heart of Darkness: A Journey into the Dark Matter of the Art World." In *Visual Worlds*, edited by Lisa Tamiris Becker, John R. Hall, and Blake Stimson, 91–108. New York: Routledge, 2006.

Smith, Terry. *The Architecture of Aftermath*. Chicago: University of Chicago Press, 2006.

Sontag, Susan. "Fascinating Fascism." In *Under the Sign of Saturn*, 73–105. New York: Farrar, Straus and Giroux, 1980.

Spotts, Frederic. *Hitler and the Aesthetics of Power*. Woodstock, N.Y.: Overlook Press, 2003.

Stadt Nürnberg. *Auslobungstext: Städtebaulicher Ideenwettbewerb für das ehemalige Reichsparteitagsgelände*. Nuremberg: Stadt Nürnberg, 2001.

———. *Dokumentation: Städtebaulicher Ideenwettbewerb für das ehemalige Reichsparteitagsgelände*. Nuremberg: Stadt Nürnberg, 2001.

Steinweis, Alan. *Art, Ideology, and Economics in Nazi Germany: The Reich Chambers of Music, Theater, and the Visual Arts*. Chapel Hill: University of North Carolina Press, 1993.

———. *Studying the Jew: Scholarly Antisemitism in Nazi Germany*. Cambridge, Mass.: Harvard University Press, 2006.

———. "Weimar Culture and the Rise of National Socialism: The *Kampfbund für deutsche Kultur*." *Central European History* 24, no. 4 (1991): 402–23.

Storr, Robert. *Gerhard Richter: Forty Years of Painting*. New York: Museum of Modern Art, 2002.

———. *Gerhard Richter: October 18, 1977*. New York: Museum of Modern Art, 2000.

Strom, Elizabeth A. *Building the New Berlin: The Politics of Urban Development in Germany's Central City*. Lanham, Md.: Lexington Books, 2001.

Sudhalter, Adrian. "14 Years Bauhaus: A Chronicle." In *Bauhaus: Workshops for Modernity*, edited by Barry Bergdoll and Leah Dickerman, 323–37. New York: Museum of Modern Art, 2009.

Till, Karen E. *The New Berlin: Memory, Politics, Place*. Minneapolis: University of Minnesota Press, 2005.

Tooze, Adam. *The Wages of Destruction: The Making and Breaking of the Nazi Economy*. New York: Allen Lane, 2006.

van Bruggen, Coosje. "Gerhard Richter: Painting as a Moral Act." *Artforum* 9 (May 1985): 82–91.

van Dyke, James. "Franz Radziwill: 'Die Gemeinschaft' und die nationalsozialistische 'Revolution' in der Kunst." *Georges-Bloch-Jahrbuch des Kunstgeschichtlichen Seminars der Universität Zürich* 4 (1997): 135–63.

———. *Franz Radziwill and the Contradictions of German Art History, 1919–45*. Ann Arbor: University of Michigan Press, 2011.

Vees-Gulani, Susanne. "The Politics of New Beginnings: The Continued Exclusion of the Nazi Past in Dresden's Cityscape." In Rosenfeld and Jaskot, *Beyond Berlin*, 25–47.

Verlag Hans Müller. *Nürnberger Facetten*. Nuremberg: Verlag Hans Müller, 2001.

Vidler, Anthony. *Warped Space: Art, Architecture, and Anxiety in Modern Culture*. Cambridge, Mass.: MIT Press, 2001.

Vieten, Günter C. "Fälscher." *Art*, no. 1 (January 1980): 117.

Wagner, Monika. "Bild—Schrift—Material: Konzepte der Erinnerung bei Boltanski, Sigurdsson und Kiefer." In *Mimesis, Bild und Schrift: Ähnlichkeit und Entstellung im Verhältnis der Künste*, edited by Birgit Erdle and Sigrid Weigel, 23–29. Cologne: Böhlau Verlag, 1996.

Waller, James. *Becoming Evil: How Ordinary People Commit Genocide and Mass Killing*. Oxford: Oxford University Press, 2002.

Warnke, Martin. "On Heinrich Wölfflin." *Representations* 27 (Summer 1989): 172–87.

———, ed. *Das Kunstwerk zwischen Wissenschaft und Weltanschauung*. Gütersloh: Bertelsmann, 1970.

Weinland, Martina, and Kurt Winkler. *Das Jüdische Museum im Stadtmuseum Berlin: Eine Dokumentation/The Jewish Museum in the Berlin Municipal Museum*. Berlin: Nicolai, 1997.

Weinraub, Bernard. "Reagan Joins Kohl in Brief Memorial at Bitburg Graves." In Hartman, *Bitburg in Moral and Political Perspective*, 146–49.

Weiss, Peter. *Die Ermittlung*. Frankfurt am Main: Suhrkamp, 1991.

Weizsäcker, Richard von. "Speech by Richard von Weizsäcker, President of the Federal Republic of Germany, in the Bundestag during the Ceremony Commemorating the 40th Anniversary of the End of the War in Europe and of National Socialist Tyranny, May 8, 1985." In Hartman, *Bitburg in Moral and Political Perspective*, 262–72.

Wellensiek, Hertha. "Bildersturm und Busse." *Weltkunst* 32, no. 23 (December 1, 1962): 15–16.

Welti, Alfred. "Den Stein von innen her begreifen." *Art*, no. 3 (March 1983): 72–81.

Werckmeister, O. K. "Hitler the Artist." *Critical Inquiry* 23 (Winter 1997): 270–97.

———. "Radical Art History." *Art Journal* 42, no. 4 (1982): 284–91.

Wharton, Annabelle. *Building the Cold War: Hilton International Hotels and Modern Architecture*. Chicago: University of Chicago Press, 2001.

Wiener, S. Jonathan. *West German Industry and the Challenge of the Nazi Past, 1945–1955*. Chapel Hill: University of North Carolina Press, 2001.

Wiesel, Elie. *Night*. New York: Hill and Wang, 1982.

Wilke, Jürgen, Birgit Schenk, Akiba Cohen, and Tamar Zemach. *Holocaust und NS-Prozesse: Die Presseberichterstattung in Israel und Deutschland zwischen Aneignung und Abwehr*. Cologne: Böhlau, 1995.

Wise, Michael Z. *Capital Dilemma: Germany's Search for a New Architecture of Democracy*. New York: Princeton Architectural Press, 1998.

Wittmann, Rebecca. *Beyond Justice: The Auschwitz Trial*. Cambridge, Mass.: Harvard University Press, 2005.

Wölfflin, Heinrich. *Italien und das deutsche Formgefühl*. Munich: F. Bruckmann, 1931.

———. *Kunstgeschichtliche Grundbegriffe*. 7th ed. Munich: F. Bruckmann, 1929.

Young, James E. *At Memory's Edge: After-Images of the Holocaust in Contemporary Art and Architecture*. New Haven, Conn.: Yale University Press, 2000.

———. "The Biography of a Memorial Icon: Nathan Rapoport's Warsaw Ghetto Monument." *Representations*, no. 26 (Spring 1989): 69–106.

———. *The Texture of Memory: Holocaust Memorials and Meaning*. New Haven, Conn.: Yale University Press, 1993.

Zelnhefer, Siegfried. *Die Reichsparteitage der NSDAP: Geschichte, Struktur und Bedeutung der grössten Propagandafeste im nationalsozialistischen Feierjahr*. Nuremberg: Korn und Berg, 1991.

"Zu diesem Heft." *Tendenzen* 24, no. 141 (January/March 1983): 4.

"Zu diesem Heft." *Tendenzen* 25, no. 147 (July/Sept 1984): 4.

Zuschlag, Christoph. "An 'Educational Exhibition': The Precursors of *Entartete Kunst* and Its Individual Venues." In *"Degenerate Art": The Fate of the Avant-Garde in Nazi Germany*, edited by Stephanie Barron, 83–97. New York: Abrams, 1991.

———. *"Entartete Kunst": Ausstellungsstrategien im Nazi-Deutschland*. Worms: Wernersche Verlagsgesellschaft, 1995.

Zweite, Armin. "Gerhard Richters 'Atlas der Fotos, Collagen und Skizzen.'" In *Gerhard Richters Atlas*, 7–20. Munich: Verlag Fred Jahn, 1989.

INDEX

PAUL B. JASKOT is professor of art history at DePaul University. He is author of *The Architecture of Oppression: The SS, Forced Labor, and the Nazi Monumental Building Economy* and coeditor of *Beyond Berlin: Twelve German Cities Confront the Nazi Past.*